AF576710

ABANDONED TOWNS

ABANDONED TOWNS

CHRIS McNAB

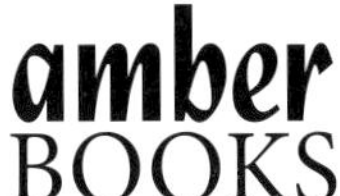

Previously published as *Ghost Towns*

Published by
Amber Books Ltd
United House
London N7 9DP
United Kingdom

www.amberbooks.co.uk
Facebook: amberbooks
YouTube: amberbooksltd
Instagram: amberbooksltd
X(Twitter): @amberbooks

ISBN: 978-1-83886-373-9

Project Editor: Sarah Uttridge
Designer: Mark Batley
Picture Research: Terry Forshaw

Printed in China

Contents

Introduction

The name 'ghost town' actually does much of the explaining about why such places continue to draw our fascination. Abandoned towns have an undeniably haunted aura, the sense that the hollow rooms, wind-swinging doors and silent roads still bear the imprint of those who once lived there, sometimes with unnerving immediacy (think Pompeii or Chernobyl). Whether we are looking at ancient Italian ruins, or a ramshackle old mining settlement in the American Midwest, our exploration of ghost towns brings mixed feelings – fascination to be wandering freely among people's former homes and places and work, and also a sense of trespass for the very same reason. Yet ghost towns are also invaluable historical sources, true (and in some cases literal) windows on our past. What seems to distinguish a ghost town from bare ruins is that enough of the authentic fabric remains, allowing us to step into the lives of people now long gone, having passed through time decades or centuries ago.

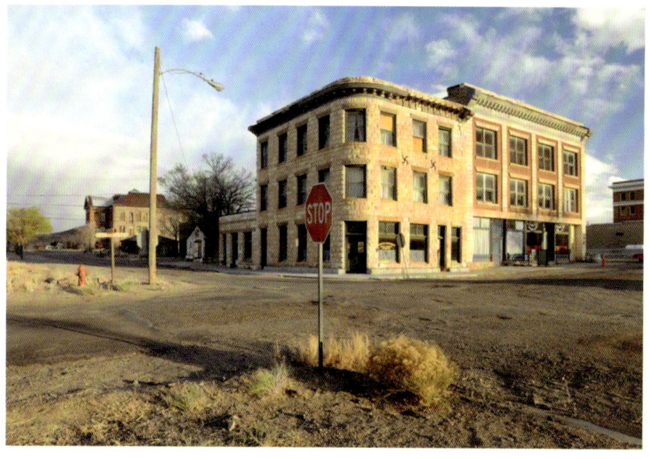

ABOVE:
The town of Goldfield, Nevada, USA, was once home to 30,000 people, but a collapse in the supporting gold-mining industry brought decline and abandonment.
RIGHT:
Crumbling away in the Western Desert, the fortress city of Shali in the Siwa Oasis has origins back in the 10th century BCE.

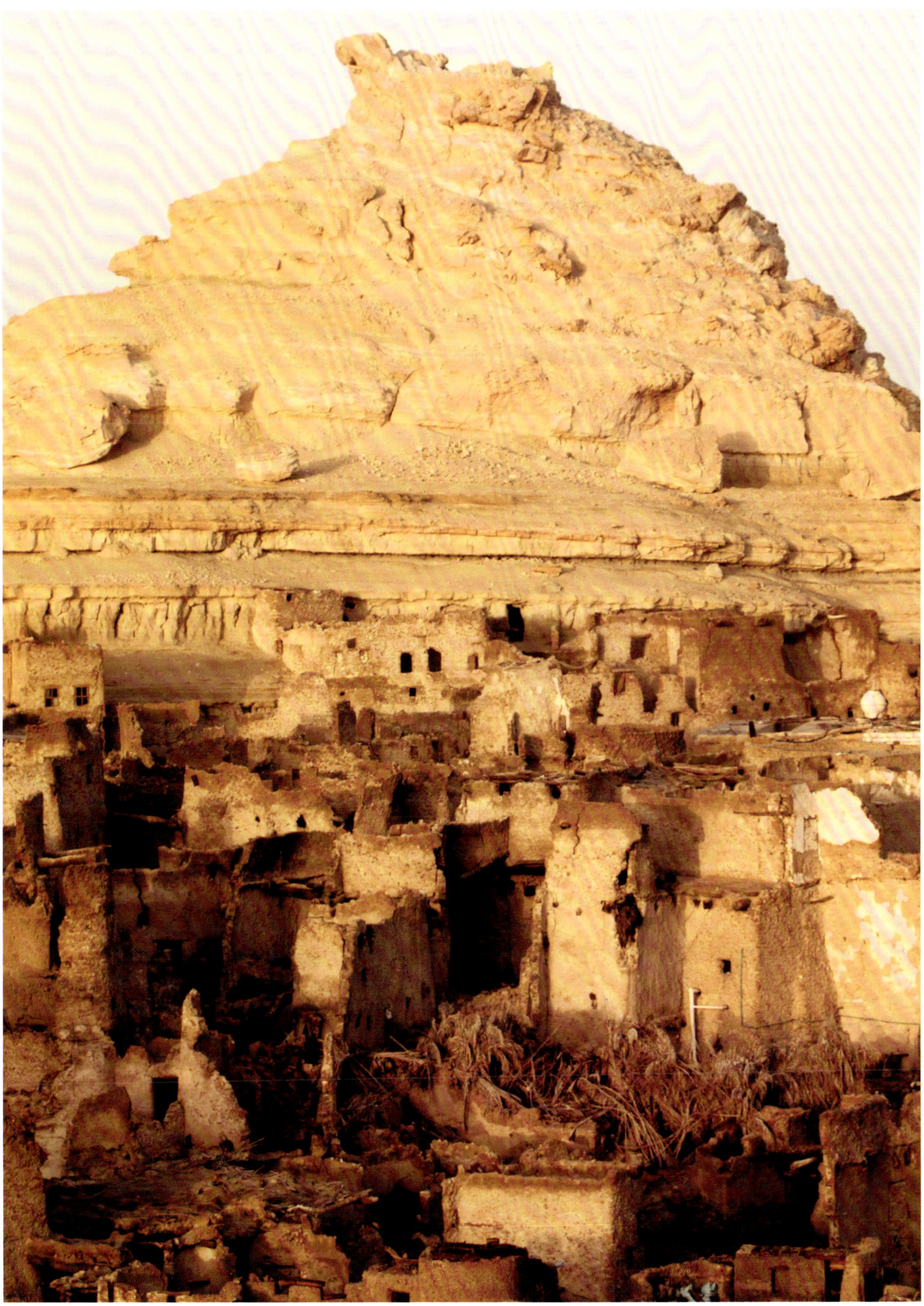

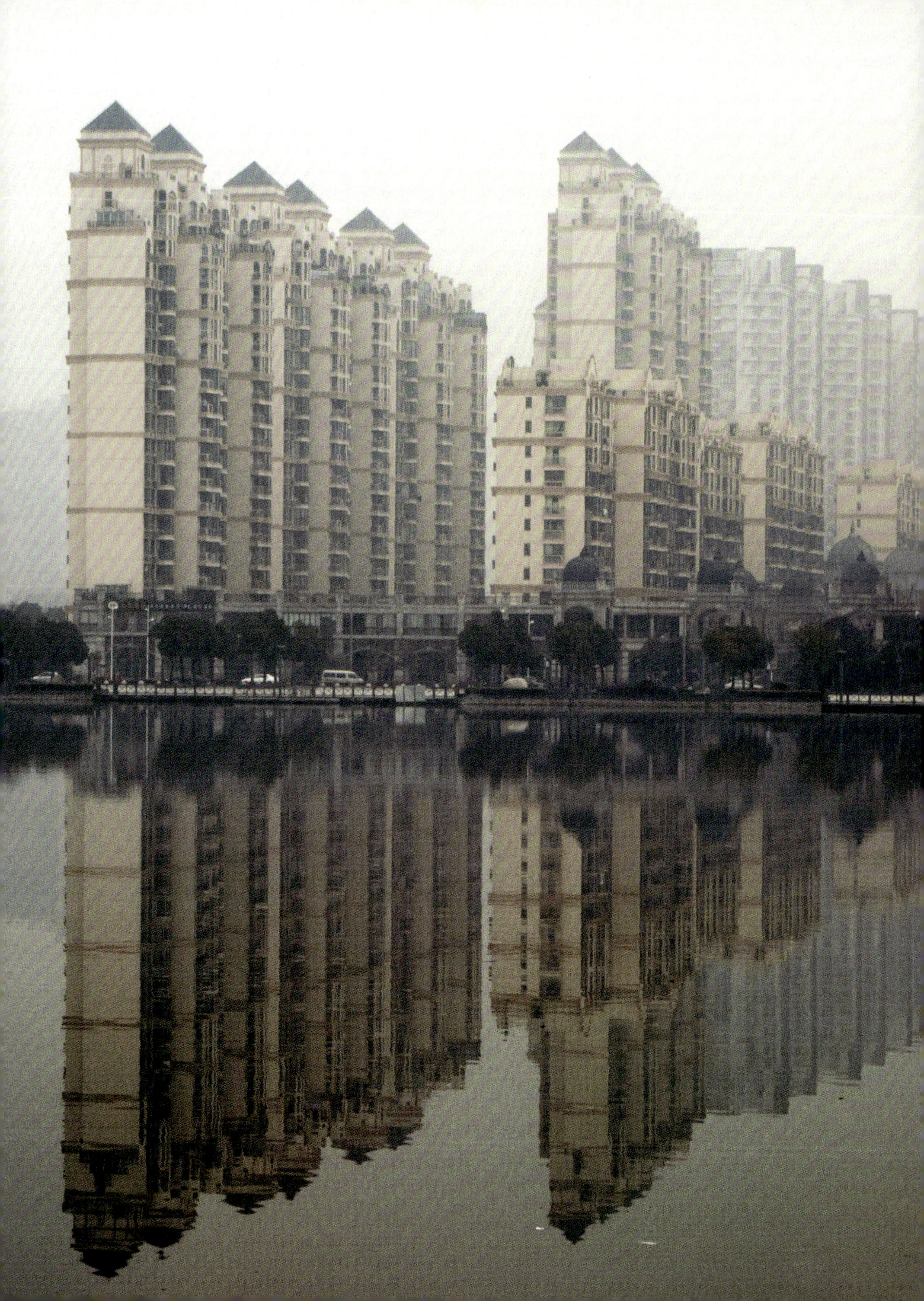

East Asia

The ghost towns of East Asia have highly diverse backstories. Many of these places laid their foundations in ancient or medieval history, often centred around temples that anchored the spirituality of the local community and its rulers. Wat Phra Si Sanphet, the old Royal Palace in Thailand's ancient capital of Ayutthaya, and featured in this chapter, is a prime example, its 400-year history brought to an end in 1767 by Burmese invasion. At least the intrinsic beauty and historical importance of such sites has made them continually attractive to travellers and tourists. In strange contrast, however, are the many modern ghost towns that now flourish across East Asia. Some of these are the by-product of economic changes, particularly the decline of key industries that underpinned the viability of towns and cities in the first place. Others are – and often spectacularly so – the products of misplaced enthusiasm for building development. China, for example, added 23,700 square kilometres (10,695 square miles) of urban land in 2000–2010 alone, the expansion fuelled by a growing economy, the ready availability of financial credit and dramatic expectations for the growth of urban populations. Yet in reality, urban population densities have actually shrunk in many regions of China, the result being futuristic but gaunt city complexes standing empty, waiting for people who might not, in fact, arrive at all.

LEFT:
Thames Town, Songjiang New City, Shanghai, China
Thames Town is one of many underpopulated new developments that have sprung up across China in the last 20 years. The 'Thames Town' name reflects the fact that many of the streets and buildings are a pastiche of quintessential English architectural styles.

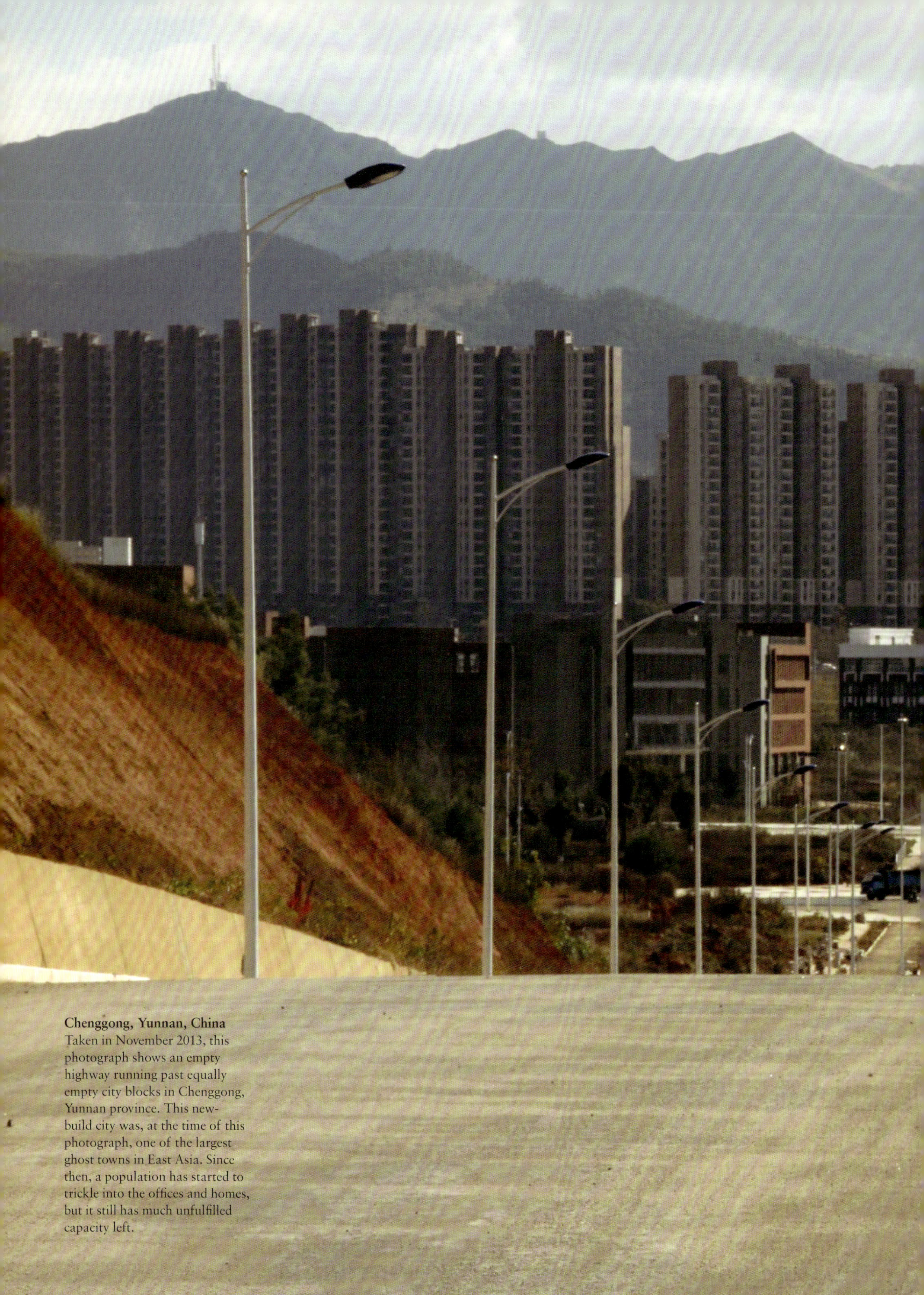

Chenggong, Yunnan, China
Taken in November 2013, this photograph shows an empty highway running past equally empty city blocks in Chenggong, Yunnan province. This new-build city was, at the time of this photograph, one of the largest ghost towns in East Asia. Since then, a population has started to trickle into the offices and homes, but it still has much unfulfilled capacity left.

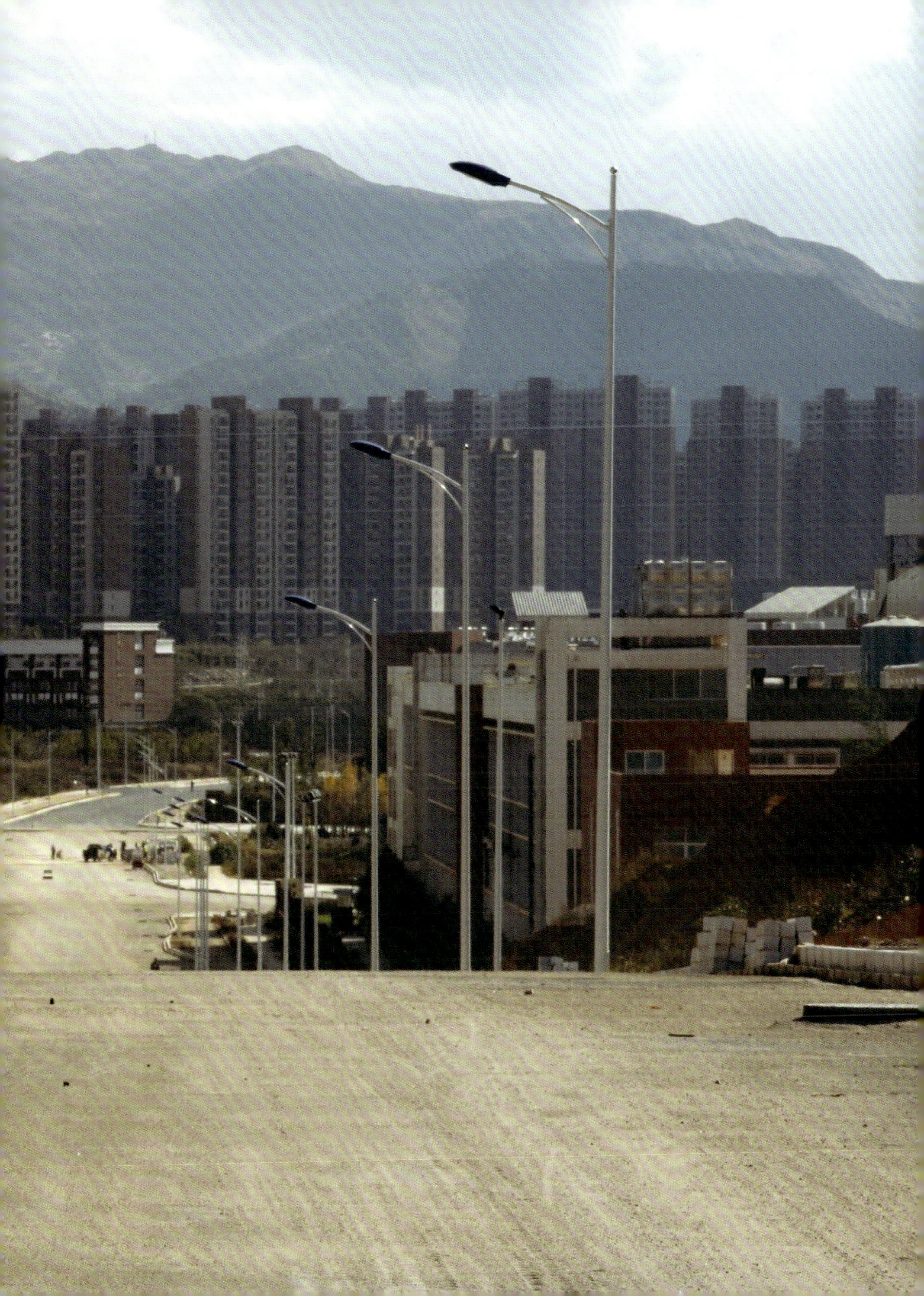

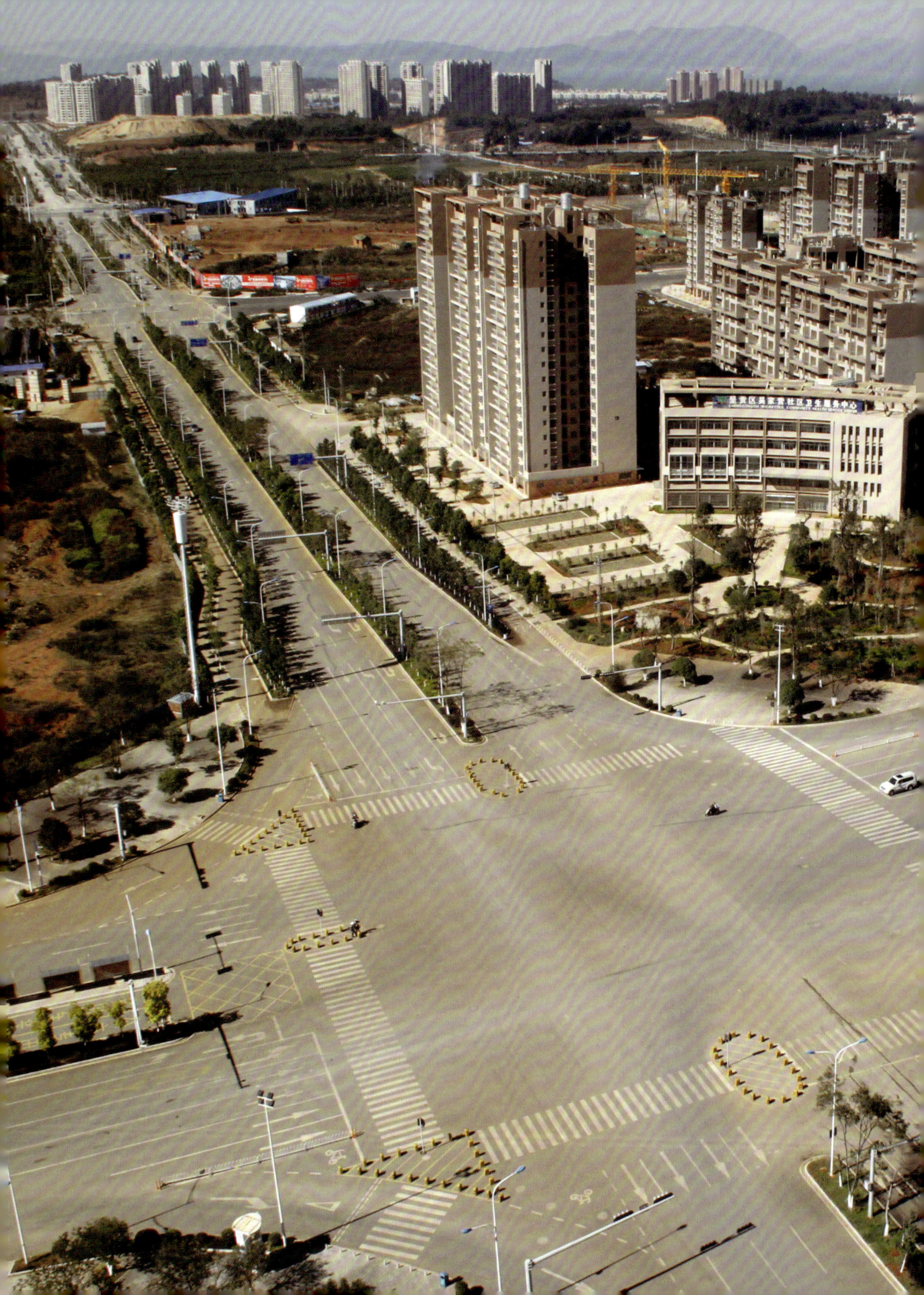
呈贡区吴家营社区卫生服务中心

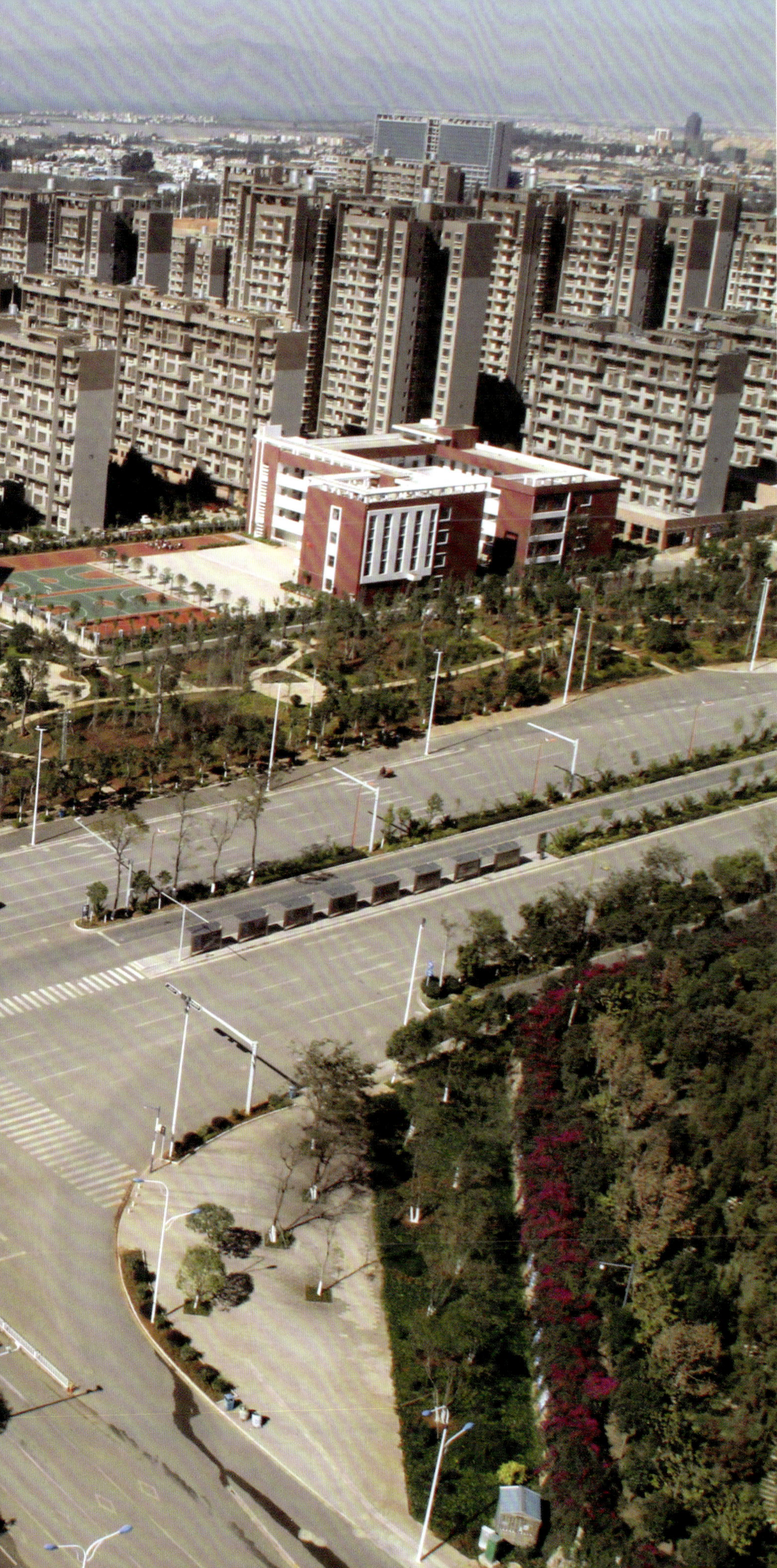

Chenggong, Yunnan, China
Another, rather eerie, view across the streets and buildings of Chenggong. Like many of the big ghost-town developments across modern China, Chenggong was developed to provide space for population overspill from other, overcrowded cities. In the case of Chenggong, it is a satellite city located just south of Kunming.

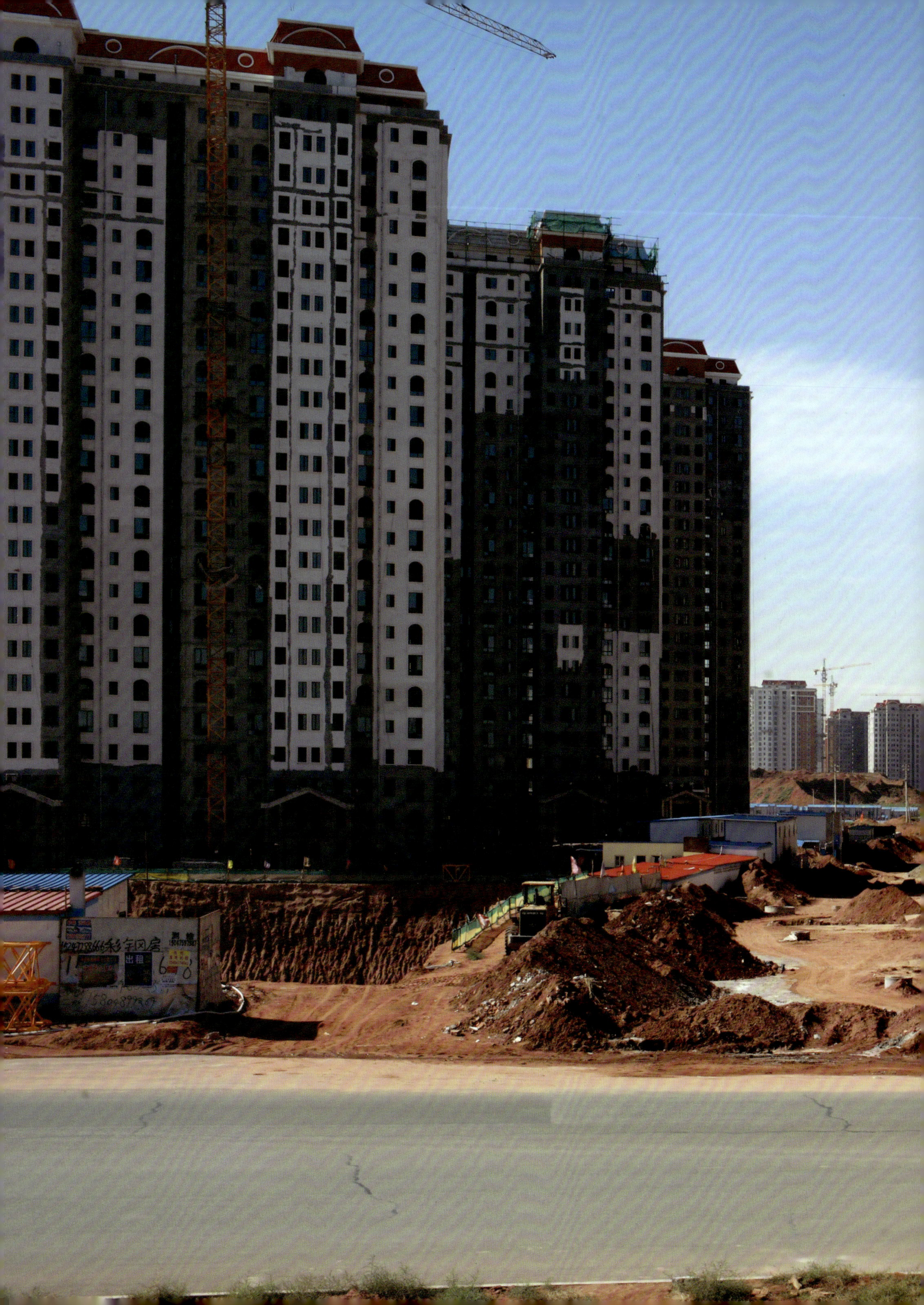
出租

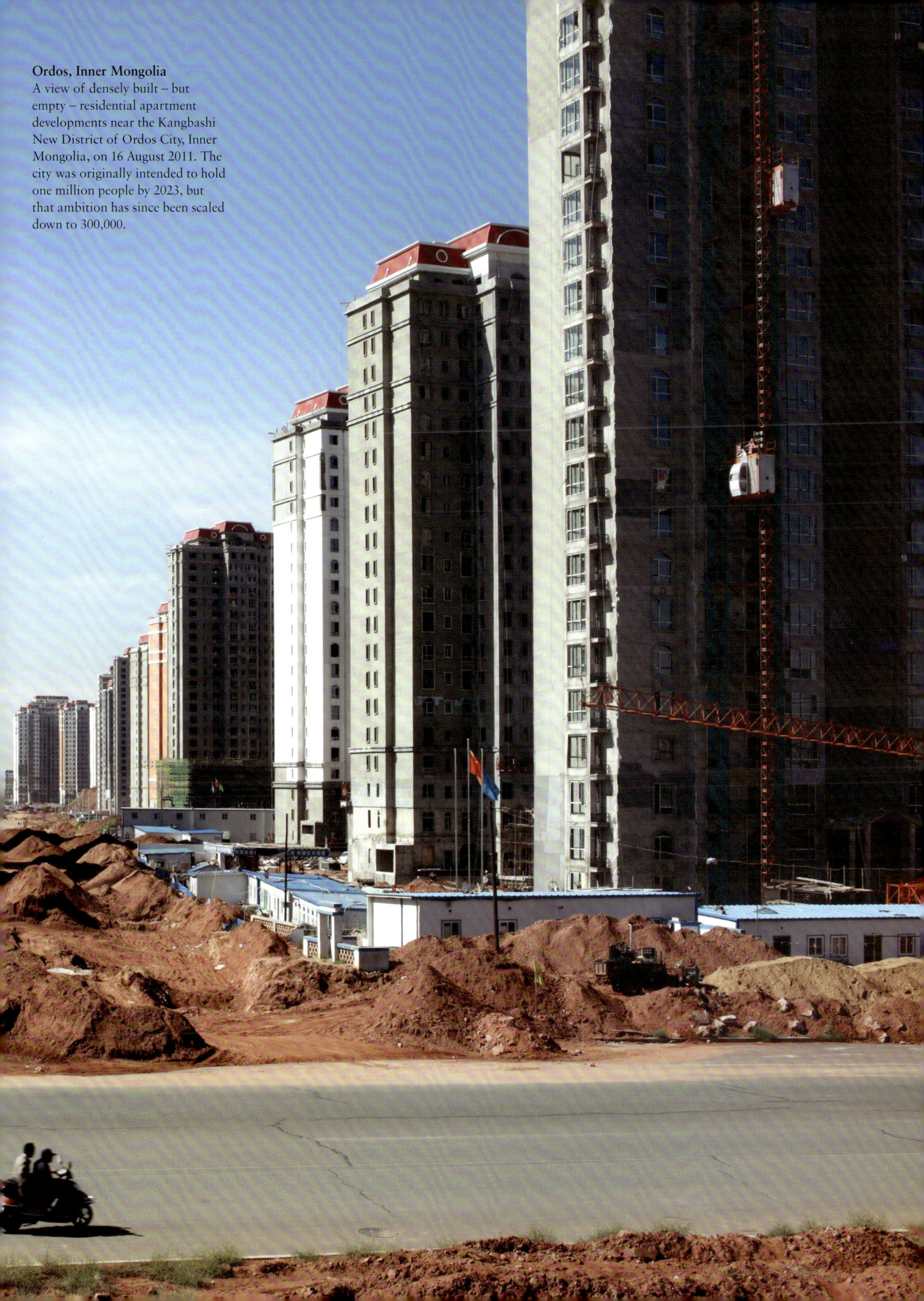

Ordos, Inner Mongolia
A view of densely built – but empty – residential apartment developments near the Kangbashi New District of Ordos City, Inner Mongolia, on 16 August 2011. The city was originally intended to hold one million people by 2023, but that ambition has since been scaled down to 300,000.

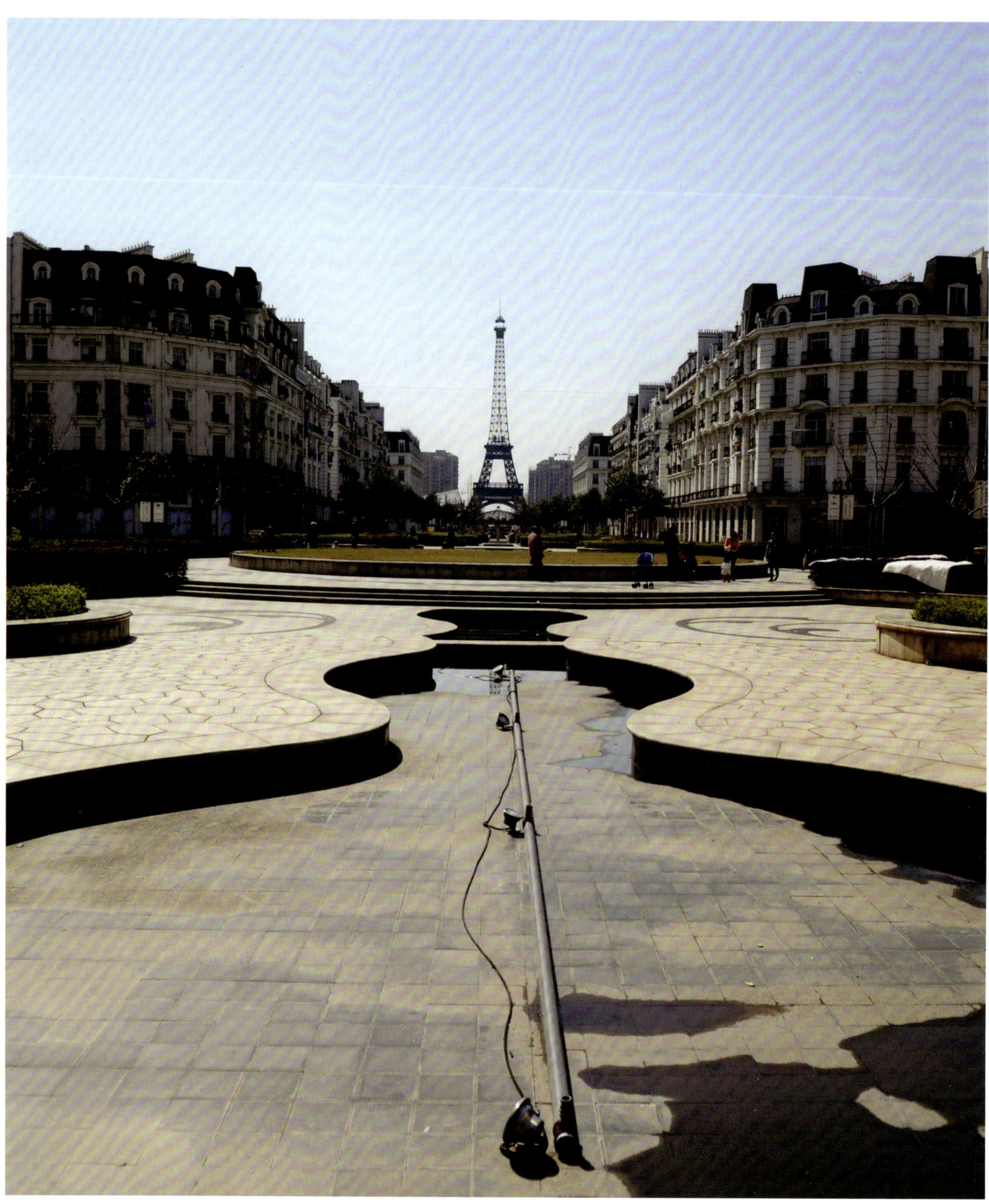

ALL PHOTOGRAPHS:

Tianducheng, Hangzhou, China
The Parisian theme behind the city of Tianducheng, China, is readily apparent from these photographs, not least in the 108m (354ft) replica of the Eiffel Tower, standing at the end of a long boulevard (above), and the lakeside château (opposite right). Other facilities include open-air theatre spaces (opposite top), fountains and landscaped parks. The city was opened for habitation in 2007, but by 2013 only about 2000 people had moved in; the total capacity of the town was 10,000. Like Thames Town featured previously, Tianducheng reflects Chinese developers' affection for iconic Western cities, although the architectural styles are often imbued with a certain idealistic and Disney-like quality, rather than realism.

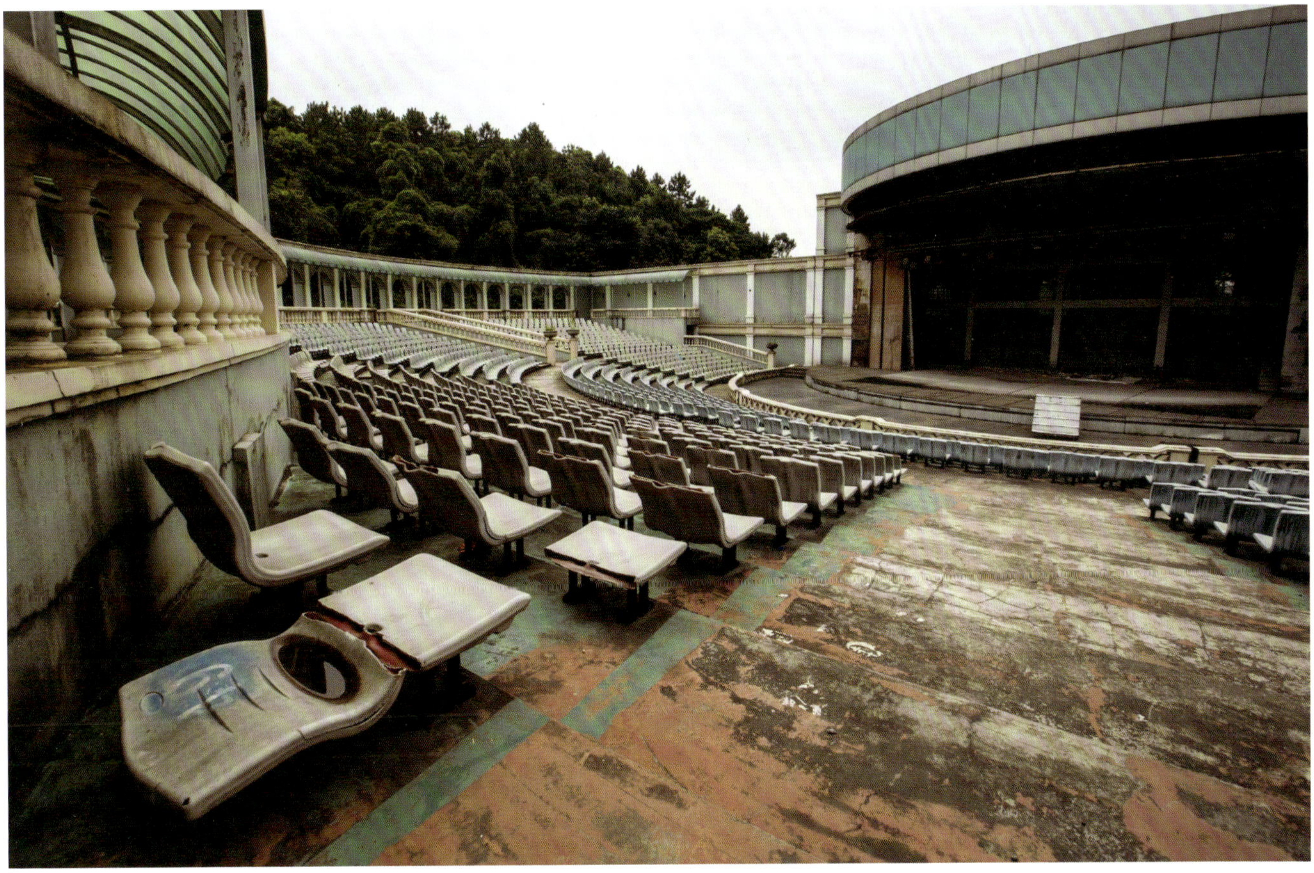

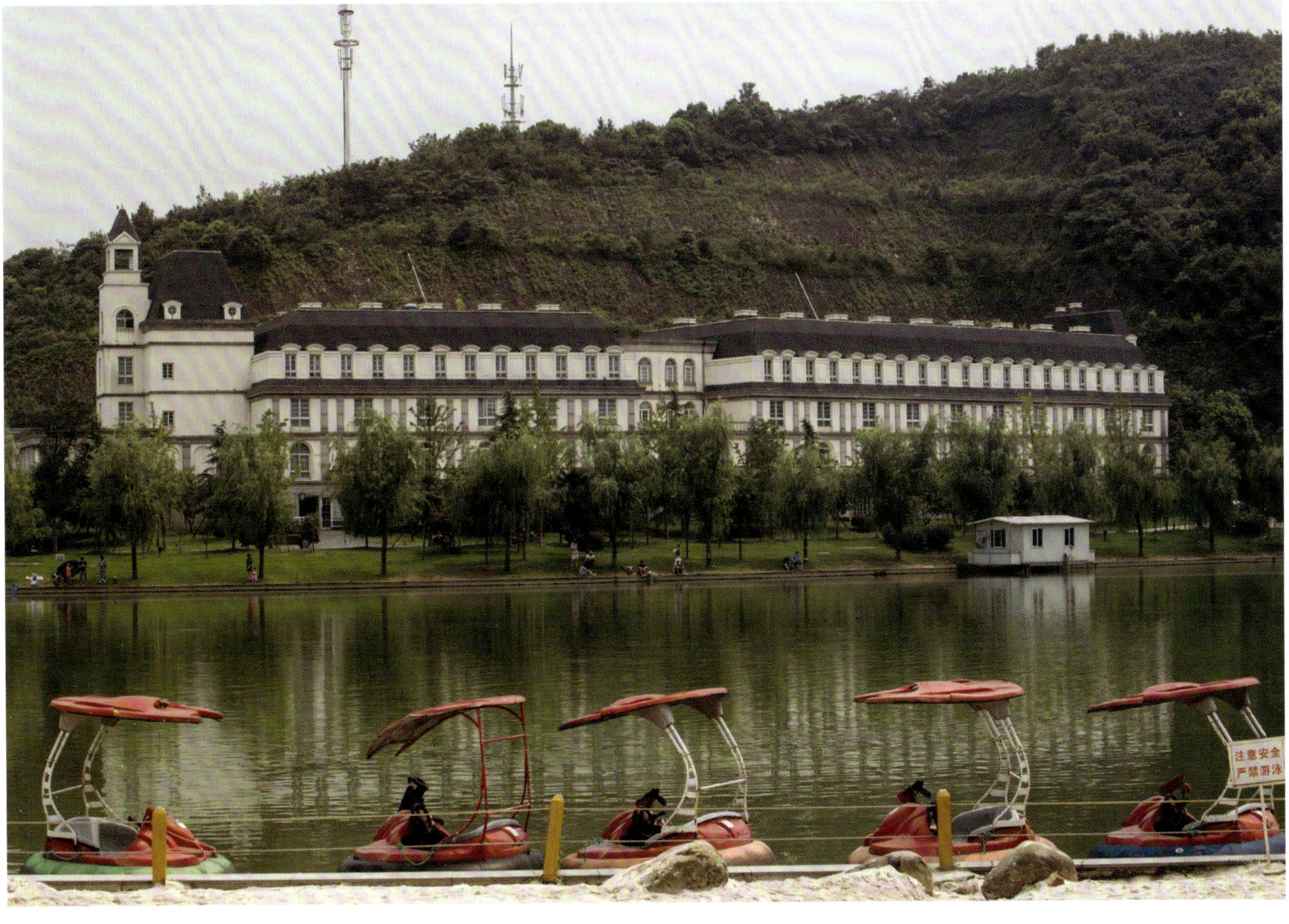

Bokor Hill Station, Preah Monivong National Park, Cambodia
French imperial architecture is to be found throughout much of Southeast Asia, especially in the countries that previously formed French Indochina (Vietnam, Cambodia, Laos). The Bokor Hill Station was originally built by the French in the 1920s as a colonial mountain resort, in what is today the Preah Monivong National Park. The building was abandoned by the French in the late 1940s; here we see the entrance to the complex's casino.

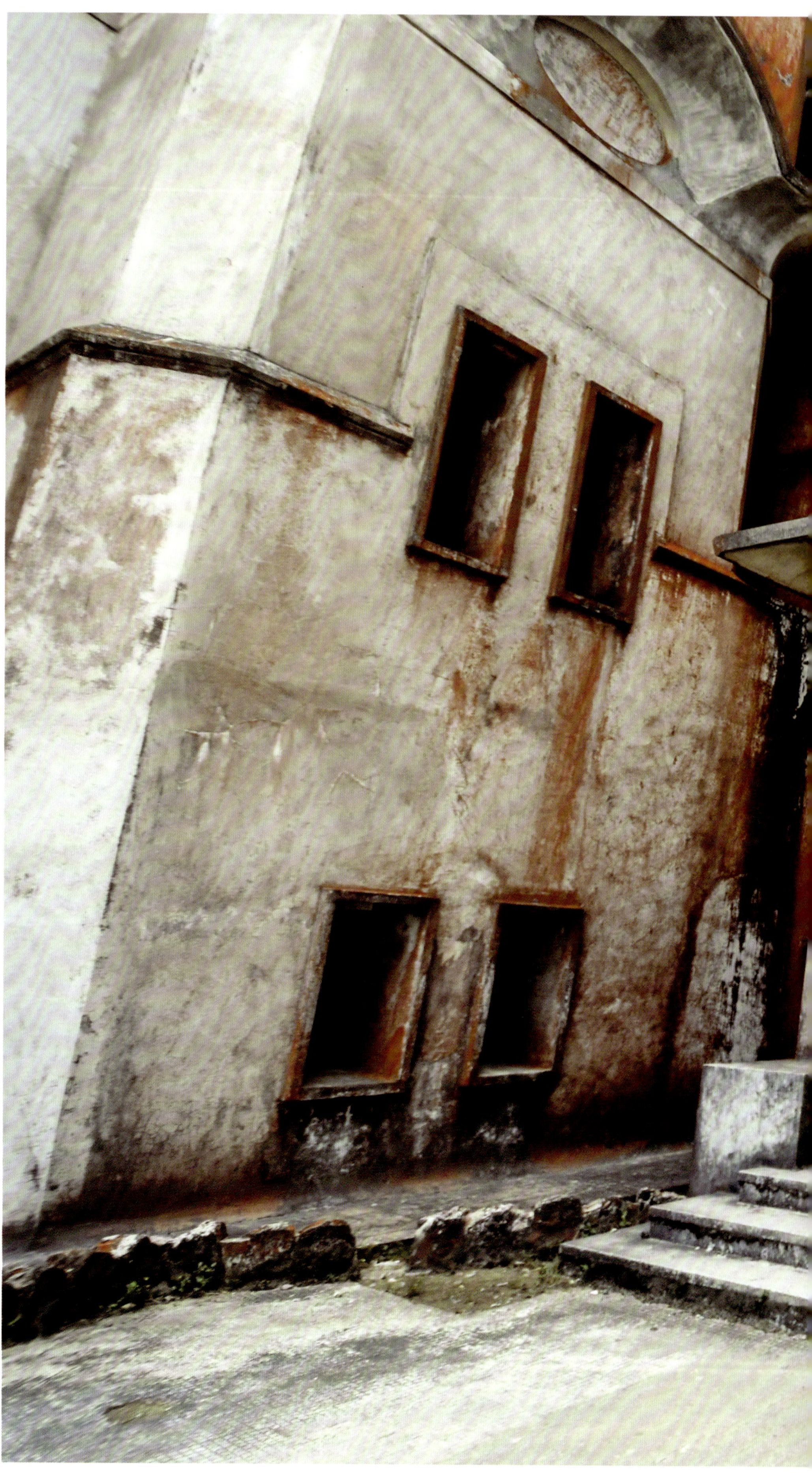

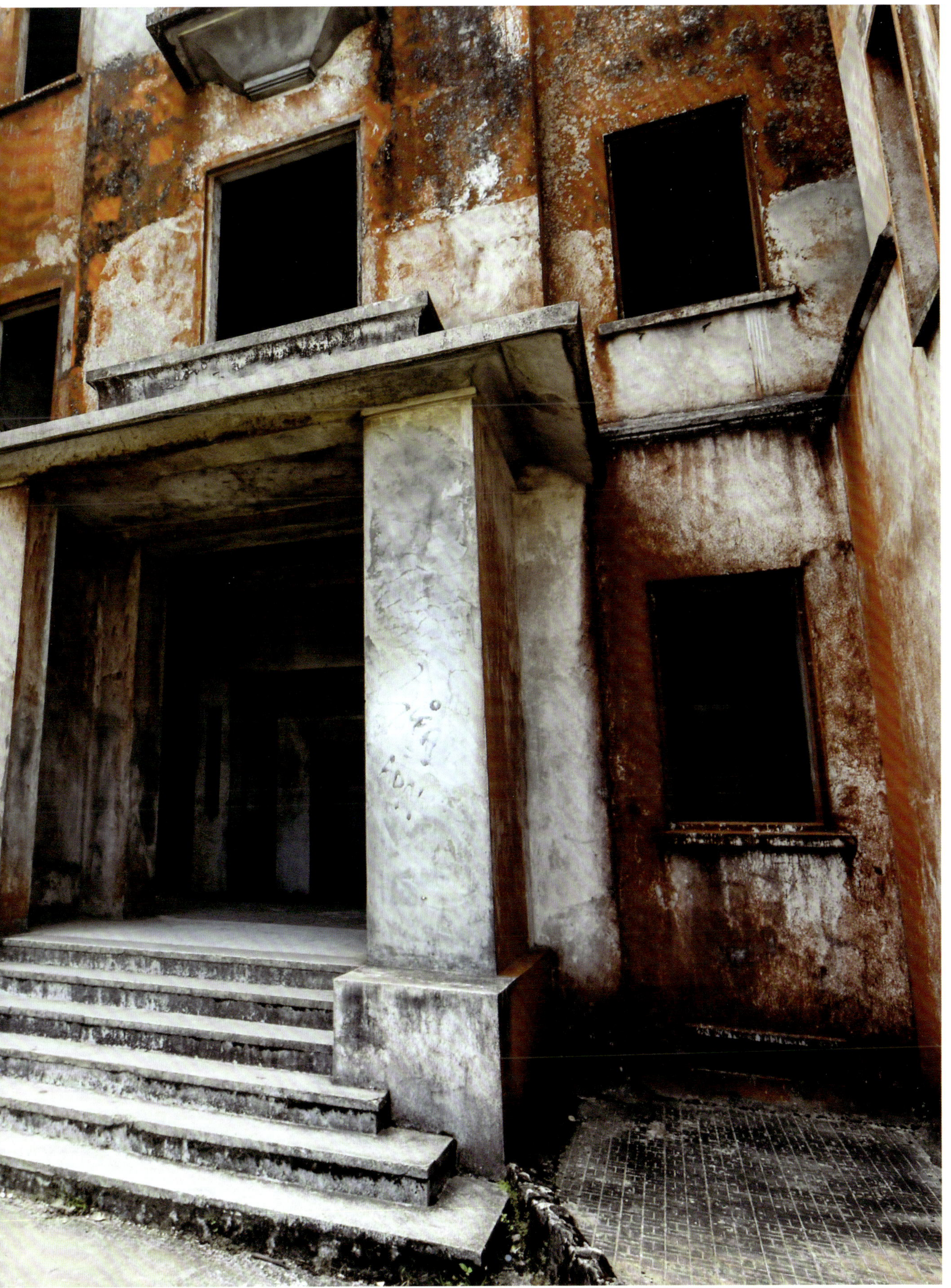

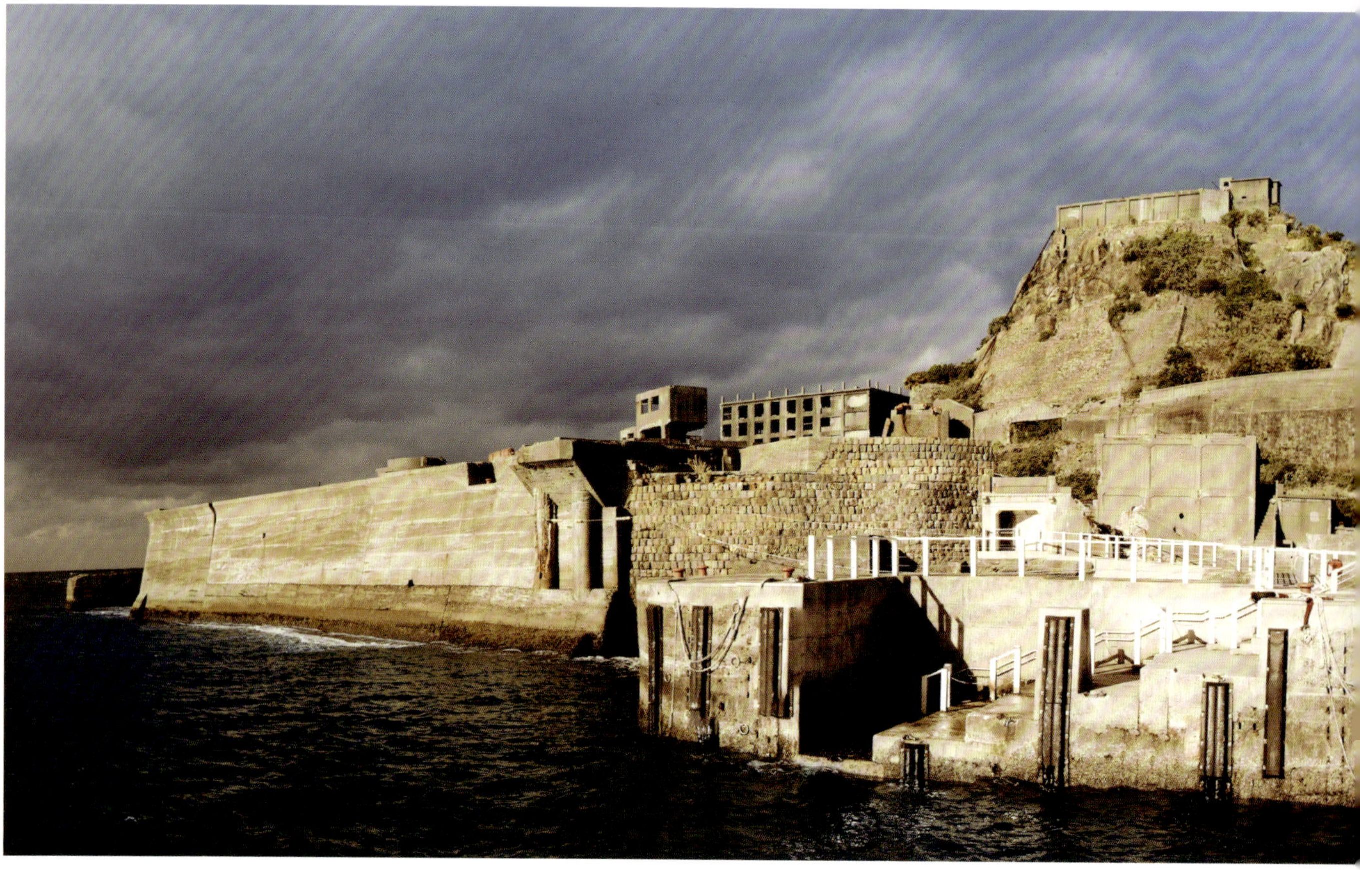

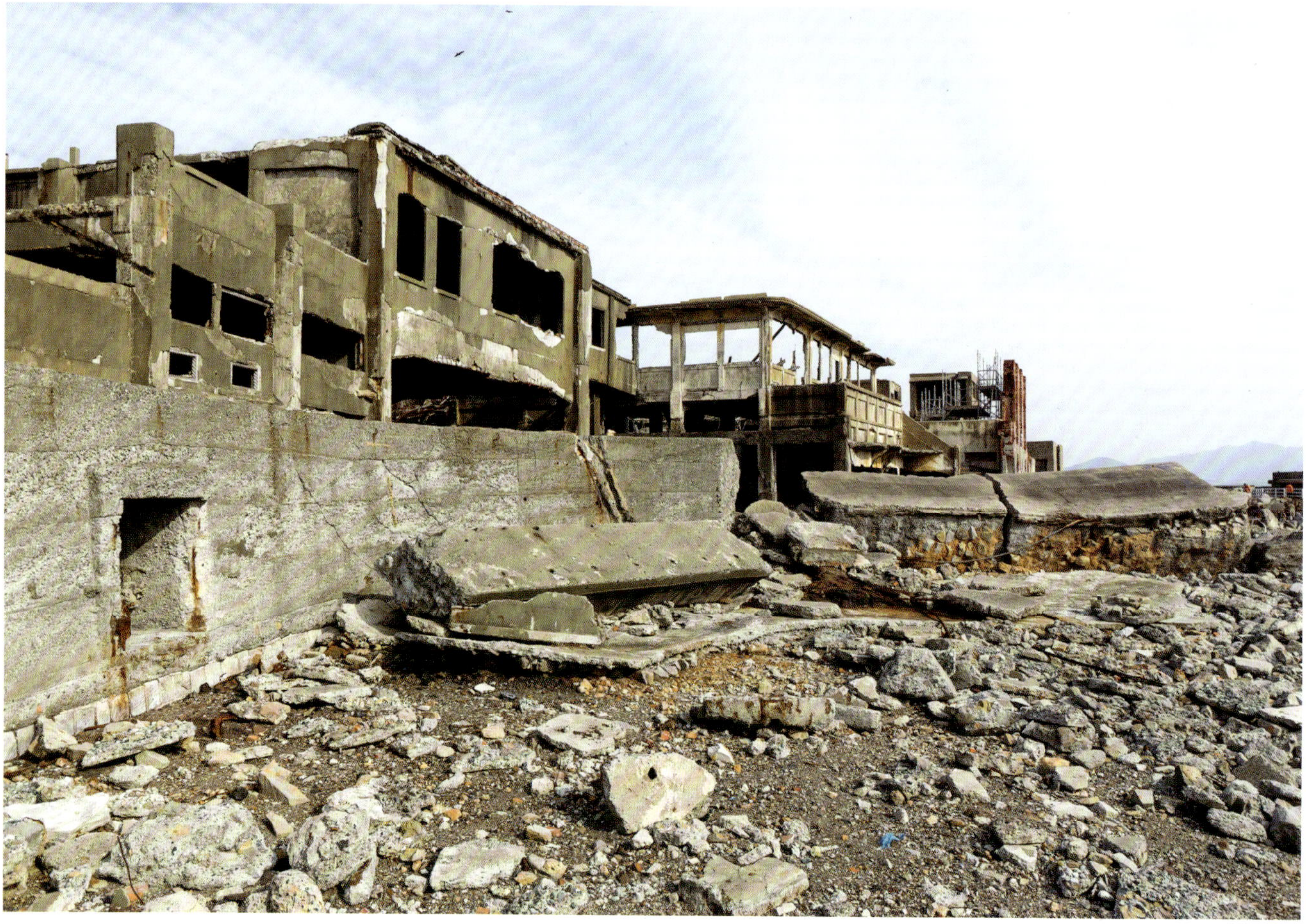

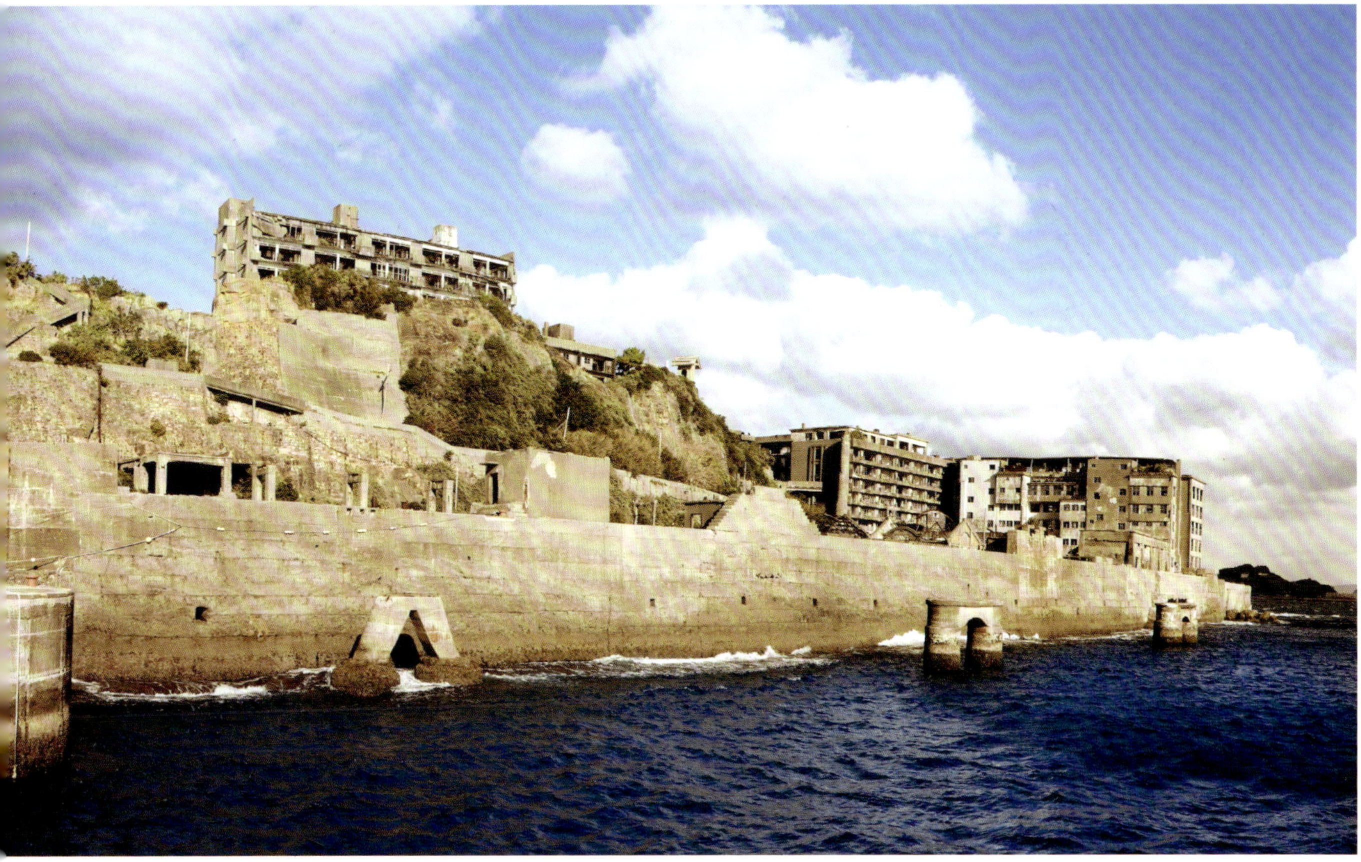

ABOVE & OPPOSITE:
Hashima Island, Nagasaki, Japan
Nicknamed 'Battleship Island' on account of its shape when viewed from above, Hashima lies 15km (9 miles) offshore from the city of Nagasaki. The island was essentially a huge seabed coal-mining installation established in the late 19th century, and finally abandoned in 1974 following the collapse in Japan's reliance upon that particular resource. For dark periods of the island's history, slave labour formed a major part of the island's population.

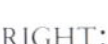

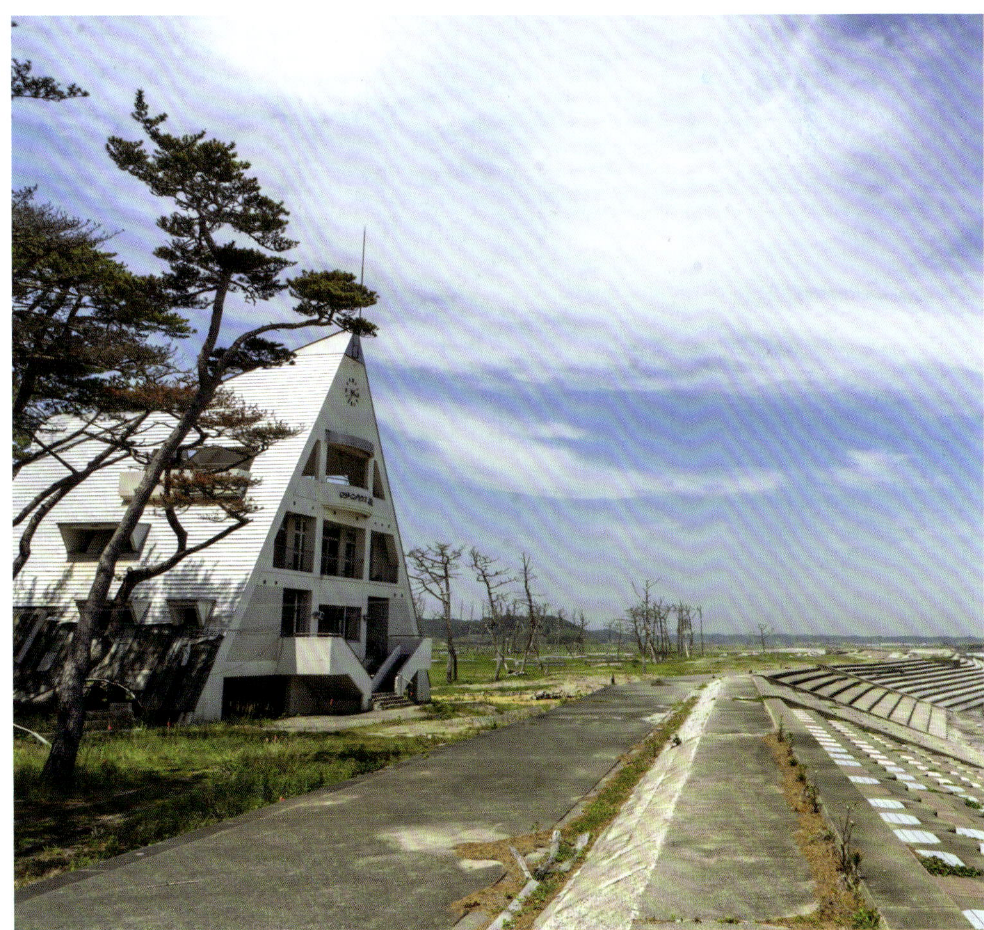

RIGHT:
Fukushima Prefecture, Japan
The Fukushima Prefecture in Japan was terribly affected by the 2011 Tohoku earthquake and tsunami and the subsequent Fukushima Daiichi nuclear disaster. Here we see an abandoned coastal house in a highly contaminated area. Slowly the population has been returning to the region, but about 3 per cent of the prefecture, concentrated around the nuclear plant, remains a no-go area.

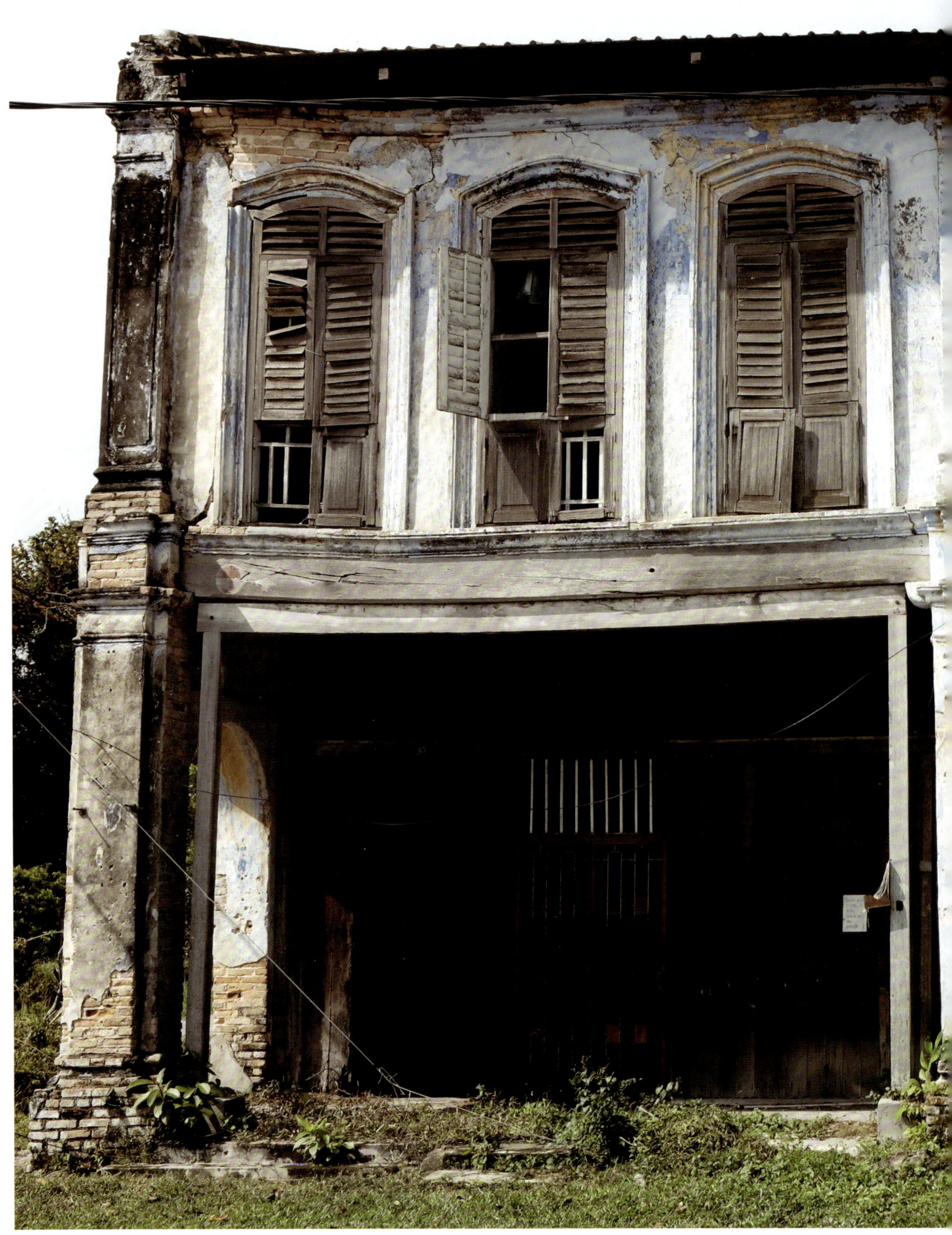

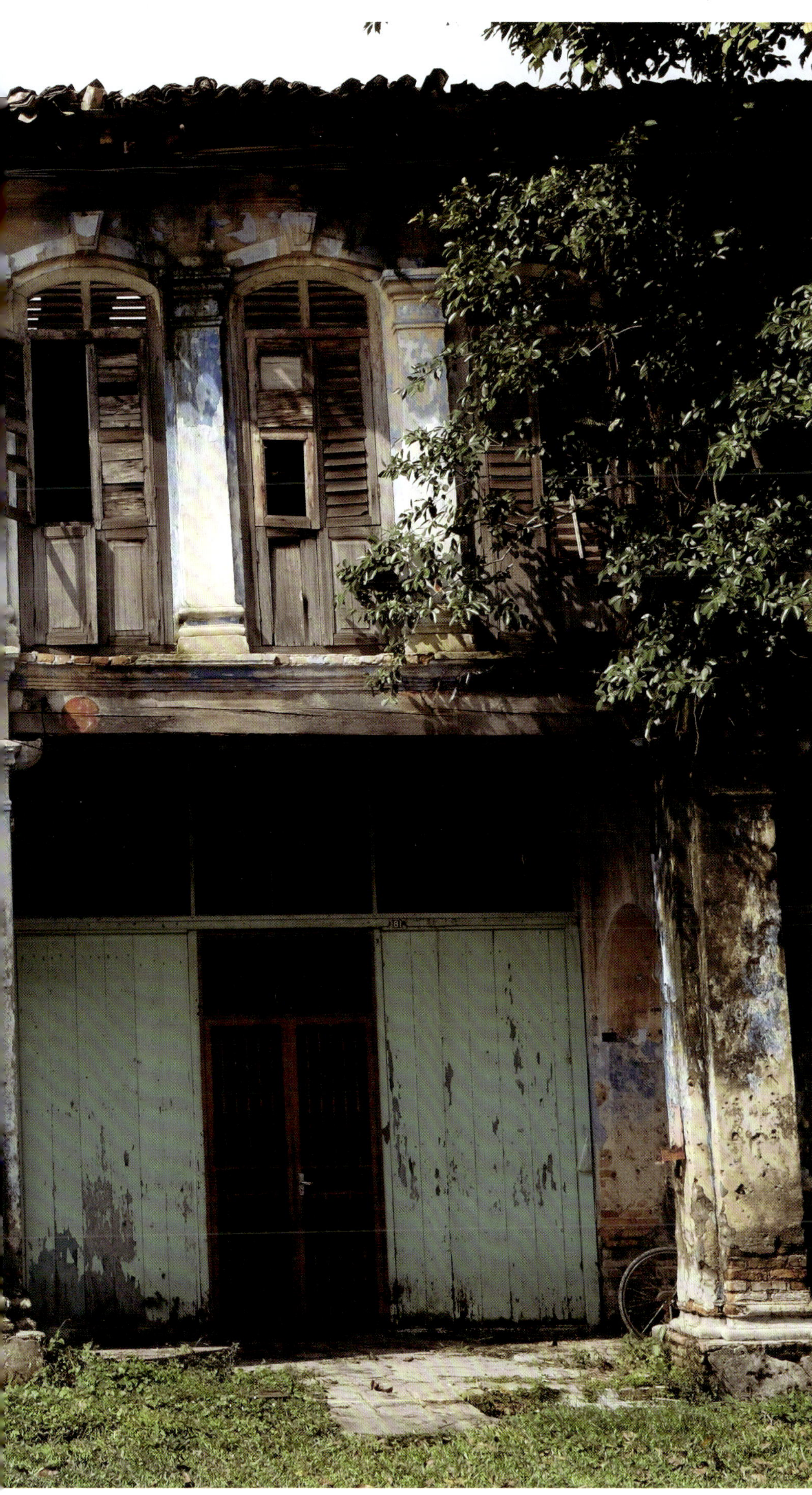

LEFT:

Papan, Perak, Malaysia

Pekan Papan, or Papan Town, is a small town in Perak, Malaysia, that flared into existence in the 19th century, first through the timber industry and later (in the early 20th century) on the back of local tin mining. The town's decline began with the Japanese occupation during World War II and with the collapse of tin-mining prosperity in the 1980s. Among nearby peoples, Papan has a reputation for supernatural activity.

OVERLEAF:

Sungai Lembing, Pahang, Malaysia

Another victim of the decline of tin-mining in Malaysia is the town of Sungai Lembing in Kuantan District, Pahang. At its height in the first half of the 20th century, the town was one of the richest in the region. It also boasted one of the longest and deepest mines in the world. Today it is severely underpopulated, and subject to periodic heavy flooding.

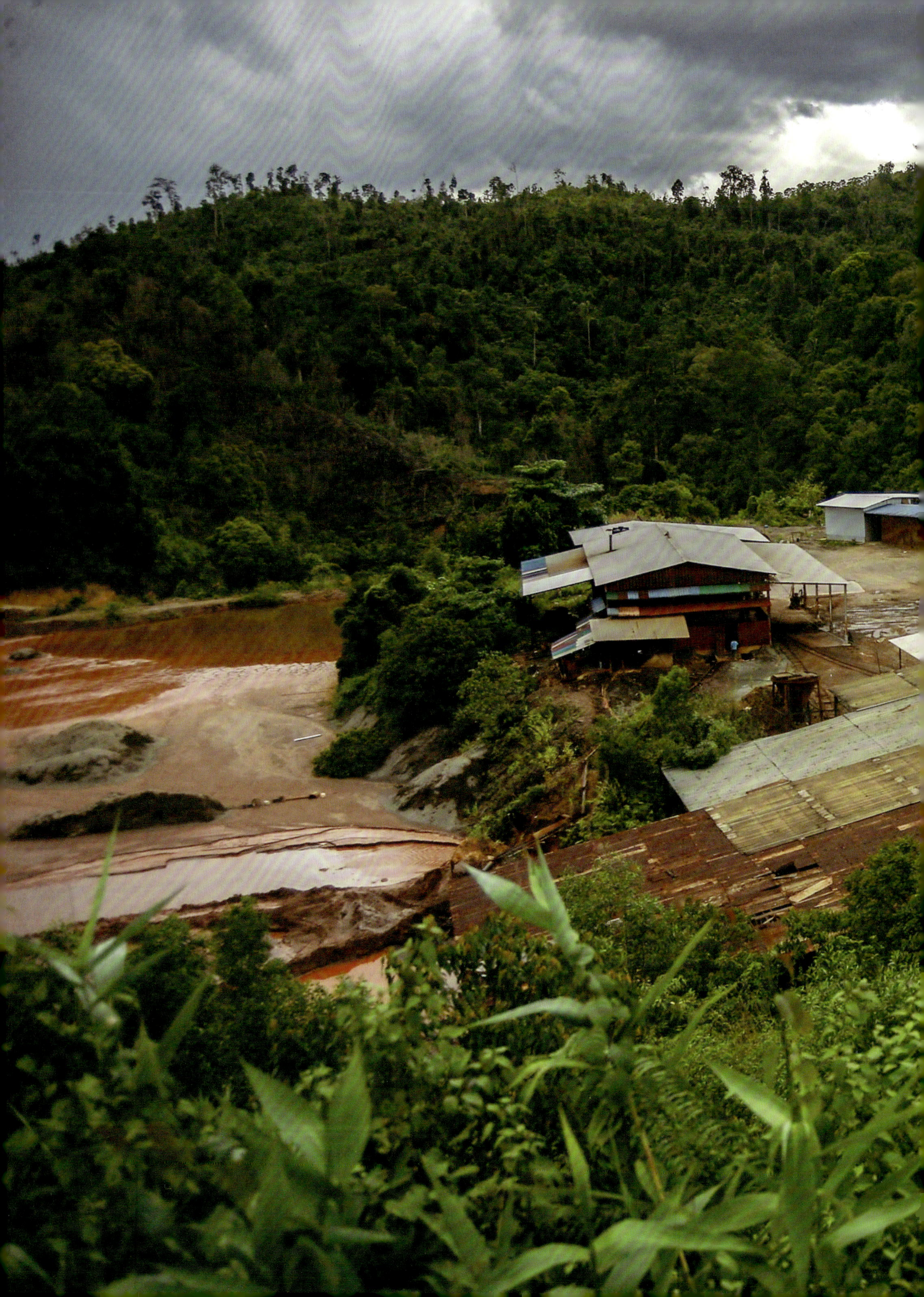

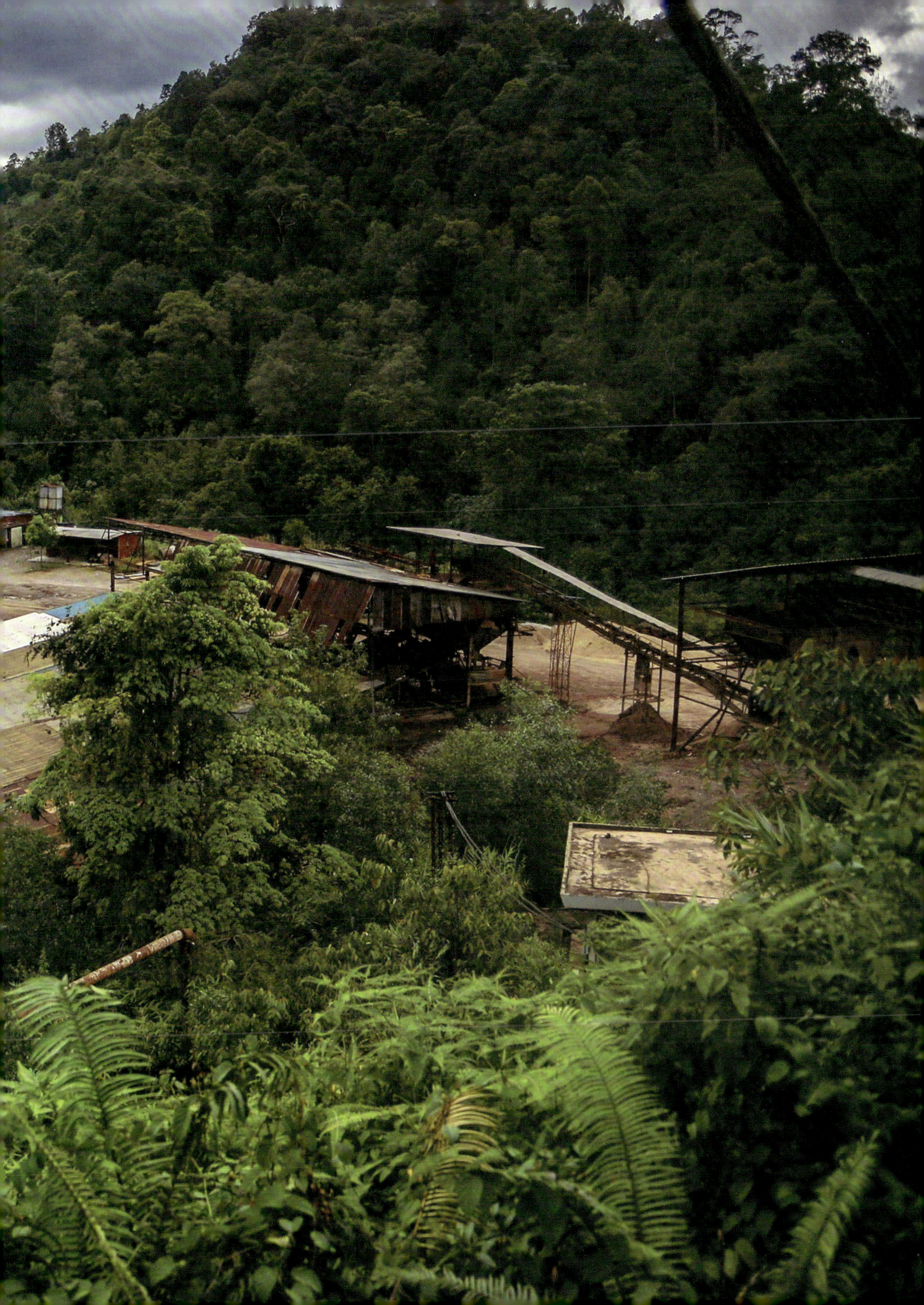

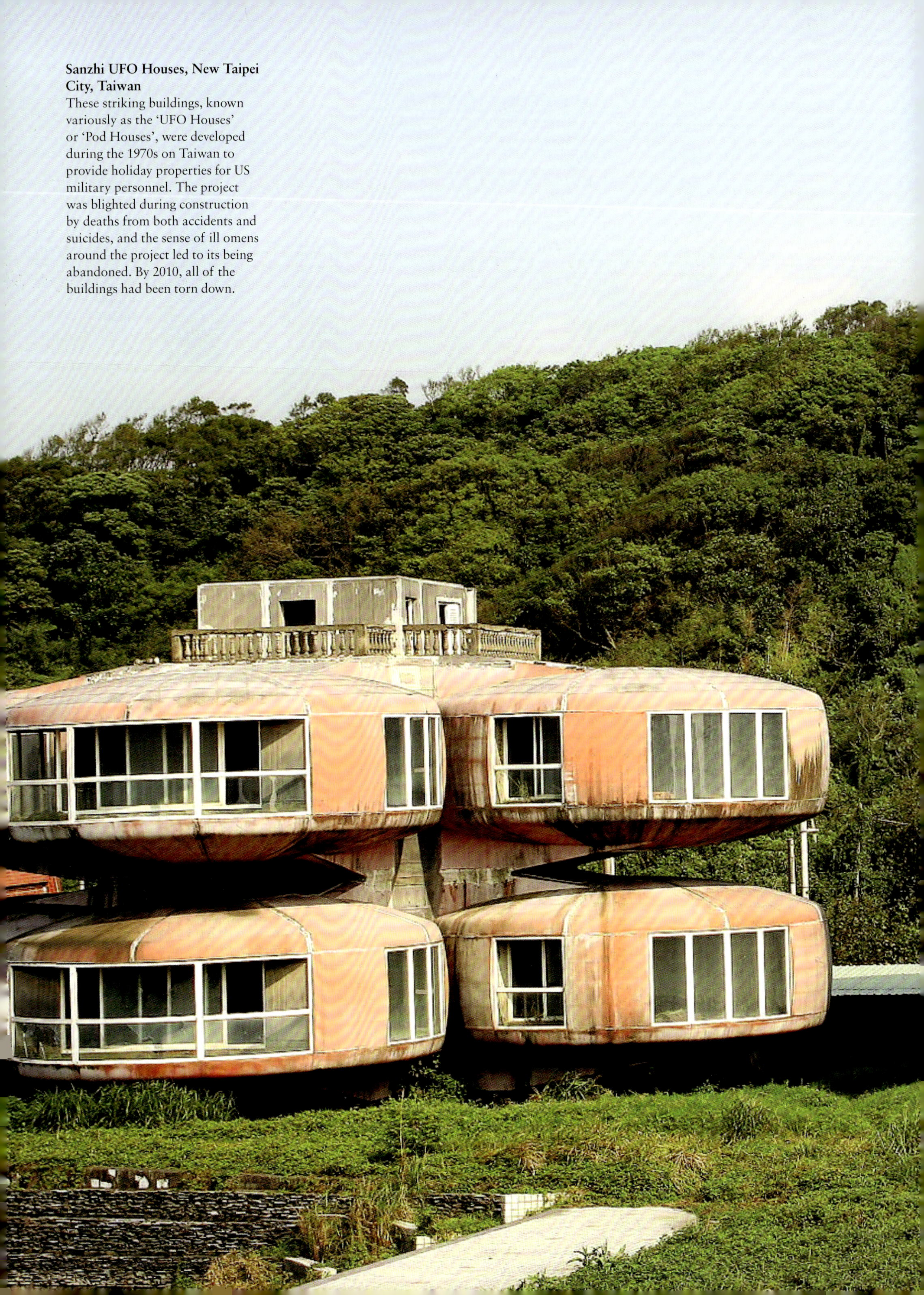

Sanzhi UFO Houses, New Taipei City, Taiwan
These striking buildings, known variously as the 'UFO Houses' or 'Pod Houses', were developed during the 1970s on Taiwan to provide holiday properties for US military personnel. The project was blighted during construction by deaths from both accidents and suicides, and the sense of ill omens around the project led to its being abandoned. By 2010, all of the buildings had been torn down.

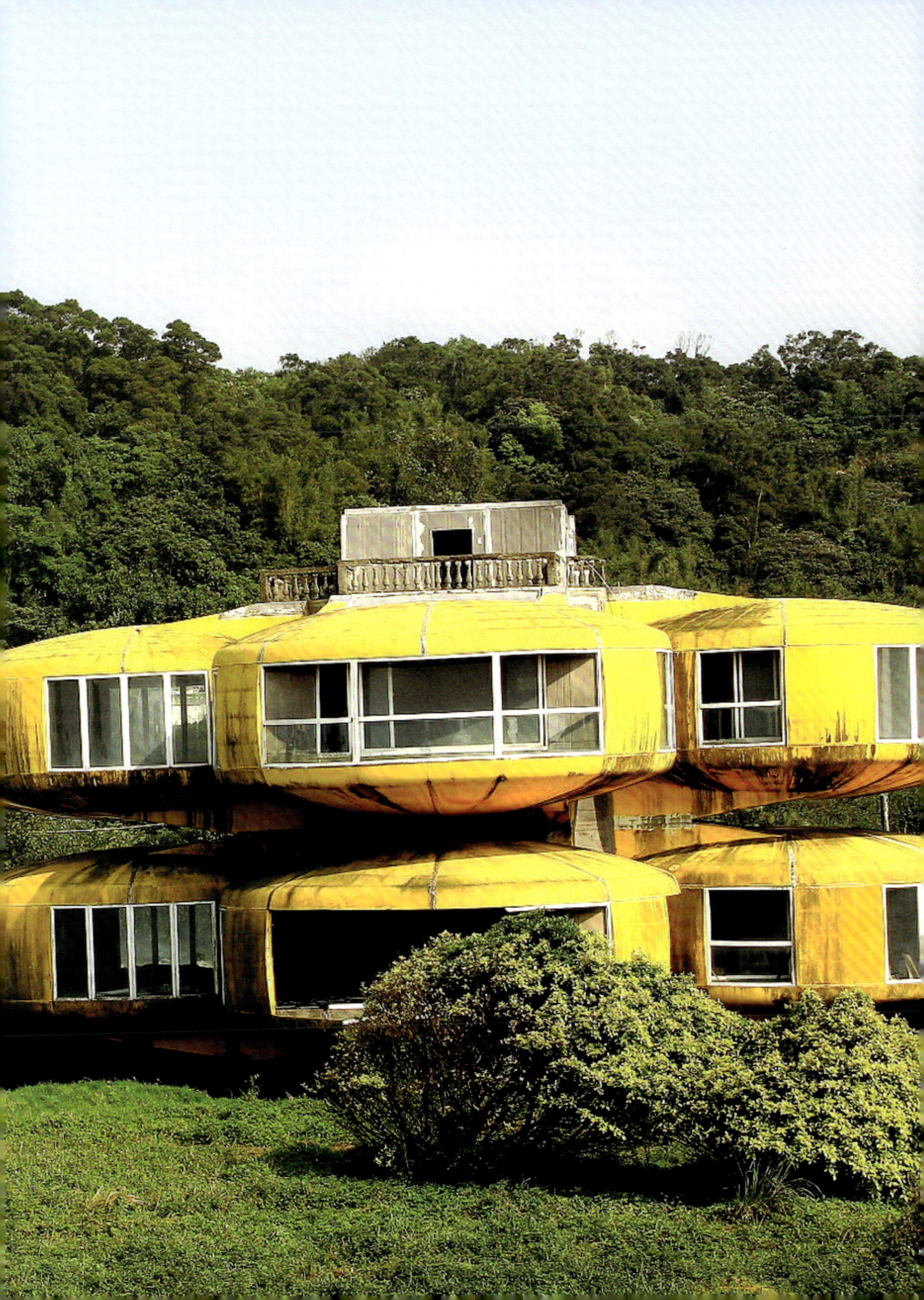

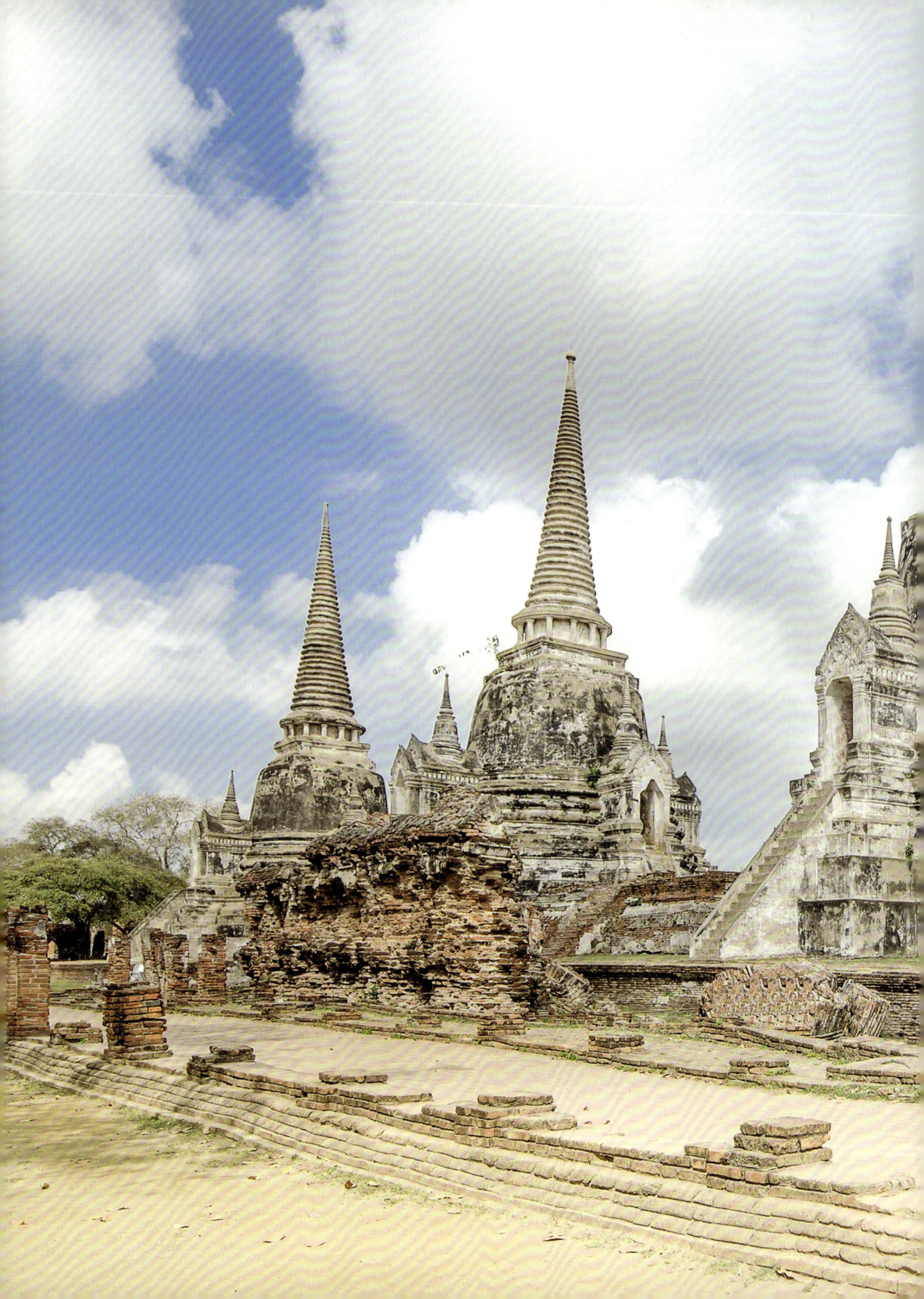

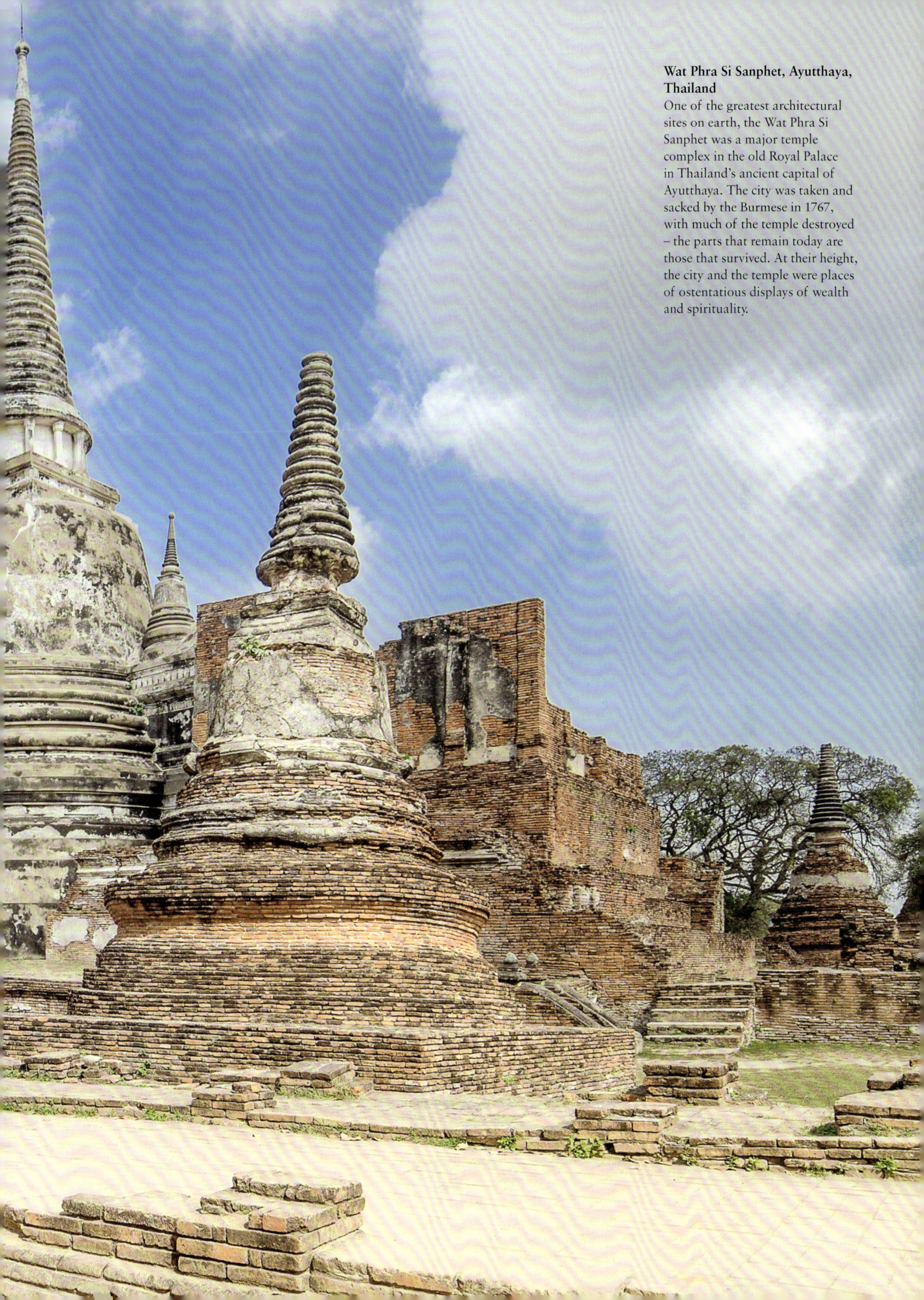

Wat Phra Si Sanphet, Ayutthaya, Thailand
One of the greatest architectural sites on earth, the Wat Phra Si Sanphet was a major temple complex in the old Royal Palace in Thailand's ancient capital of Ayutthaya. The city was taken and sacked by the Burmese in 1767, with much of the temple destroyed – the parts that remain today are those that survived. At their height, the city and the temple were places of ostentatious displays of wealth and spirituality.

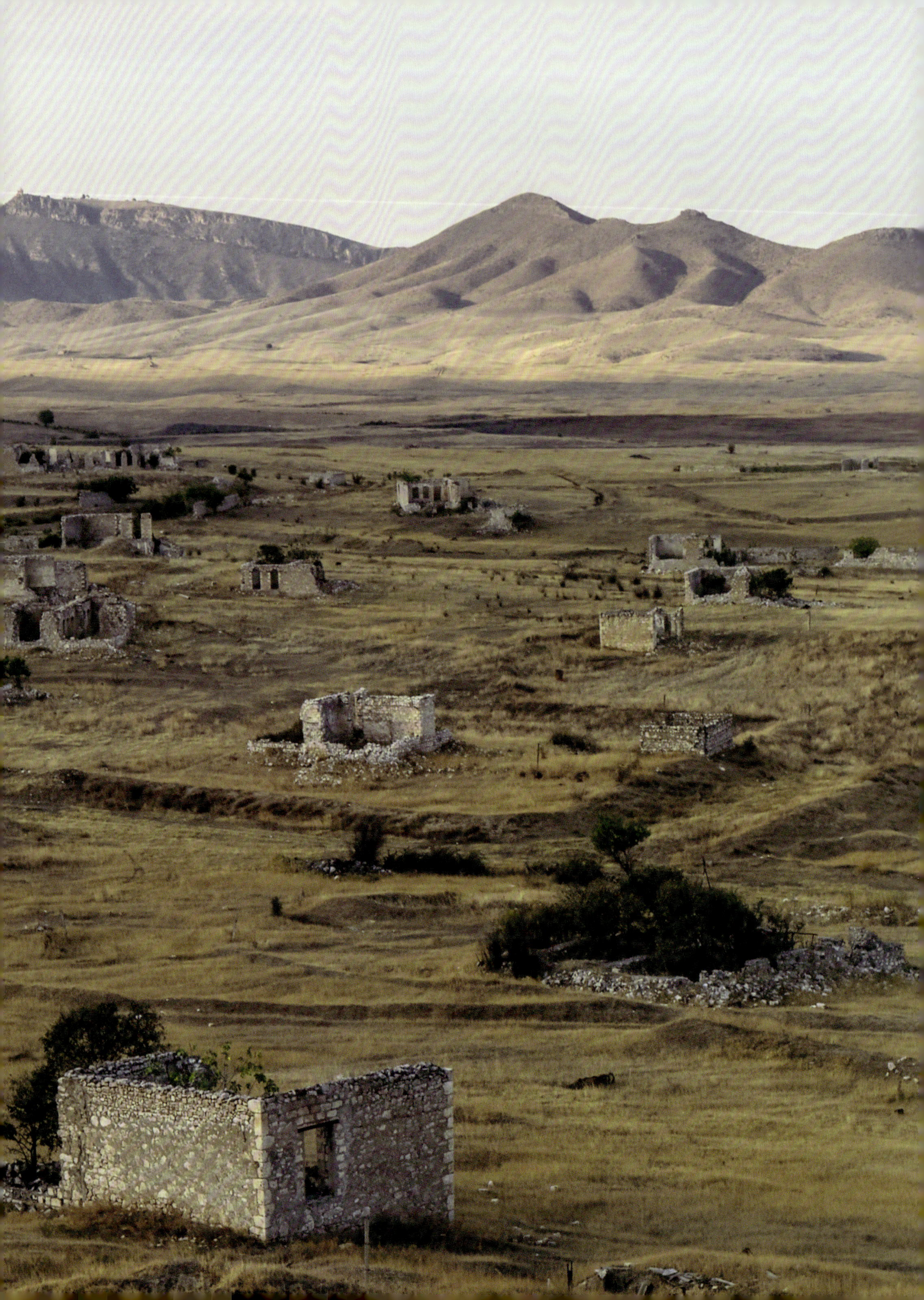

Central Asia

Central Asia covers a vast portion of the planet, and includes some regions that have particularly low population densities. The state of Kazakhstan, for example, is roughly the same size as the whole of Western Europe – which has a population of nearly 500 million – but the entirety of that great country has just 18 million people. Central Asia is also a region that has been through tumultuous economic, political and geographical changes. Entire empires have risen and fallen within the region, and once mighty trade routes – not least the ancient Silk Road – have laced its deserts, steppes and mountains. In the 20th century, many of the Central Asian states fell under the ideological umbrella of the Soviet Union, a period that produced cruel social engineering, particularly under Stalin's reign, with whole ethnic communities deported out to gulags or unpromising locations further east. Wars and genocides rippled across the landscape. Even after the fall of the USSR, the faultlines carved into Central Asia by that period have spawned numerous conflicts in places such as Georgia, Nagorno-Karabakh, Chechnya and, most conspicuously, Afghanistan. Combine such turmoil with major environmental, population and economic shifts, and it is little wonder that Central Asia is littered with ghost towns, some of ancient origins and others dating back mere decades, but all testaments to the vagaries of time.

LEFT:
Agdam, Nagorno-Karabakh Republic/Azerbaijan
Looking at Agdam today, it is hard to imagine that in 1989 it was a thriving town of c. 29,000 inhabitants. During the Nagorno-Karabakh War of 1991, it was captured by Armenian forces and subsequently destroyed. Looting and the stripping of houses for building materials finished the job.

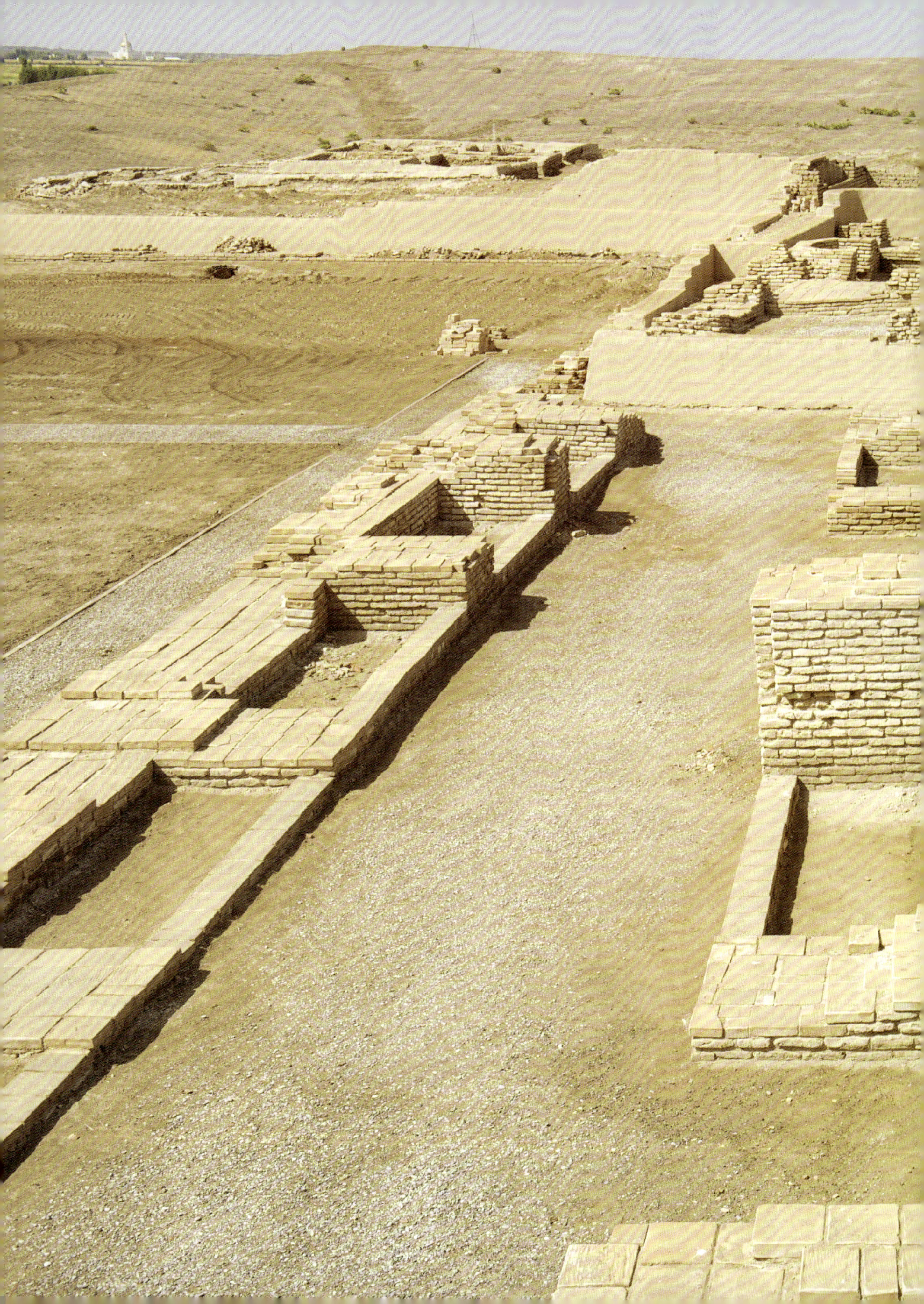

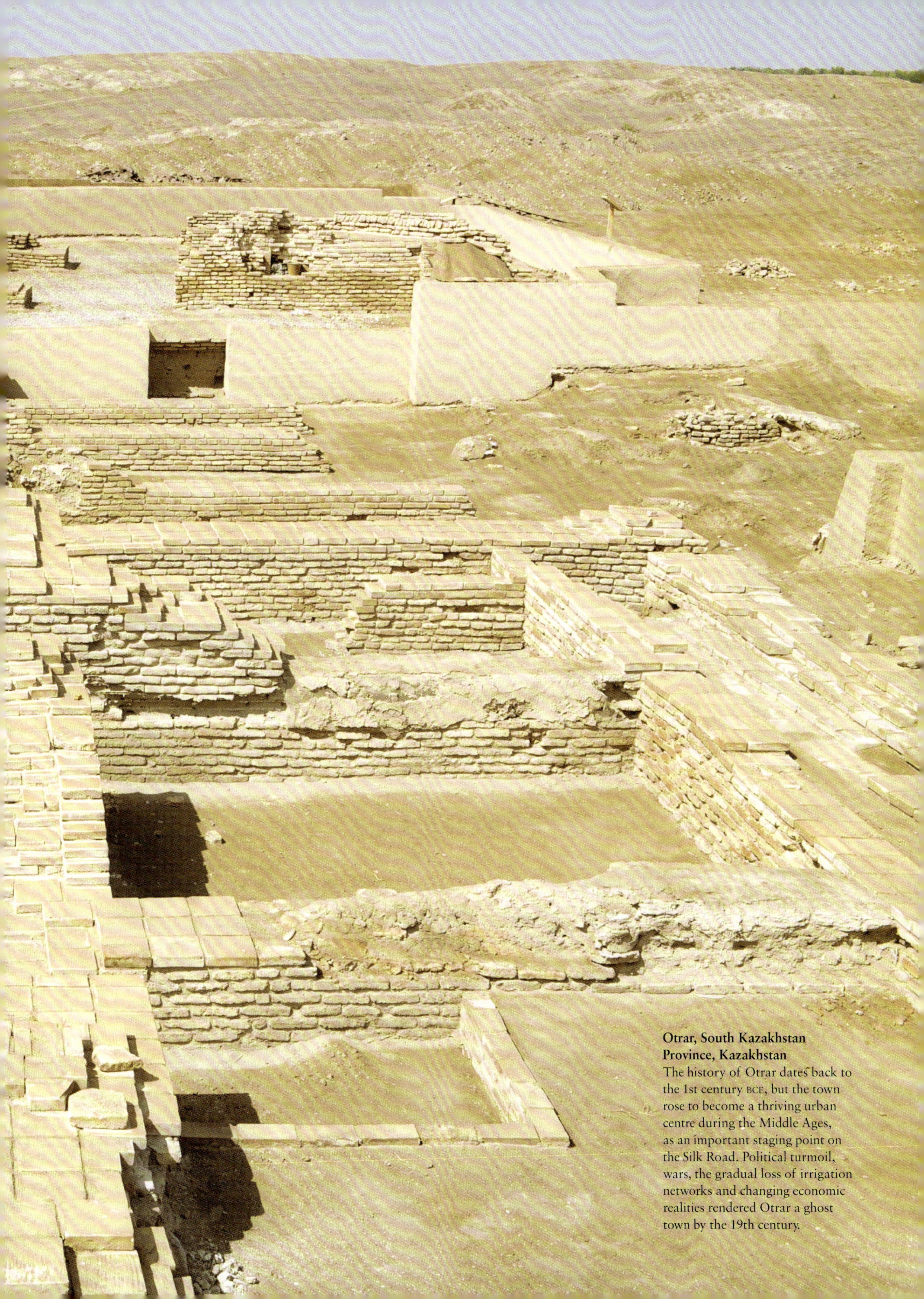

Otrar, South Kazakhstan Province, Kazakhstan
The history of Otrar dates back to the 1st century BCE, but the town rose to become a thriving urban centre during the Middle Ages, as an important staging point on the Silk Road. Political turmoil, wars, the gradual loss of irrigation networks and changing economic realities rendered Otrar a ghost town by the 19th century.

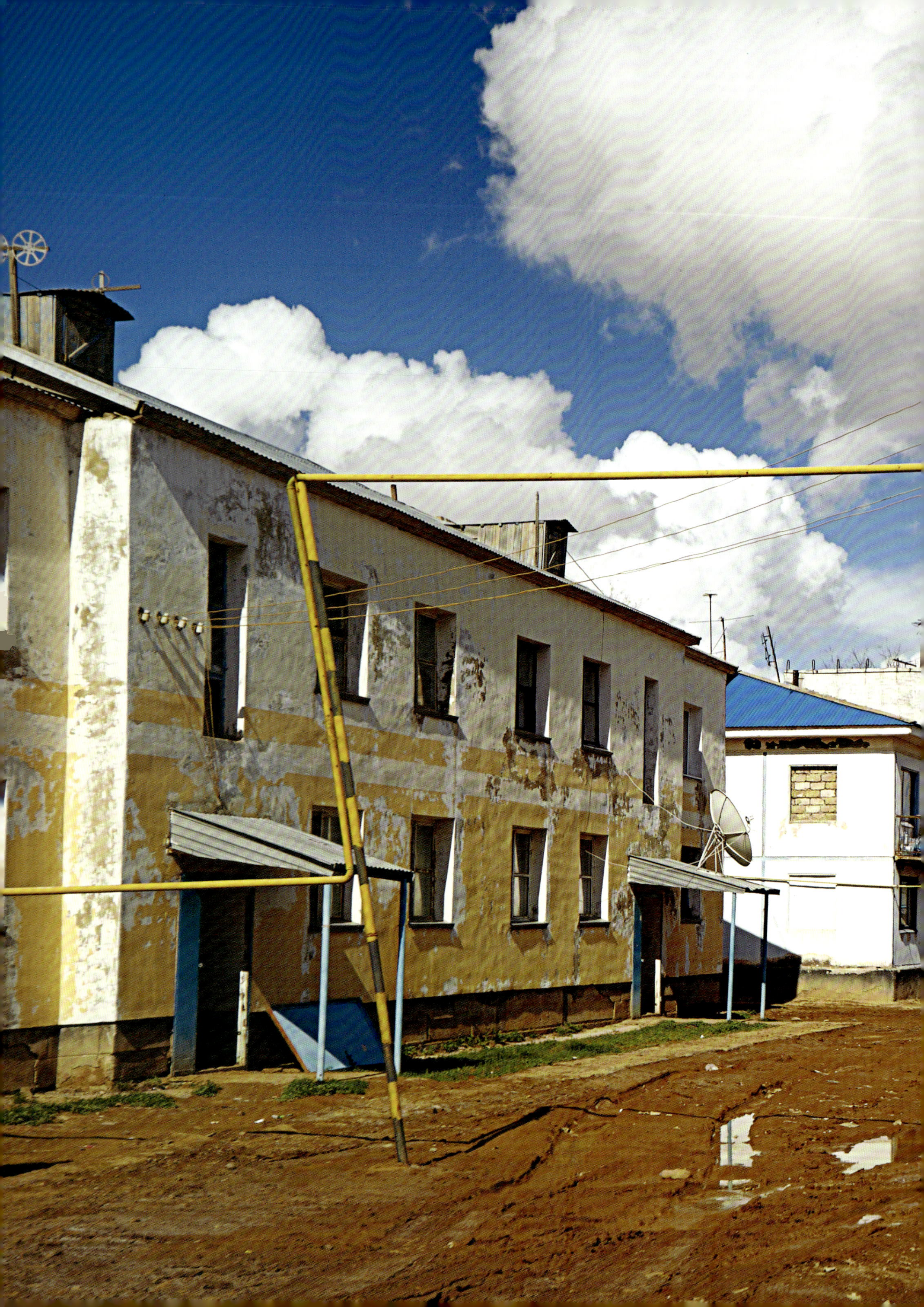

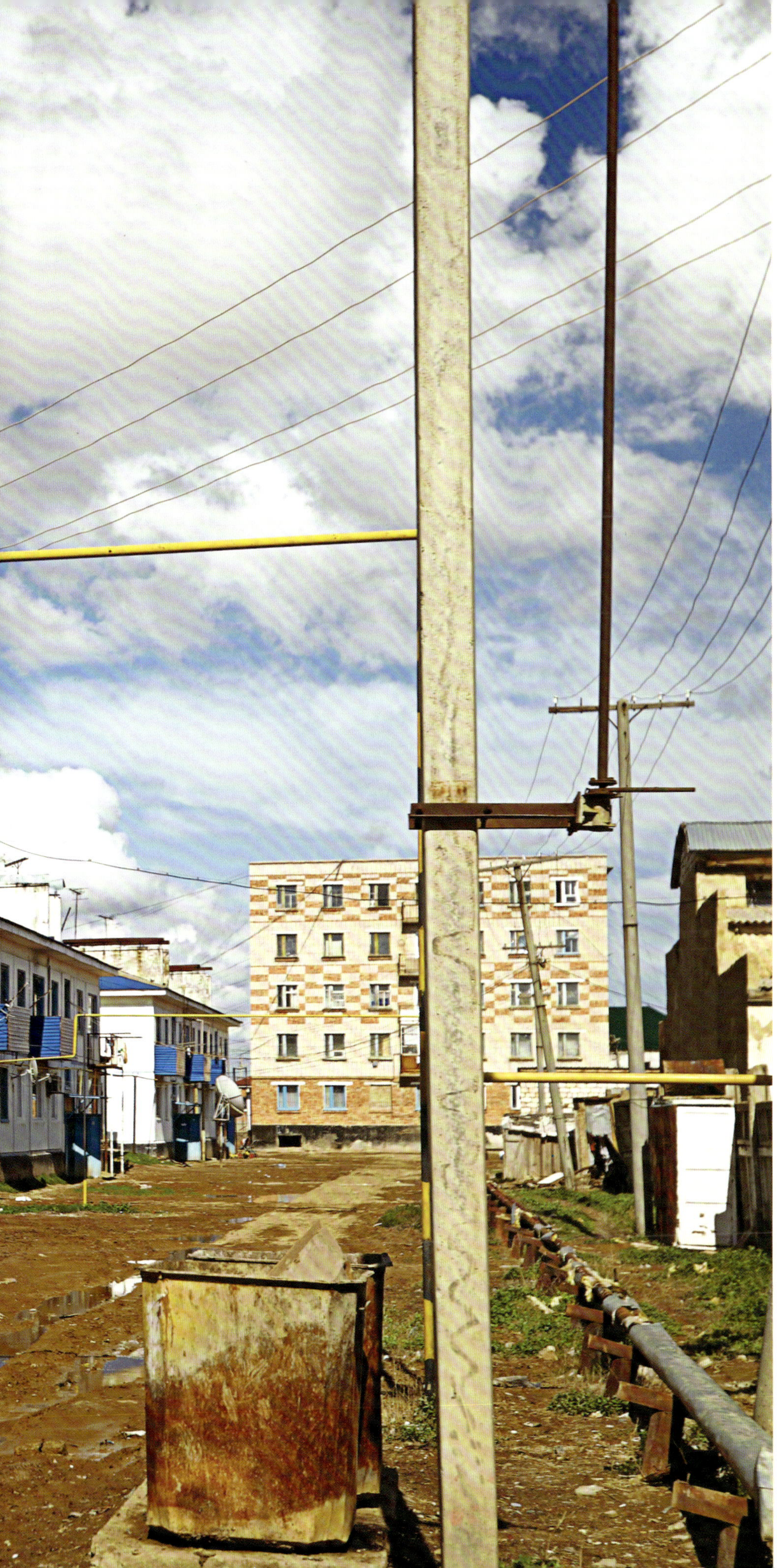

Dosser, Kazakhstan
This abandoned street in Dosser, Kazakhstan, is defined by its Soviet-era housing. Kazakhstan has been through huge social and political change since the 1990s, especially with its independence from the Soviet Union. There has been much population movement, often dictated by the development of the petrochemical industry, and some once-thriving towns and settlements have emptied out as work and opportunity gravitated elsewhere in the vast country.

Abkhazia
A selection of animals bring some life to a deserted urban zone in Abkhazia, a partially recognized state to the northwest of Georgia in southern Central Asia. The washing on the line, and the livestock, indicates some level of habitation. Hundreds of thousands of ethnic Georgians were expelled from the territory during and following the Abkhazian War (1992–93).

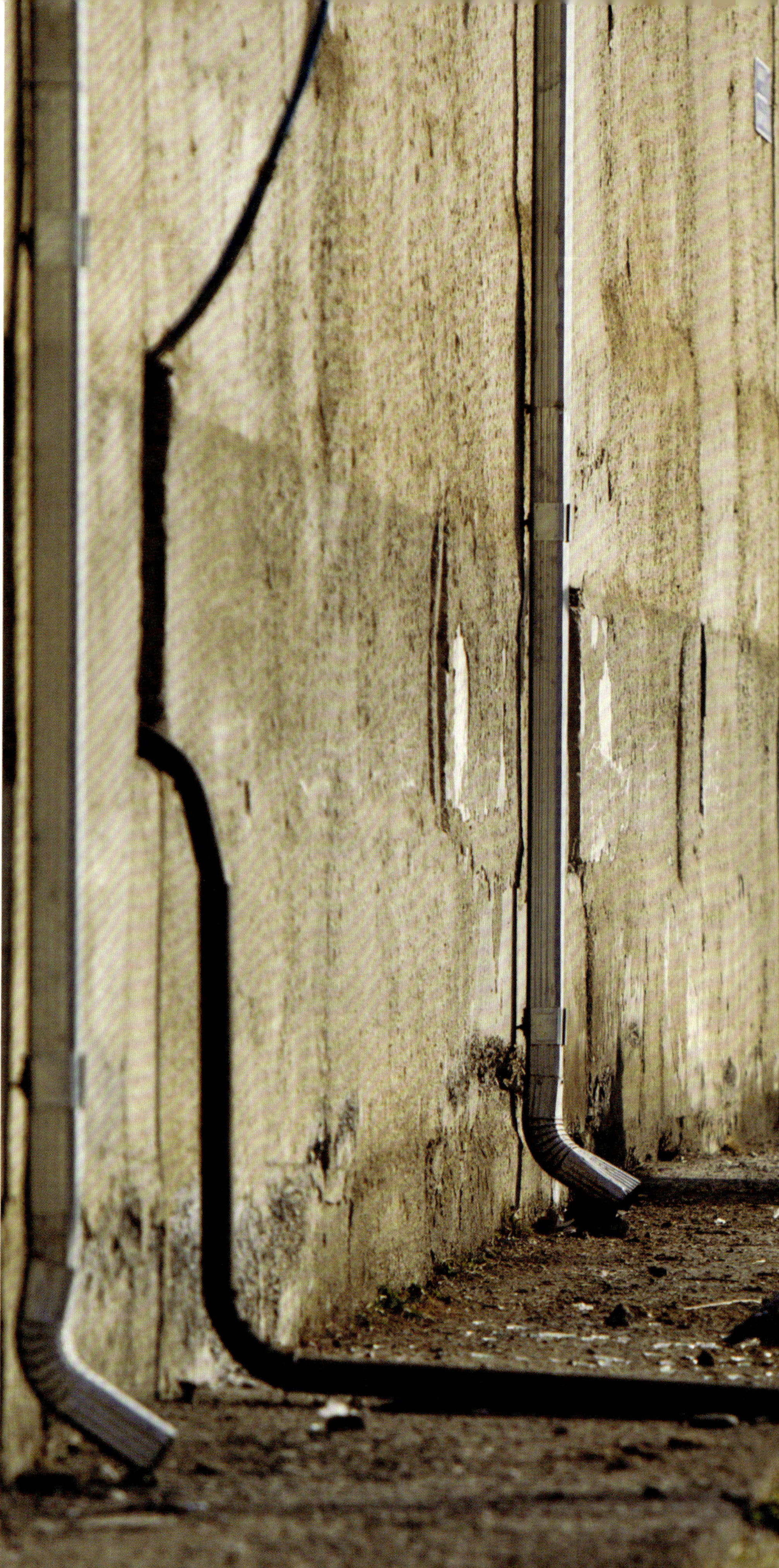

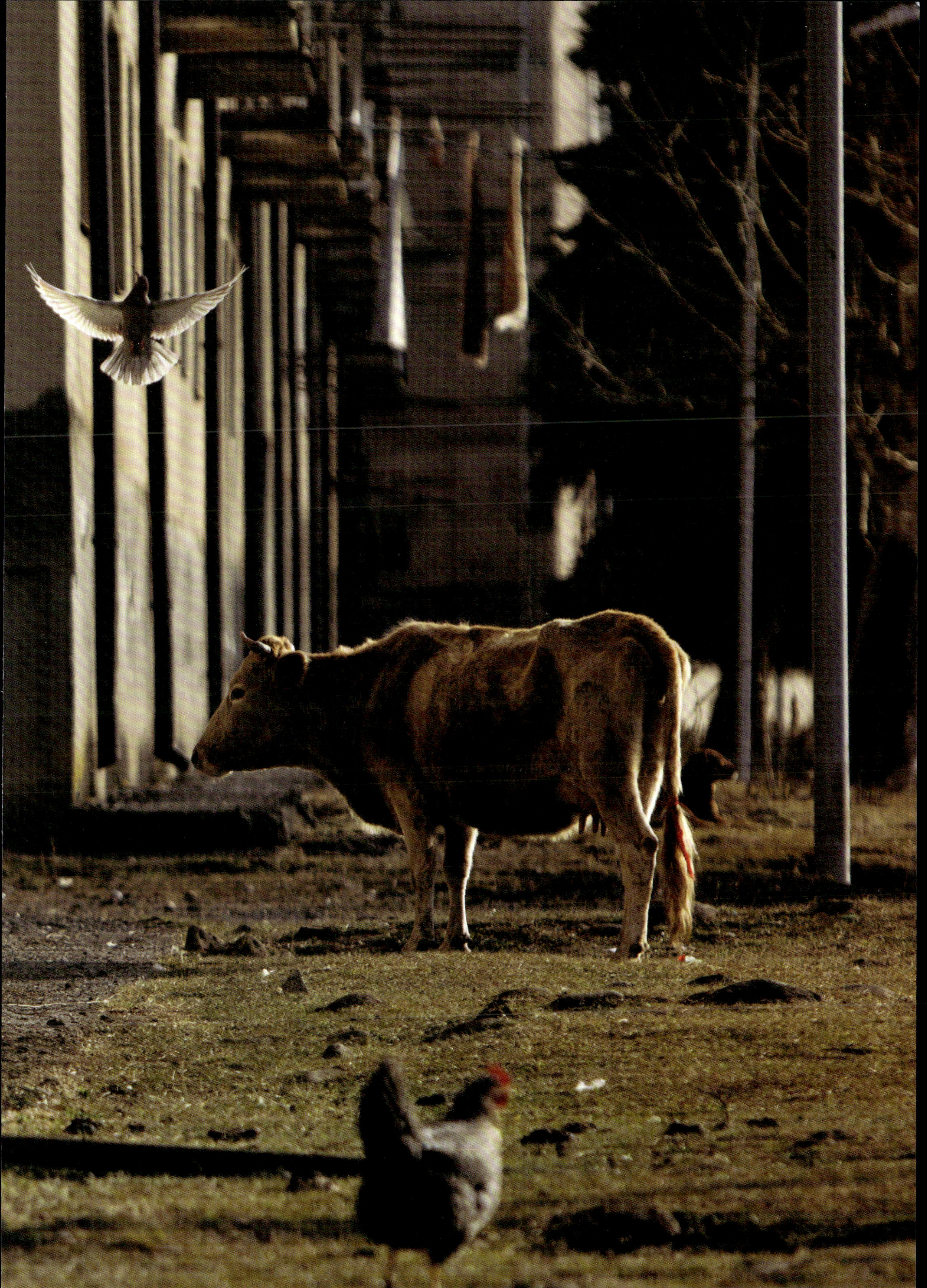

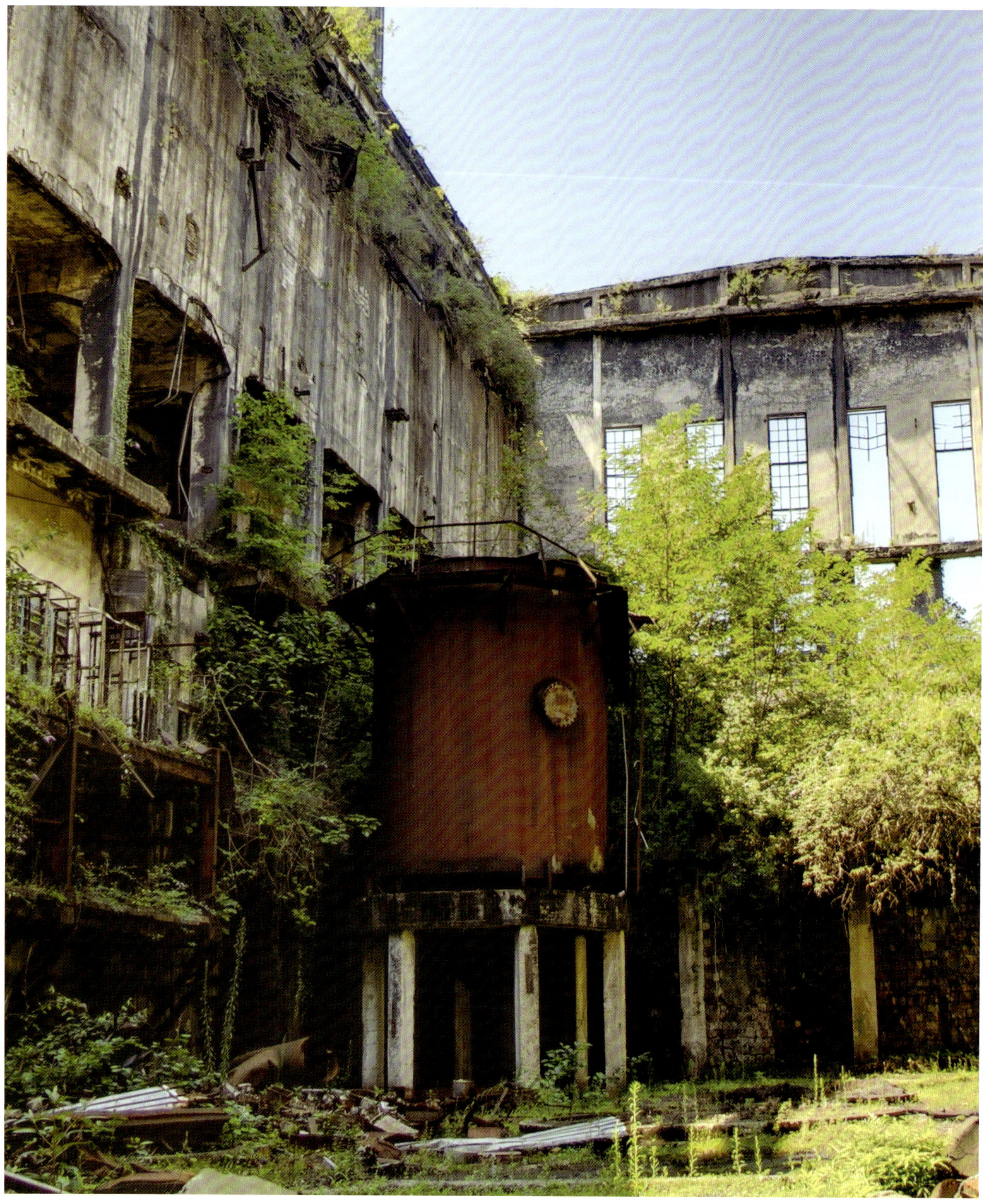

BOTH PHOTOGRAPHS:
Tkvarcheli power plant, Abkhazia
During the war in Abkhazia in the 1990s, Tkvarcheli was held under siege by Georgian forces. Although the city withstood the siege, it subsequently never recovered from the human and economic trauma, and fell into a precipitous decline. From a population of nearly 22,000 in 1989, the city's inhabitants dropped to just a few thousand (c. 5000 by 2011). Large parts of the city and the surrounding districts lie uninhabited. Here we see the rusting remains of Tkvarcheli thermal power plant, which was bombed silent in the first year of the siege, stripping the population of electricity for more than a year.

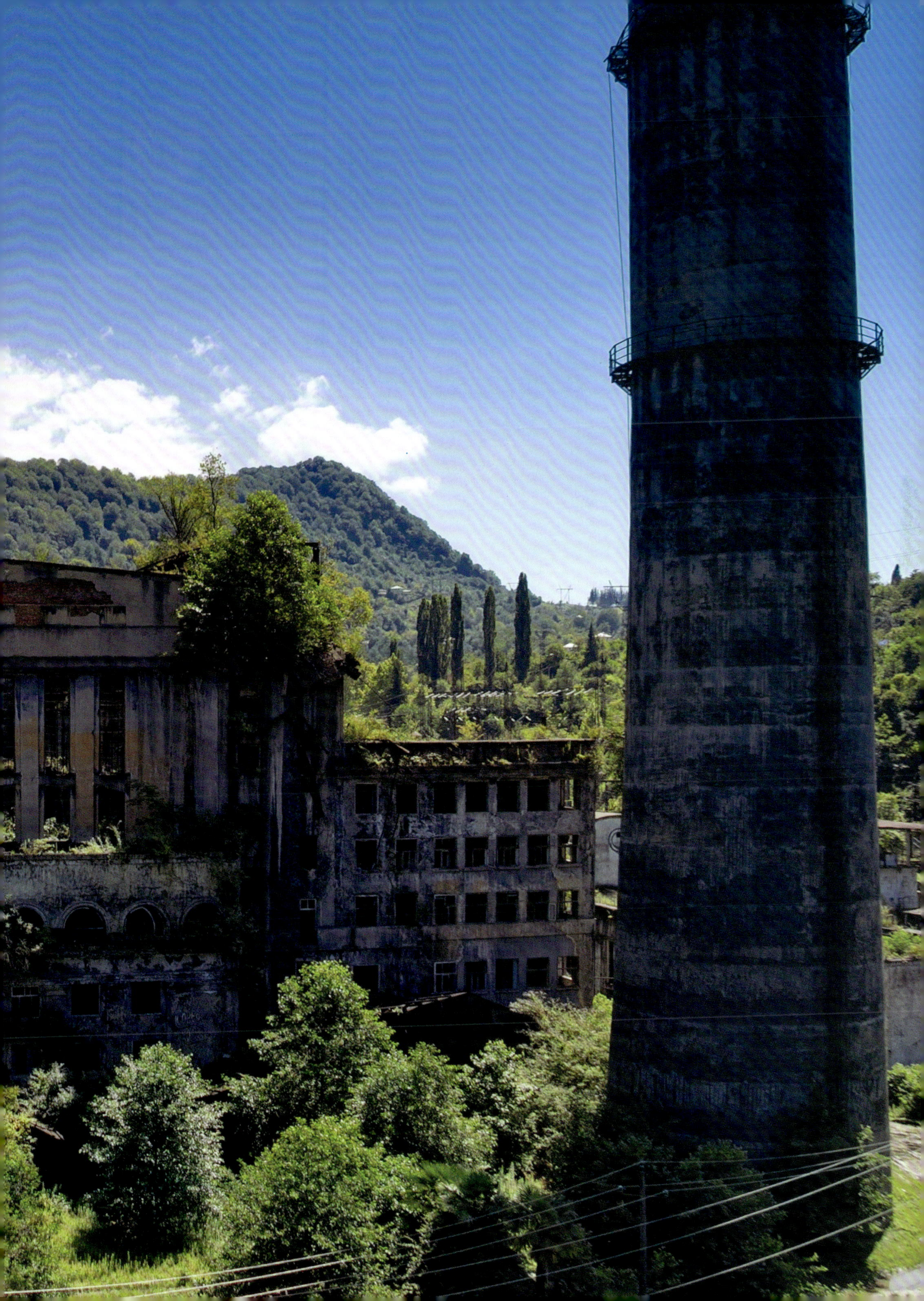

Polyana, Abkhazia
The settlement of Polyana in Abkhazia was formerly a mining community. The decline of that industry in the area, however, plus the destruction unleashed by war, has reduced the town to a haunted shadow of its former self. Many of Abkhazia's ghost towns actually still have a handful of residents, scratching out an existence in ramshackle housing.

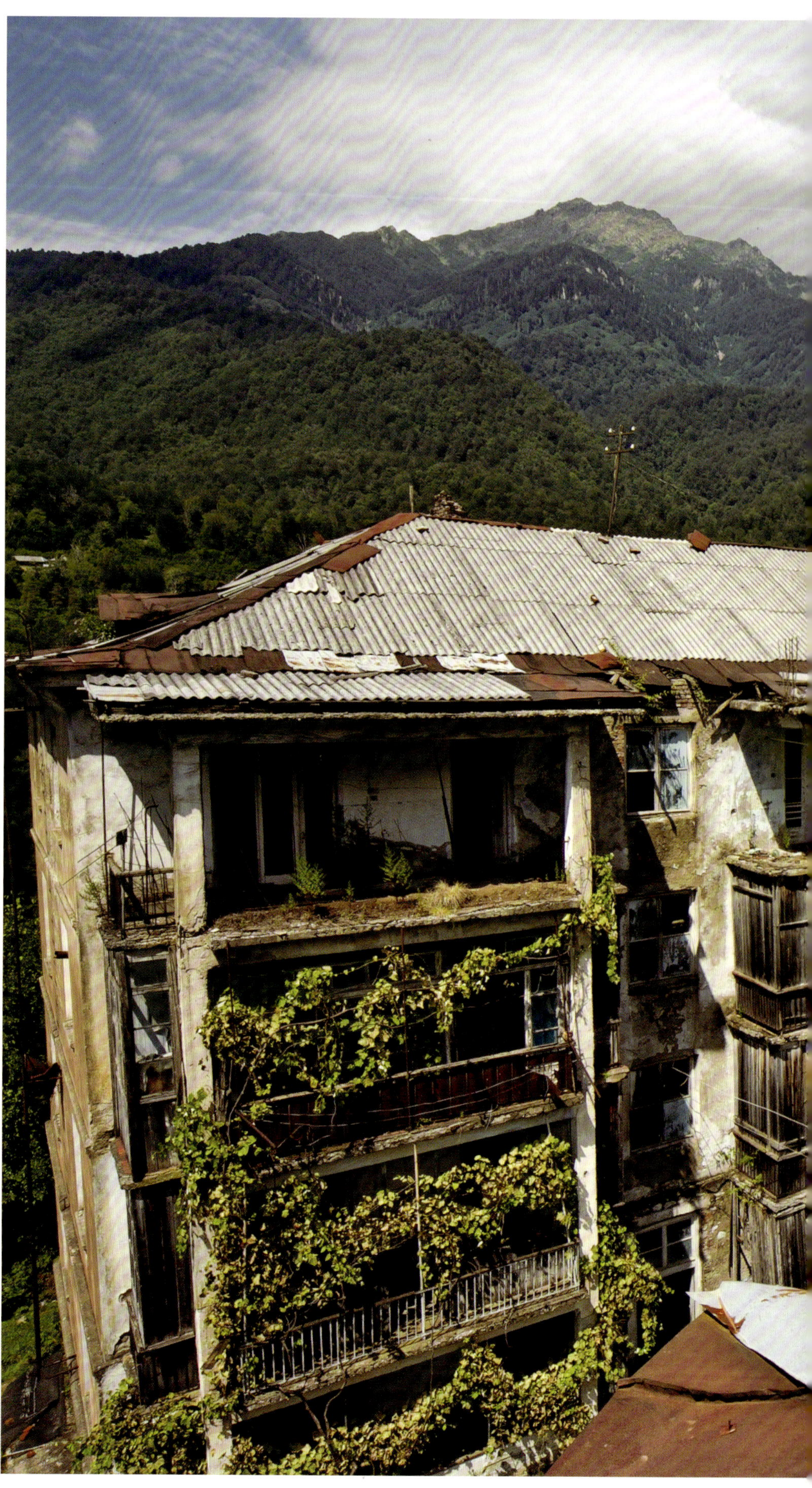

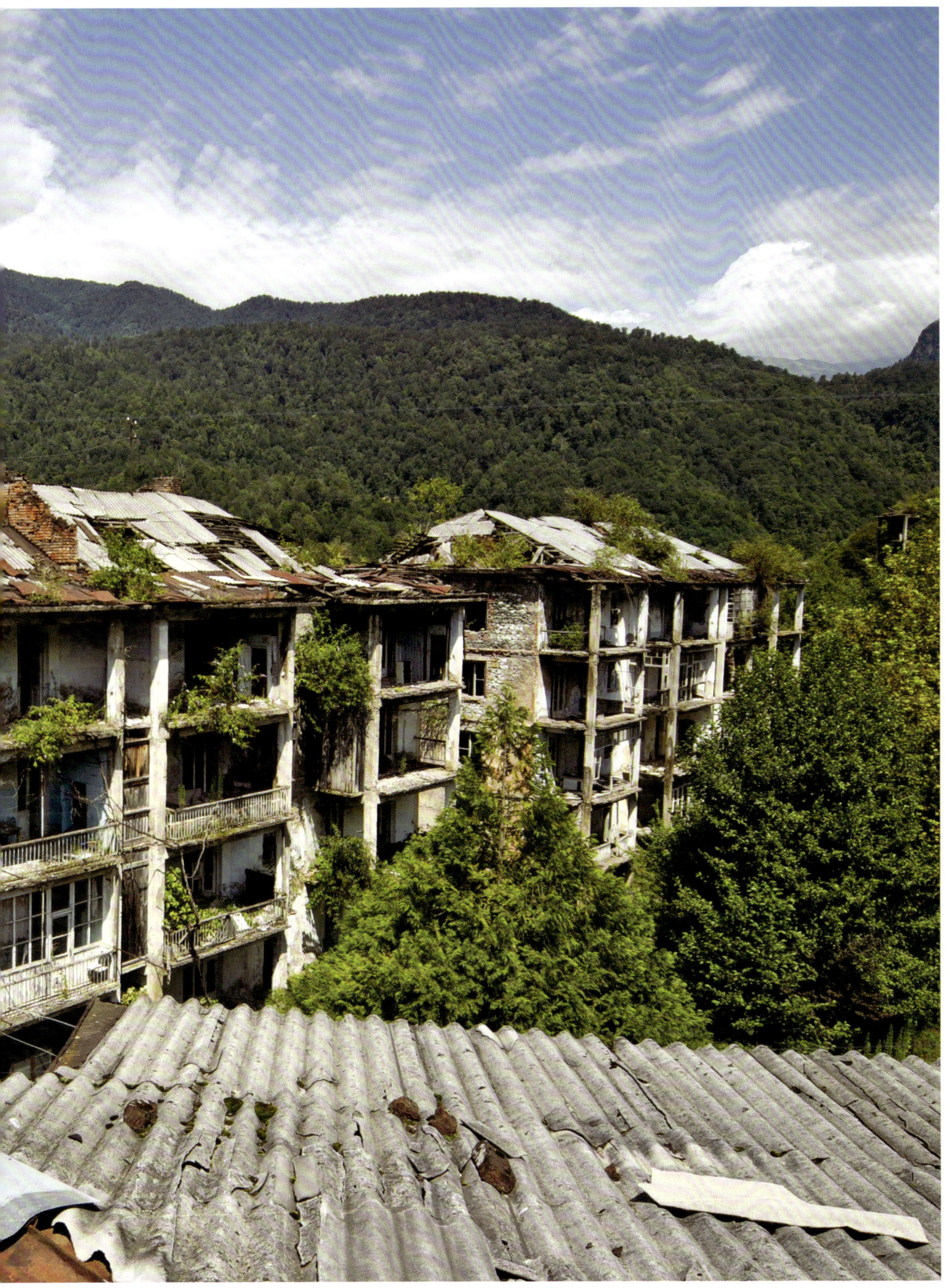

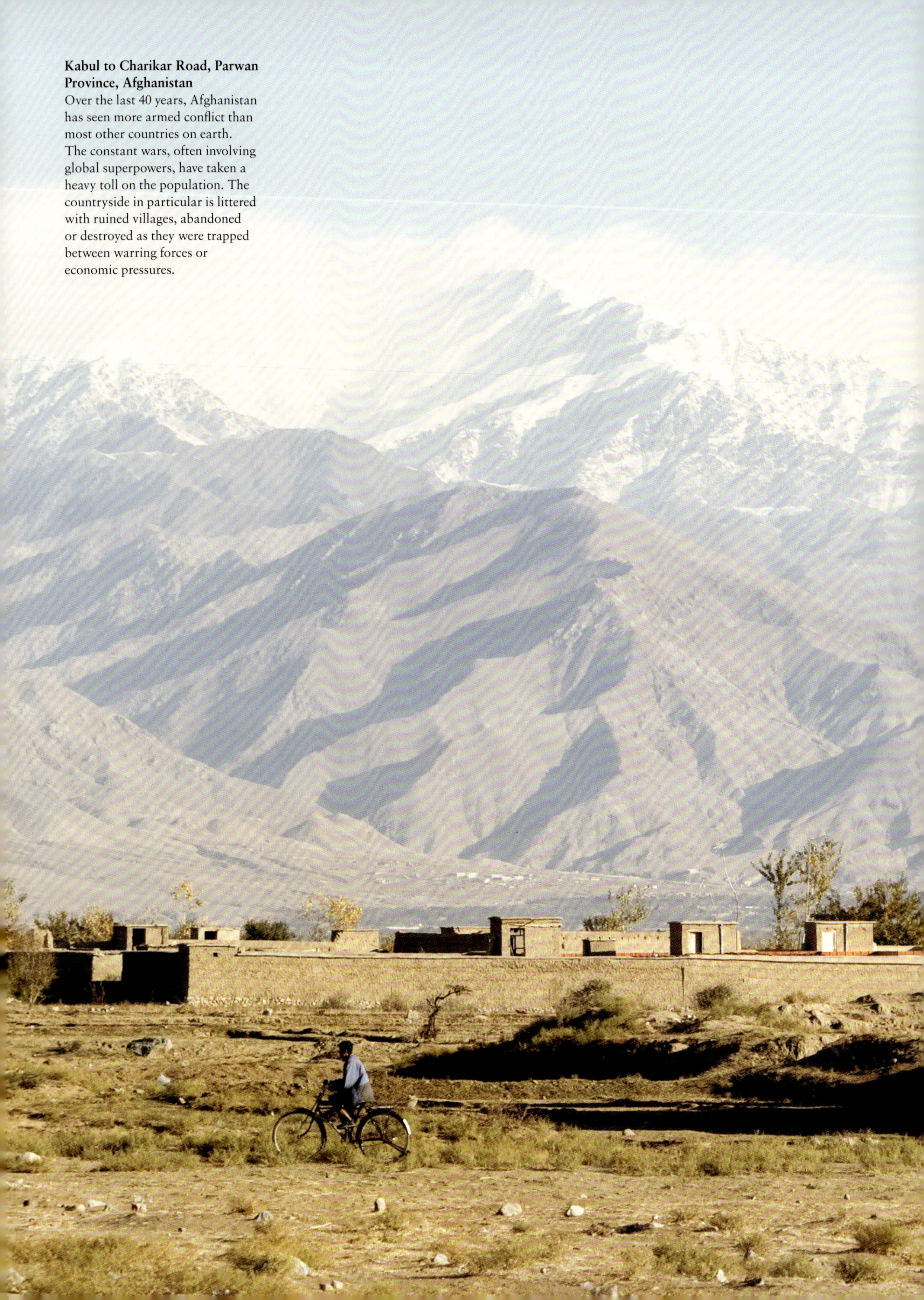

Kabul to Charikar Road, Parwan Province, Afghanistan
Over the last 40 years, Afghanistan has seen more armed conflict than most other countries on earth. The constant wars, often involving global superpowers, have taken a heavy toll on the population. The countryside in particular is littered with ruined villages, abandoned or destroyed as they were trapped between warring forces or economic pressures.

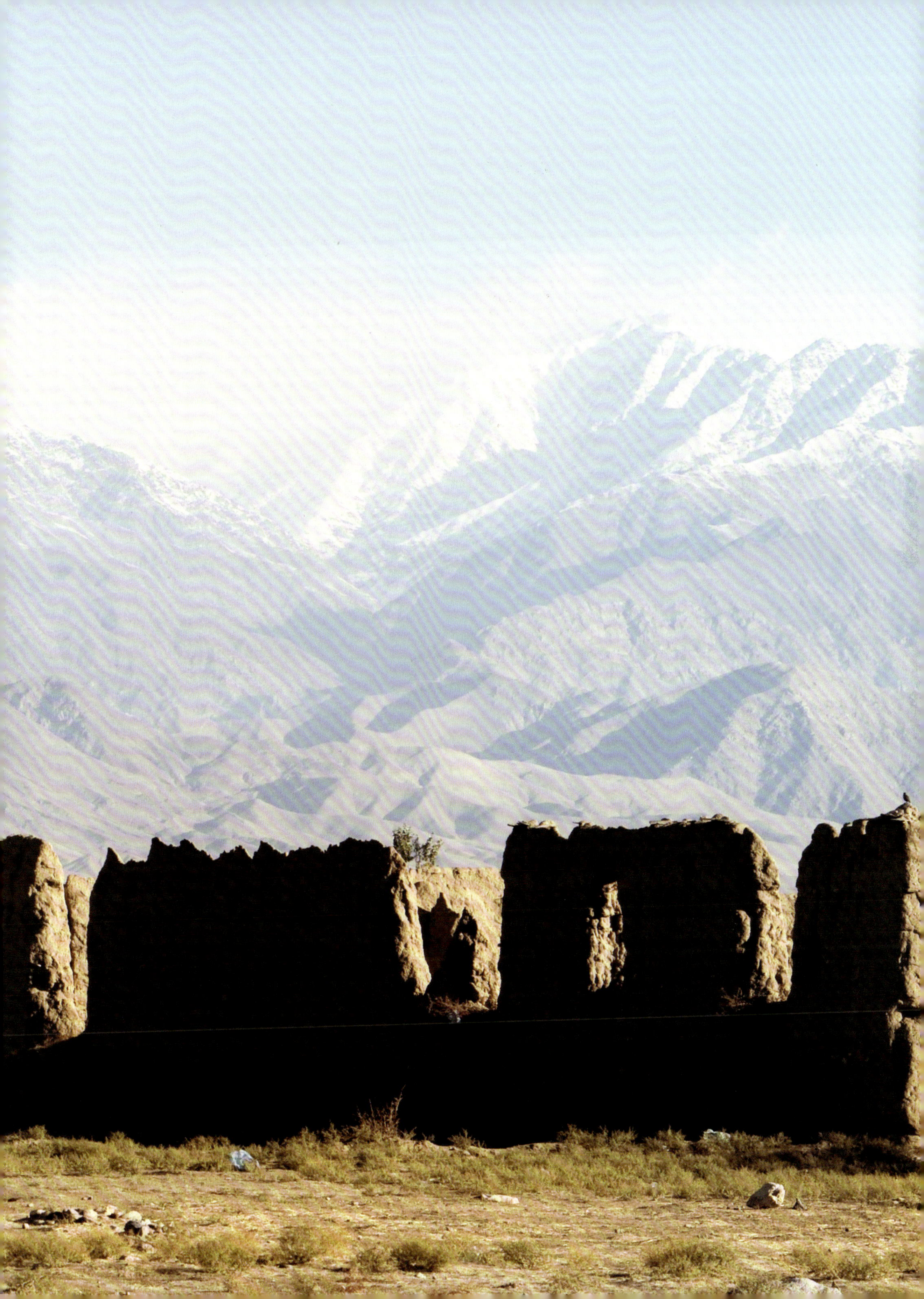

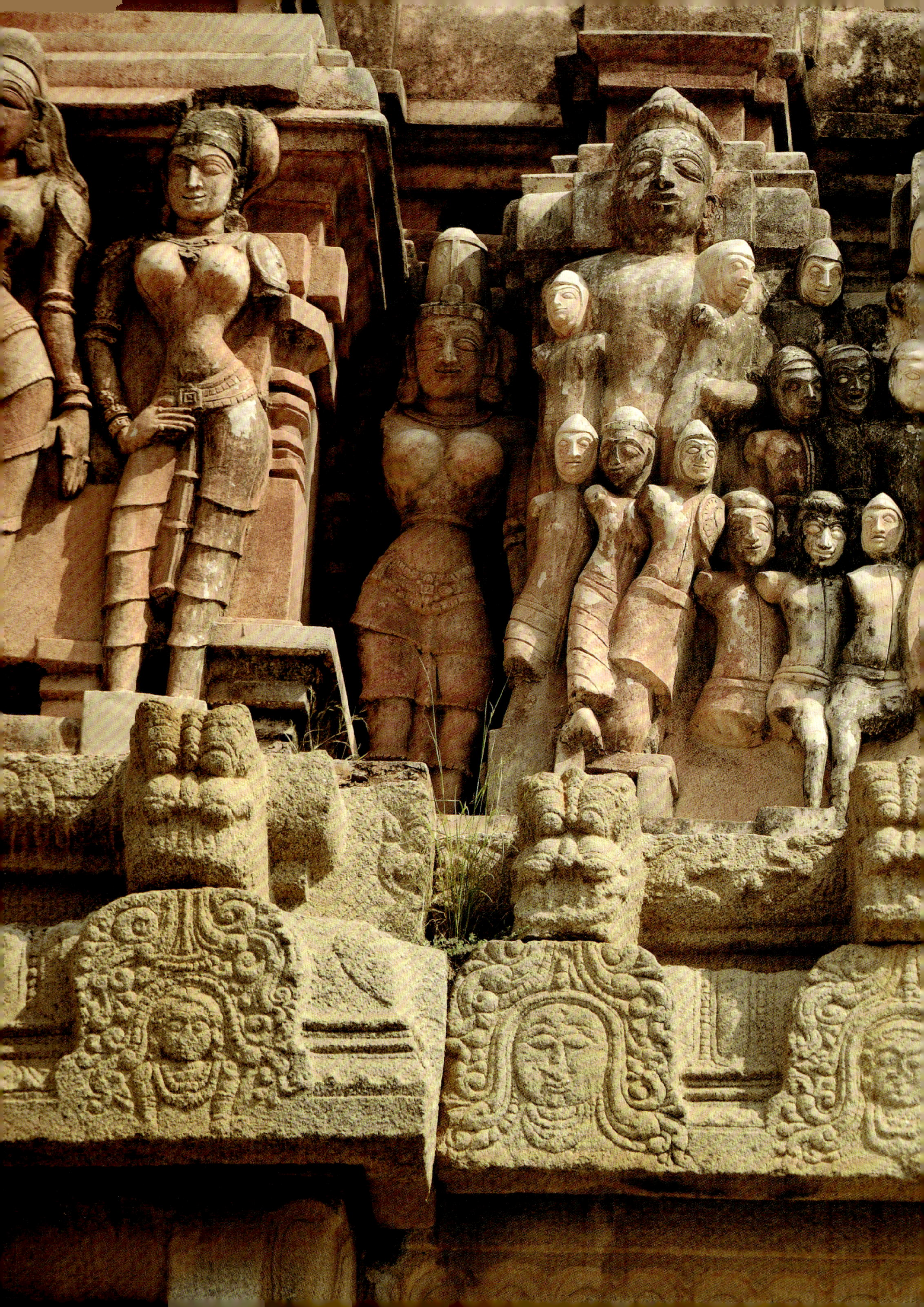

Indian Continent

The Indian subcontinent is a vast land with an epic history. Much of that history is that of the rise and fall of empires – Maurya, Mughal, Gupta, Maratha, Kushan, British, to name but a few. Some of these empires defined entire swathes of what is today India, Pakistan and Bangladesh for many hundreds of years, while others were relative flashes in the pan, shining brightly for a few decades before burning out abruptly.

Because of this imperial past, India is replete with ruins and ghost towns of unusual majesty and splendour, known for their architectural opulence and rich sculptural references to Indian politics, legend and spirituality. The Vijayanagara, capital city of the former Vijayanagara Empire, for example, extends over an area of 40 square kilometres (15.4 square miles), and in its heyday had more than 140 sacred sites alone, still referenced today in dozens of temples and statues.

India is a world region shaped by huge forces of commerce, war, geography, faith and population, these influences reshaping its history and leaving a lasting legacy in its architecture and infrastructure. Many of the abandoned towns and cities in this chapter, furthermore, also testify to the importance of legend and superstition. Curses placed on settlements centuries previously can still have resonance for many for modern populations nearby; hence such places remain abandoned and avoided to this day.

LEFT:
Vijayanagara, Ballari District, Karnataka, India
Vijayanagara, surrounding the modern Indian village of Harampi, was previously the capital city of the Vijayanagara Empire of southern India. Although much of the original extent of the city has gone, incredible sculptures and monuments remain, featuring mythical and social scenes.

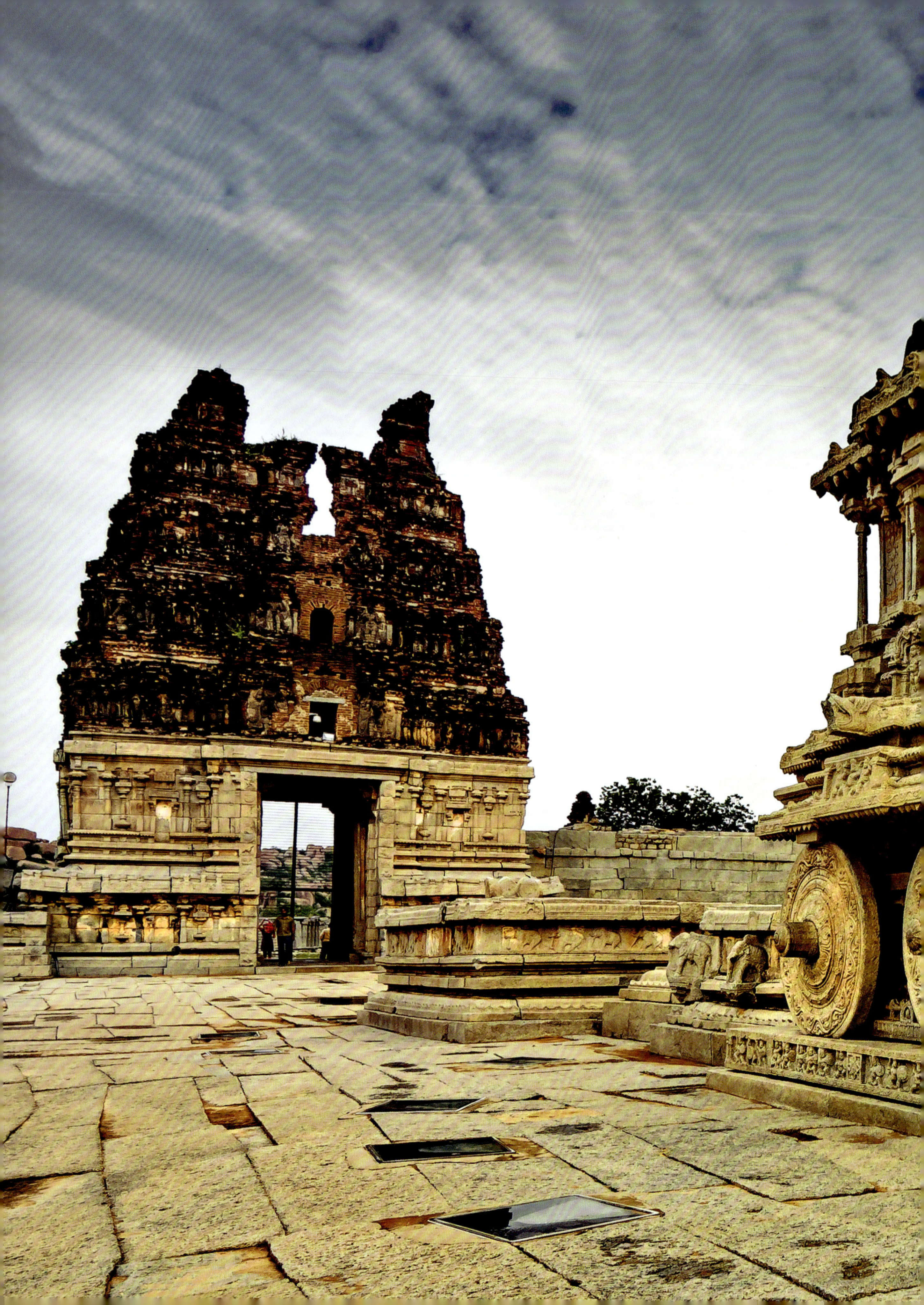

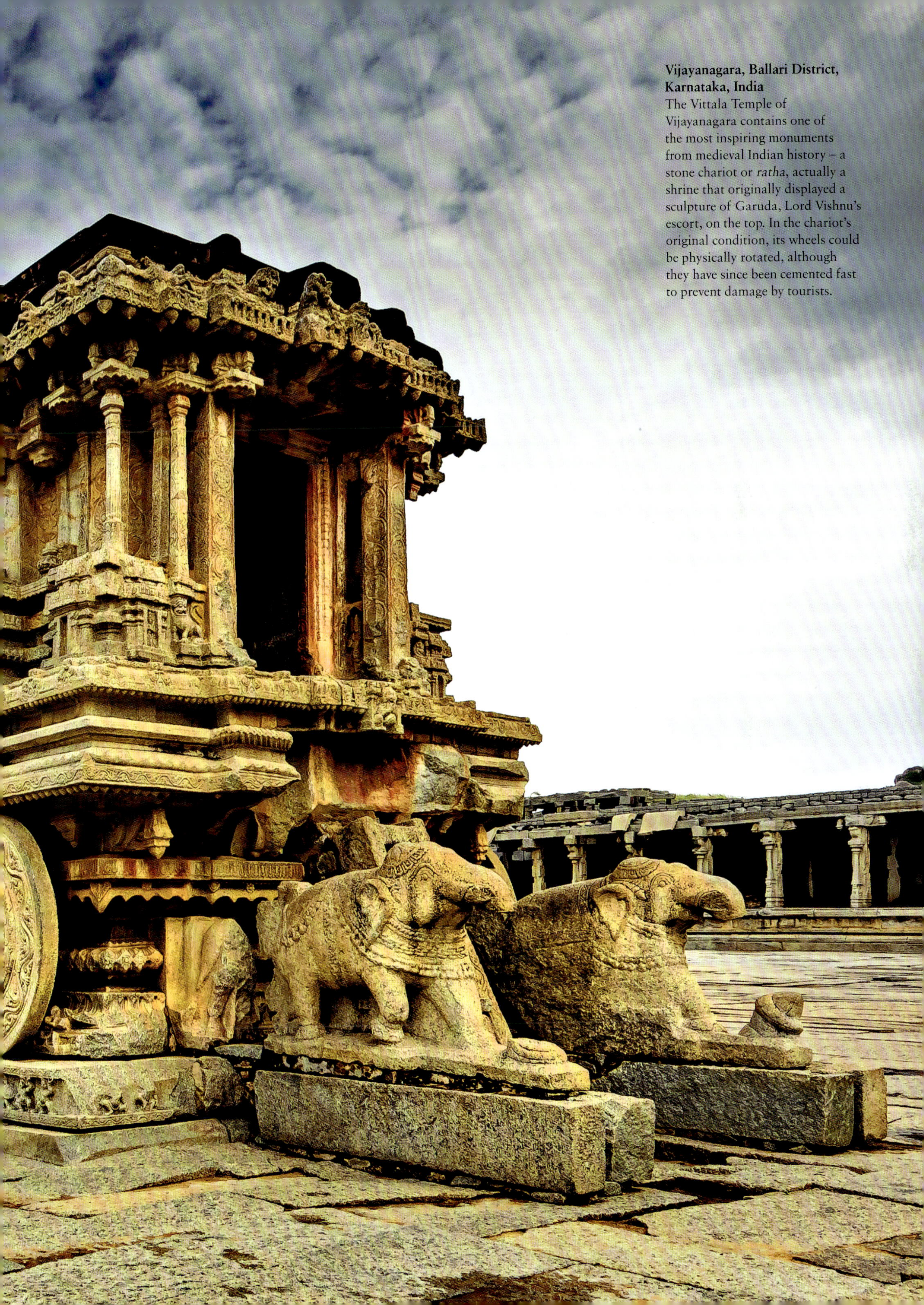

Vijayanagara, Ballari District, Karnataka, India
The Vittala Temple of Vijayanagara contains one of the most inspiring monuments from medieval Indian history – a stone chariot or *ratha*, actually a shrine that originally displayed a sculpture of Garuda, Lord Vishnu's escort, on the top. In the chariot's original condition, its wheels could be physically rotated, although they have since been cemented fast to prevent damage by tourists.

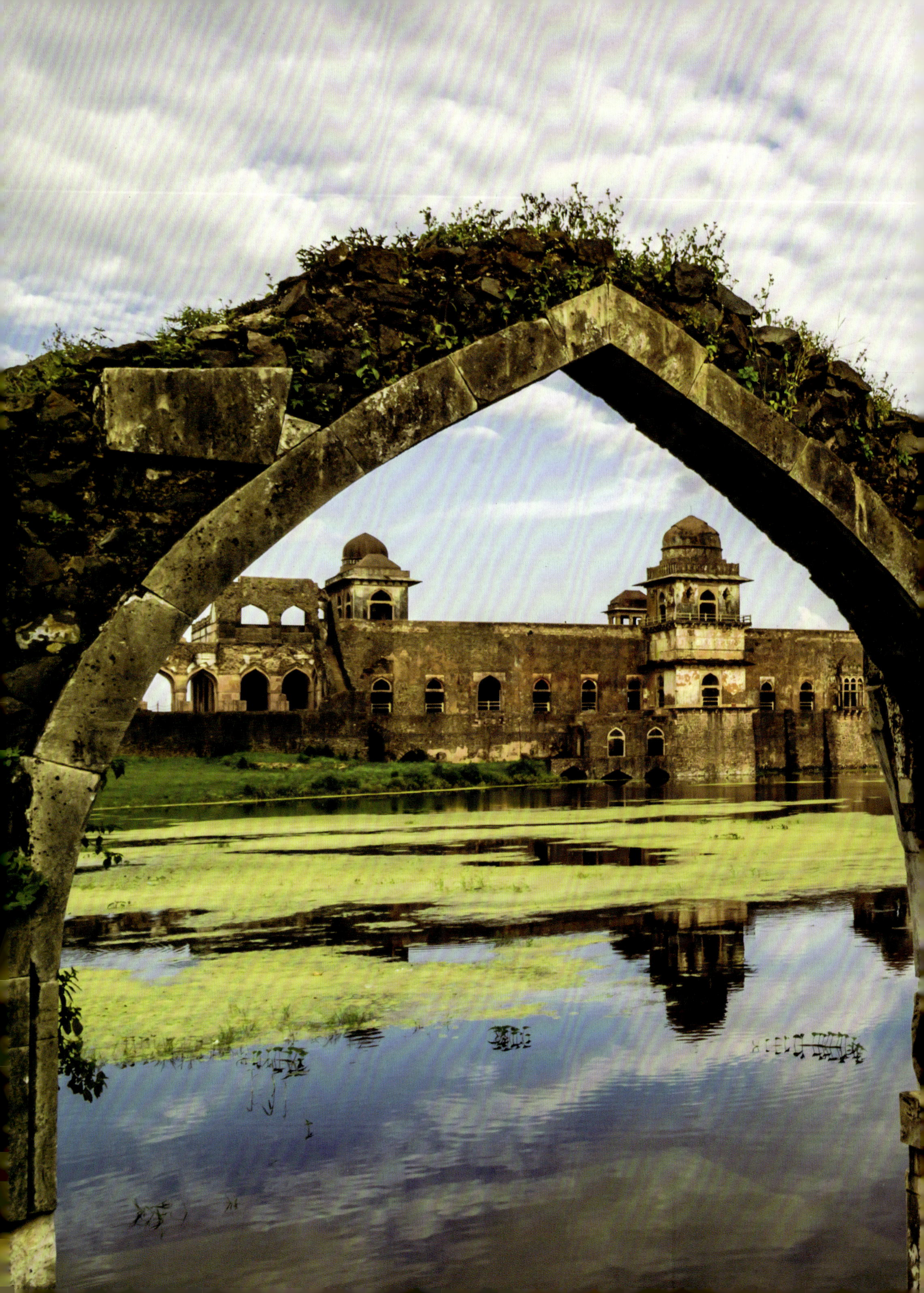

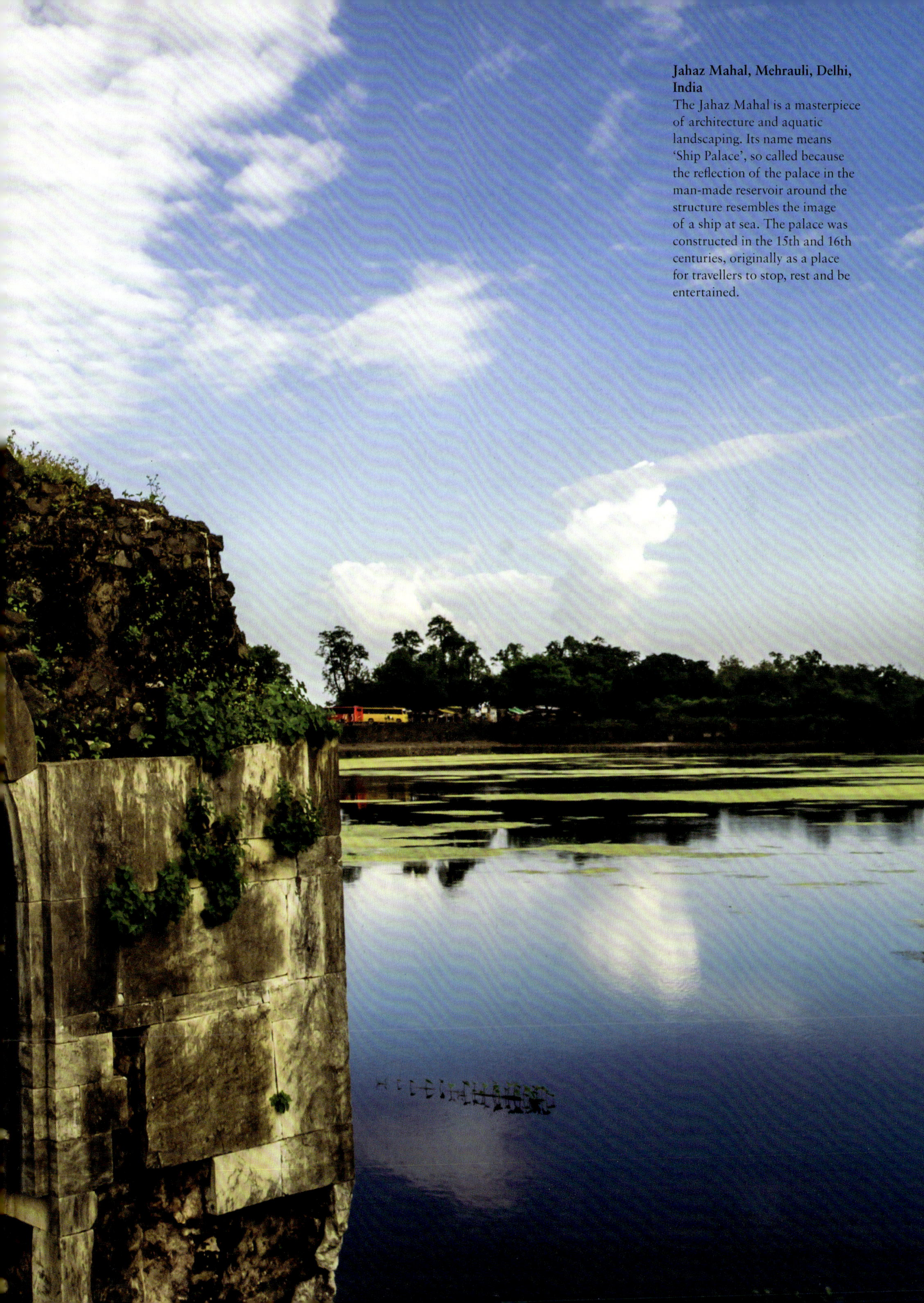

Jahaz Mahal, Mehrauli, Delhi, India
The Jahaz Mahal is a masterpiece of architecture and aquatic landscaping. Its name means 'Ship Palace', so called because the reflection of the palace in the man-made reservoir around the structure resembles the image of a ship at sea. The palace was constructed in the 15th and 16th centuries, originally as a place for travellers to stop, rest and be entertained.

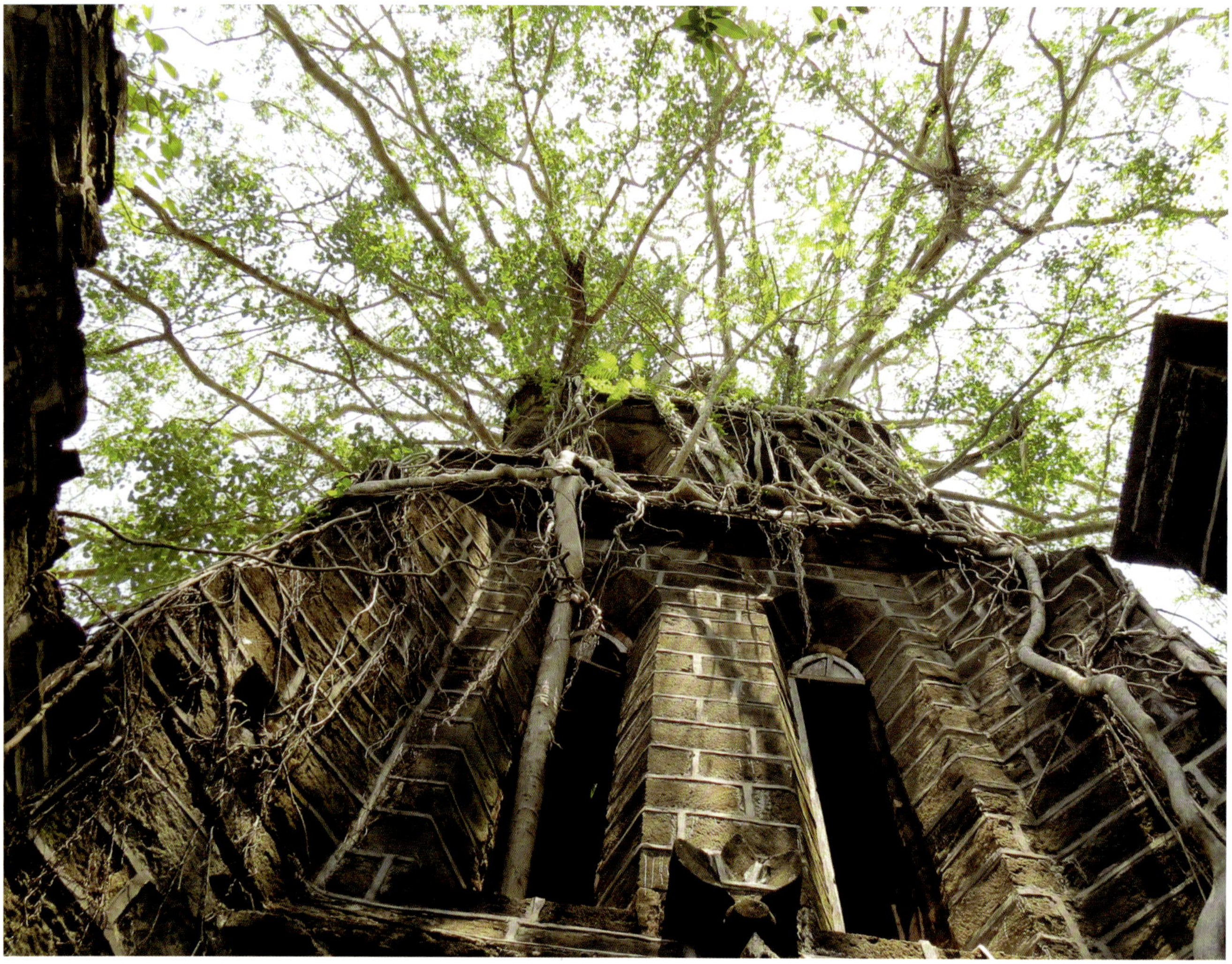

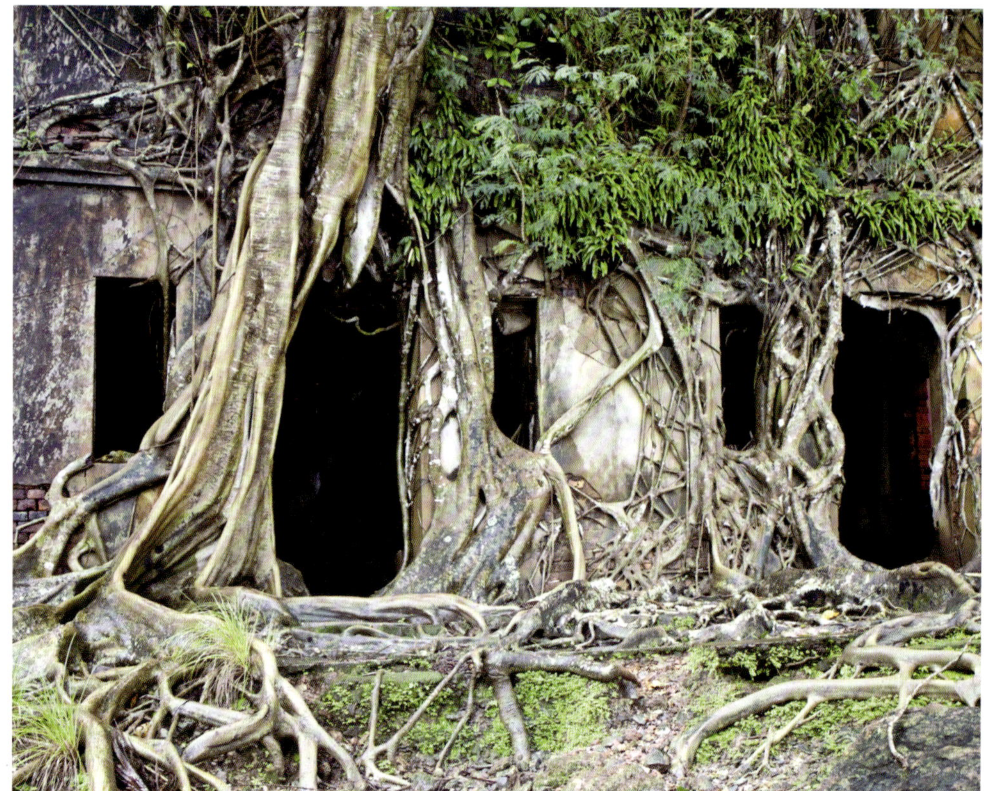

ALL PHOTOGRAPHS:

Port Blair, Ross Island, Andaman and Nicobar Islands, India

Nature progressively reclaims an old abandoned Presbyterian church, with vines and tree roots swarming over foundations and walls, and out through windows previously decorated with elaborate teak window frames. The church is located in Port Blair on Ross Island, part of the Andaman and Nicobar Islands situated in the Indian Ocean. A British settlement was established at Port Blair in the late 18th century, part of the spreading British colonization of the Indian subcontinent. Although in its heyday Port Blair sparkled with high-society lives, the islands also proved to be difficult outposts for the British over their c. 150-year occupation. Disease claimed many lives, and there was periodic violence between the colonists and the local inhabitants. From 1858 the island was also home to the Ross Island Penal Colony, a brutal establishment housing political prisoners from India.

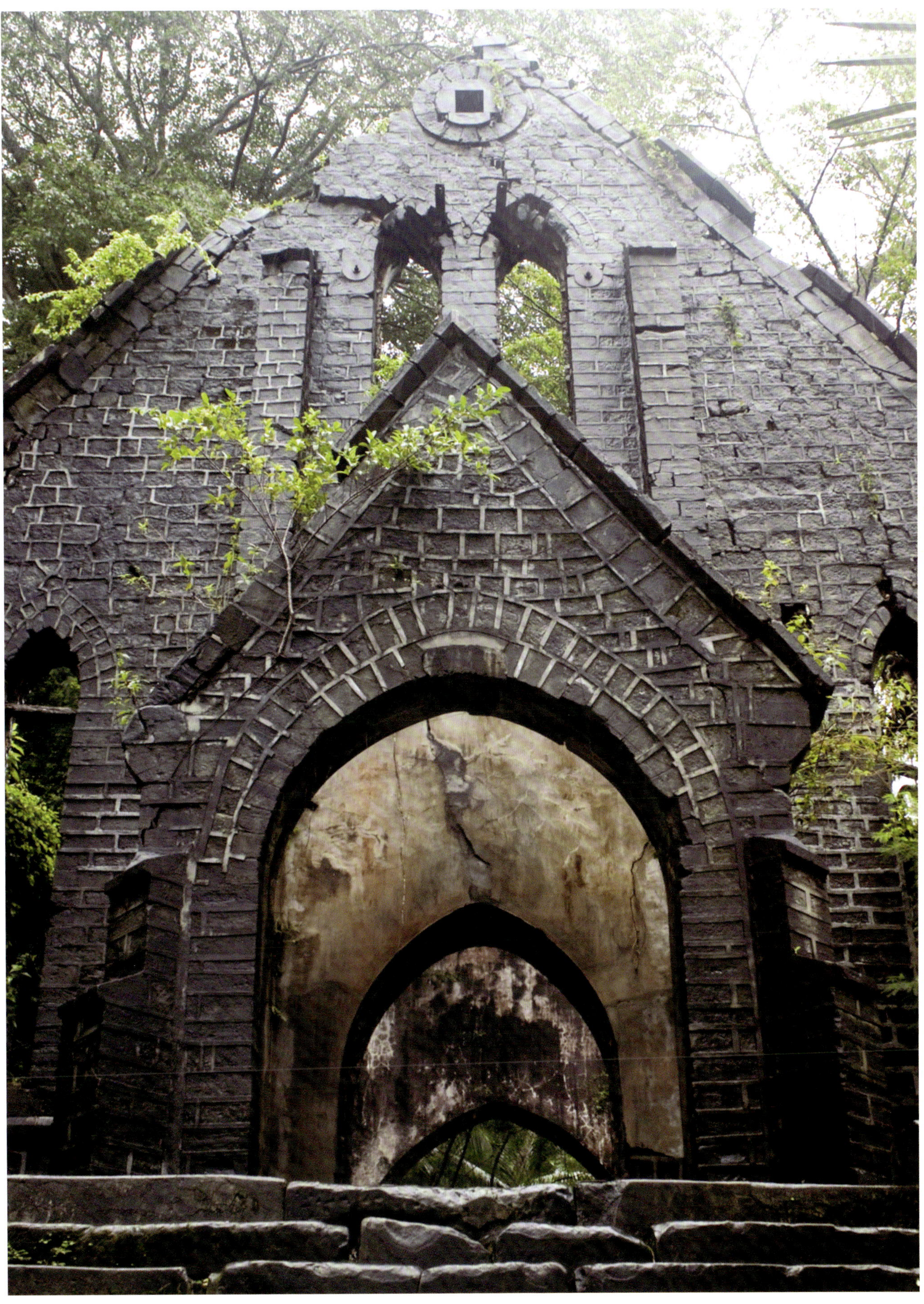

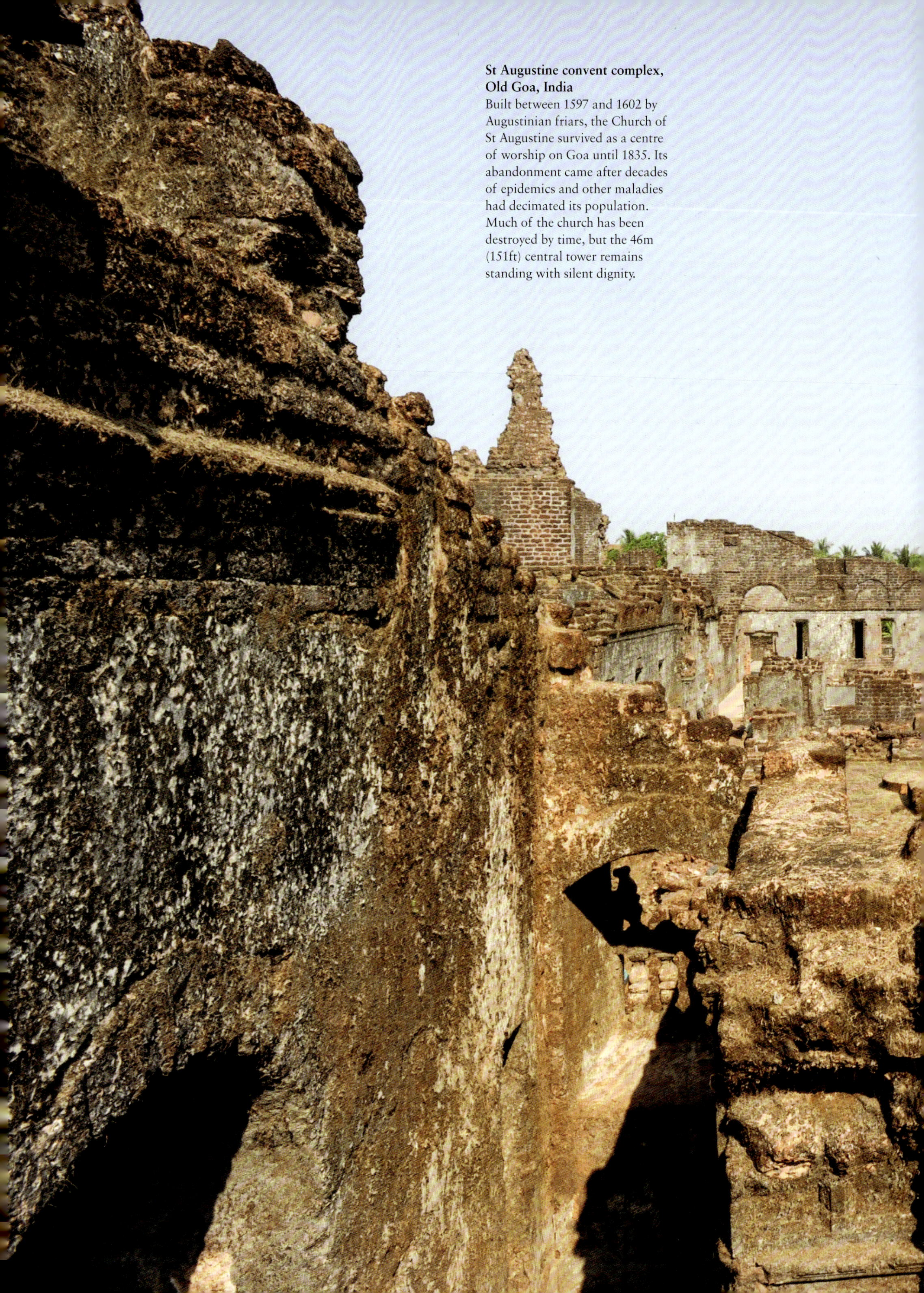

St Augustine convent complex, Old Goa, India
Built between 1597 and 1602 by Augustinian friars, the Church of St Augustine survived as a centre of worship on Goa until 1835. Its abandonment came after decades of epidemics and other maladies had decimated its population. Much of the church has been destroyed by time, but the 46m (151ft) central tower remains standing with silent dignity.

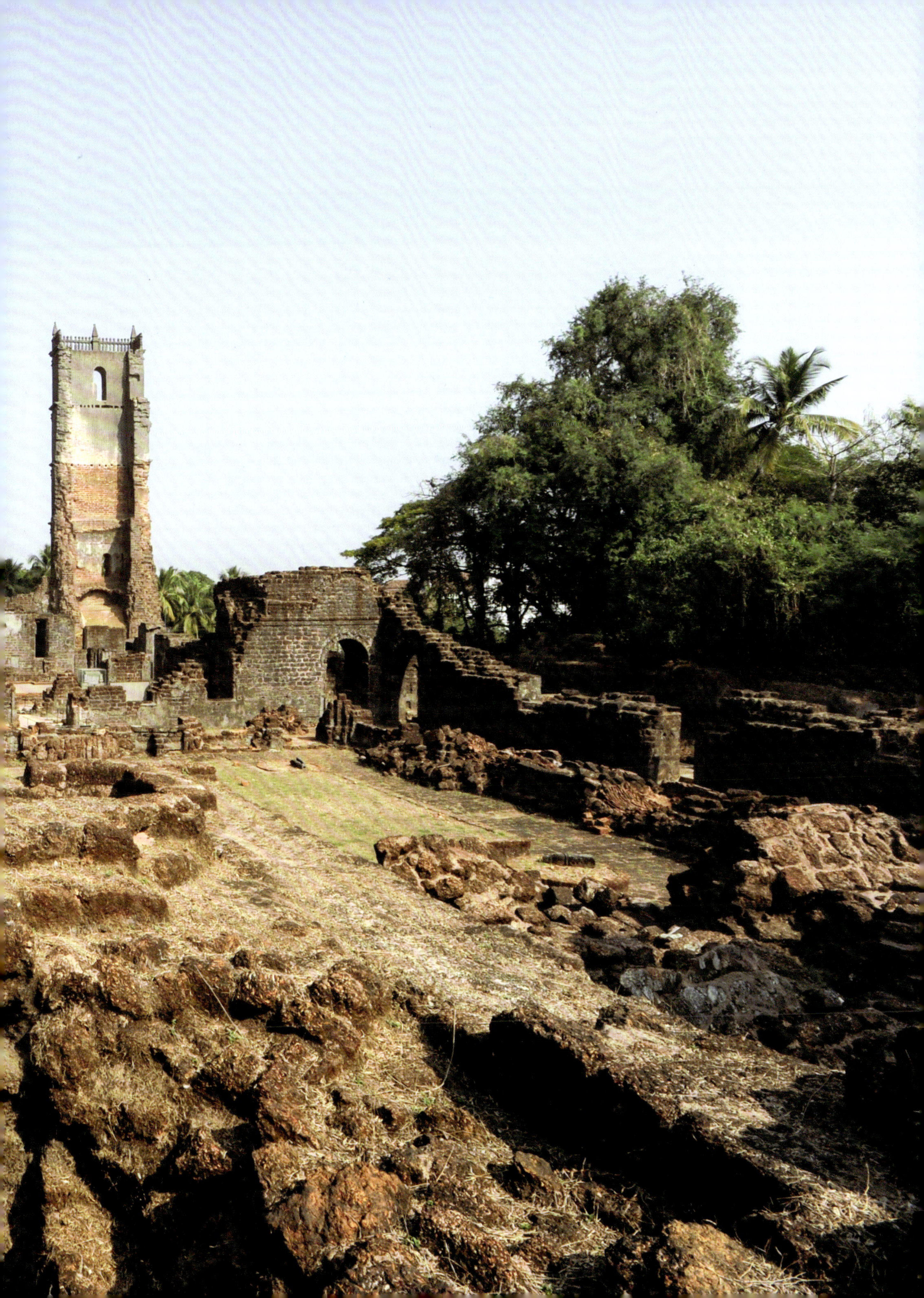

Kuldhara, near Jaisalmer, Rajasthan, India

Lying some 20km (12.4 miles) to the west of Jaisalmer, Kuldhara is an eerie and desolate space. Established in the 13th century, it was a thriving settlement of about 1000 inhabitants until, in the 19th century, it was mysteriously and rapidly abandoned. Local legends tell of a curse brought on the village by evil local officials, but more prosaic explanations could revolve around problems with irrigation. Either way, the idea of a curse placed upon the village means that it has never been repopulated.

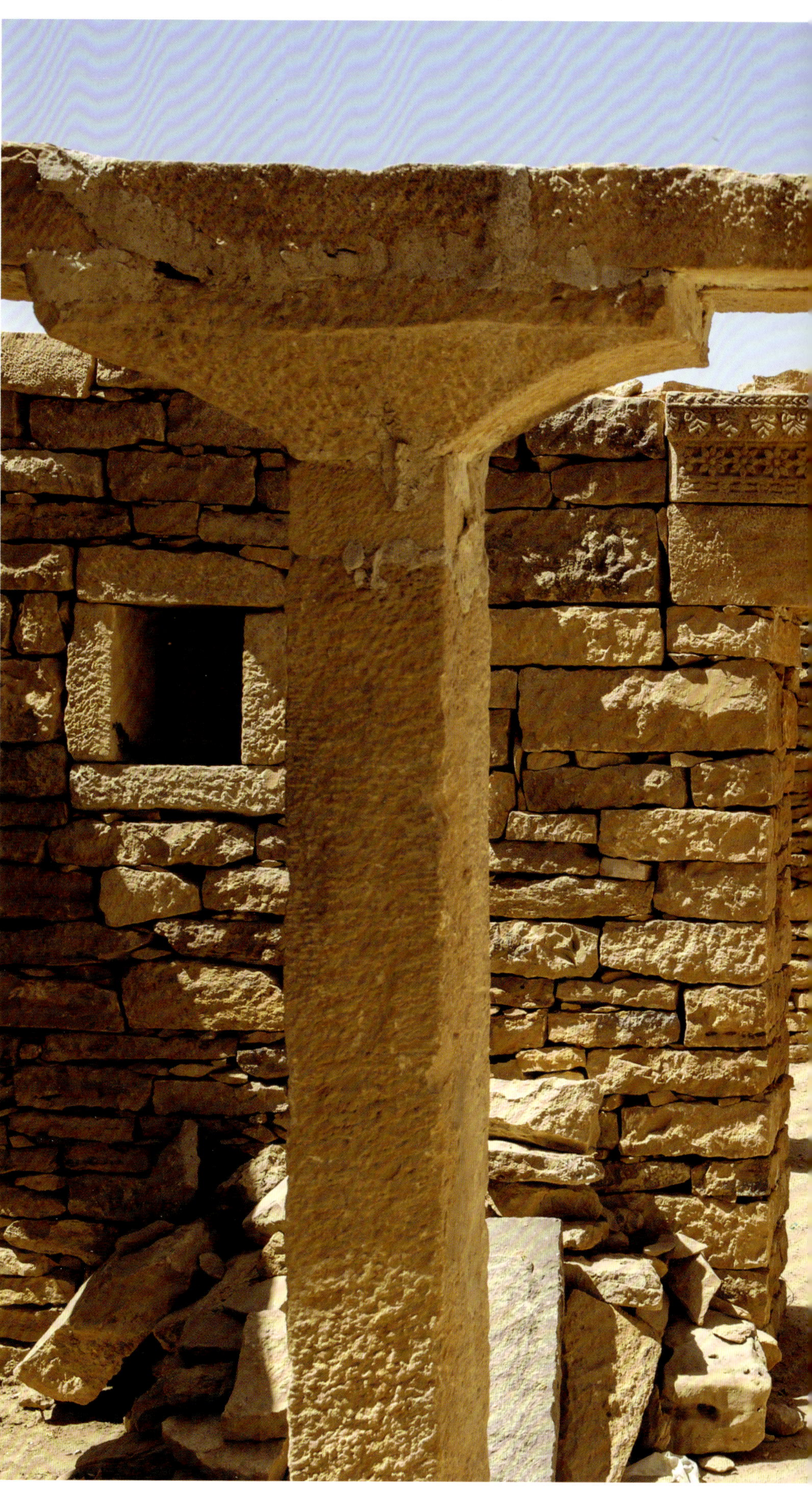

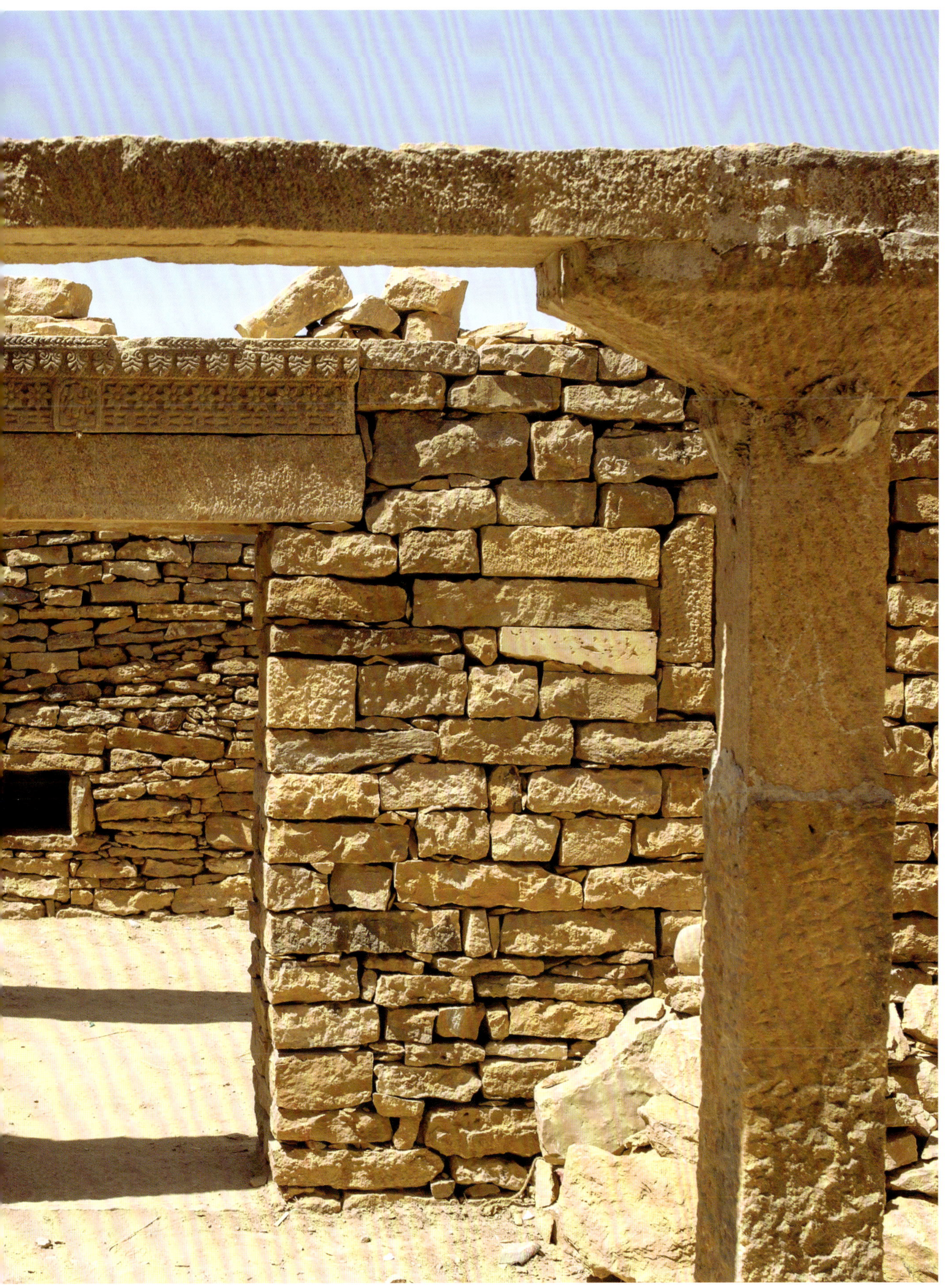

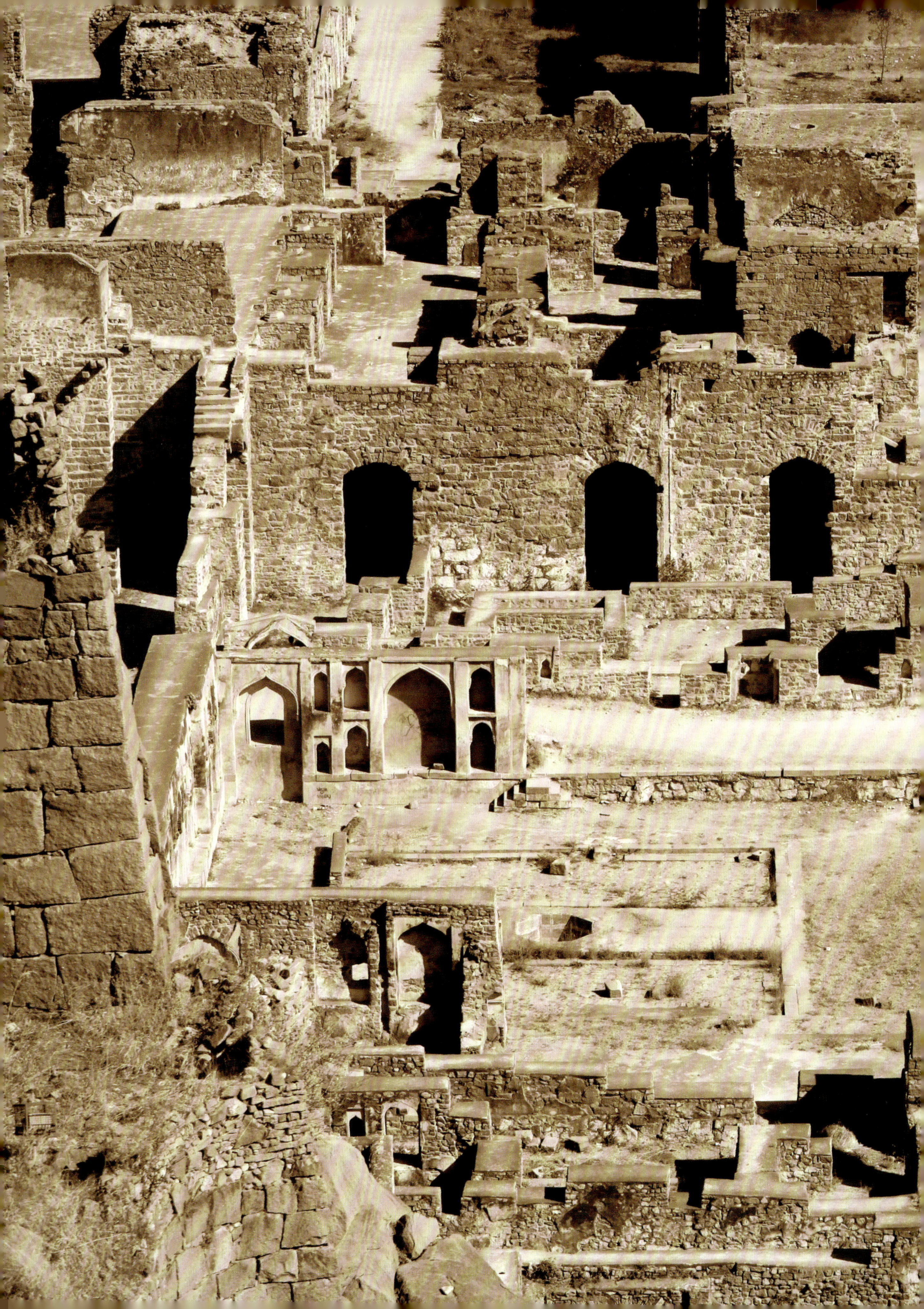

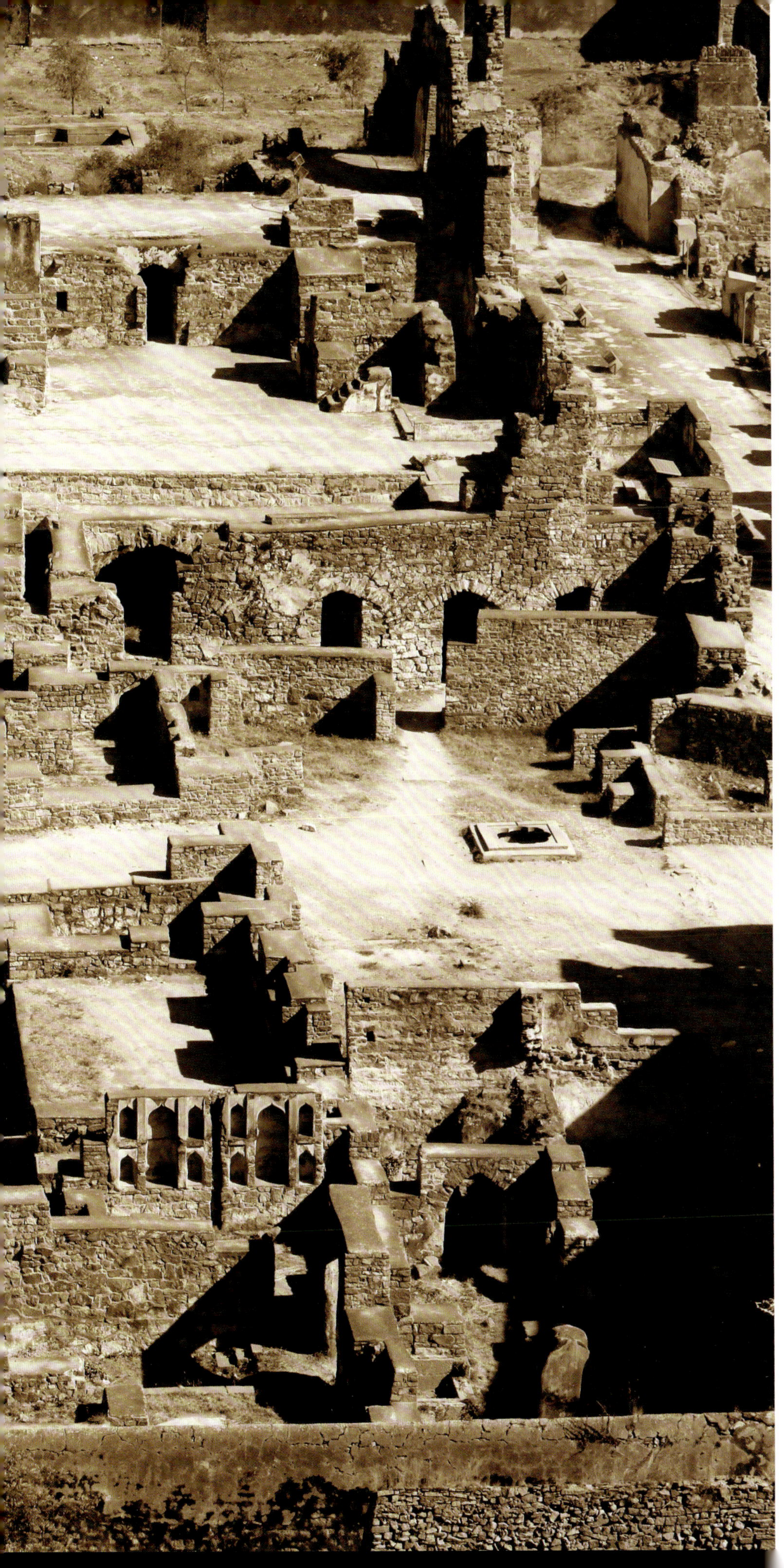

Golkonda Fort, Hyderabad, India

Situated 11km (6.8 miles) from Hyderabad, the Golkonda Fort formed the capital of the kingdom of Golkonda in the 14th–17th centuries. Built initially of mud-brick, the fortress was expanded with granite structures during the 16th century. During the 17th century, the fortress resisted a nine-month siege by the Mughal prince Aurangzeb, only succumbing when a traitor nefariously opened a gate from the inside.

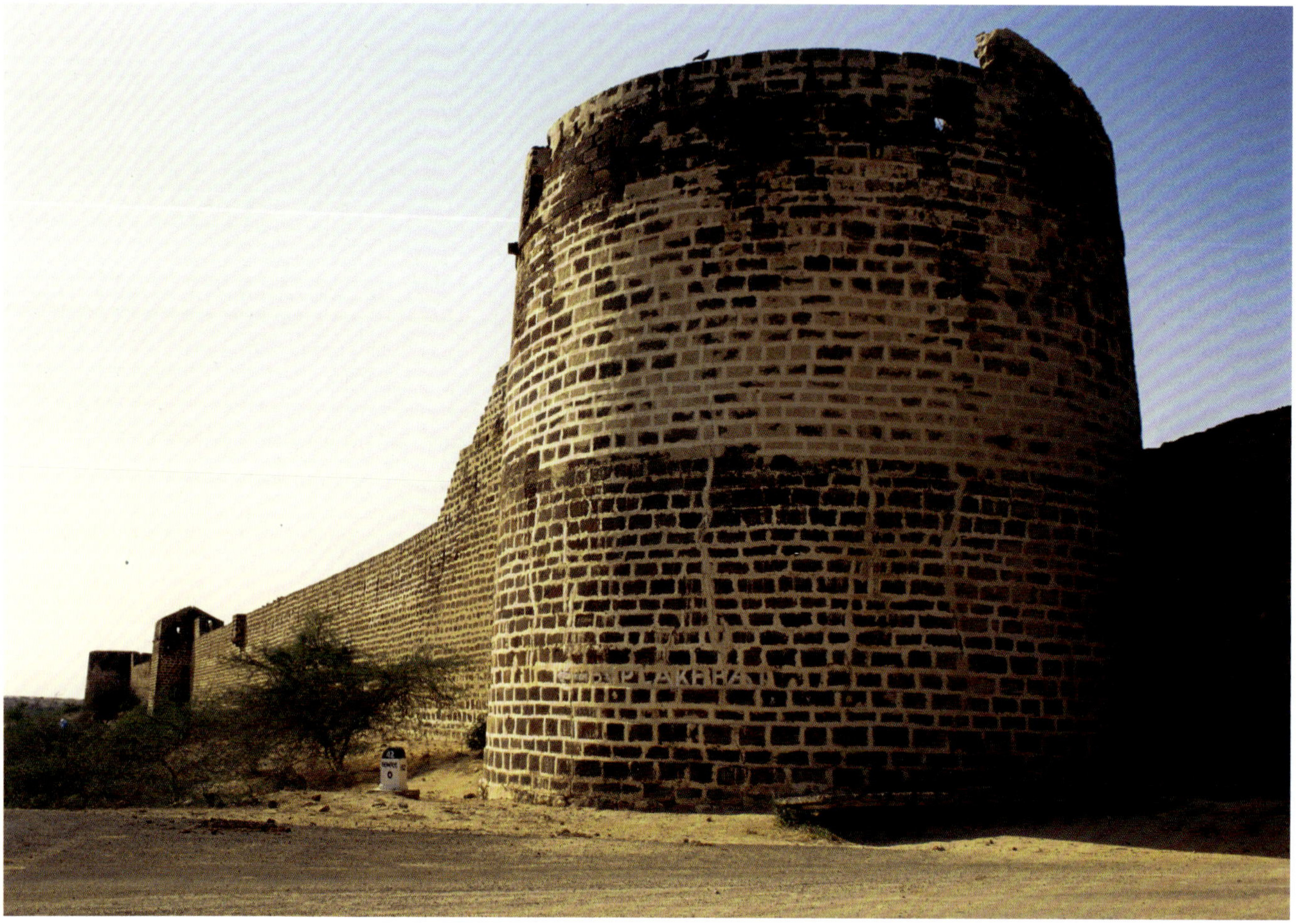

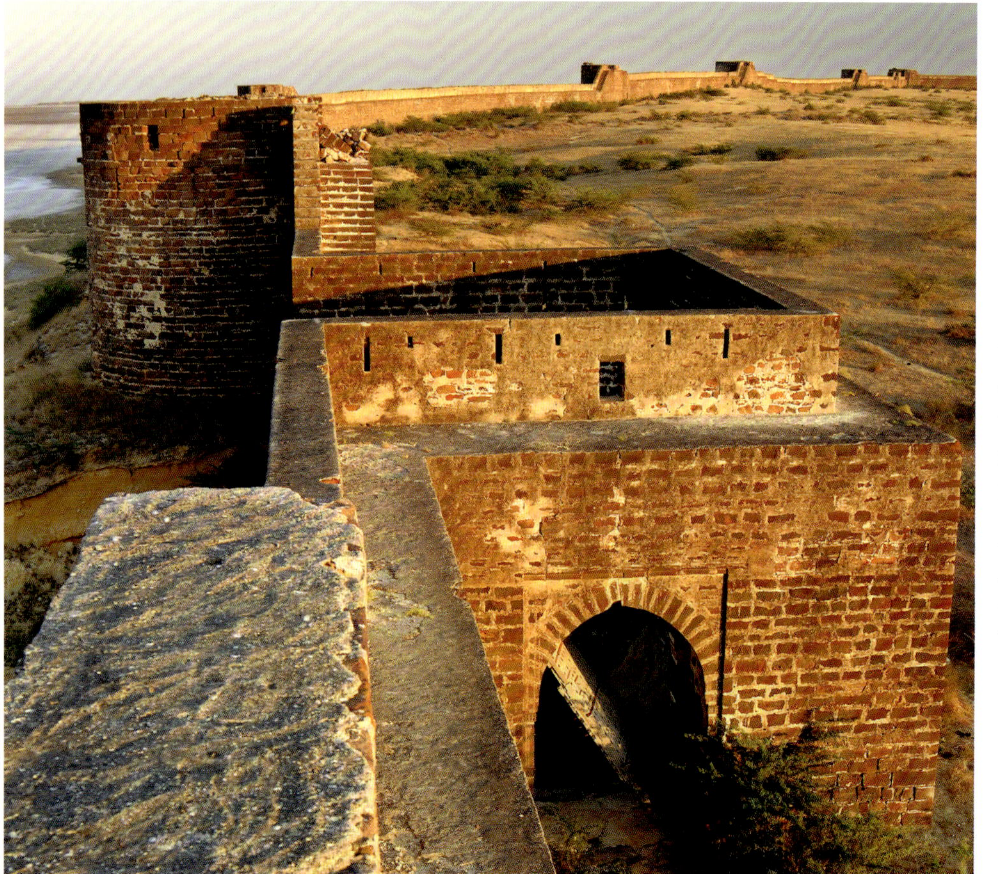

ALL PHOTOGRAPHS:

Lakhpat Fort, Kutch Kachchh, Gujarat, India

Lakhpat Fort sits majestic but silent on the border between India and Pakistan, its curtain walls, towers and bastions now just home to animal life rather than a watchful military garrison. The walls, which measure 7km (4.3 miles) long, previously enclosed a thriving town, one that built its prosperity on the rice trade and on maritime commerce. After an 1819 earthquake changed the course of the Indus River, however – previously the river flowed through the city itself – the fortunes of Lakhpat began their sad and rapid decline. The main visitors to Lakhpat today are tourists plus religious pilgrims – the town has important connections to Sikhism, Sufism and Hinduism.

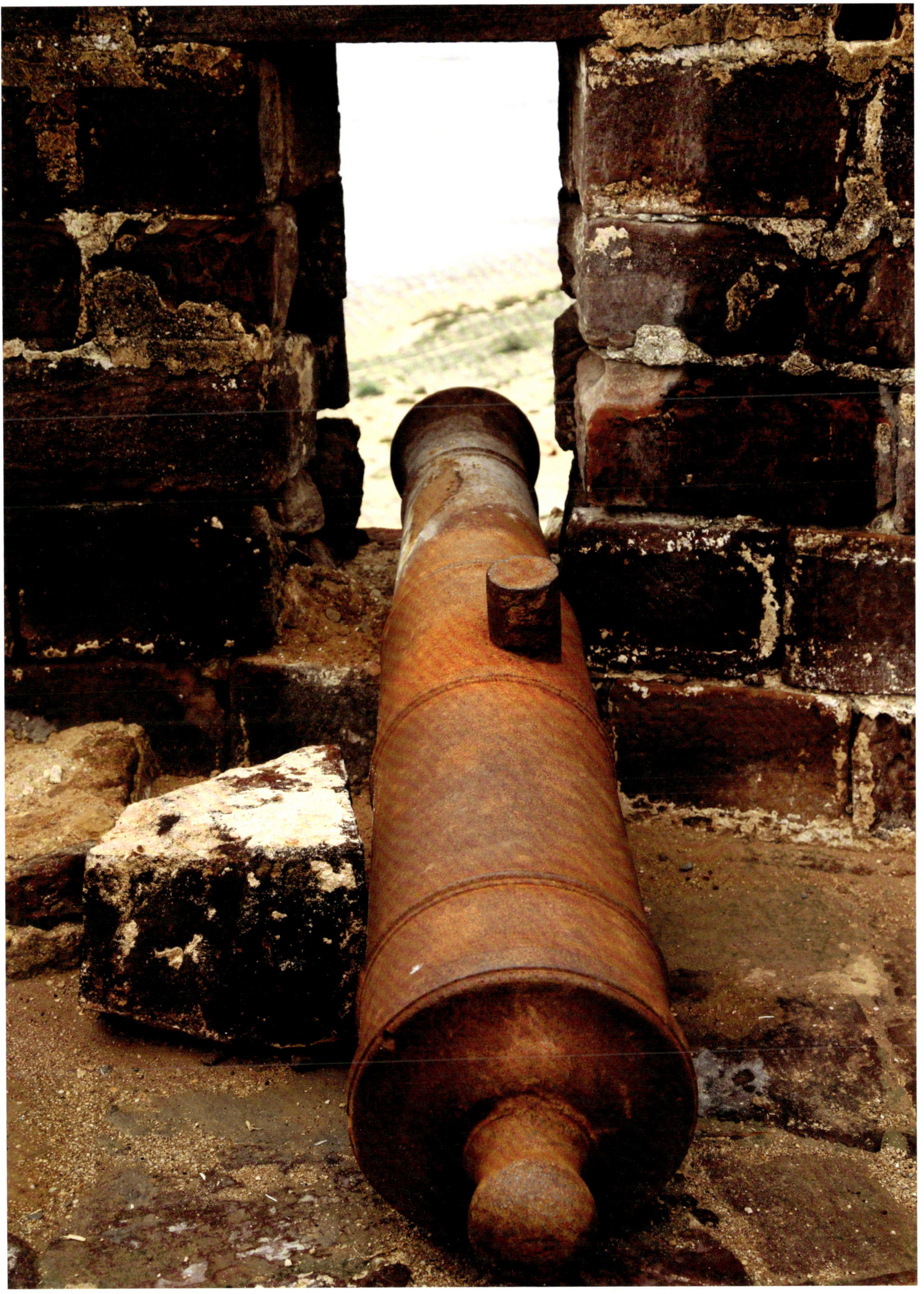

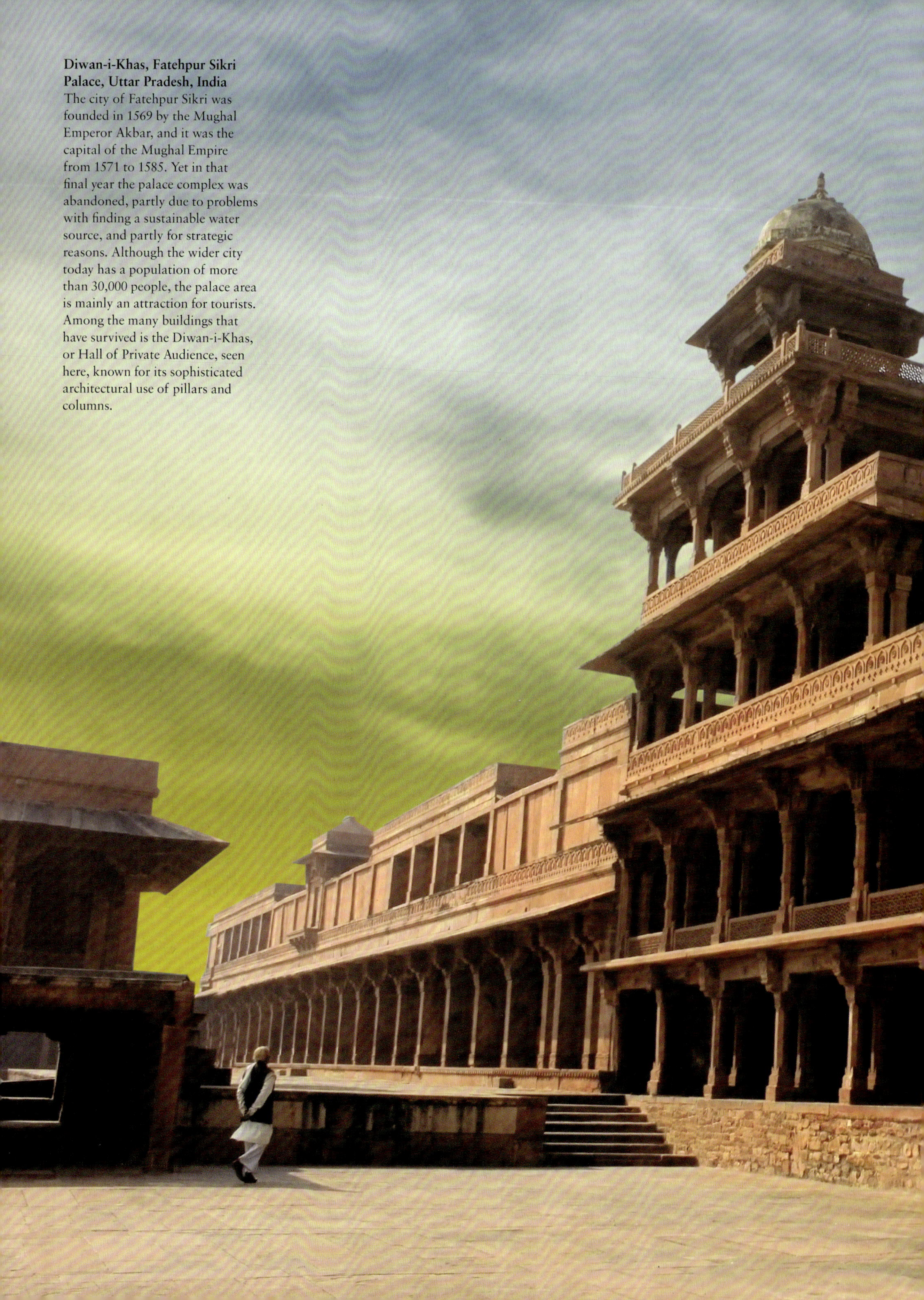

Diwan-i-Khas, Fatehpur Sikri Palace, Uttar Pradesh, India
The city of Fatehpur Sikri was founded in 1569 by the Mughal Emperor Akbar, and it was the capital of the Mughal Empire from 1571 to 1585. Yet in that final year the palace complex was abandoned, partly due to problems with finding a sustainable water source, and partly for strategic reasons. Although the wider city today has a population of more than 30,000 people, the palace area is mainly an attraction for tourists. Among the many buildings that have survived is the Diwan-i-Khas, or Hall of Private Audience, seen here, known for its sophisticated architectural use of pillars and columns.

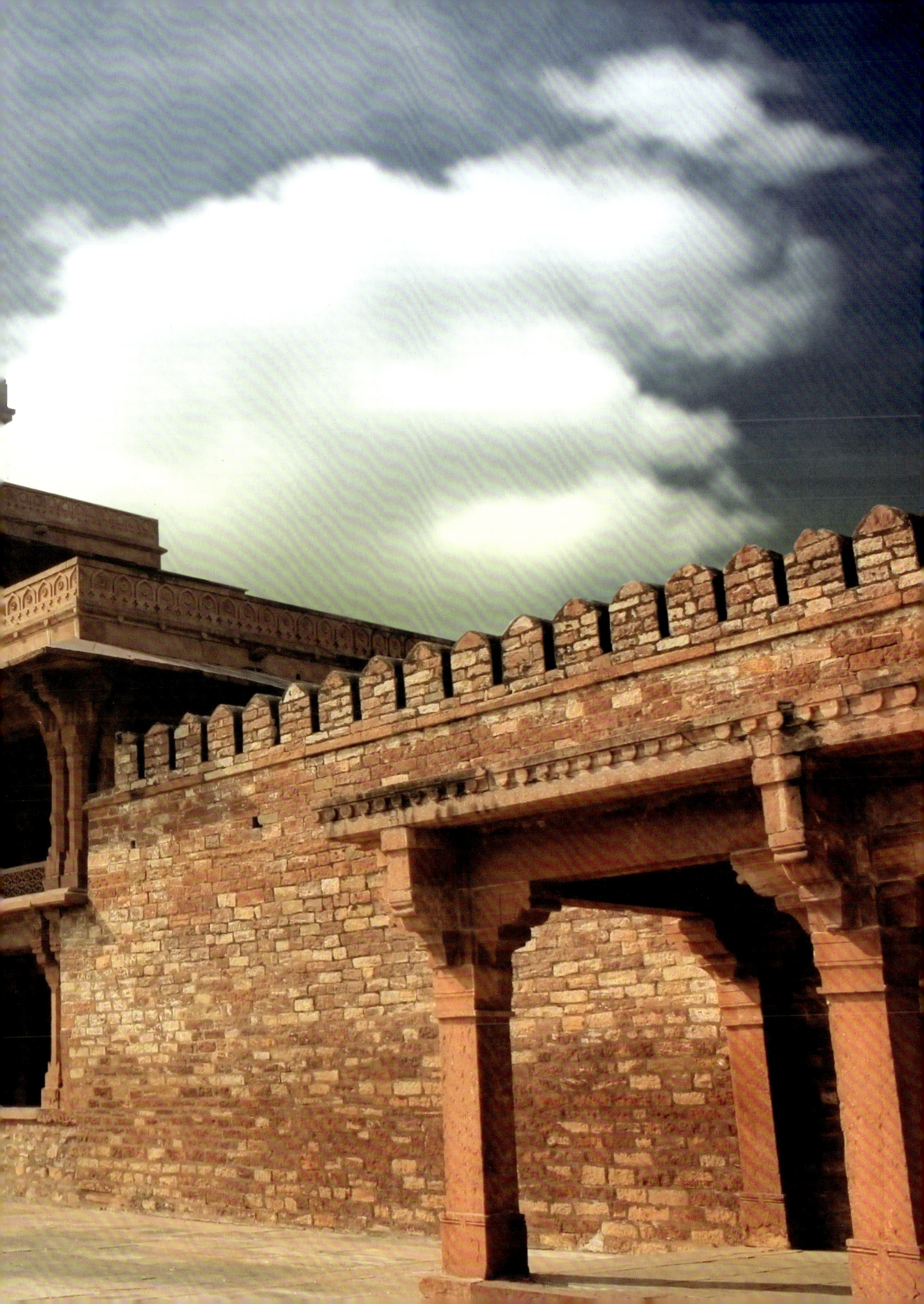

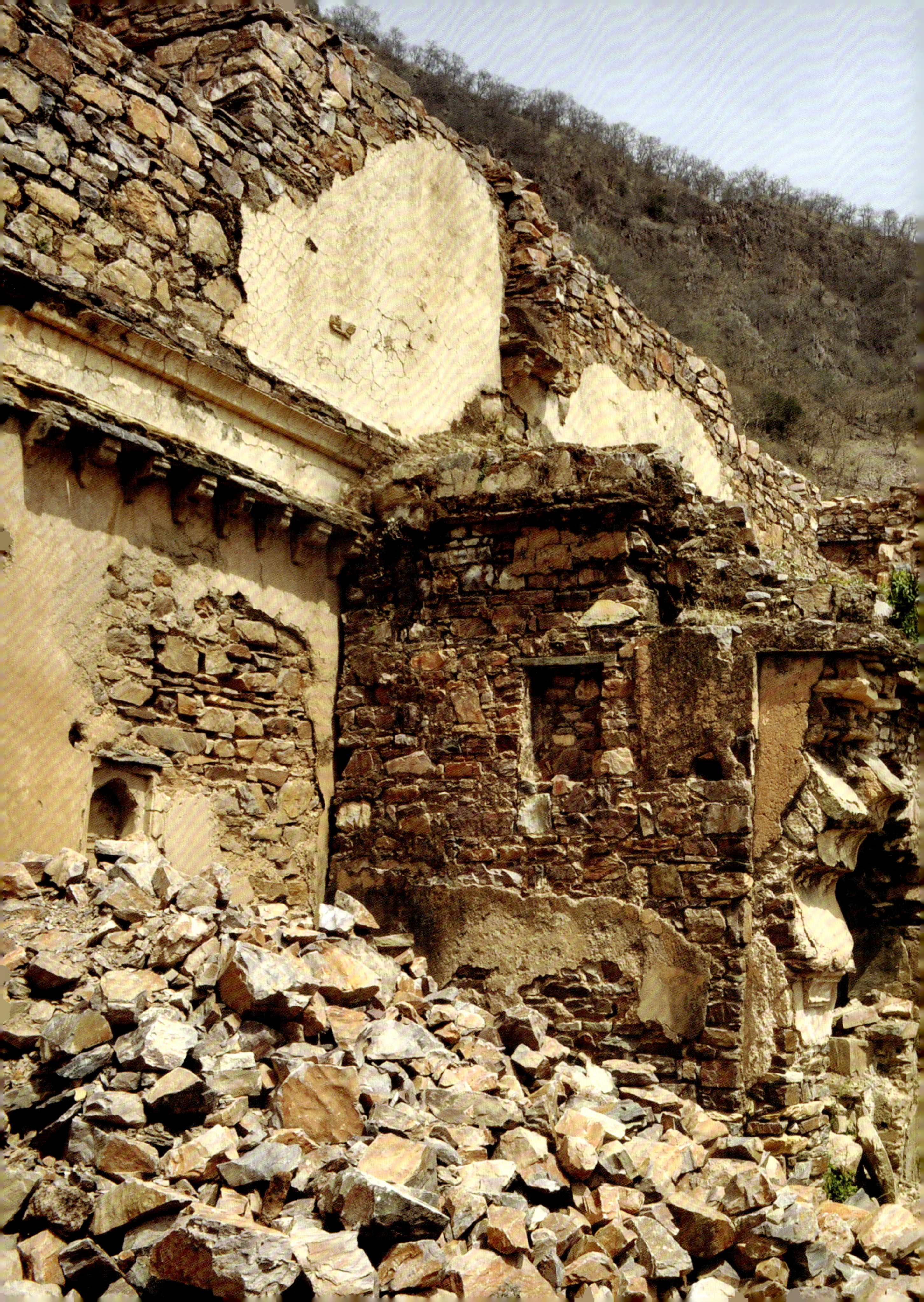

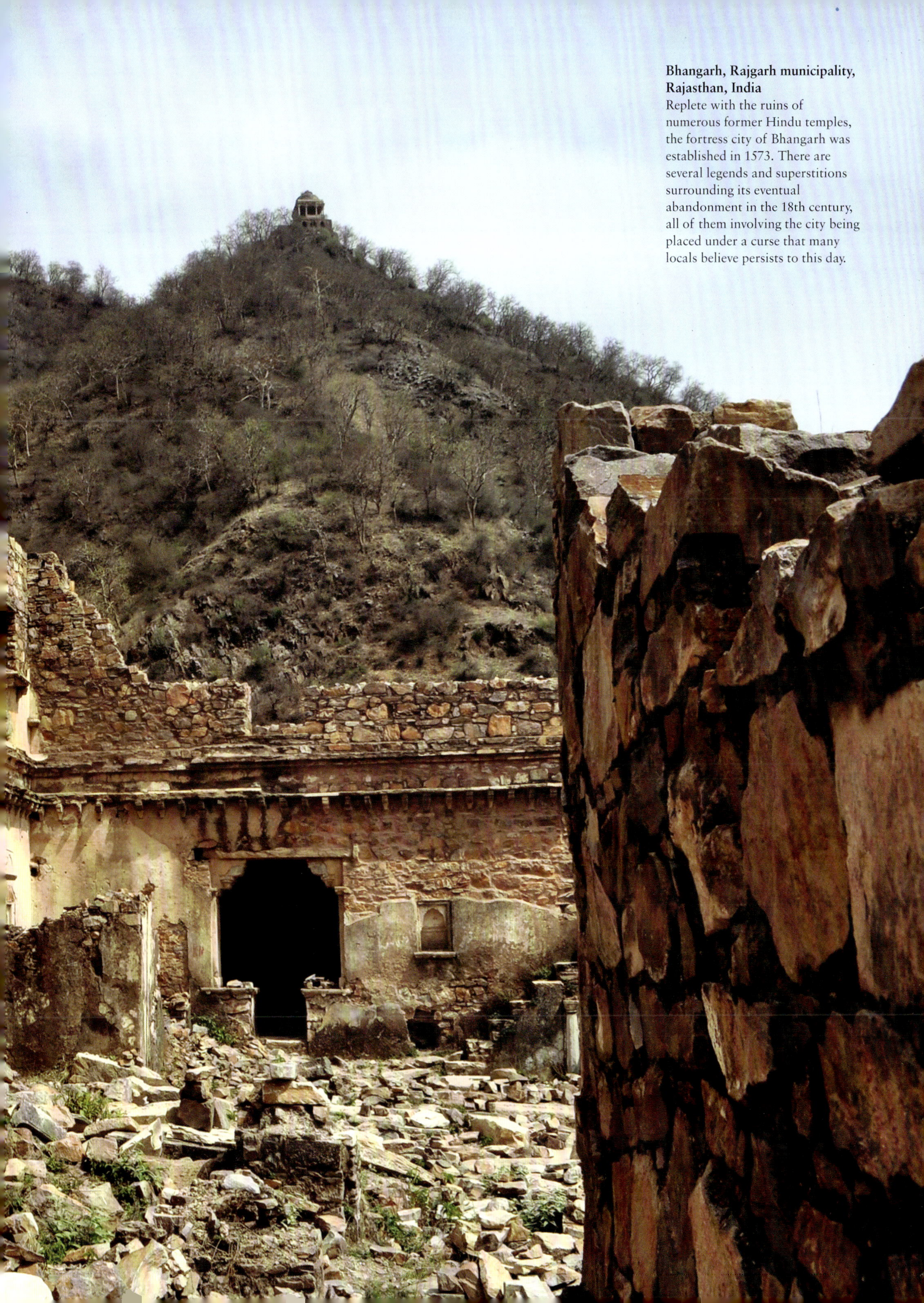

Bhangarh, Rajgarh municipality, Rajasthan, India
Replete with the ruins of numerous former Hindu temples, the fortress city of Bhangarh was established in 1573. There are several legends and superstitions surrounding its eventual abandonment in the 18th century, all of them involving the city being placed under a curse that many locals believe persists to this day.

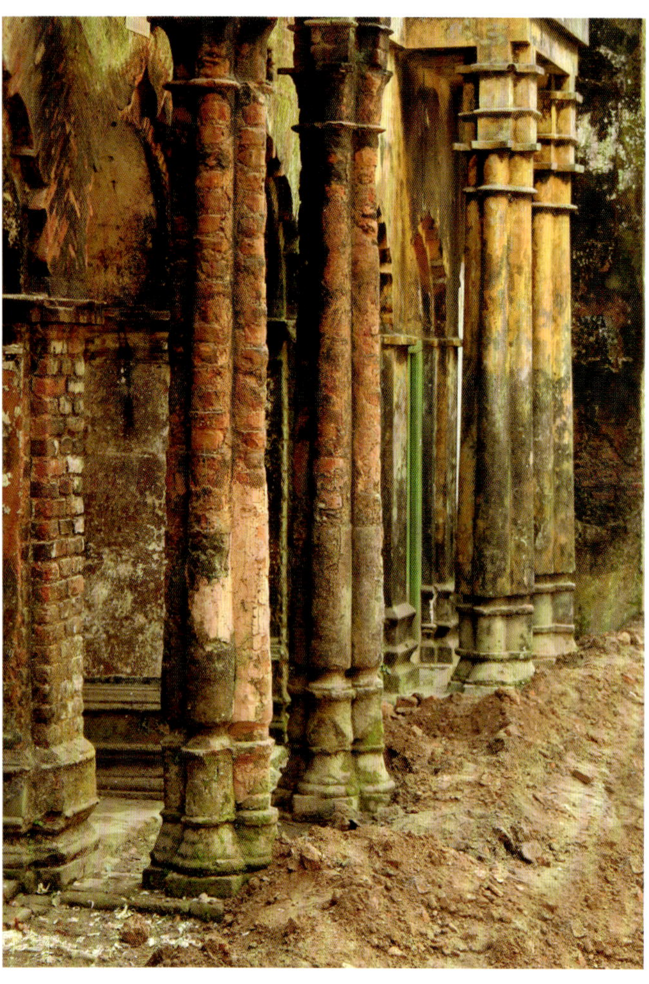

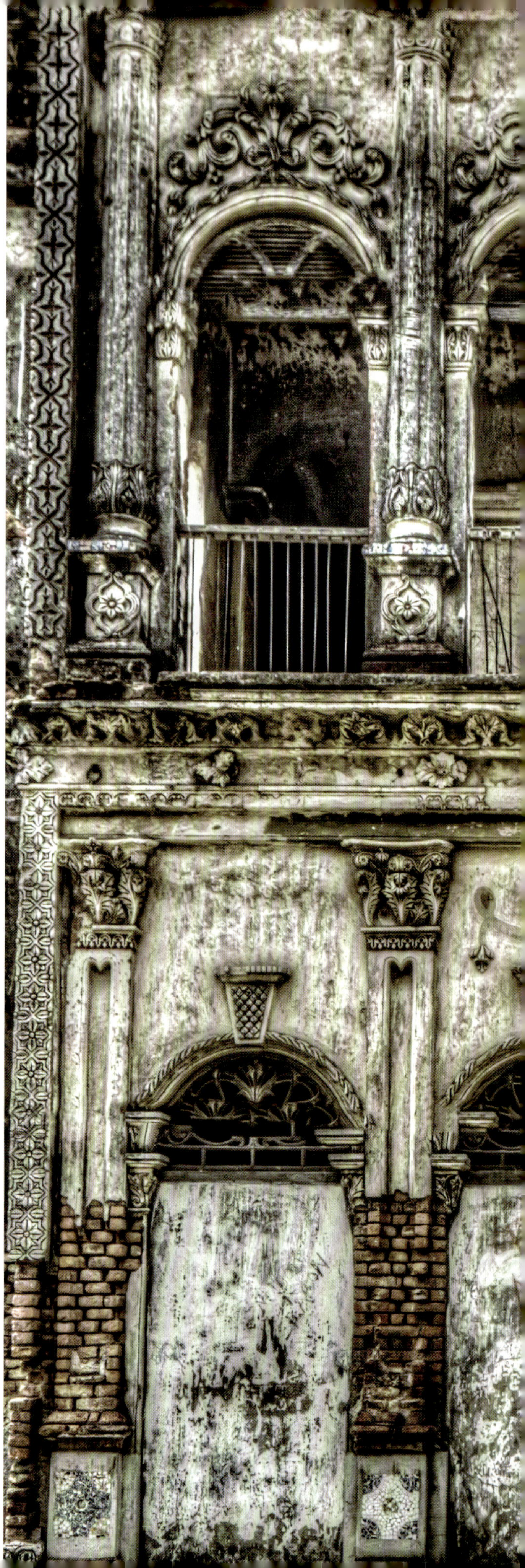

BOTH PHOTOGRAPHS:

Panam City, Sonargaon, Narayanganj, Bangladesh

Panam City was a major part of the Sonargaon, a huge commercial and trading centre in the Bengal, and the capital of the 15th-century Bengal ruler Isa Khan. Although the Sonargaon dated back to the medieval period, Panam City was actually established during the 19th century by the British, as a place for the trading of cotton fabrics, a hugely profitable enterprise for the British Empire. Today, as these photographs attest, many of Panam City's imperial buildings are now ghostly ruins, relics of a former affluent past. Some restoration work has been undertaken by the country's Department of Archaeology.

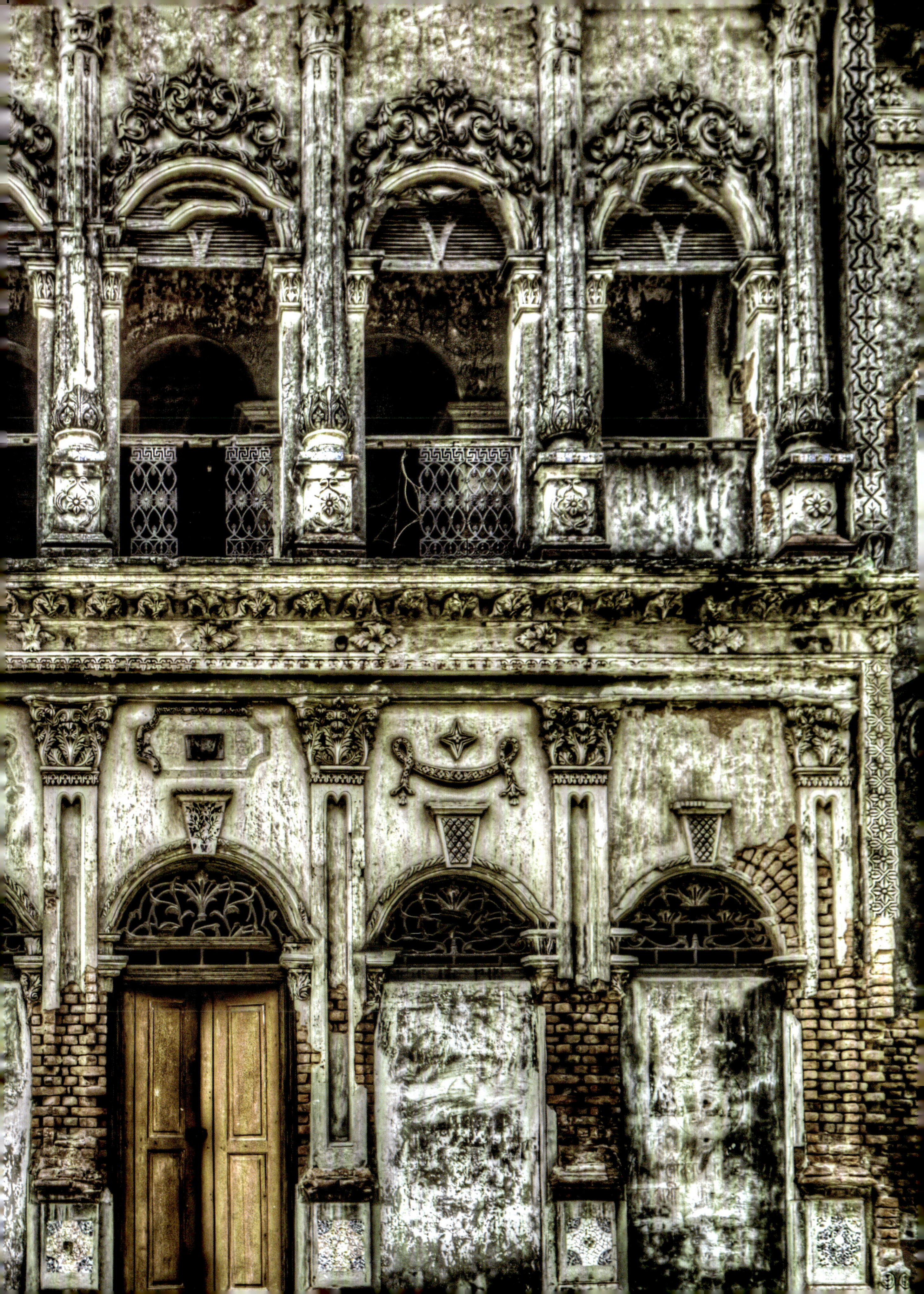

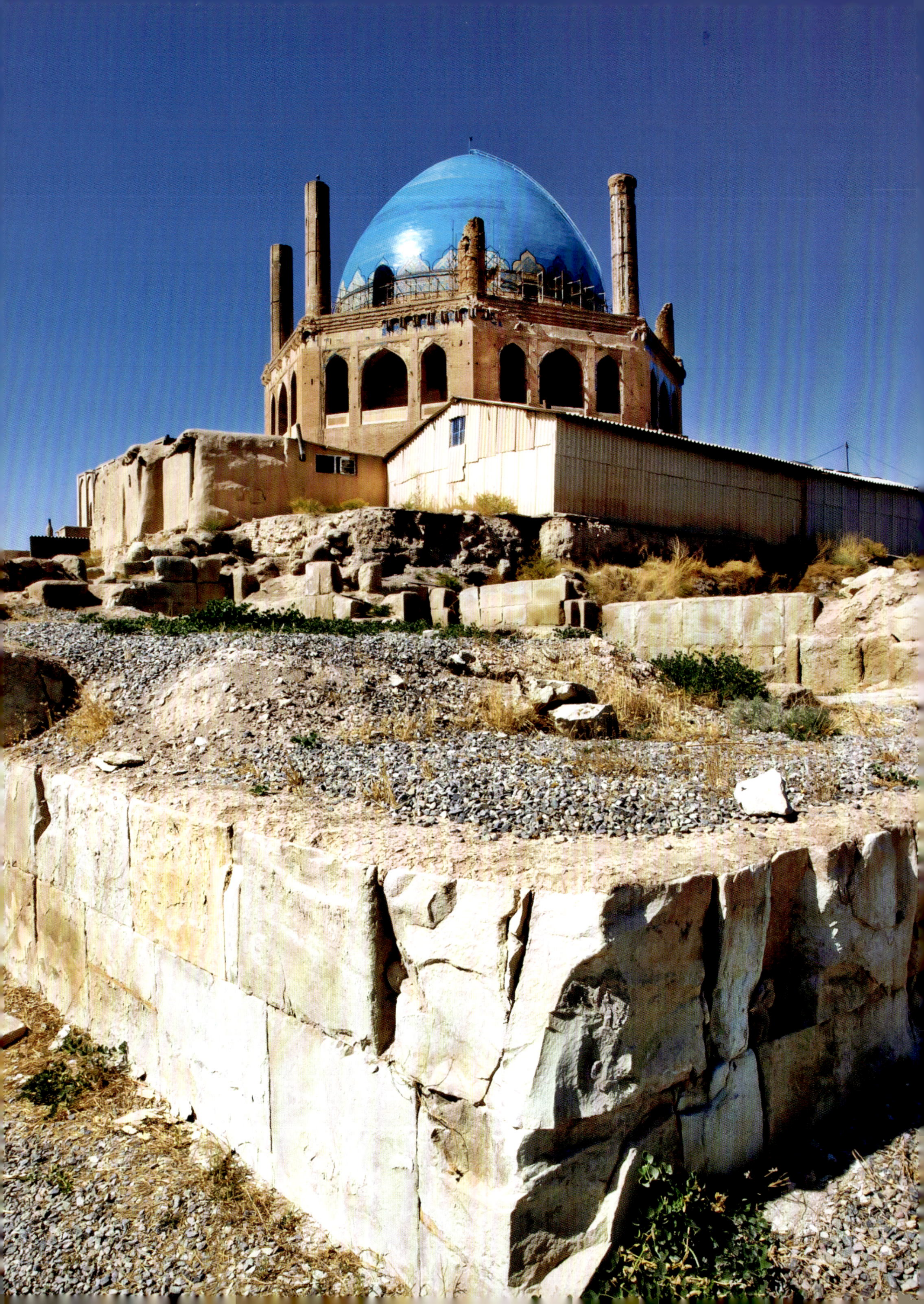

Middle East

The Middle East is a place of harsh physical beauty. Much of it is open and arid, with sand and stone baking under a tropical sun for many months of the year. Yet other regions – particularly those around major rivers or mountainous areas – can be lush and fertile. What is certain, however, is that the climate and terrain have historically been harsh upon human beings, particularly in relation to their access to water. Some of the ghost habitations of the Middle East are simply the product of that most vital of substances running dry over time, the citizens of a town forced to travel miles to obtain drinking water or no longer able to irrigate their crops.

Despite the adversity, across the millennia of Middle Eastern history and culture there have flowered civilizations and empires at the very forefront of human developments in art, architecture, town planning, mathematics, metallurgy, science and education. The region is also the cradle for the world's great monotheistic religions – Judaism, Christianity and Islam. Yet time has been hard on many Middle Eastern towns and cities, retarding or undoing many of their historical gains. Some previously opulent or vibrant urban areas are now empty shells, populated temporarily by tourists. Furthermore, regular and dreadful wars have continually played their part in creating the ghost towns of the future.

LEFT:
Soltaniyeh, Iran
Standing out in sharp relief against the Iranian sky, the Mausoleum of Oljaytu at Soltaniyeh was built in 1302–12, as the tomb of the eighth Ilkhanid ruler. Its salient feature is the 50m (164ft) dome, covered with turquoise-blue faience tiles that have not faded with age. Although abandoned, the monument is protected by the Iranian national government.

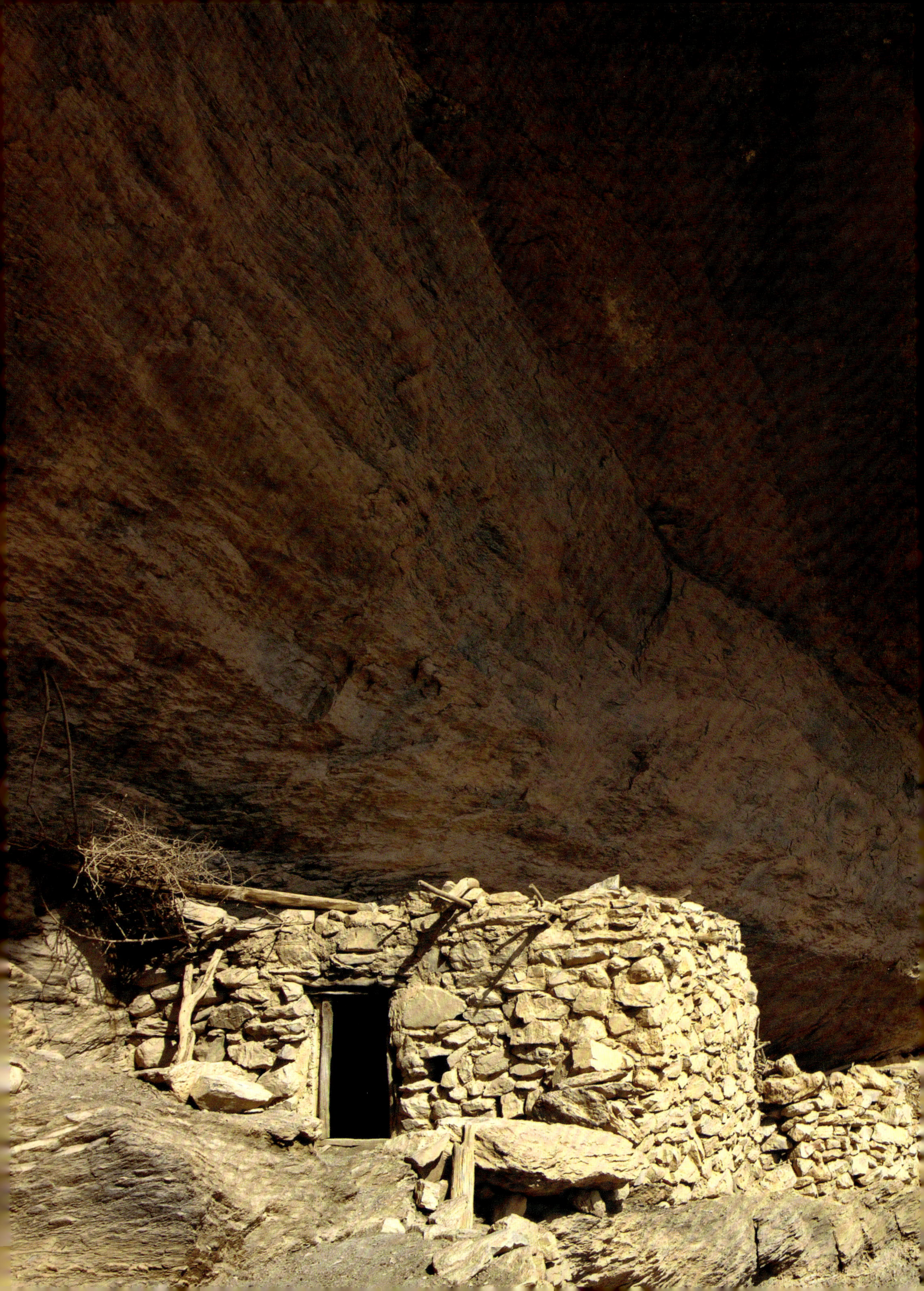

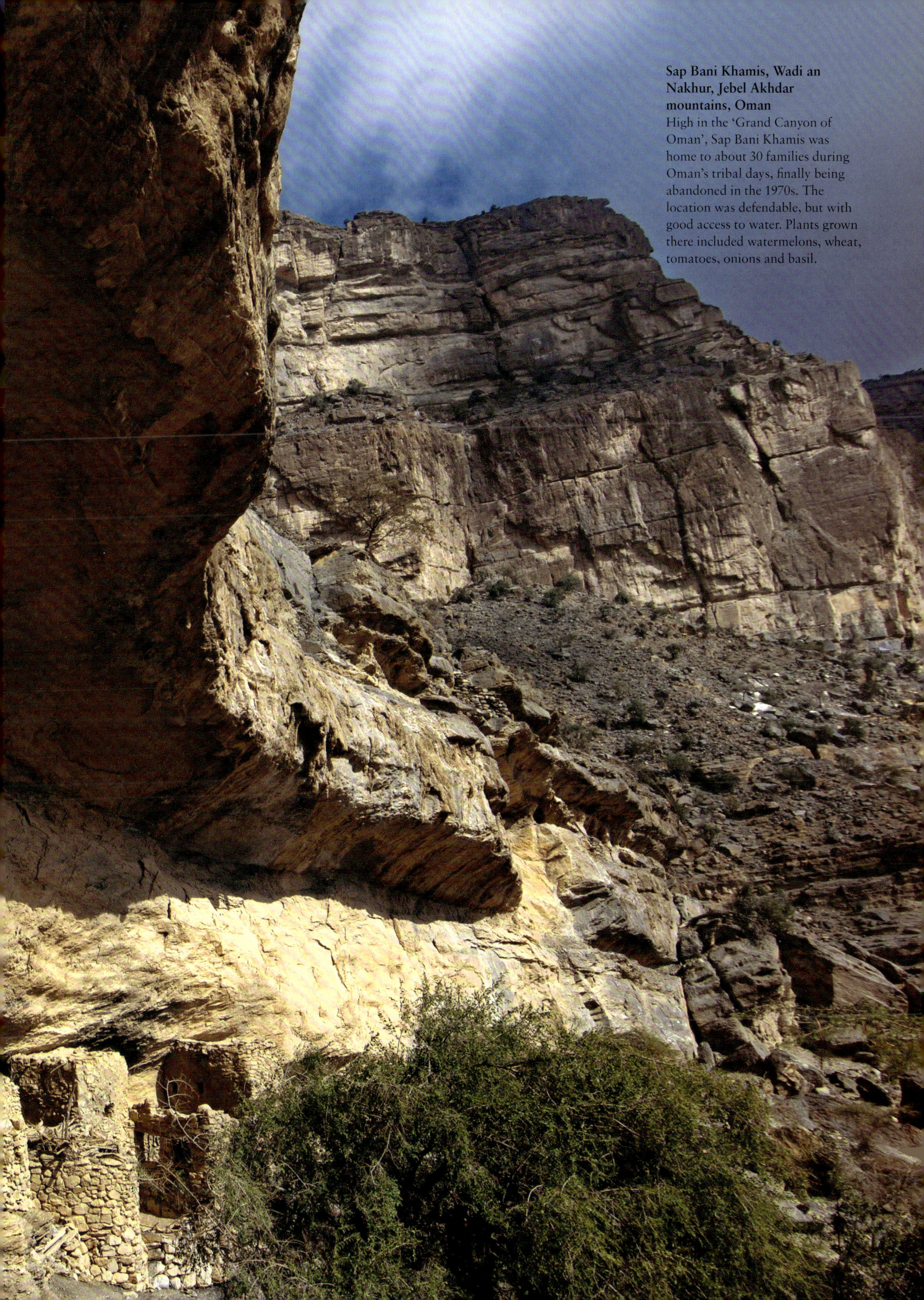

Sap Bani Khamis, Wadi an Nakhur, Jebel Akhdar mountains, Oman
High in the 'Grand Canyon of Oman', Sap Bani Khamis was home to about 30 families during Oman's tribal days, finally being abandoned in the 1970s. The location was defendable, but with good access to water. Plants grown there included watermelons, wheat, tomatoes, onions and basil.

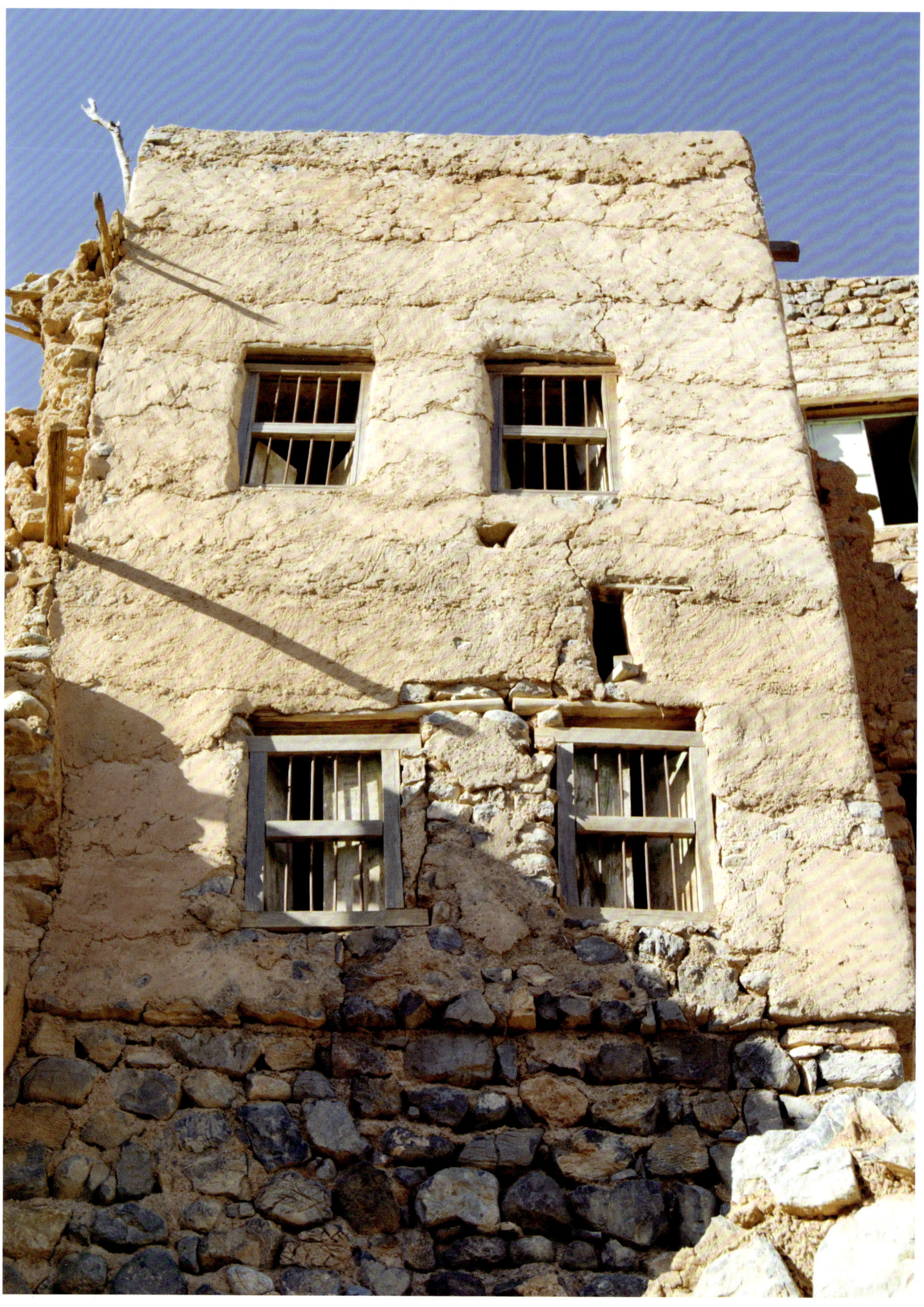

OPPOSITE:

Wadi Bani Habib, Oman

An abandoned village at Wadi Bani Habib is one of many architectural legacies on the Jebel Akhdar (lit. 'Green Mountain'), roughly 150km (93 miles) from the Omani capital, Muscat. Peaking at 3000m (9842ft), the Jebel Akhdar was the scene of a bitter war in the 1950s, during which time many mountain villages were abandoned.

RIGHT AND BELOW:

Al Khuwayr, Ash Shamal, Qatar

The fishing village of Al Khuwayr sits on the far northern coastline of Qatar. Like several other villages on this part of the Qatari coastline, Al Khuwayr was abandoned in the 1970s after its inhabitants finally gave up the struggle of scratching out a difficult living from the sea. The remnants of the buildings speak of traditional architecture in this extremely hot part of the world, with thick coral rock and limestone walls helping to keep the interiors cool, and multi-layer roofs providing insulation from both heat and cold.

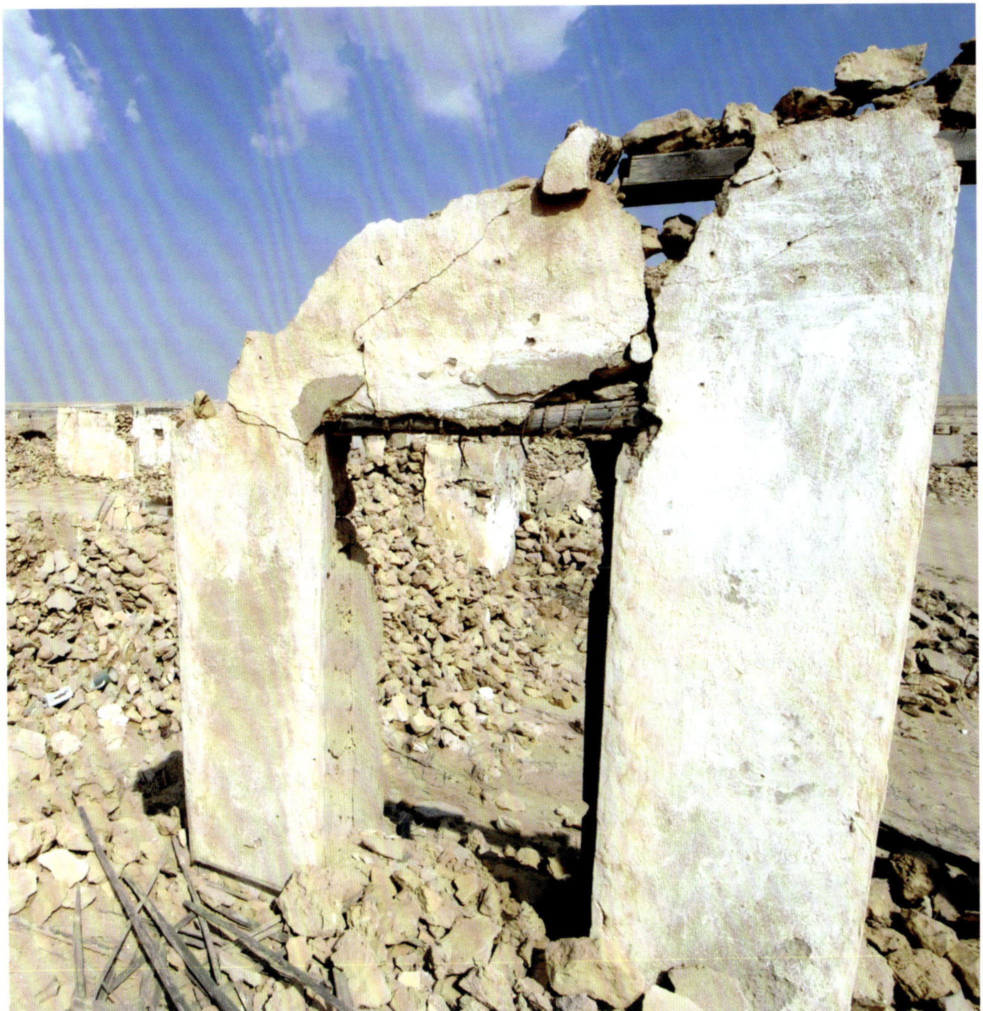

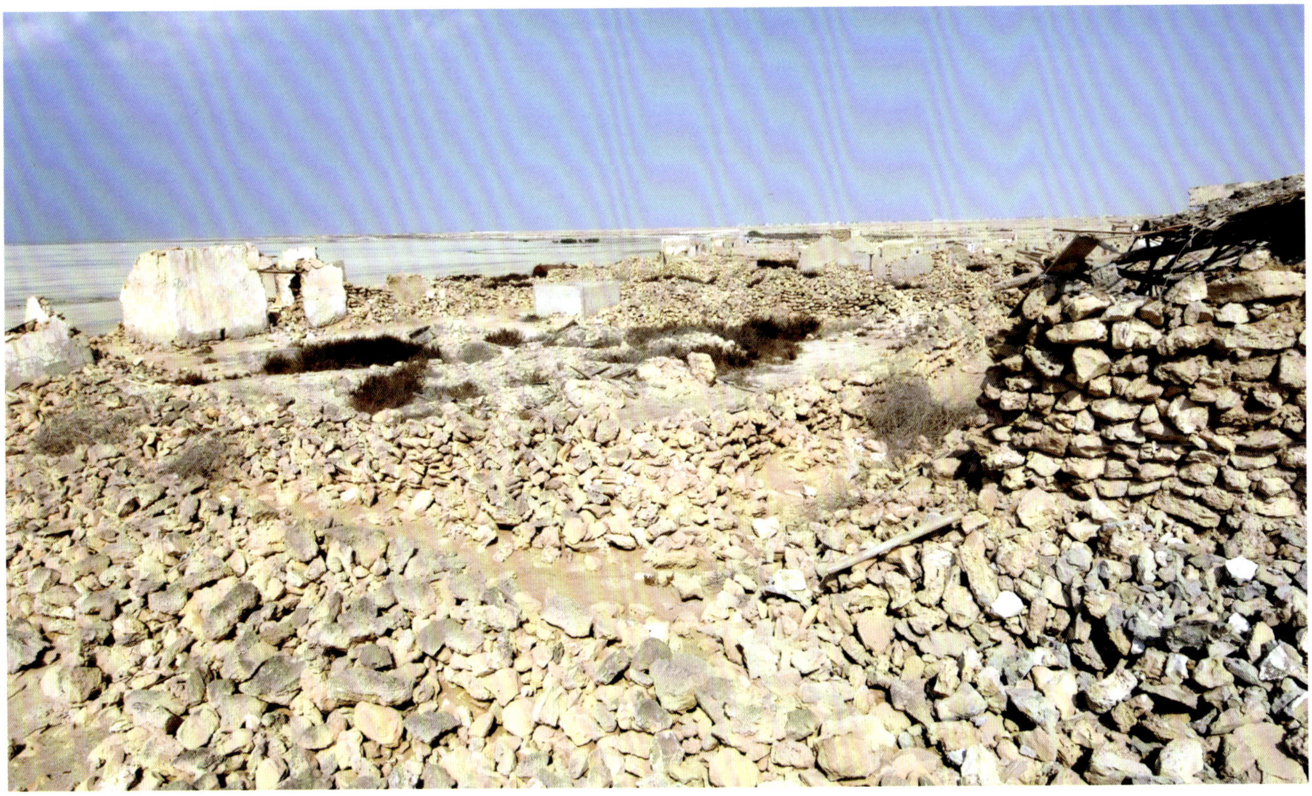

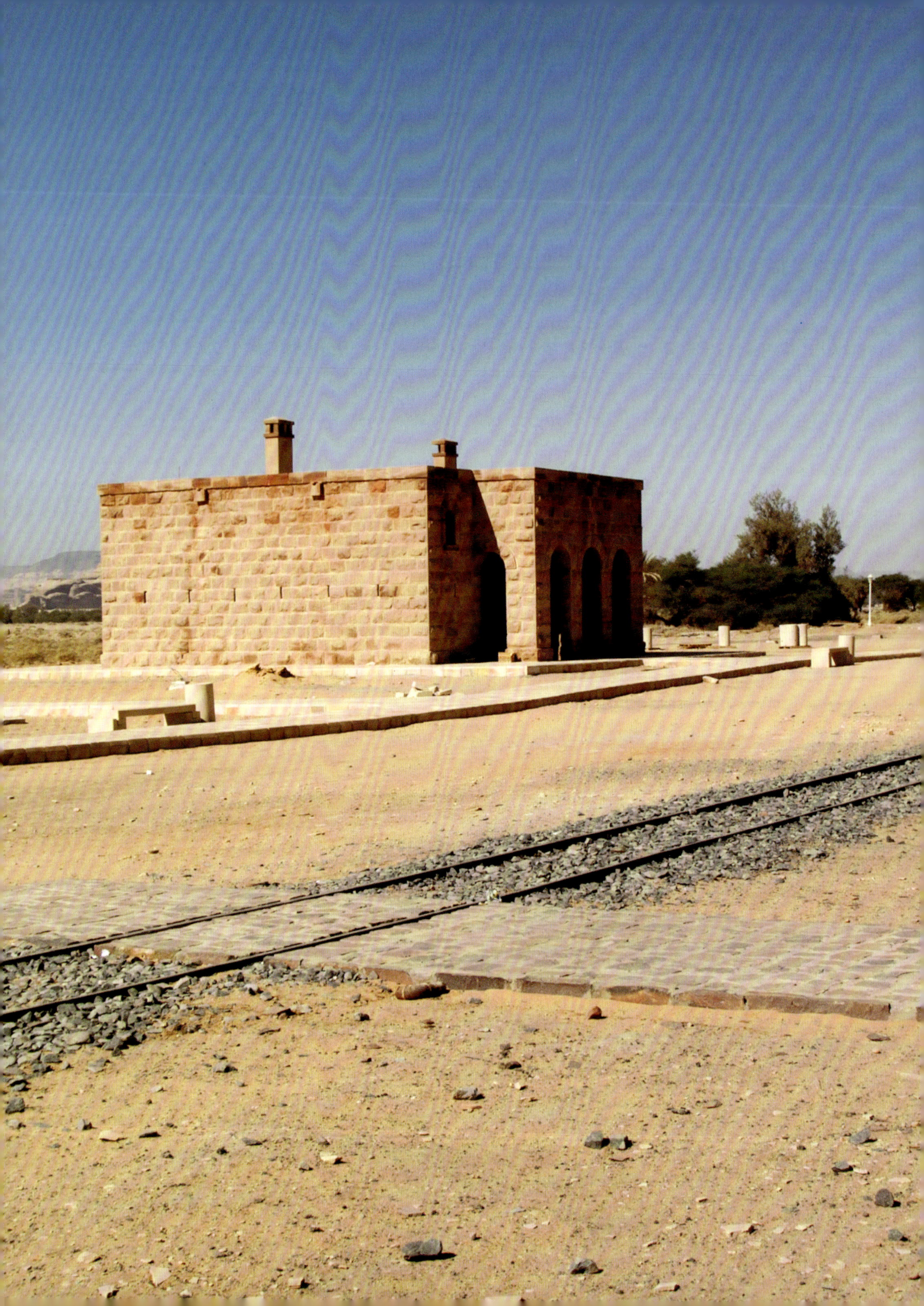

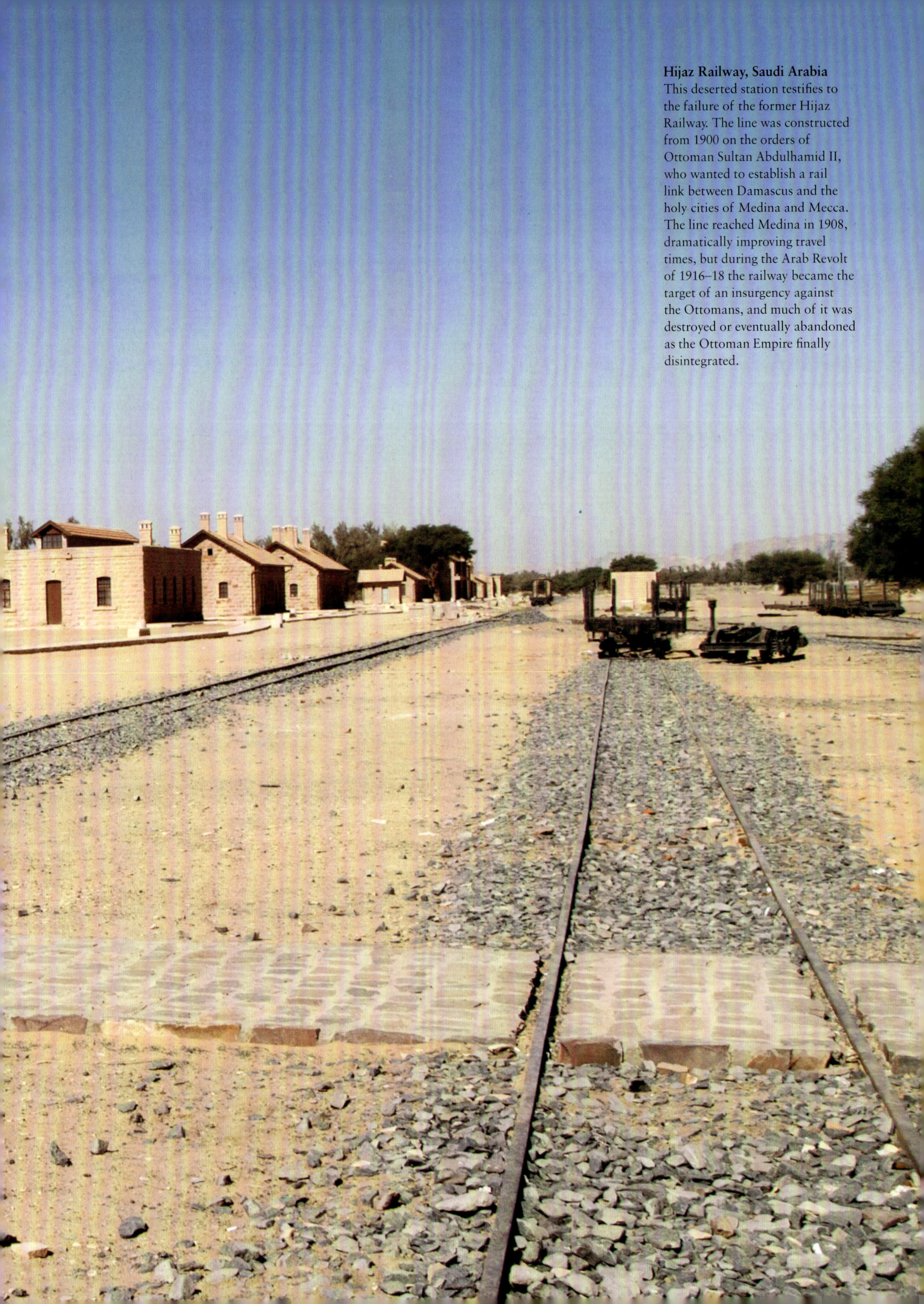

Hijaz Railway, Saudi Arabia
This deserted station testifies to the failure of the former Hijaz Railway. The line was constructed from 1900 on the orders of Ottoman Sultan Abdulhamid II, who wanted to establish a rail link between Damascus and the holy cities of Medina and Mecca. The line reached Medina in 1908, dramatically improving travel times, but during the Arab Revolt of 1916–18 the railway became the target of an insurgency against the Ottomans, and much of it was destroyed or eventually abandoned as the Ottoman Empire finally disintegrated.

Al- 'Ula, Saudi Arabia

Al- 'Ula is an astonishing spectacle even after the passage of more than 2500 years. Established in the 6th century BCE, and extensively reconstructed in the 13th century CE, the walled city grew to encompass some 800 mud-brick and stone houses, huddled together in a bewildering maze of alleys, walls and small courtyards. The last of the inhabitants left in the 1980s, moving into the modern town of Al- 'Ula nearby.

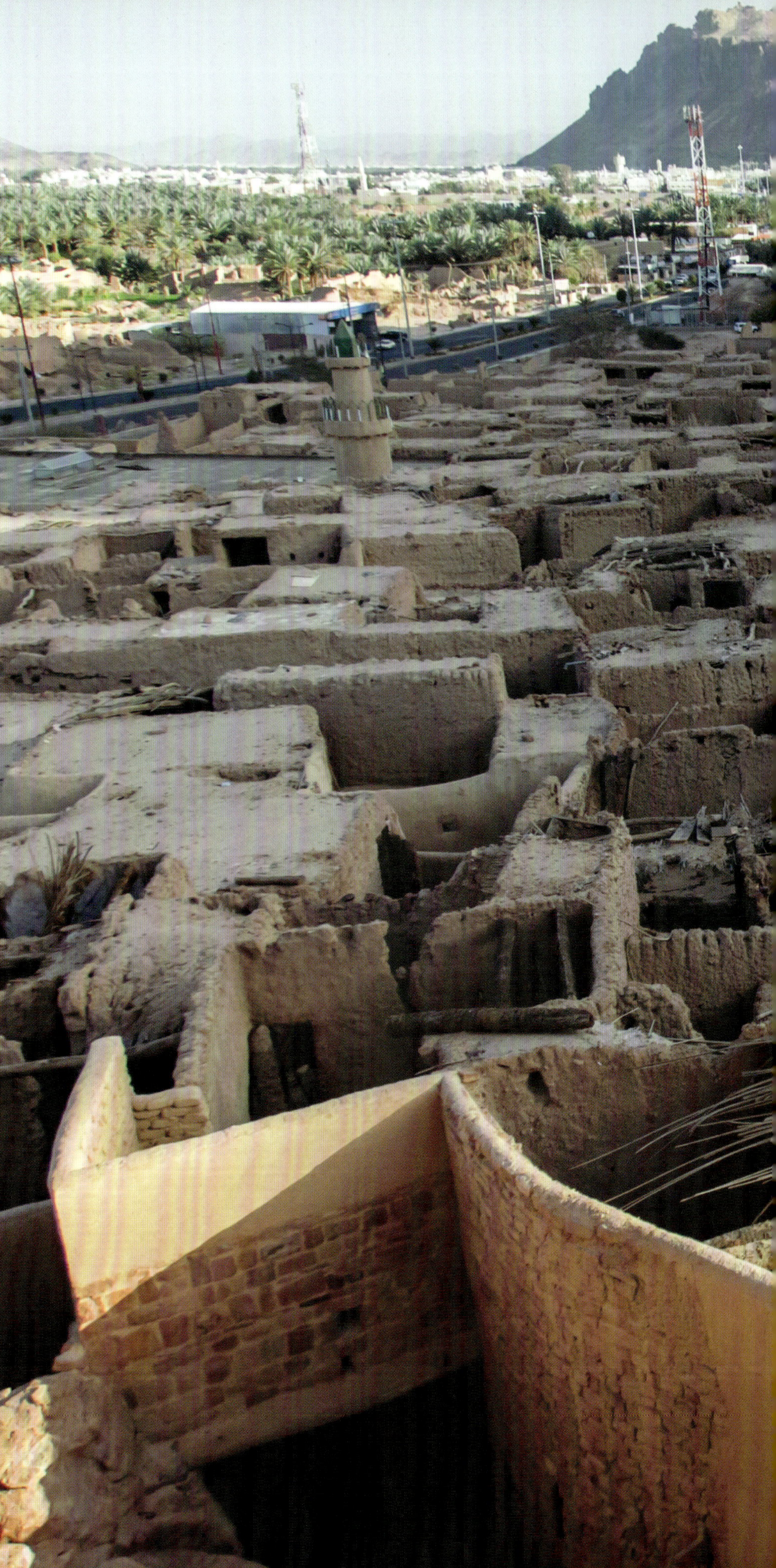

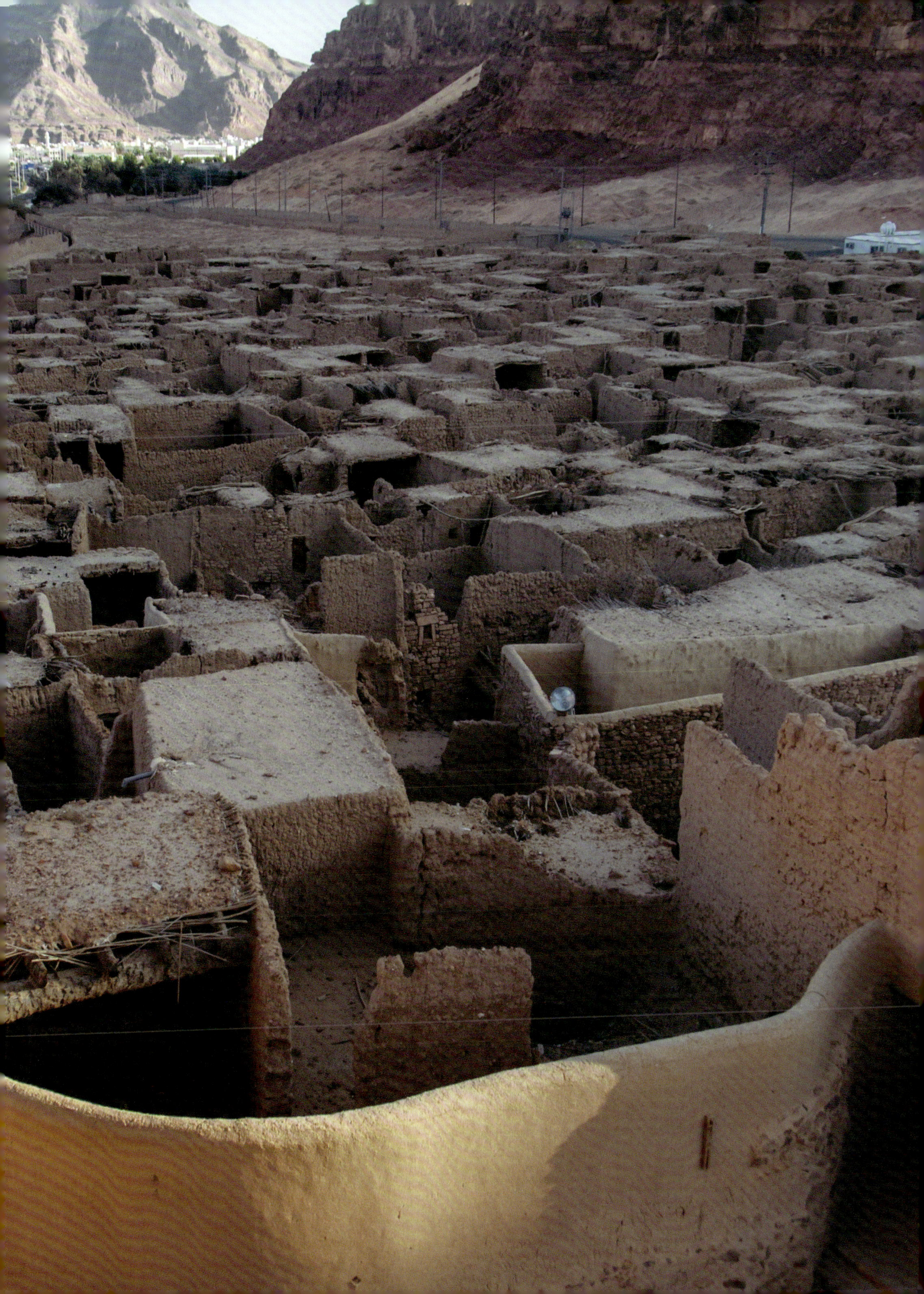

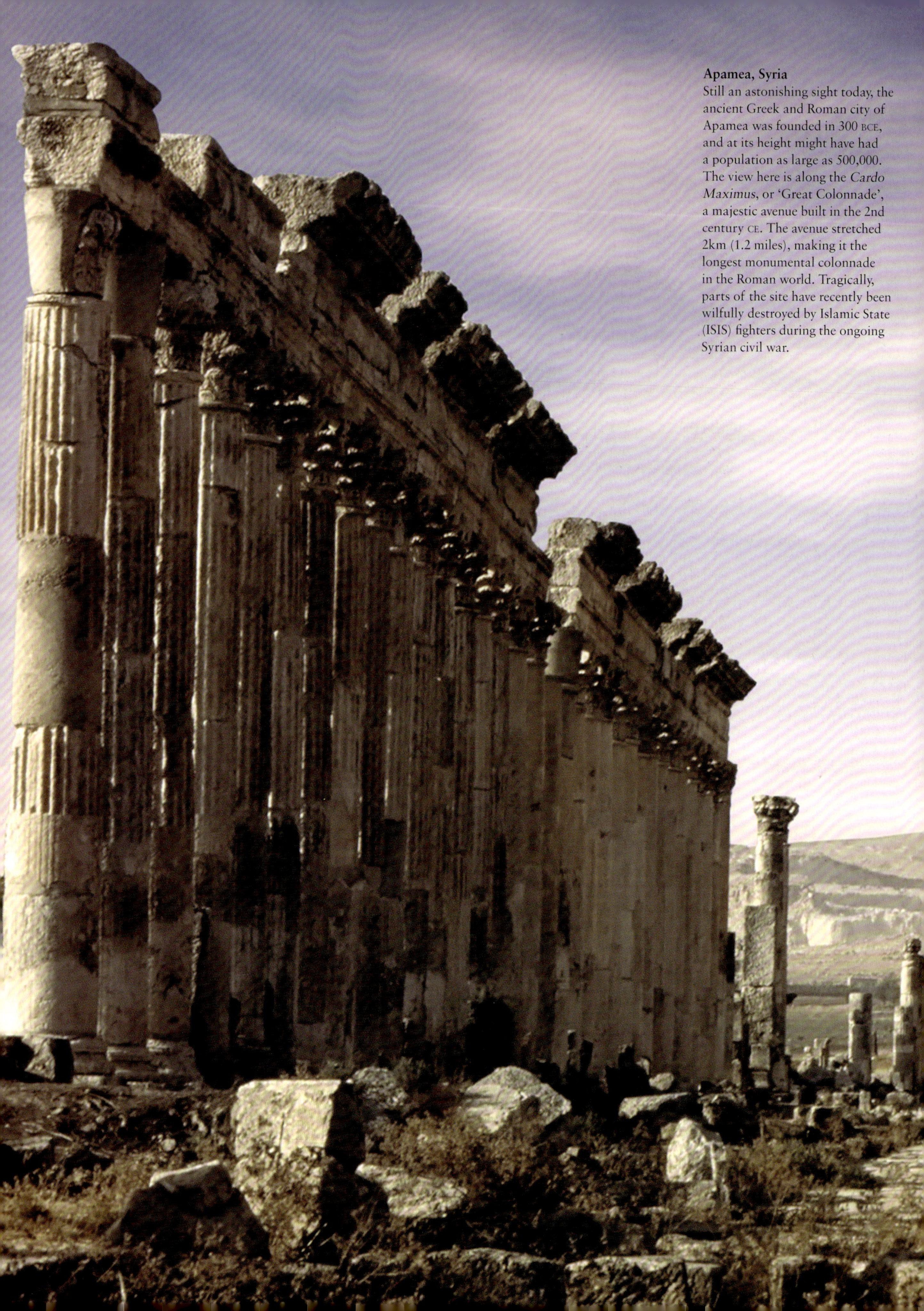

Apamea, Syria
Still an astonishing sight today, the ancient Greek and Roman city of Apamea was founded in 300 BCE, and at its height might have had a population as large as 500,000. The view here is along the *Cardo Maximus*, or 'Great Colonnade', a majestic avenue built in the 2nd century CE. The avenue stretched 2km (1.2 miles), making it the longest monumental colonnade in the Roman world. Tragically, parts of the site have recently been wilfully destroyed by Islamic State (ISIS) fighters during the ongoing Syrian civil war.

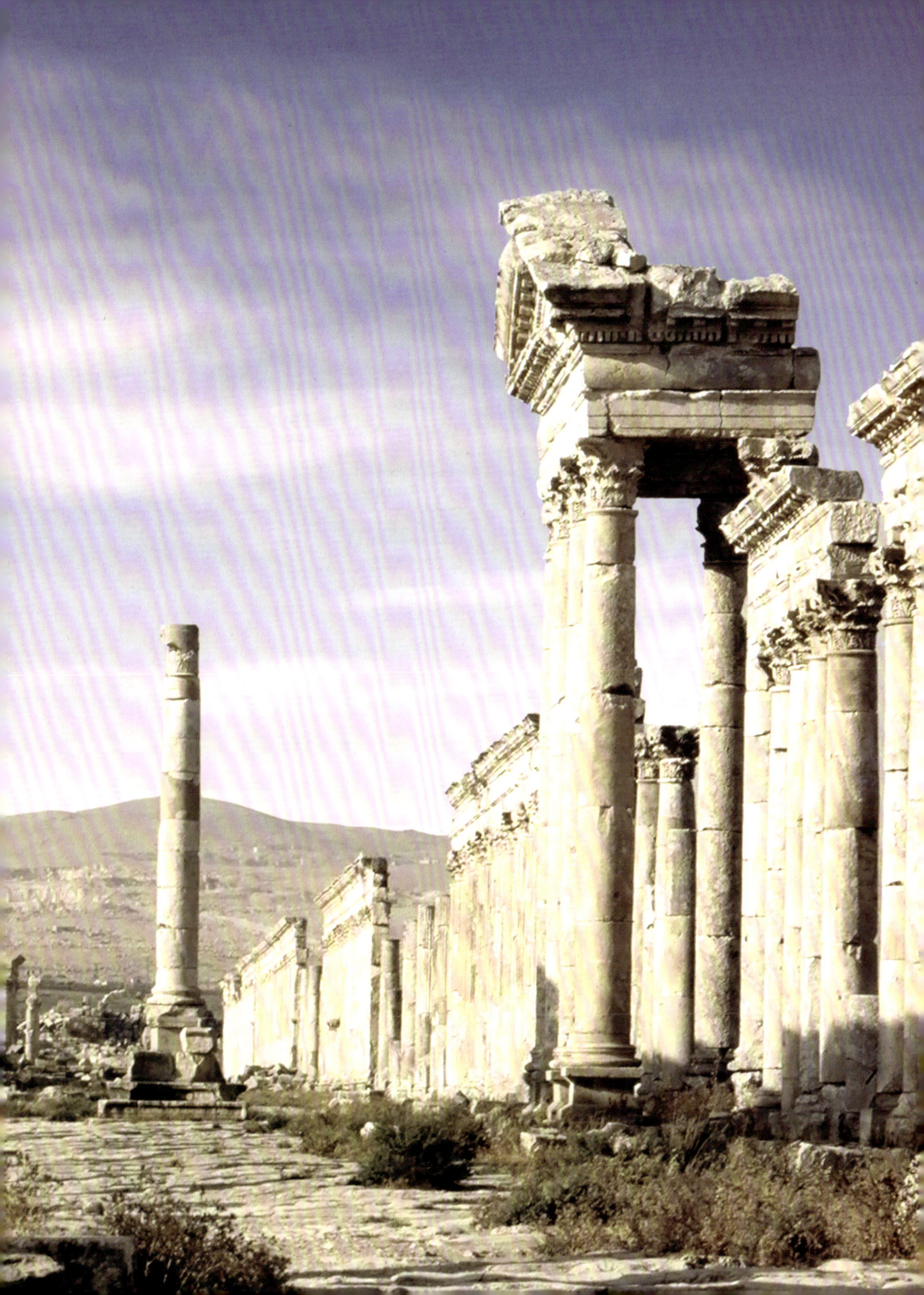

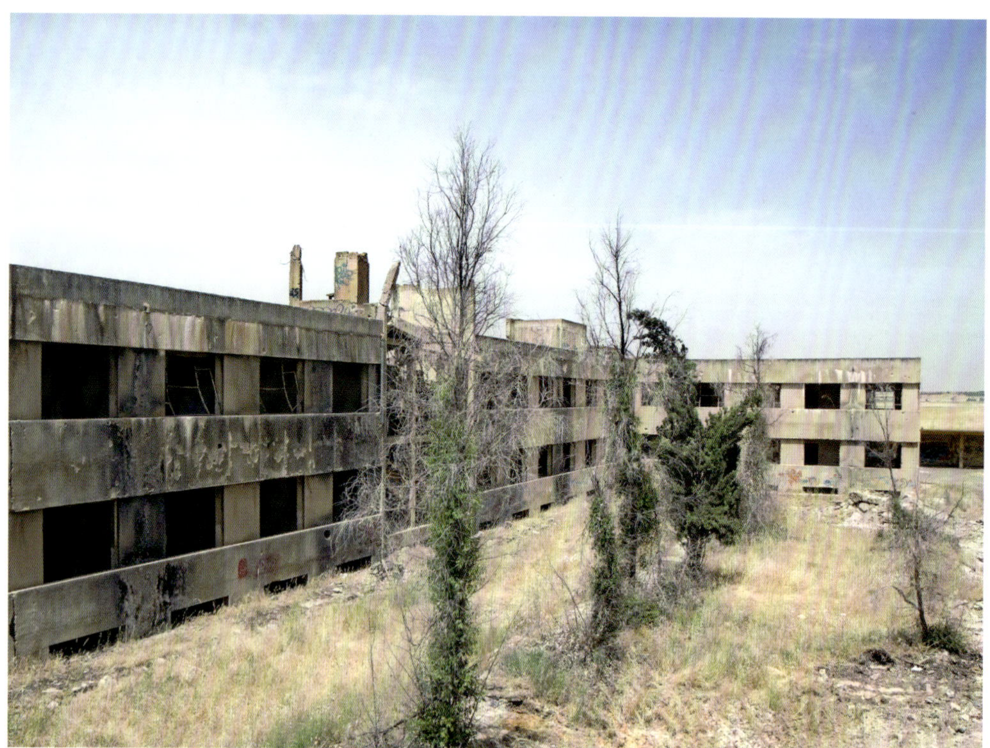

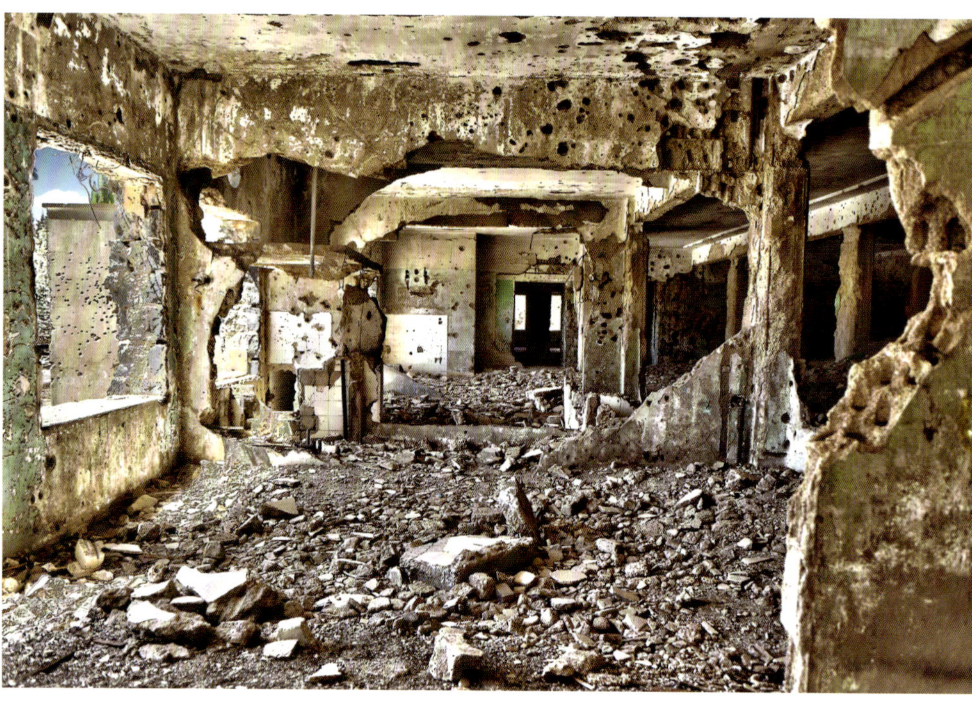

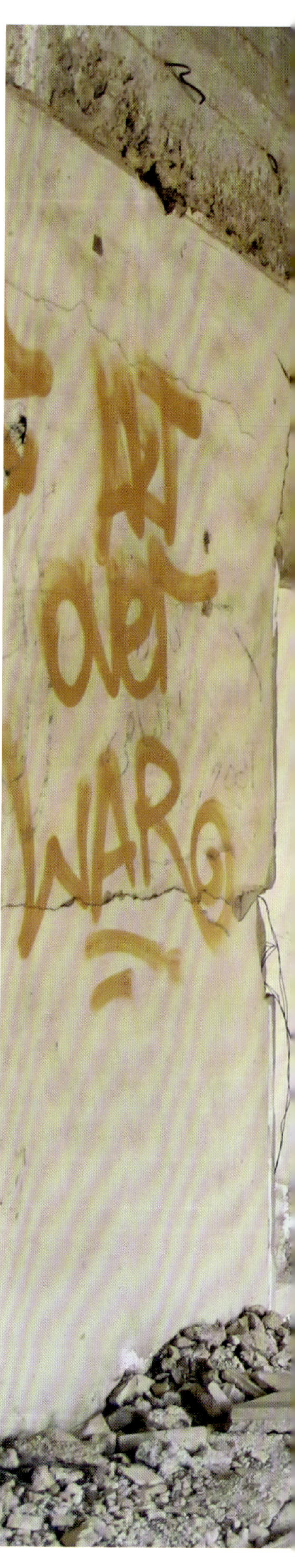

TOP:

Quneitra, Golan Heights, Syria
Quneitra's curse was to be in the frontline of the fighting between Syrian and Israeli forces on the Golan Heights during the 1967 and 1973 Arab–Israeli Wars. During those conflicts and the subsequent Israeli occupation, the city was almost entirely destroyed, and little was subsequently rebuilt. This building was the headquarters for Syrian ground forces.

ABOVE:

Quneitra, Golan Heights, Syria
This image of the interior of a building at Quneitra starkly illustrates the ragged destruction visited upon the city by artillery and air strikes. The corridor has been blasted out with high explosives, the shrapnel from the munitions peppering any of the surfaces that did not immediately collapse.

RIGHT:

Quneitra, Golan Heights, Syria
An interior view of the building seen in the top image above, with reflective graffiti bringing some measure of peace to the wrecked surroundings. In 1973–74, the already damaged city was destroyed with bulldozers, tractors and explosives by Israeli forces before their withdrawal. Today, a few dozen people attempt to live within the ruins.

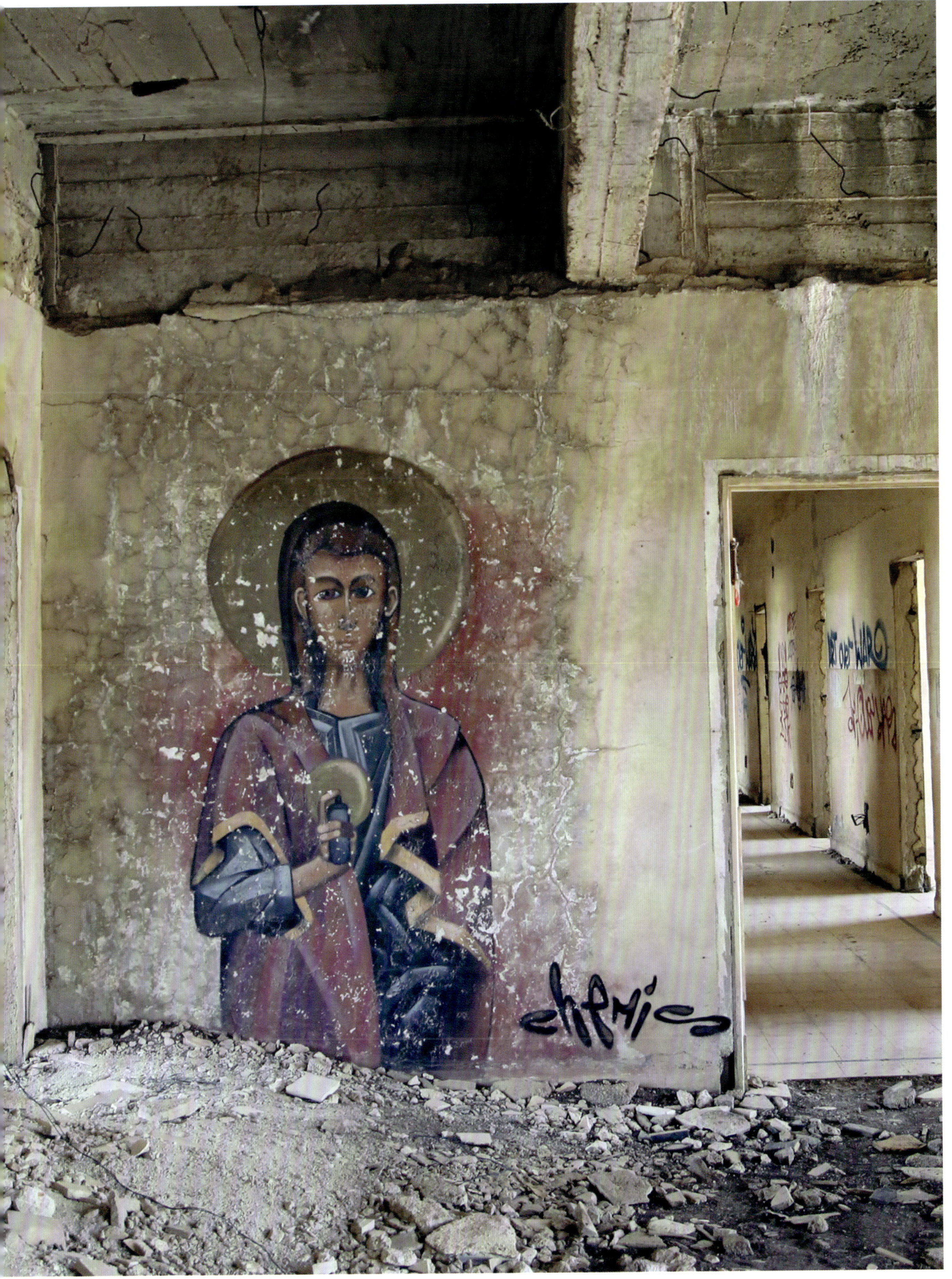

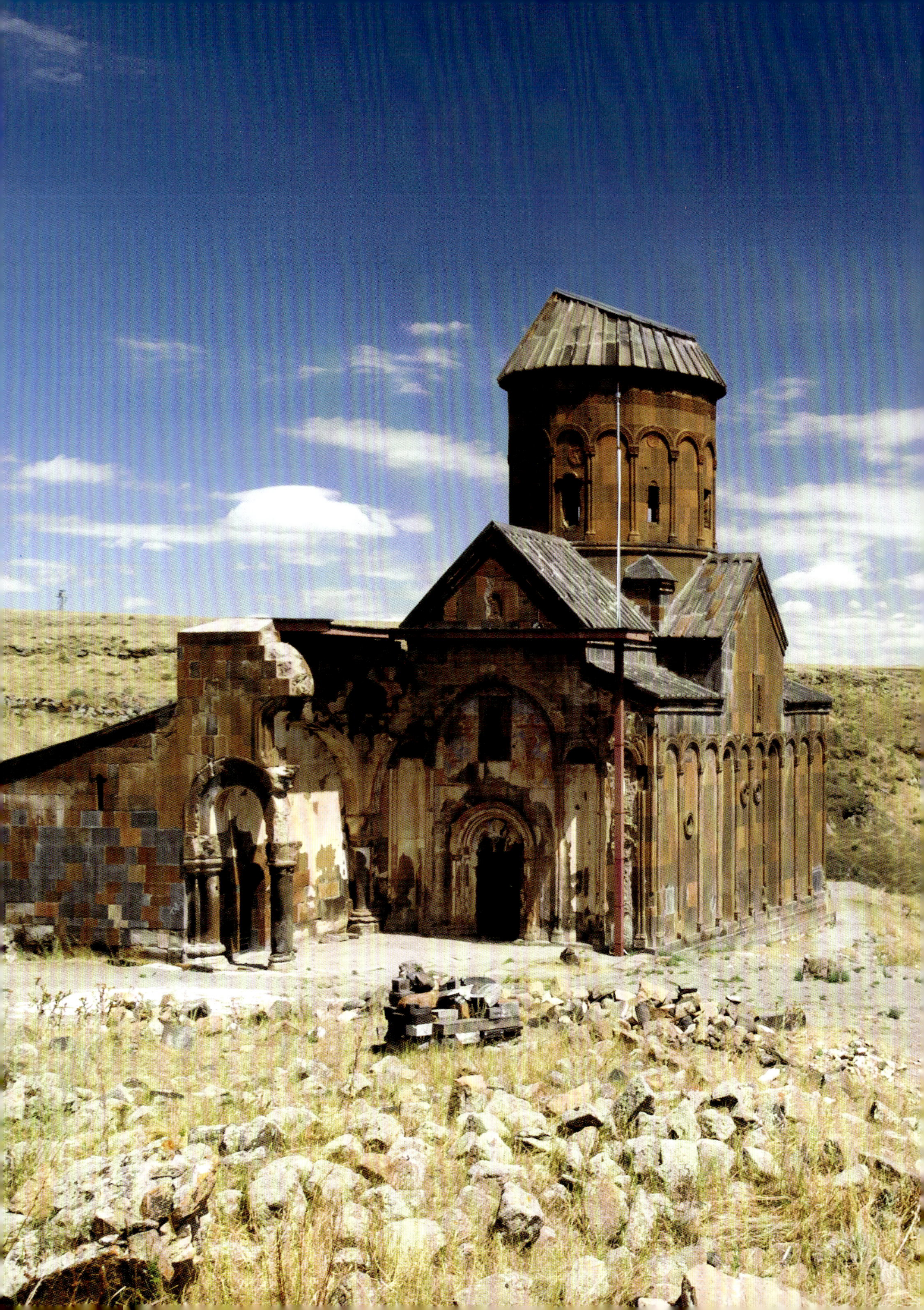

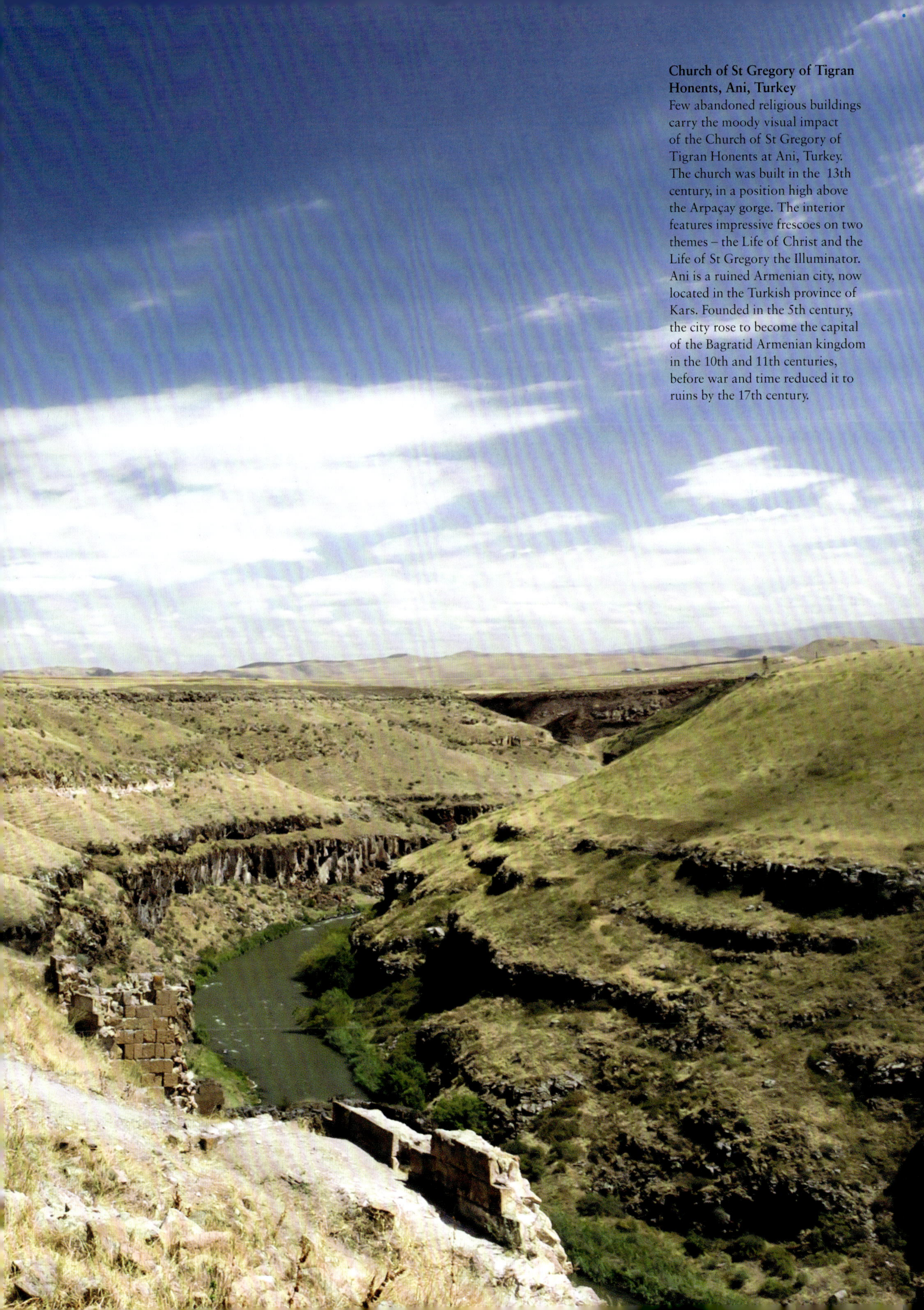

Church of St Gregory of Tigran Honents, Ani, Turkey
Few abandoned religious buildings carry the moody visual impact of the Church of St Gregory of Tigran Honents at Ani, Turkey. The church was built in the 13th century, in a position high above the Arpaçay gorge. The interior features impressive frescoes on two themes – the Life of Christ and the Life of St Gregory the Illuminator. Ani is a ruined Armenian city, now located in the Turkish province of Kars. Founded in the 5th century, the city rose to become the capital of the Bagratid Armenian kingdom in the 10th and 11th centuries, before war and time reduced it to ruins by the 17th century.

BELOW:
The Cathedral, Ani, Turkey
The ruins of a Christian past still stand poignantly in the barren yet beautiful landscape at Ani. The building here is the Cathedral, located at the southern end of the city. Originally it had a prominent central dome, which would have given the building a radically different silhouette from that which exists today.

OPPOSITE TOP & BOTTOM:
Church of the Redeemer, Ani, Turkey
Two powerful views of the famous Church of the Redeemer at Ani, or least what remains of it after hundreds of years of decay and weathering. The church's construction was completed in 1035, and it was restored at several points throughout its history before it was finally left to the elements in the mid-18th century (along with the rest of the city). The collapse of the entire eastern half of the church most likely dates to 1957 – during that year local people remember a huge storm one night, accompanied by the sound of crashing masonry in the distance as the church's neglected structure finally gave way.

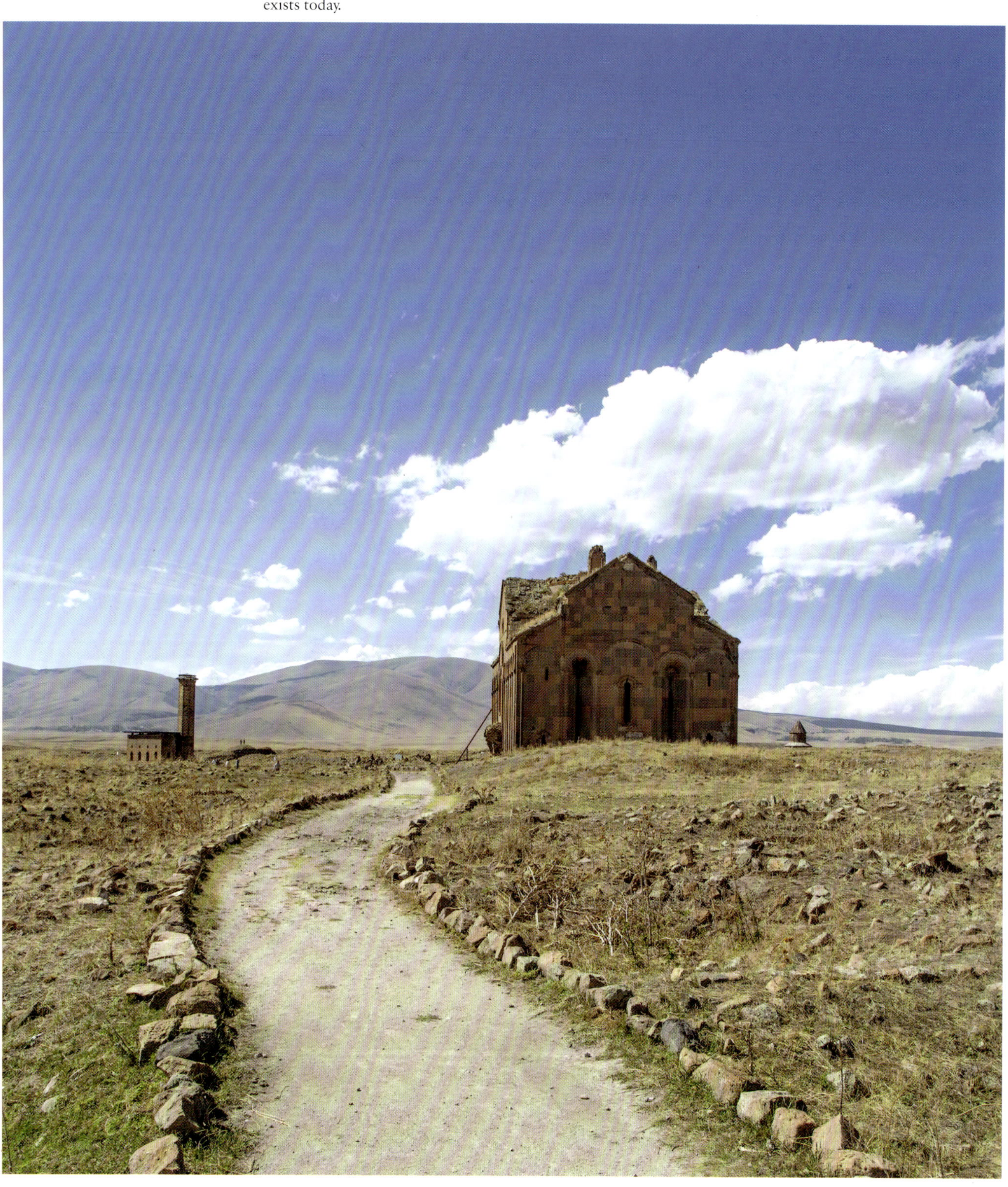

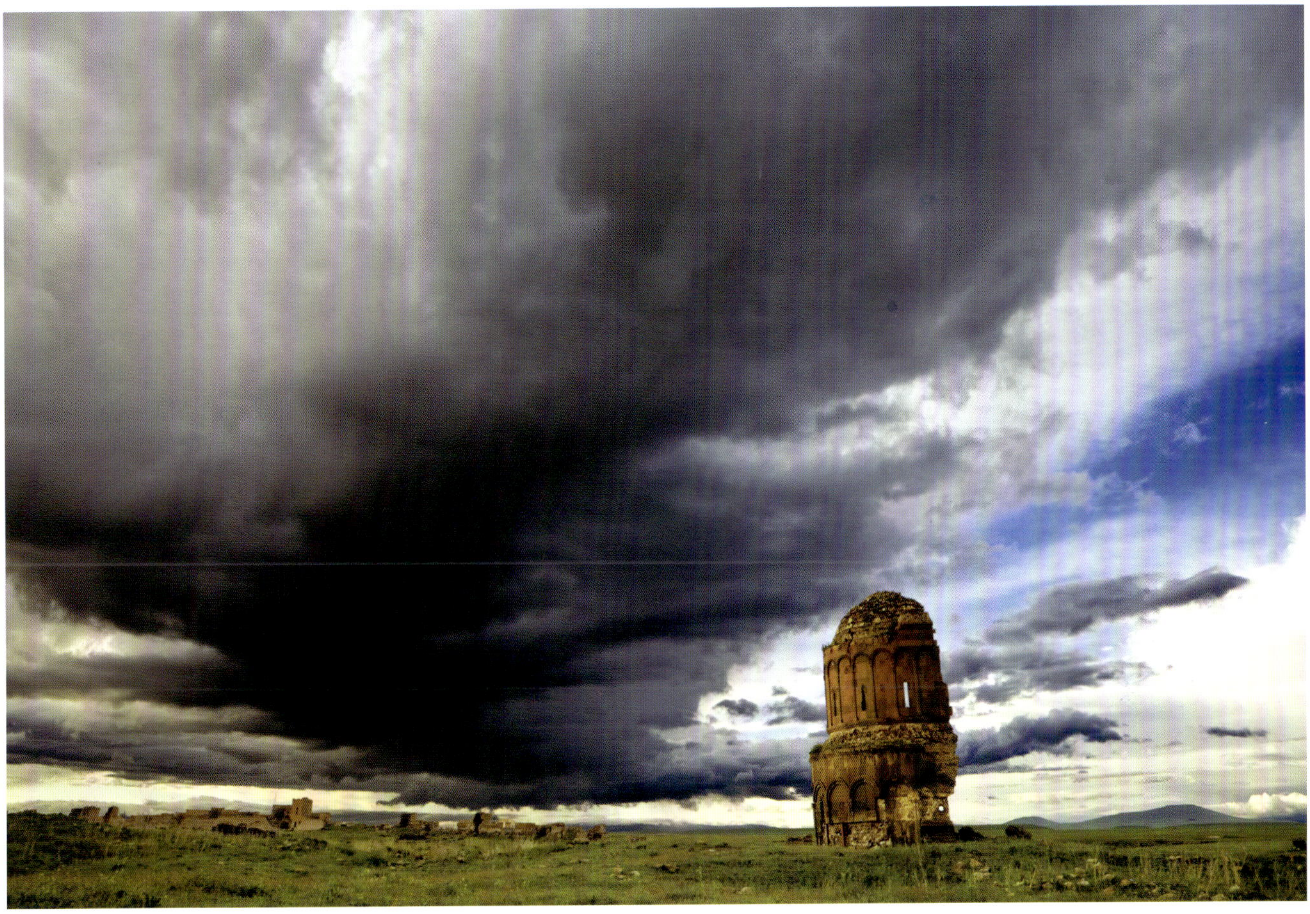

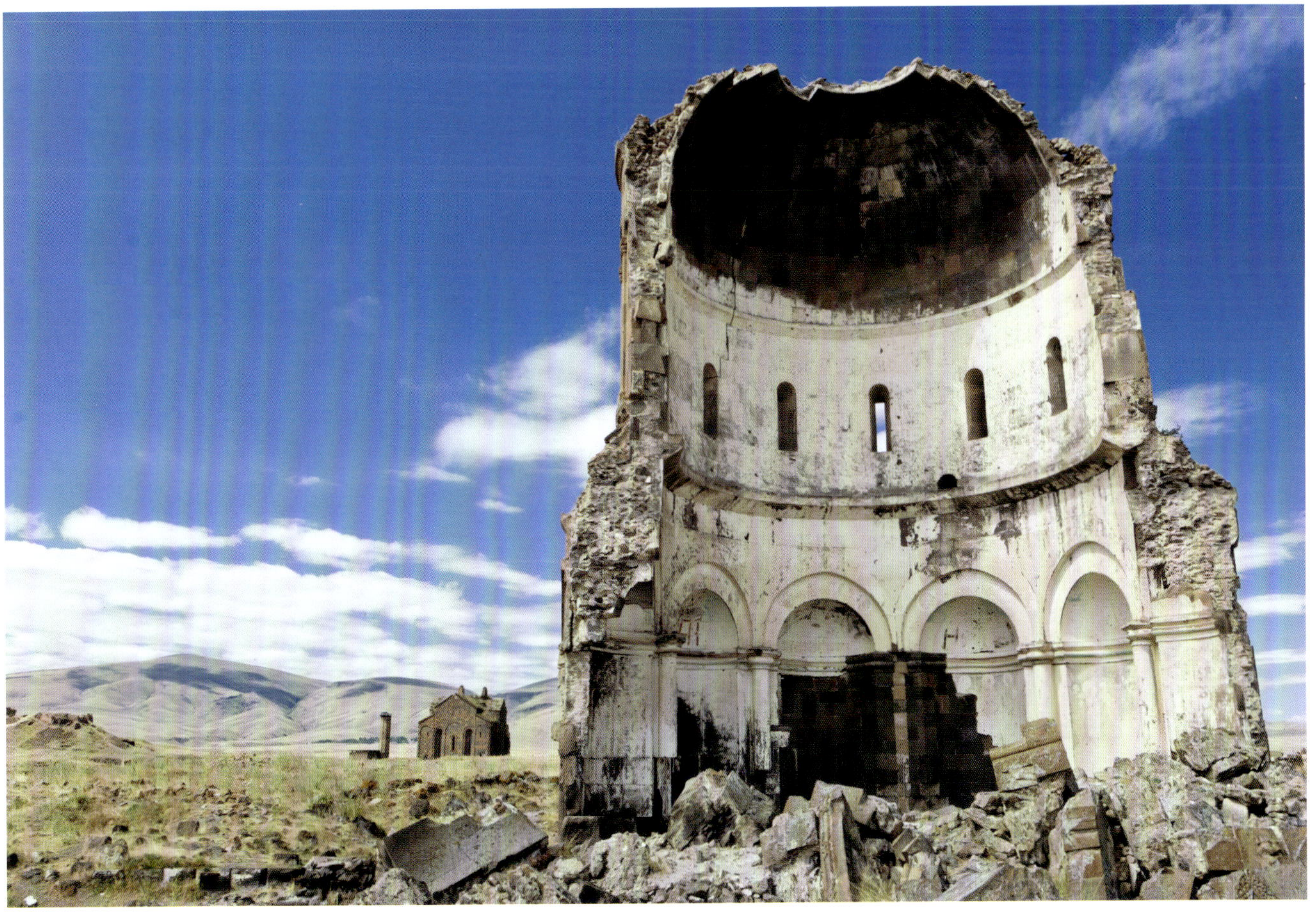

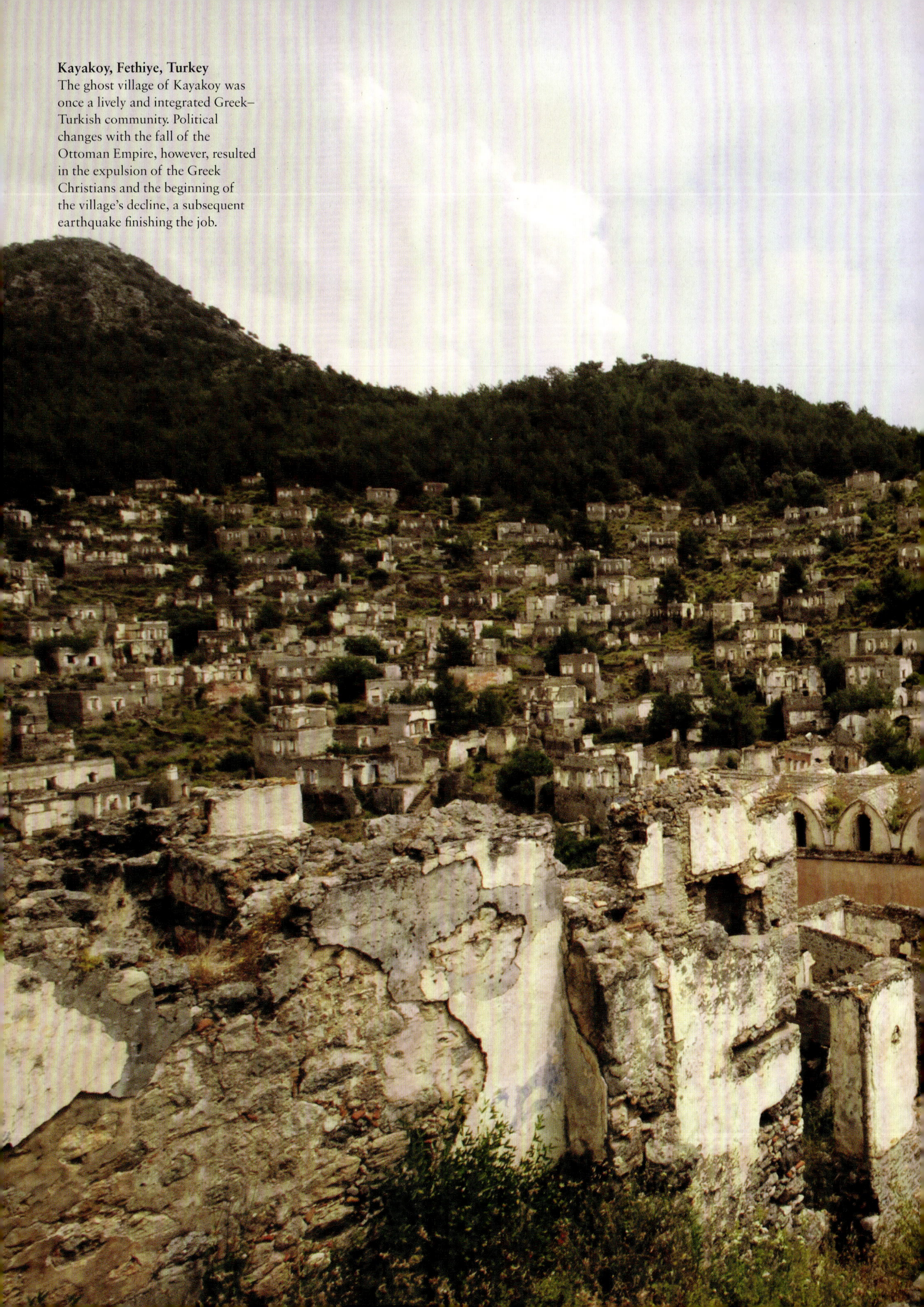

Kayakoy, Fethiye, Turkey
The ghost village of Kayakoy was once a lively and integrated Greek–Turkish community. Political changes with the fall of the Ottoman Empire, however, resulted in the expulsion of the Greek Christians and the beginning of the village's decline, a subsequent earthquake finishing the job.

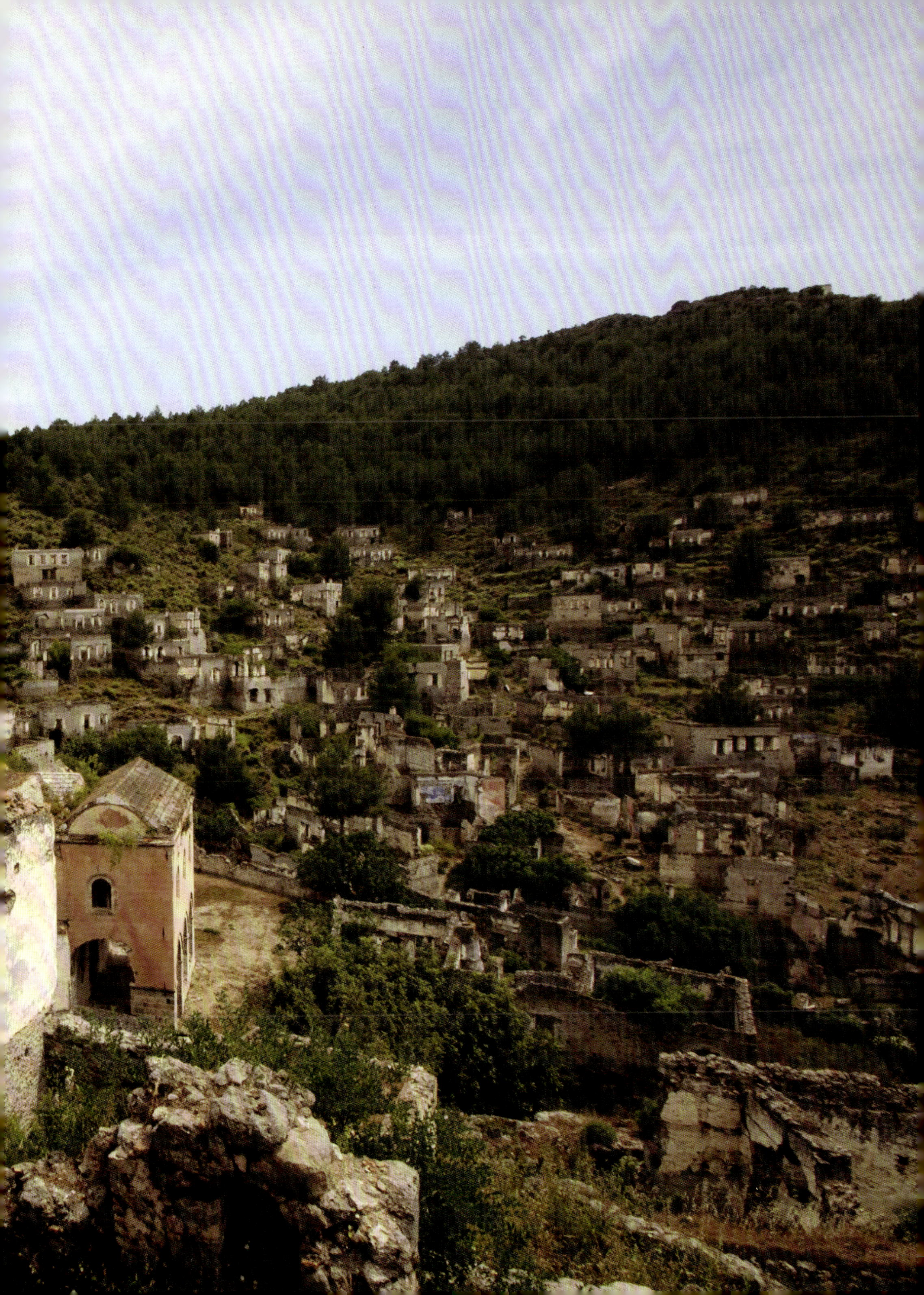

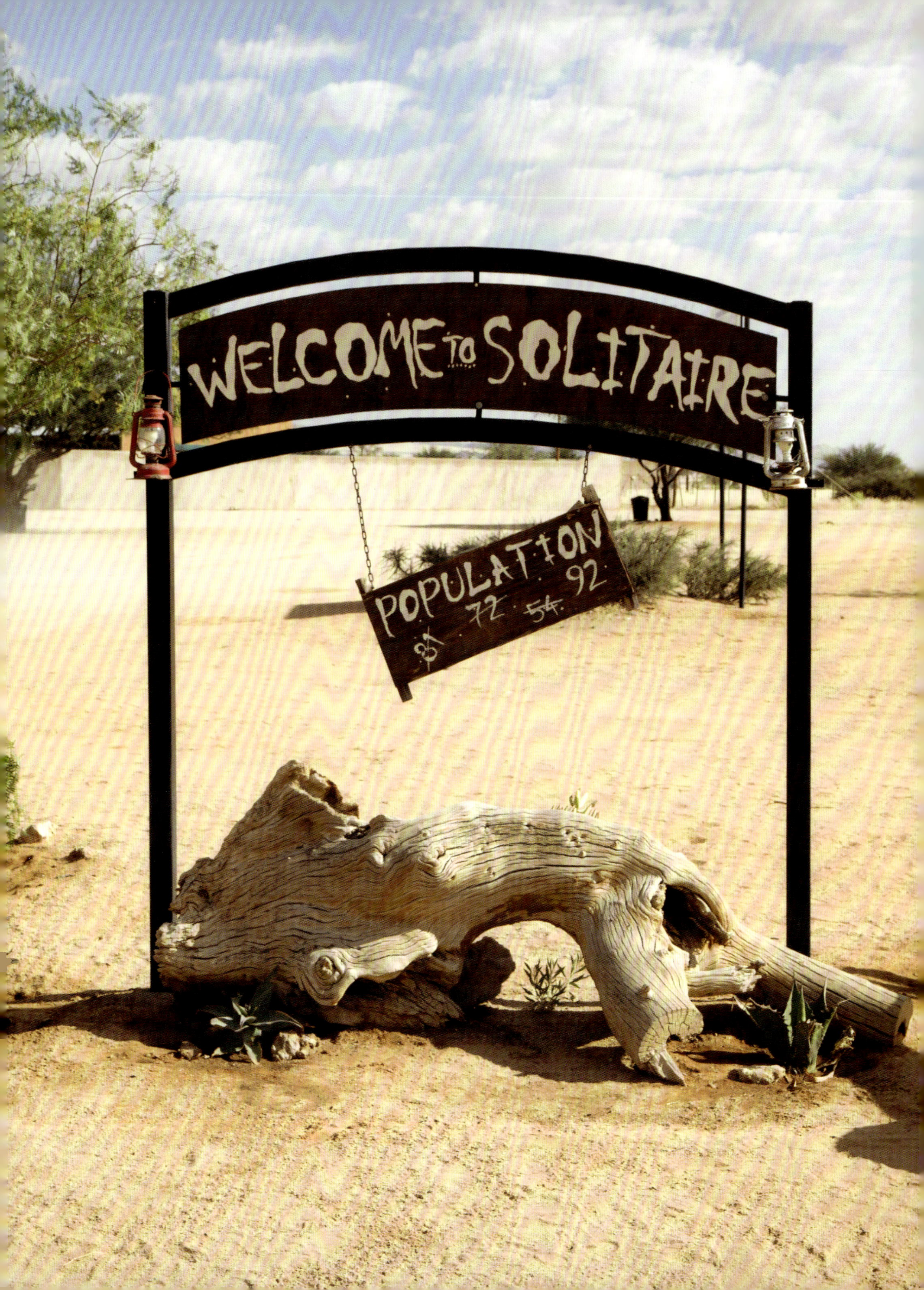
WELCOME TO SOLITAIRE
POPULATION
31 72 54 92

Africa

Africa is an astonishing continent on every level, from the diversity and extremity of its geography to the highs and lows of its history. The ghost towns featured in this chapter reflect that variety and also the huge historical forces at work across millennia of time. At one end of the narrative are the ancient ruins to be found in Egypt, monuments to some of the greatest civilizations in human history, forged well before Western narrative landmarks such as the rise of the Roman Empire or the birth of Christianity. Occupying the other end of the spectrum, however, are the new ghost towns – just a few years old – created through the brutality of recent conflicts.

Much of Africa's history over the last 300 years has been defined by the ebb and flow of imperialism, principally delivered through European colonial expansion. Carving up Africa with the aim of plundering its vast natural resources, the foreign powers (mainly Britain, France, Portugal, Italy and Germany) have left their European imprint on the face of Africa, not least in the architectural contours of many crumbling ghost towns. In some cases, these have been deemed worthy of partial or substantial preservation and even renovation. In other cases, especially when dealing with particularly remote settlements, the towns and villages have been left for nature to reclaim.

LEFT:
Solitaire, Khomas Region, Namibia
As this sign indicates, the settlement of Solitaire in Namibia is not strictly a ghost town, as it still has a small and evidently fluctuating population. Yet Solitaire's few facilities, and its placement in tens of thousands of hectares of farmland, means that it remains a desolate outpost.

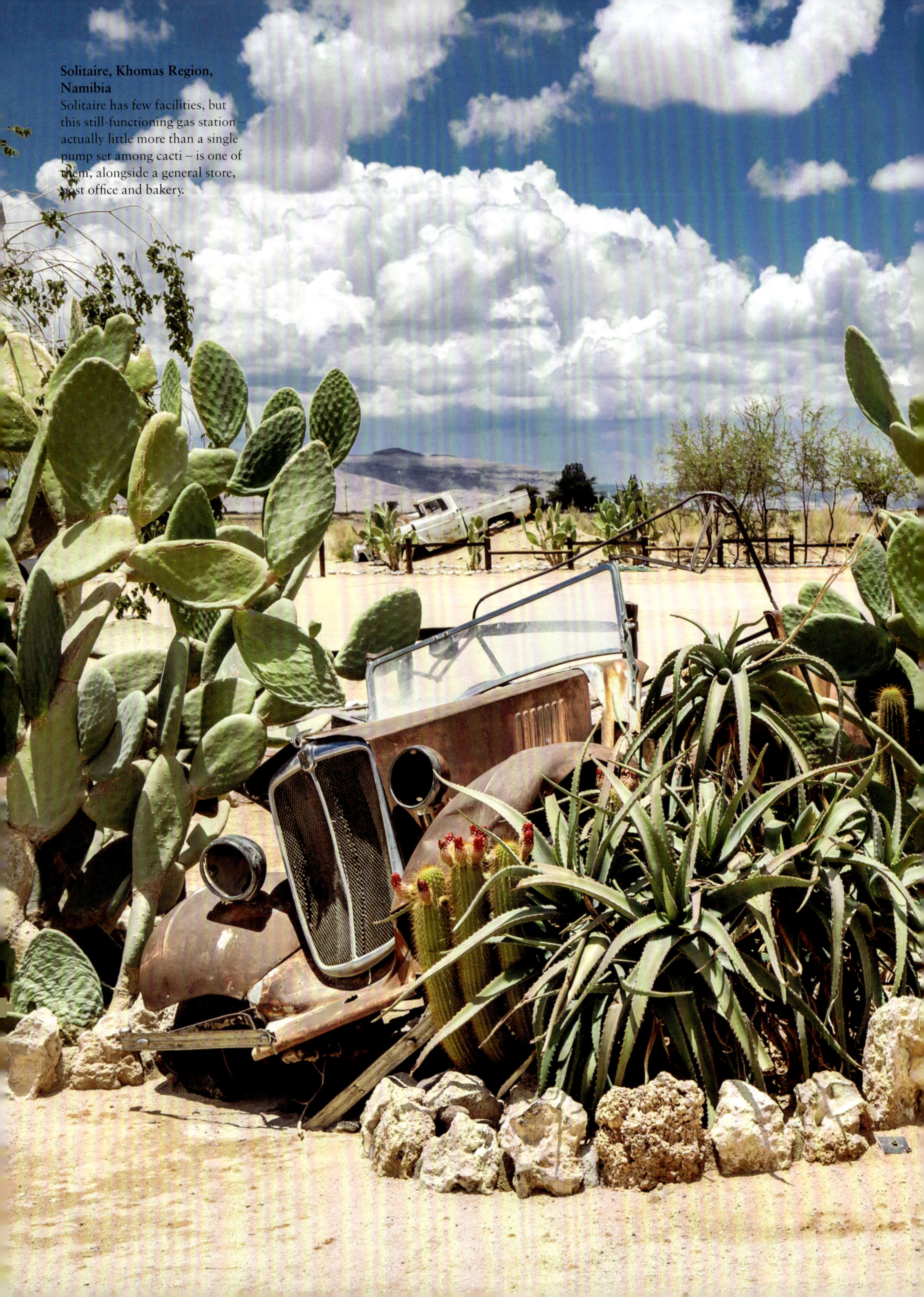

Solitaire, Khomas Region, Namibia
Solitaire has few facilities, but this still-functioning gas station – actually little more than a single pump set among cacti – is one of them, alongside a general store, post office and bakery.

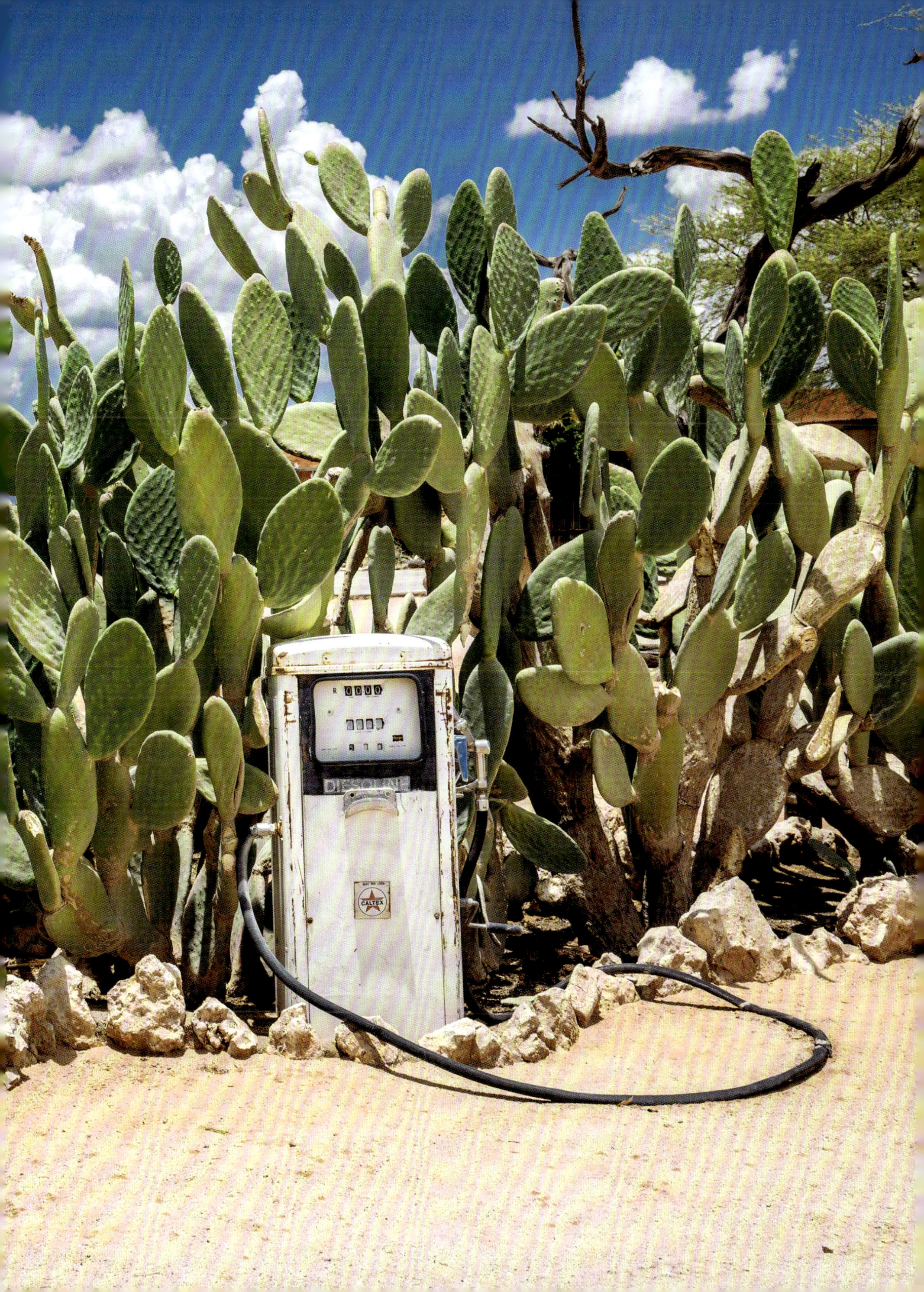
R 0000
CALTEX

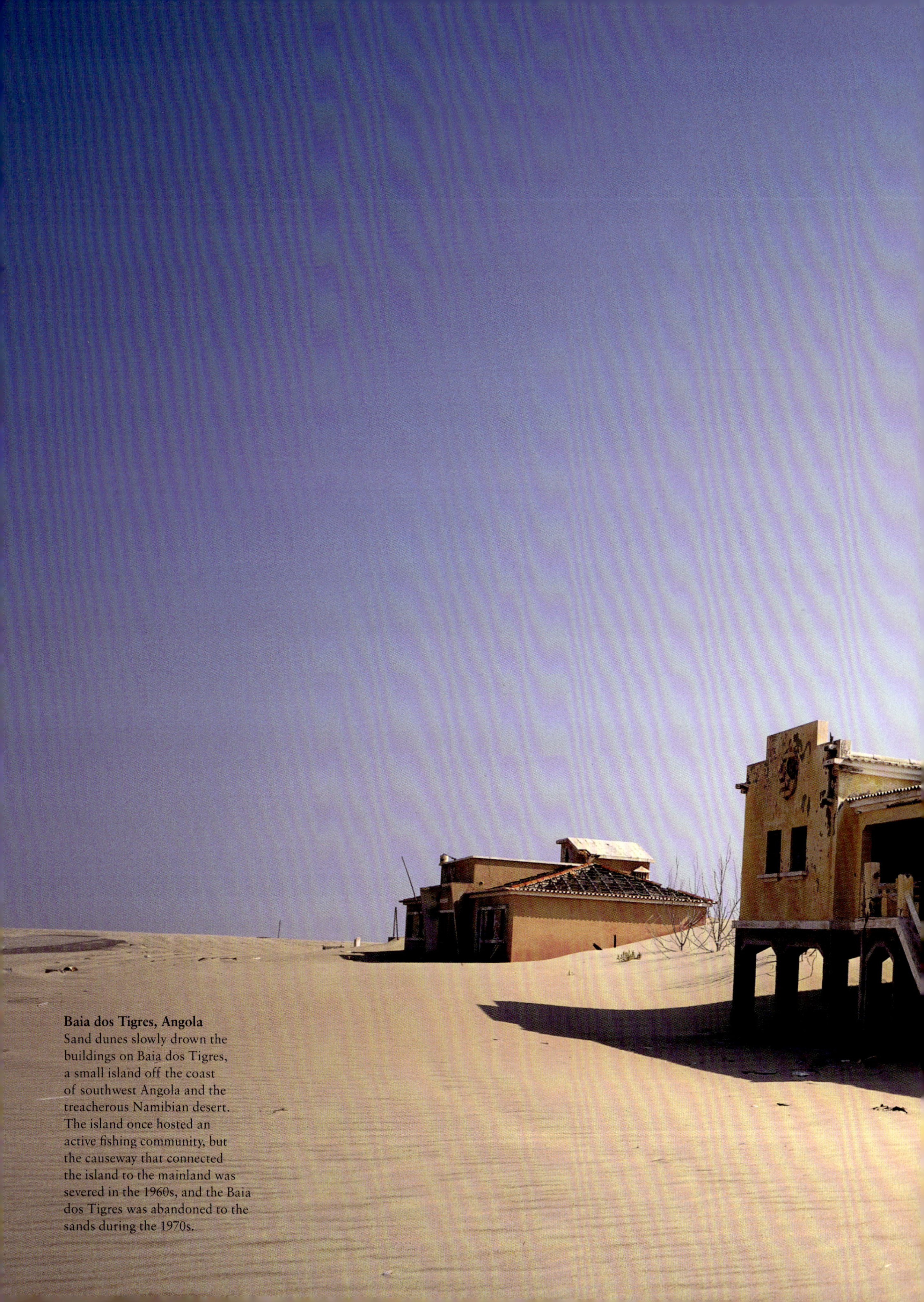

Baia dos Tigres, Angola
Sand dunes slowly drown the buildings on Baia dos Tigres, a small island off the coast of southwest Angola and the treacherous Namibian desert. The island once hosted an active fishing community, but the causeway that connected the island to the mainland was severed in the 1960s, and the Baia dos Tigres was abandoned to the sands during the 1970s.

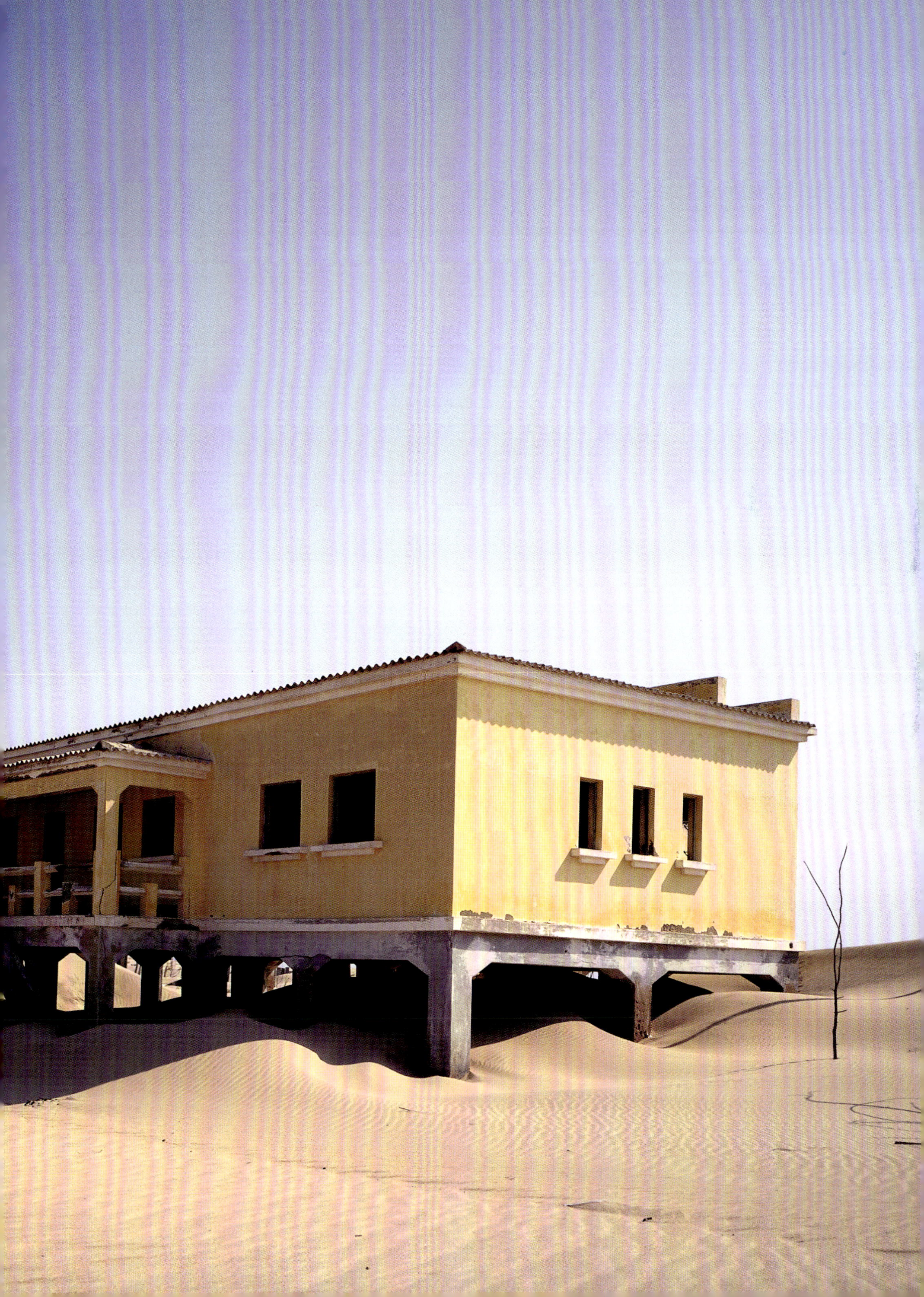

ALL PHOTOGRAPHS:

Grand-Bassam, Côte d'Ivoire

Although French explorers first visited the Ivory Coast in the 15th century, it was not until the 19th century that French rule was established over this corner of Africa. Grand-Bassam was developed by the French as a major administrative centre in the 1890s, being the French capital in the Ivory Coast until a Yellow Fever epidemic in 1896 compelled the authorities to move the capital to to Bingerville. The town is now split into two halves: an old and underpopulated French colonial district – some of its rotting colonial buildings are displayed on these pages – and a modern commercial area. The old town was named a UNESCO World Heritage Site in 2012, but its subsequent surge in tourism was hampered by an al-Qaeda terrorist shooting at a nearby beach resort in 2016, which killed 16 people and wounded 33 others.

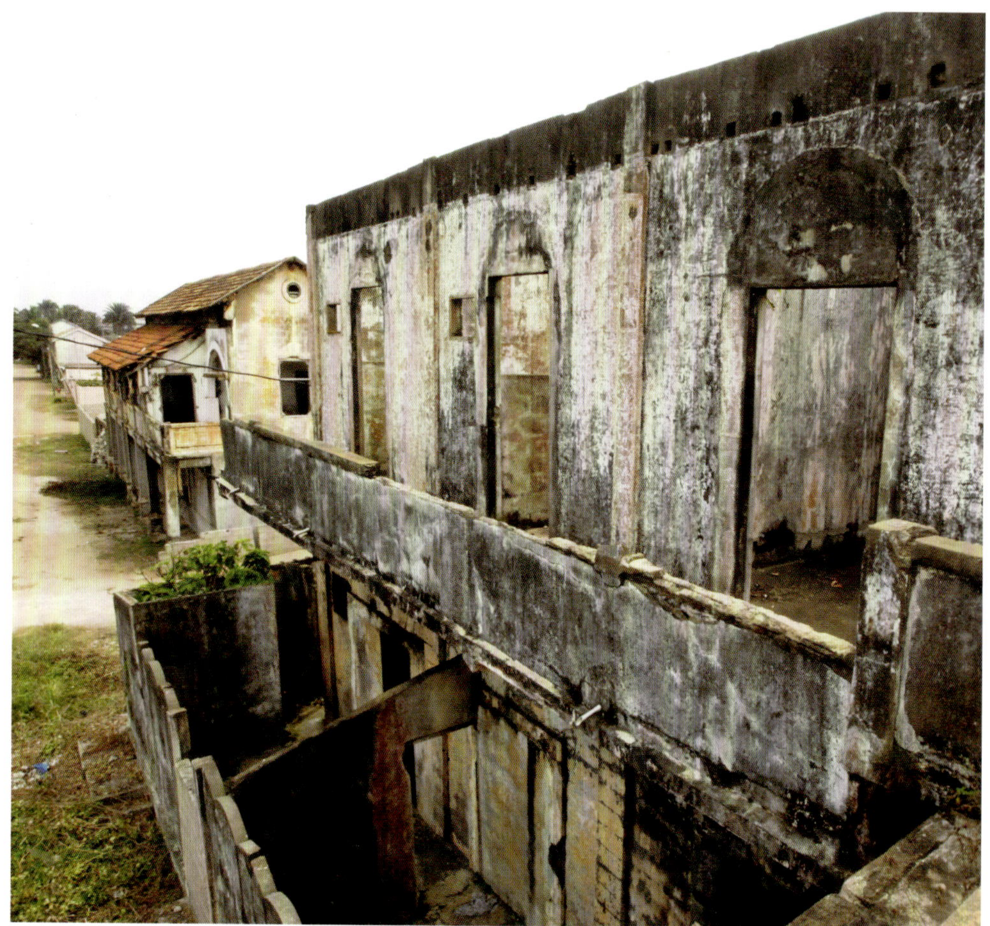

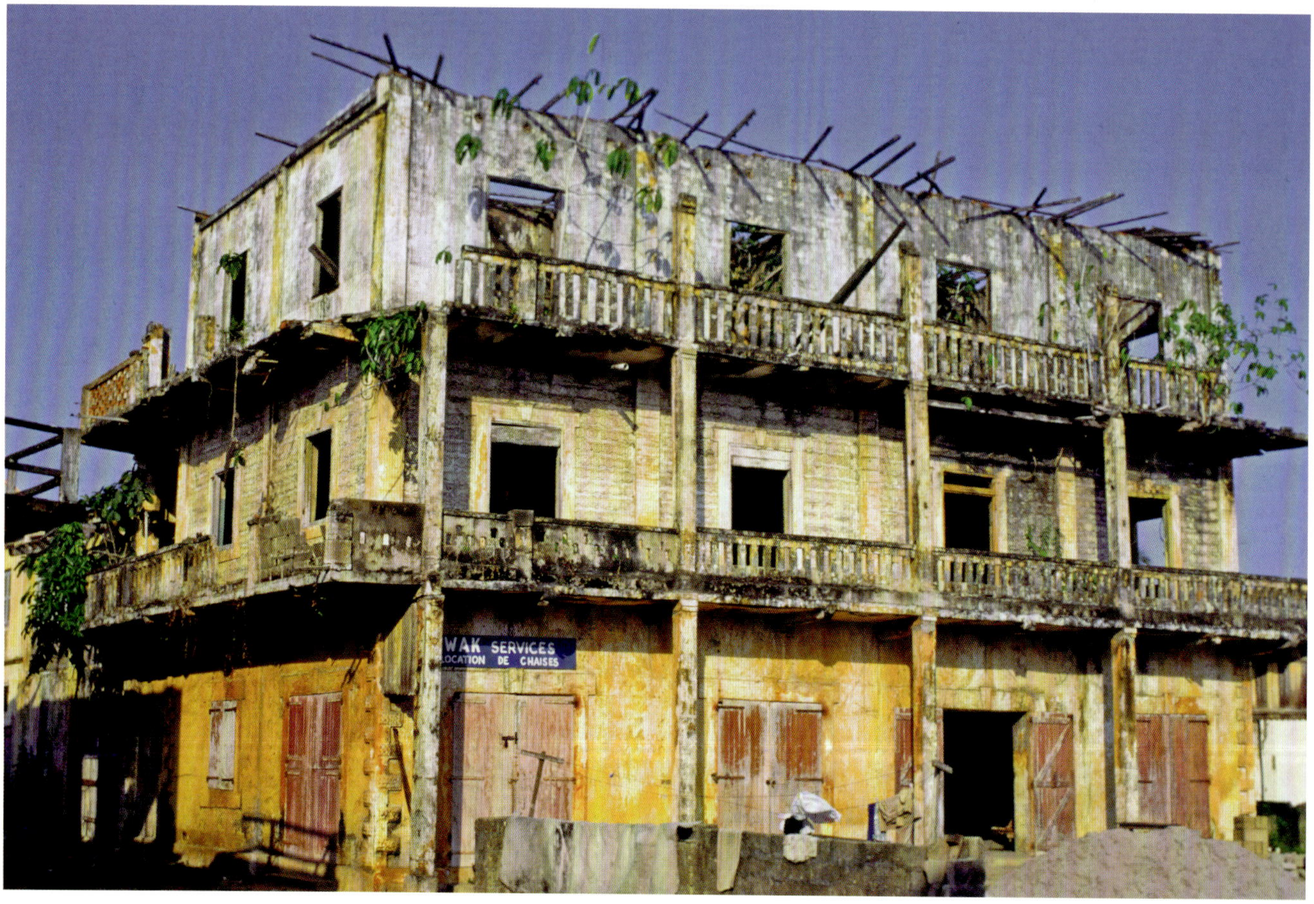

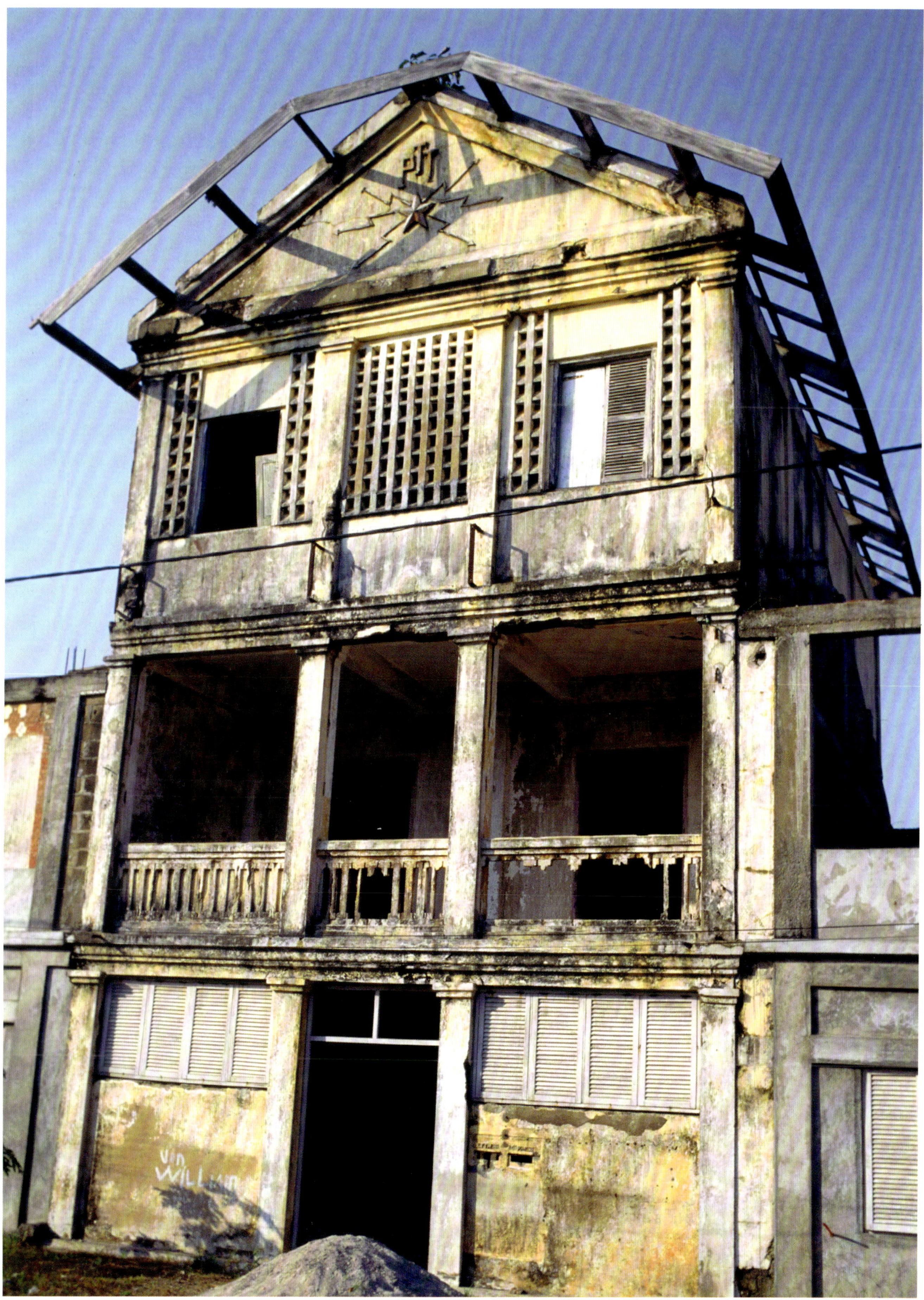

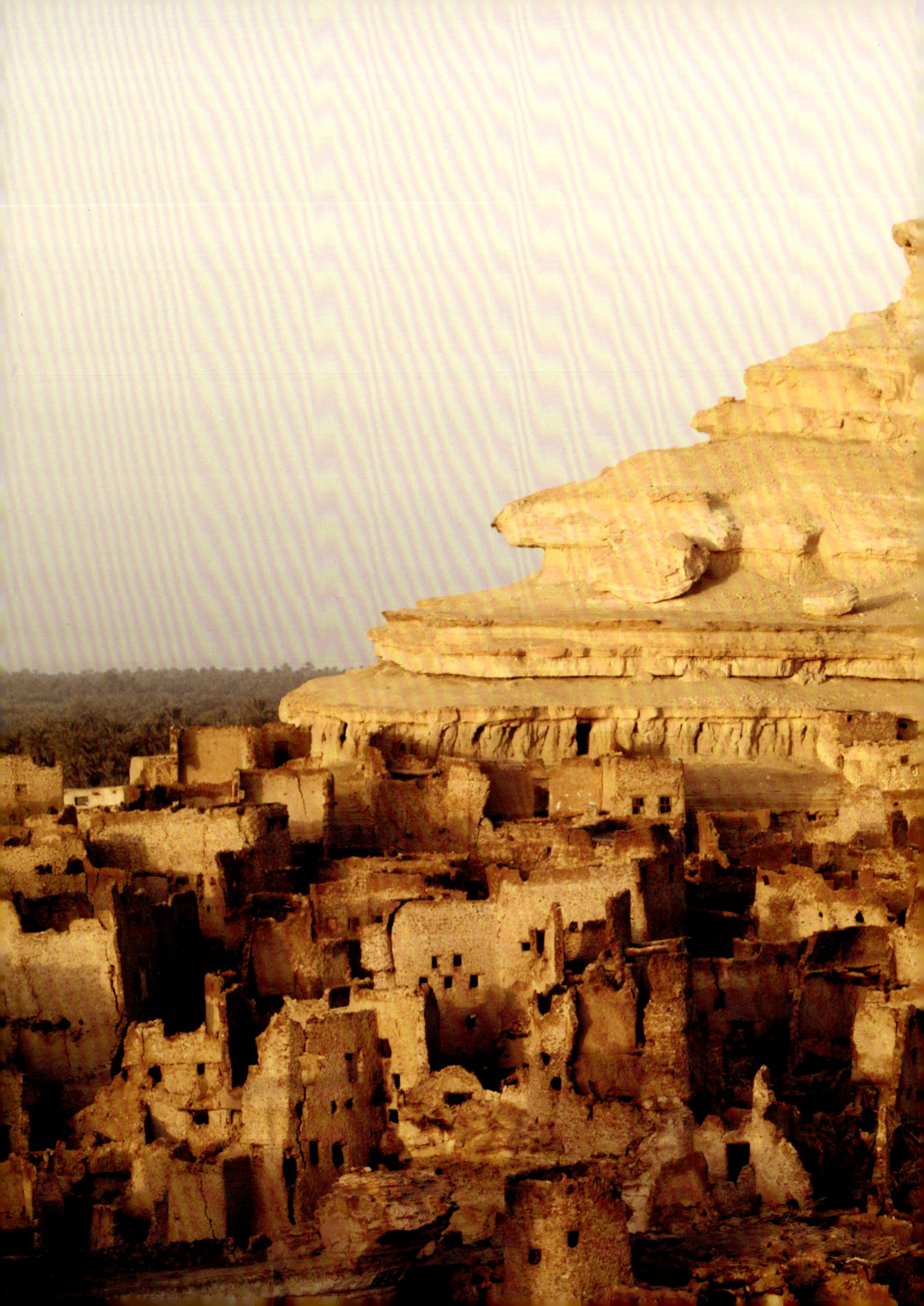

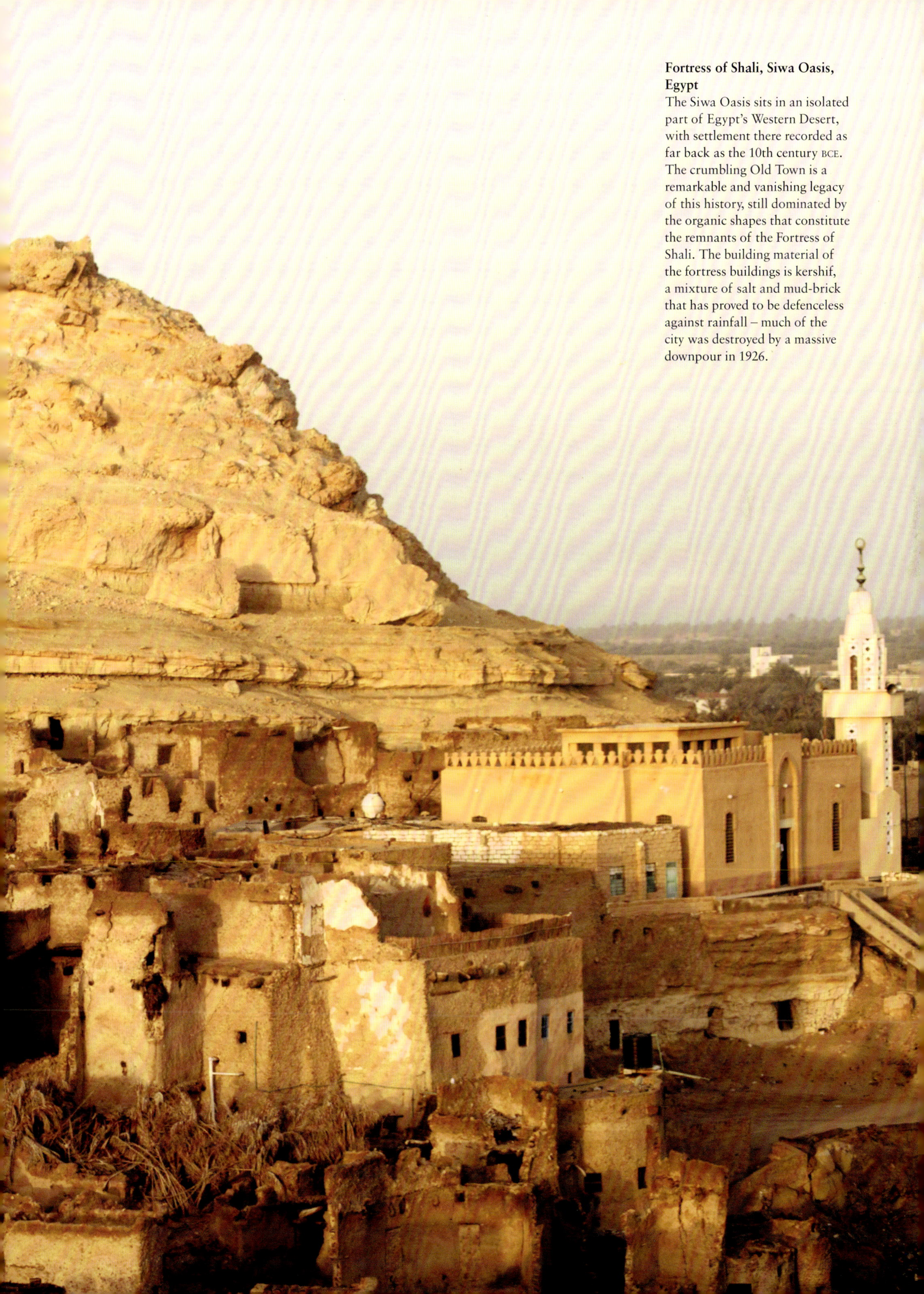

Fortress of Shali, Siwa Oasis, Egypt
The Siwa Oasis sits in an isolated part of Egypt's Western Desert, with settlement there recorded as far back as the 10th century BCE. The crumbling Old Town is a remarkable and vanishing legacy of this history, still dominated by the organic shapes that constitute the remnants of the Fortress of Shali. The building material of the fortress buildings is kershif, a mixture of salt and mud-brick that has proved to be defenceless against rainfall – much of the city was destroyed by a massive downpour in 1926.

Umm el Howeitat, Safaga, Egypt, Now nothing more than an abandoned shell, Umm el Howeitat was originally built in the early 1920s as a settlement for phosphate mine workers and their families. It grew to a substantial town of 16,000 inhabitants, complete with schools, shops, a hospital and mosques, but storm damage in 1996 caused the mines to be closed, thereby choking off the lifeblood of the town. By 2000 it had been entirely abandoned.

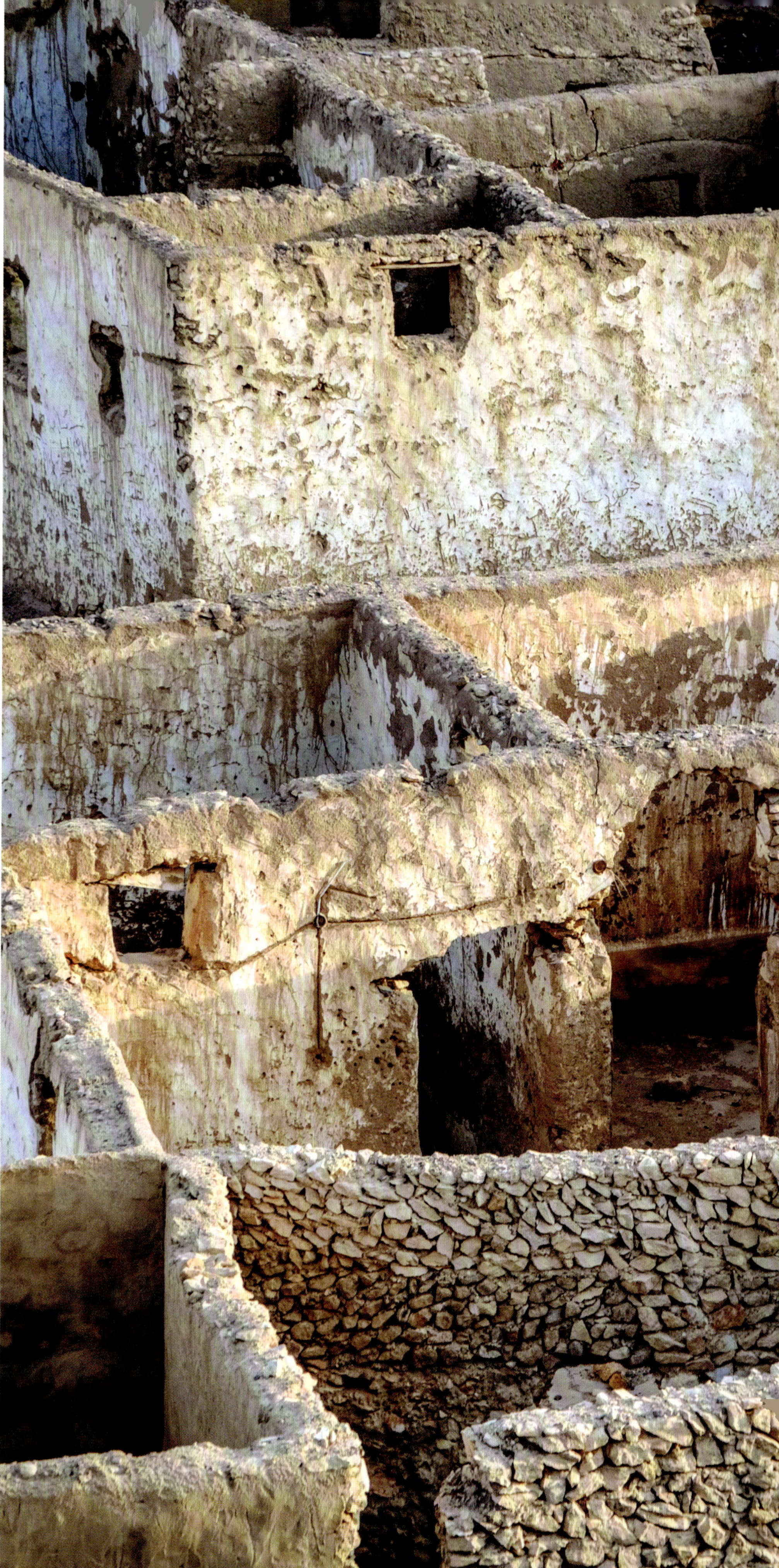

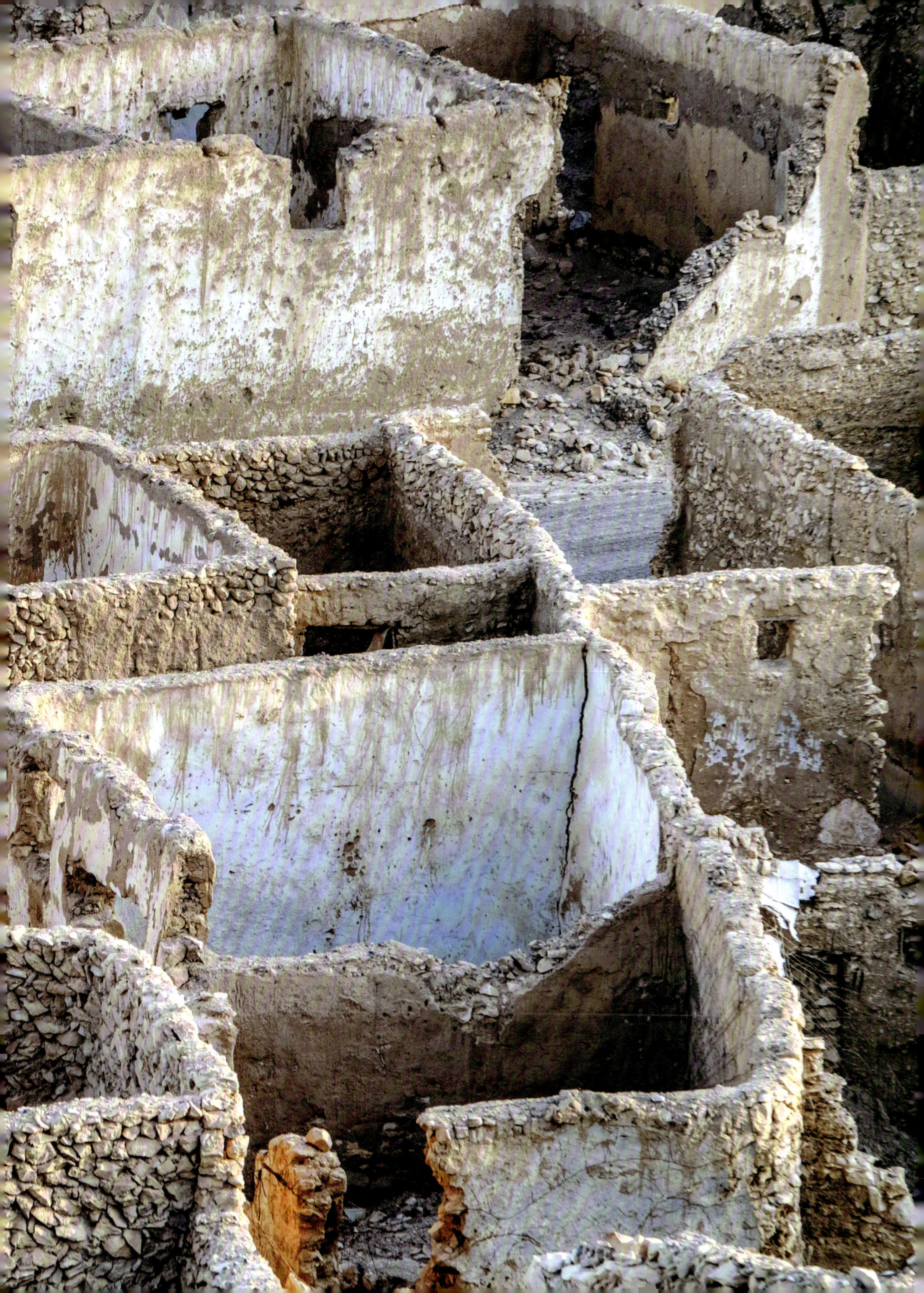

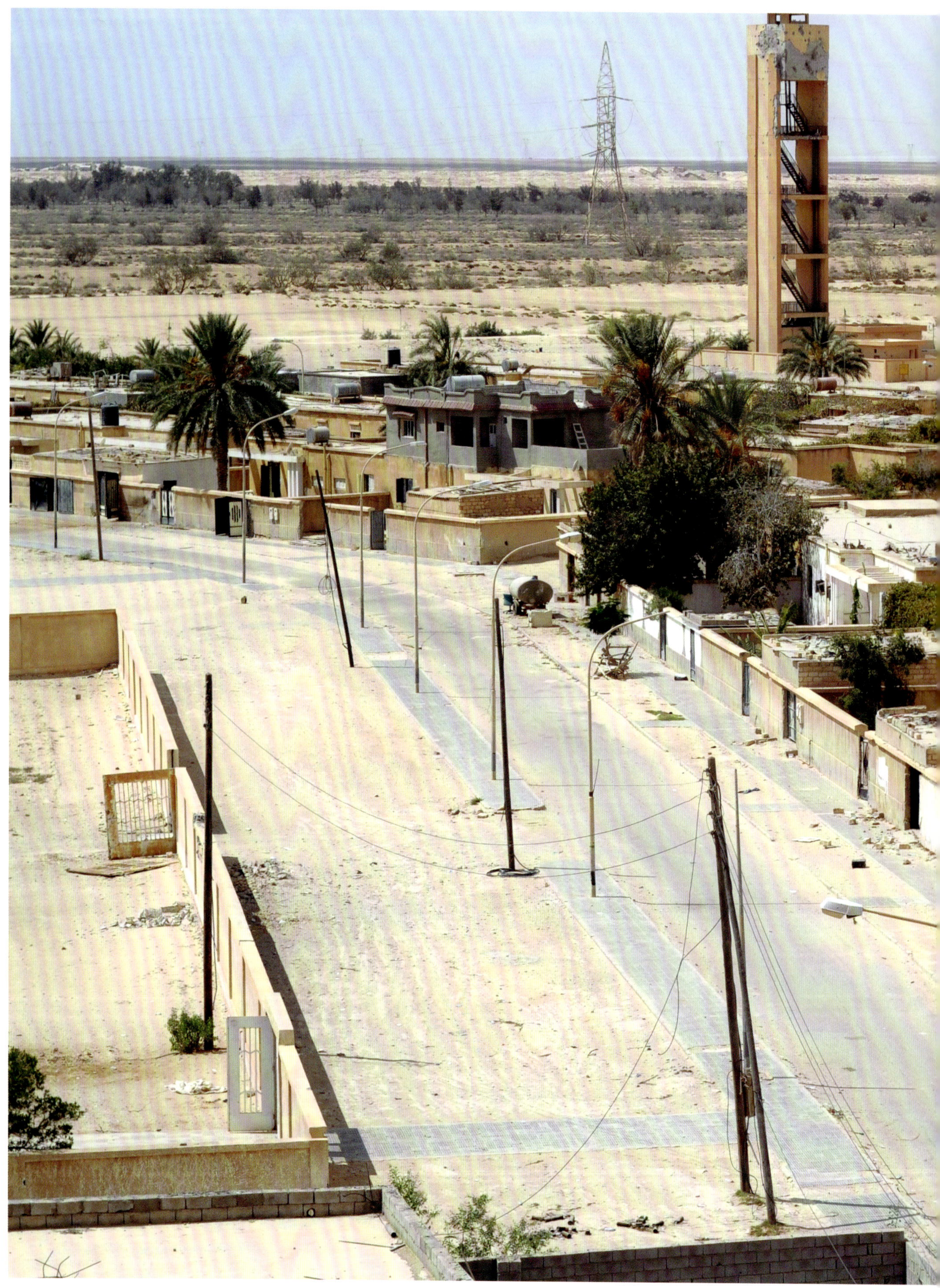

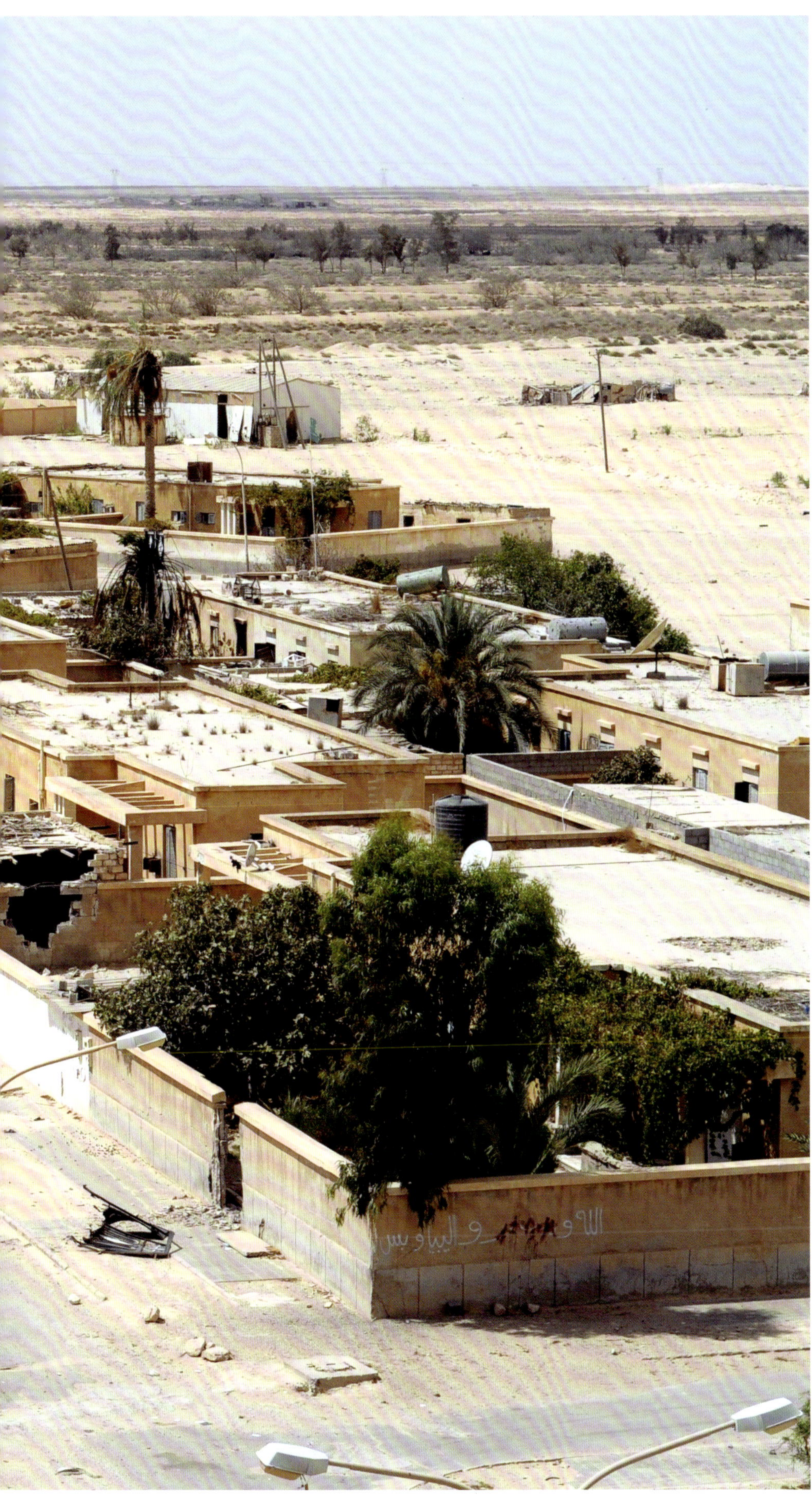

LEFT:

Tawergha, Libya

Tawergha is a modern-day ghost town, its abandonment coming abruptly in 2011 after rebel forces assaulted the government-held town during the Arab Spring uprising. The inhabitants of the town, which was heavily shelled during the fighting, were subsequently scattered out to grim refugee camps.

OVERLEAF:

Ouarzazate, Morocco

The former French outpost of Ouarzazate in Morocco may have long been abandoned by its colonial masters, but its picturesque and timeless quality has made it an ideal film set for Hollywood movie makers, particularly those wishing to depict ancient Greek, Roman or African cities.

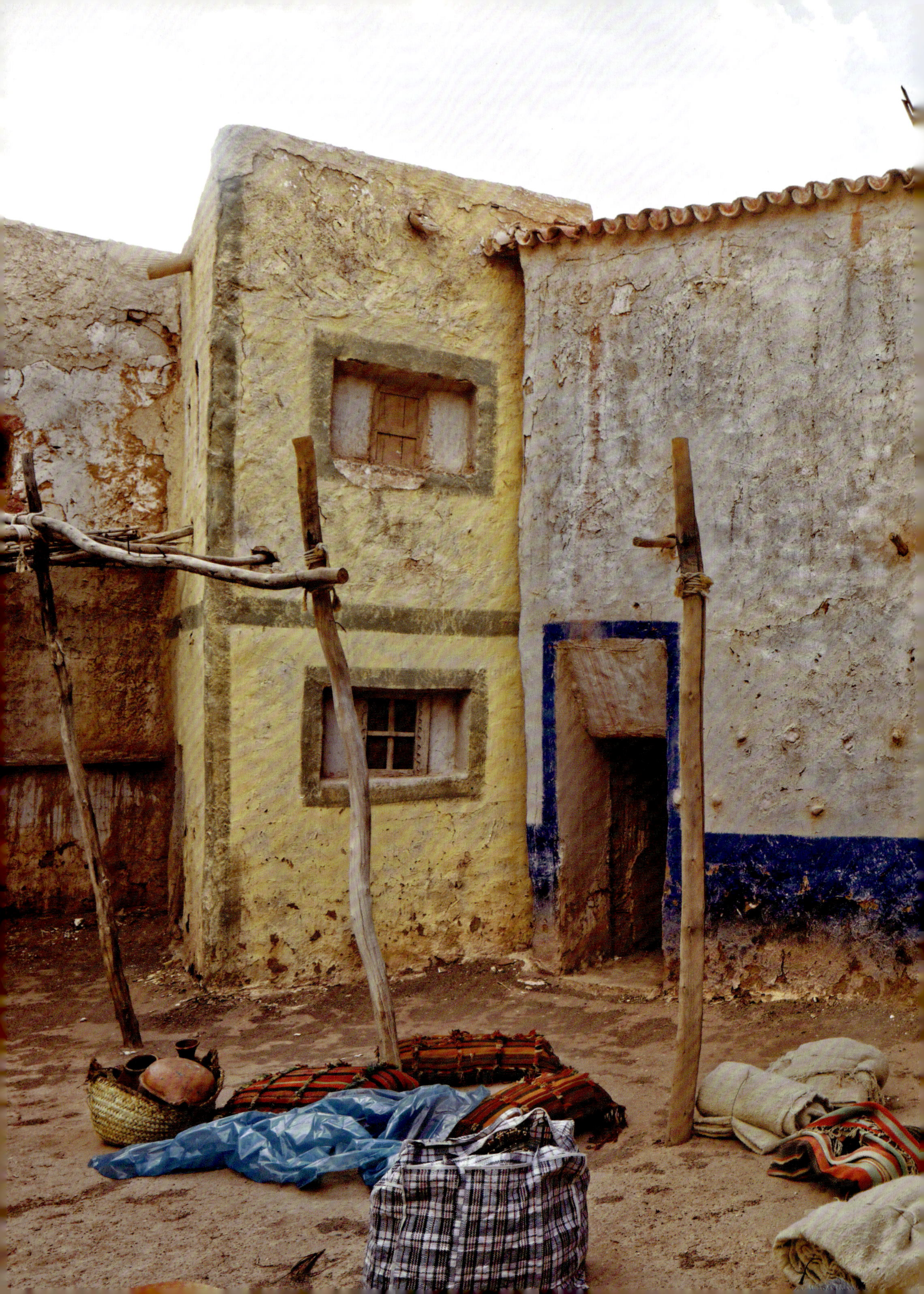

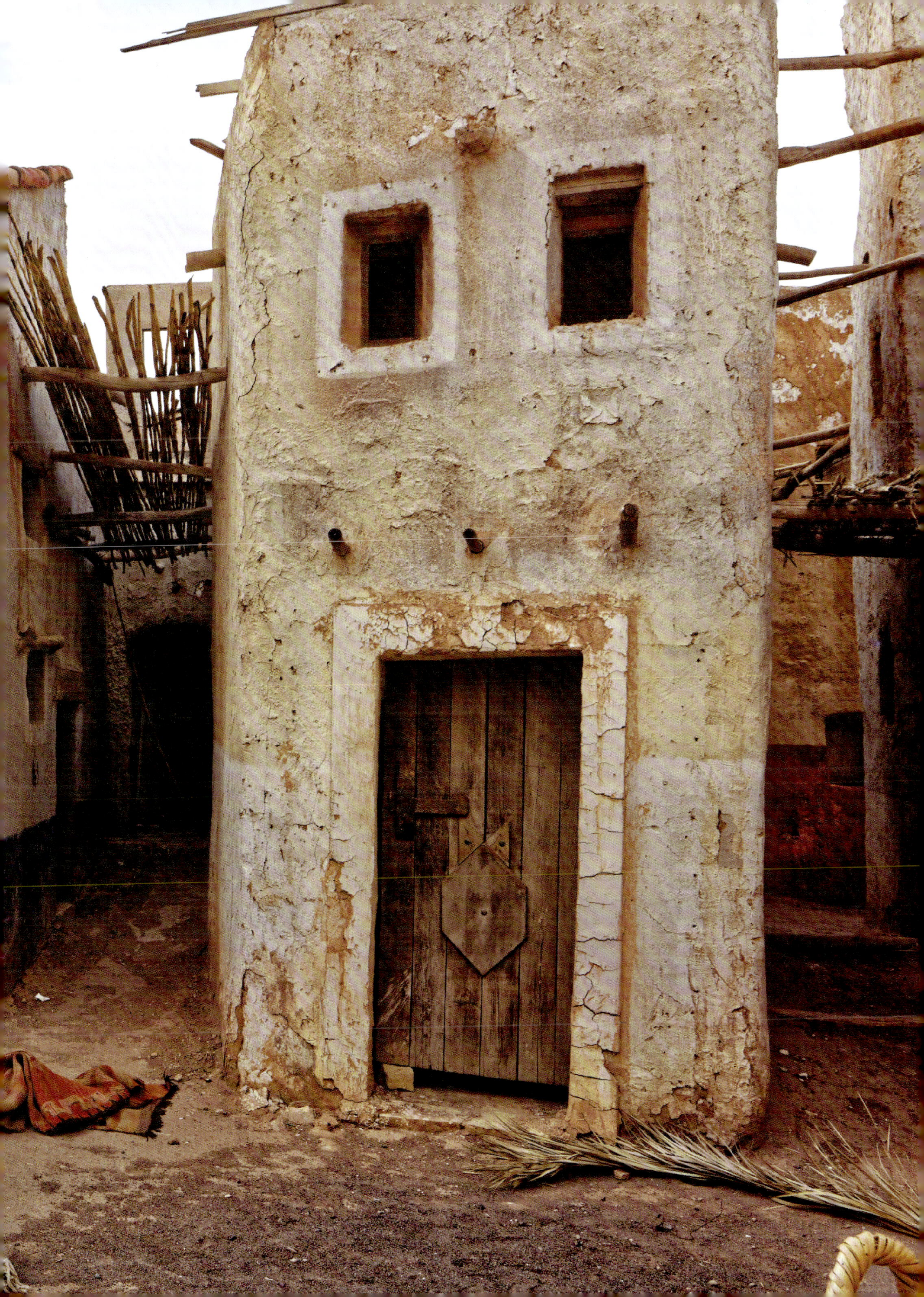

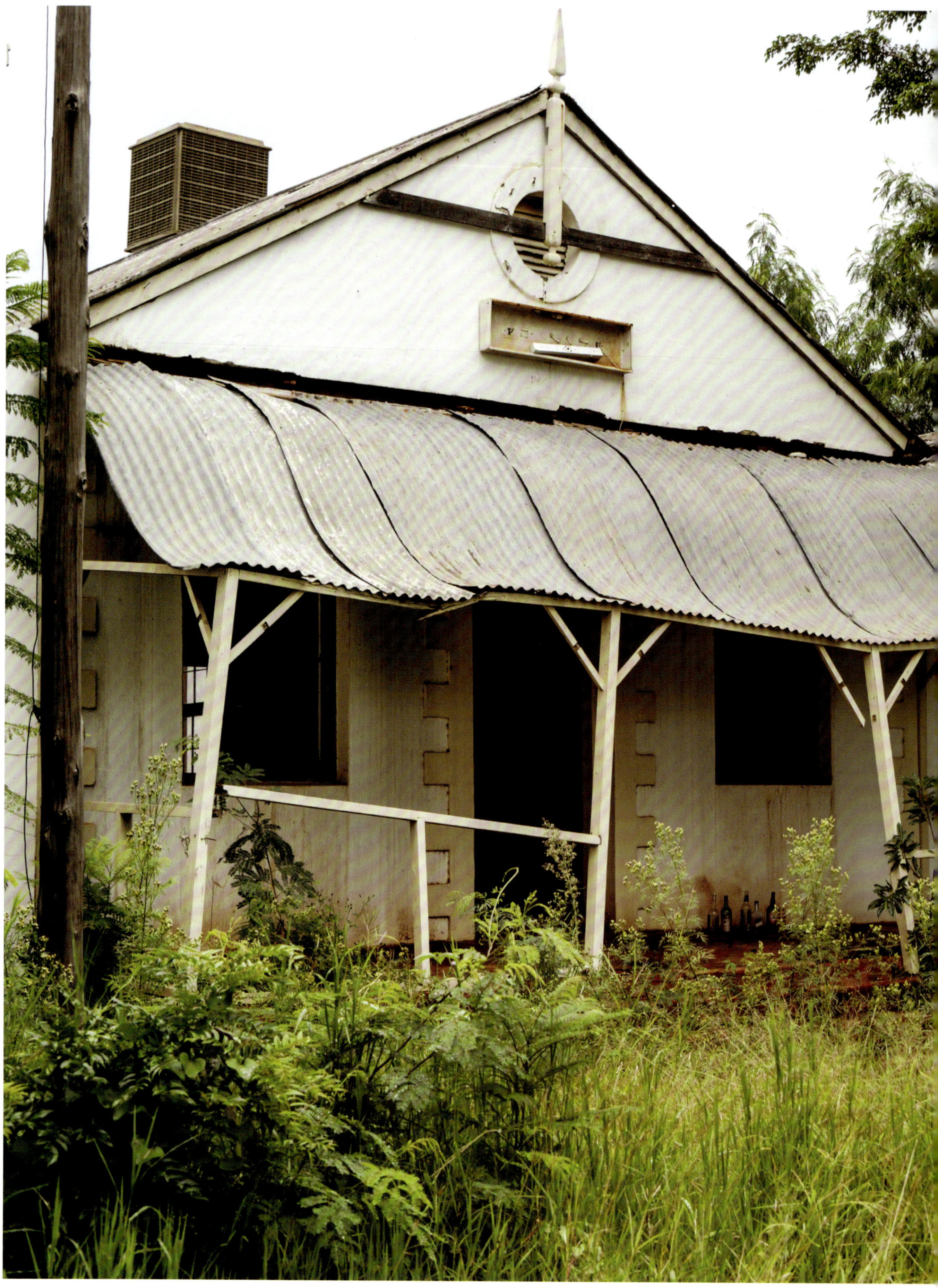

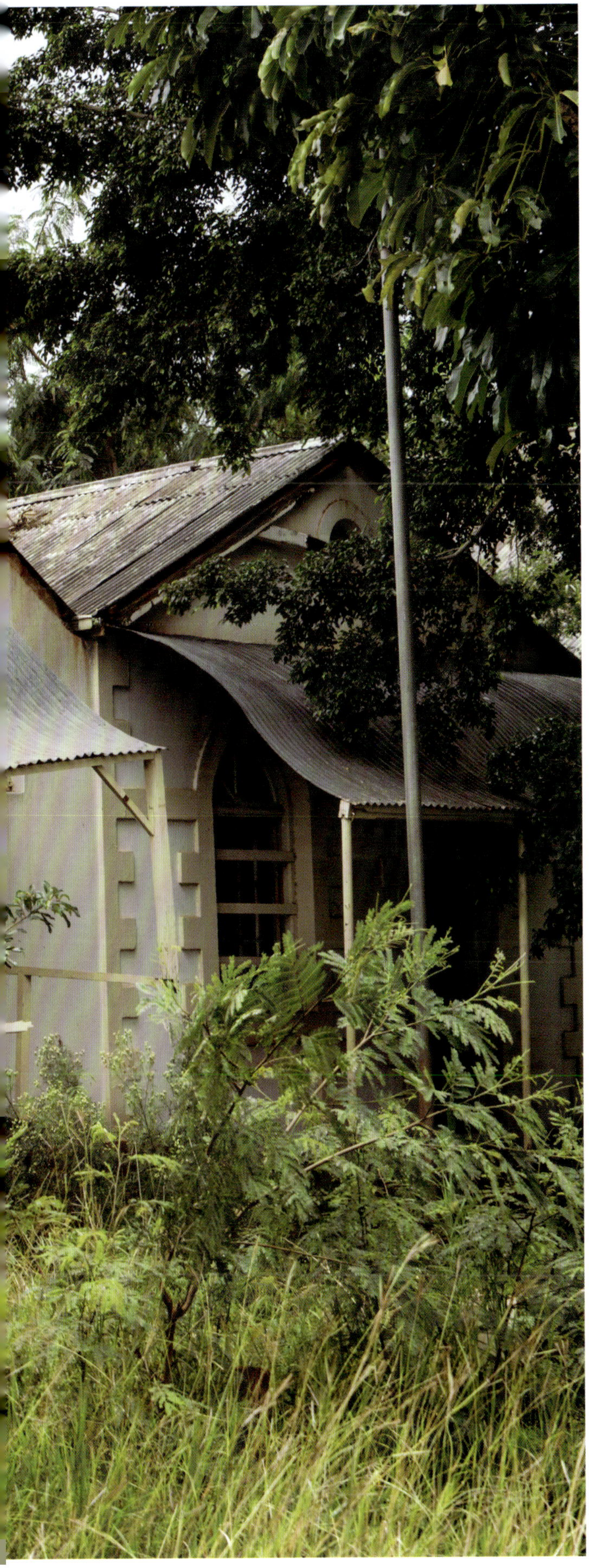

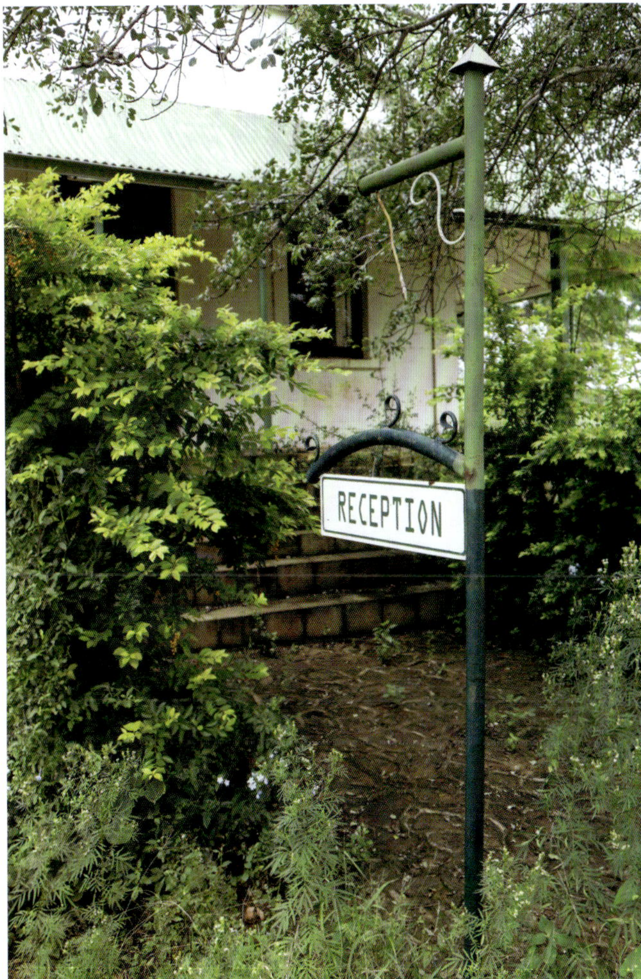

LEFT:
Leydsdorp, Limpopo province, South Africa
The now-abandoned village of Leydsdorp sprang into life in the 1880s on the back of a sudden gold rush in the nearby Murchison Range of mountains. Gold prospectors and their families quickly threw up quaint habitations, such as the whitewashed urban house seen here, and set to work in the mines, hoping to make their fortunes.

ABOVE:
Leydsdorp, Limpopo province, South Africa
The formerly smart reception area for one of the mines around Leydsdorp. Life for the c. 3000 inhabitants of Leydsdorp was hard, with many deaths from malaria and also from the endemic violence that flared up in the town's bars. Leydsdorp was quickly abandoned just years after it was founded, when better gold deposits were found on the Witwatersrand.

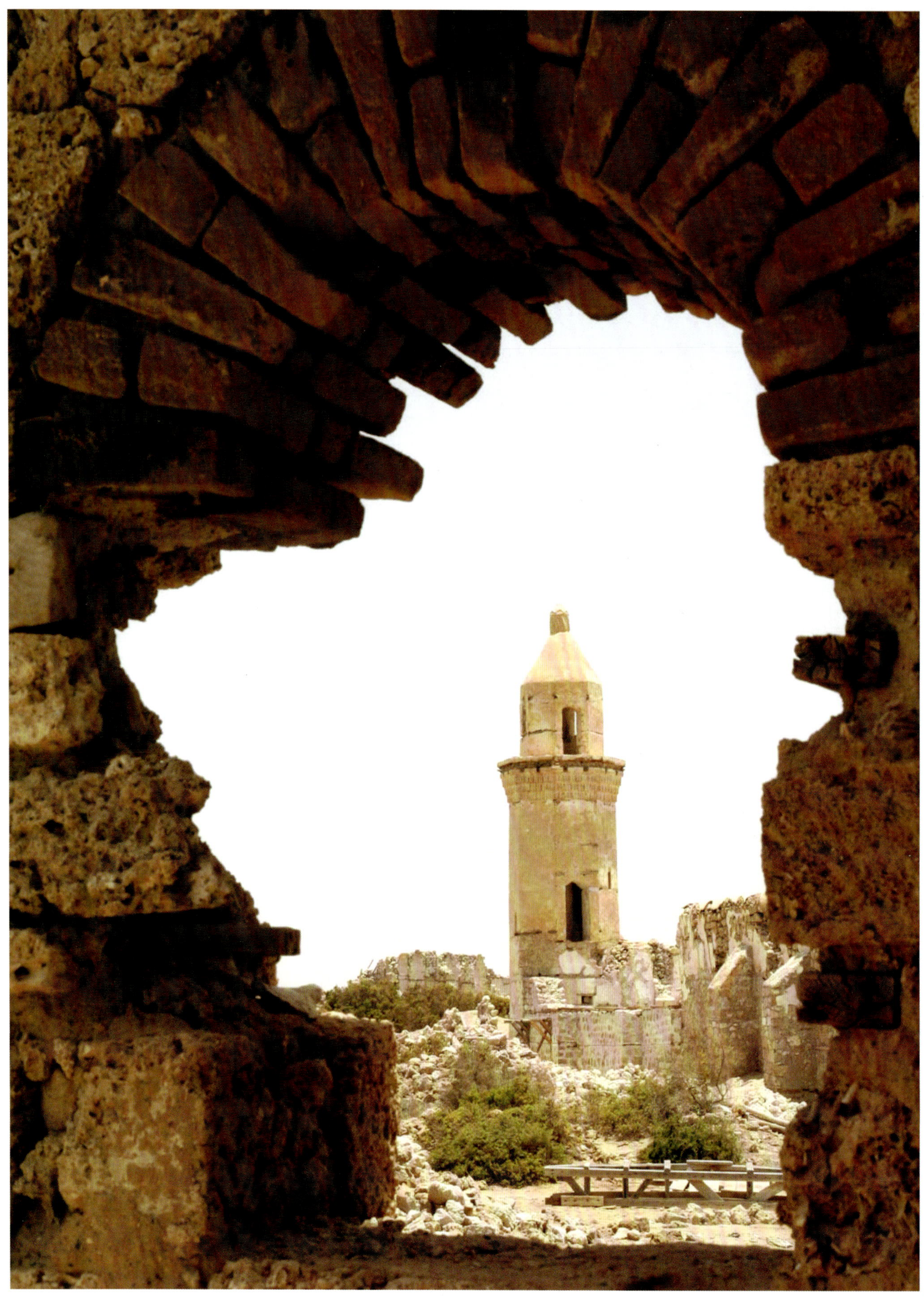

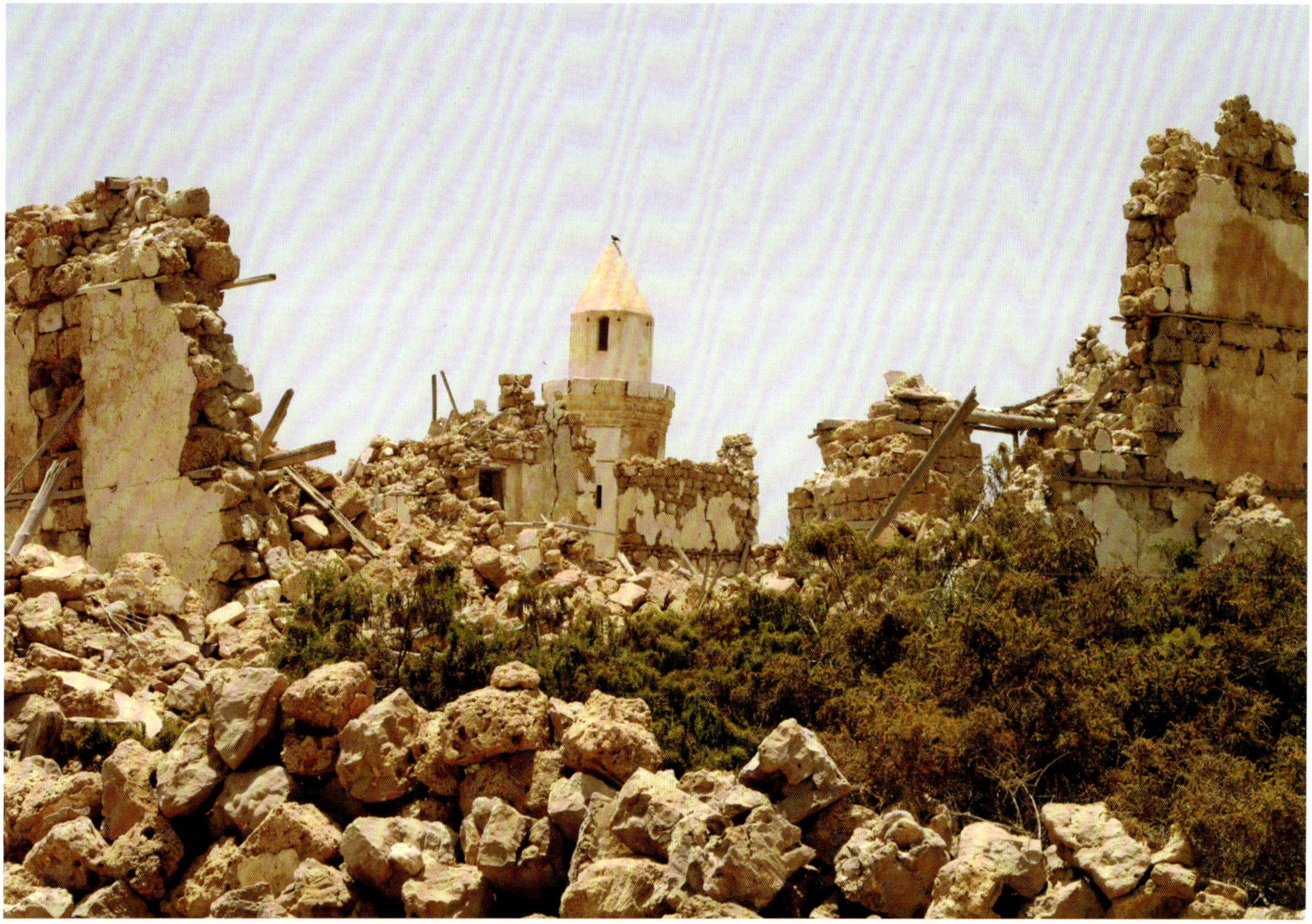

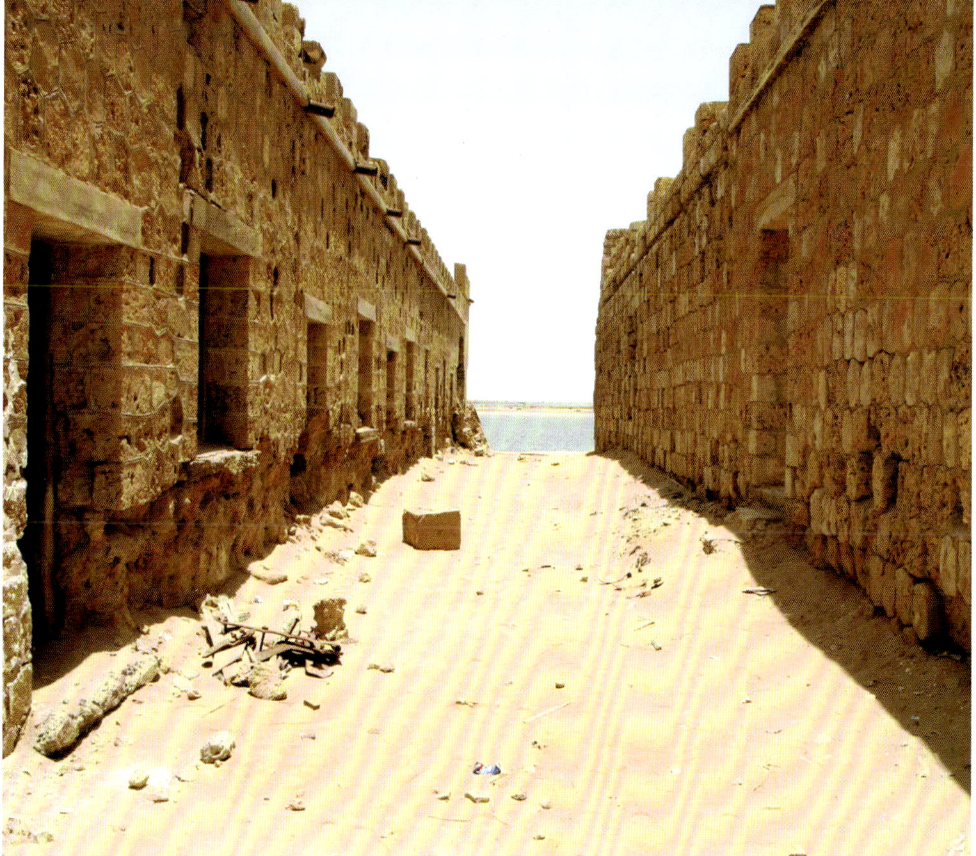

OPPOSITE:

Suakin, northeastern Sudan

Suakin, or Sawakin, was a former Red Sea port 58km (36 miles) south of Port Sudan. Indeed, it was the construction of Port Sudan that led to the abandonment of Suakin, particularly the ancient coral-built Old City.

ABOVE:

Suakin, northeastern Sudan

Although Suakin has origins back in Roman history, it was in the 10th century BCE that it began its rise as an Arab trading centre on the Red Sea. Back in medieval and Ottoman times, Suakin had a dark history as a slave port. But it also became a stop on the pilgrimage route to Mecca; here a minaret rises from amid the ruins.

LEFT:

Suakin, northeastern Sudan

The Old City of Suakin features buildings mainly constructed from coral stone, a material that is relatively easily shaped but also gives an excellent monumental finish to walls and columns.

Tamerza, Tunisia

Surrounded by the nearby mountains, the Tamerza oasis is a remarkable, fertile patch of land in an otherwise parched landscape. Because of the oasis' water supplies, courtesy of run-off from the mountains, a small town grew there. Ironically, this town was abandoned after heavy flooding destroyed many buildings during the 1960s.

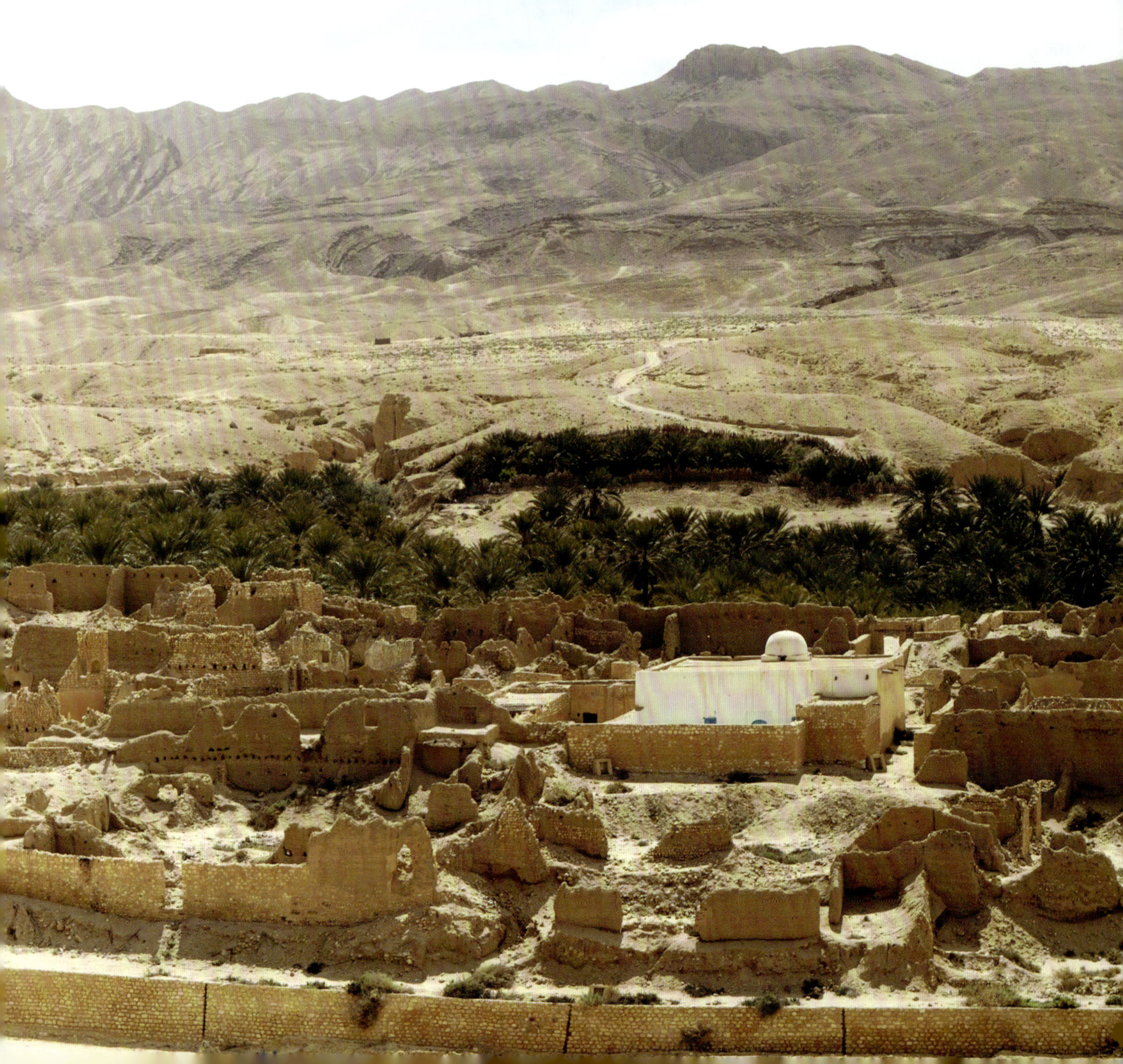

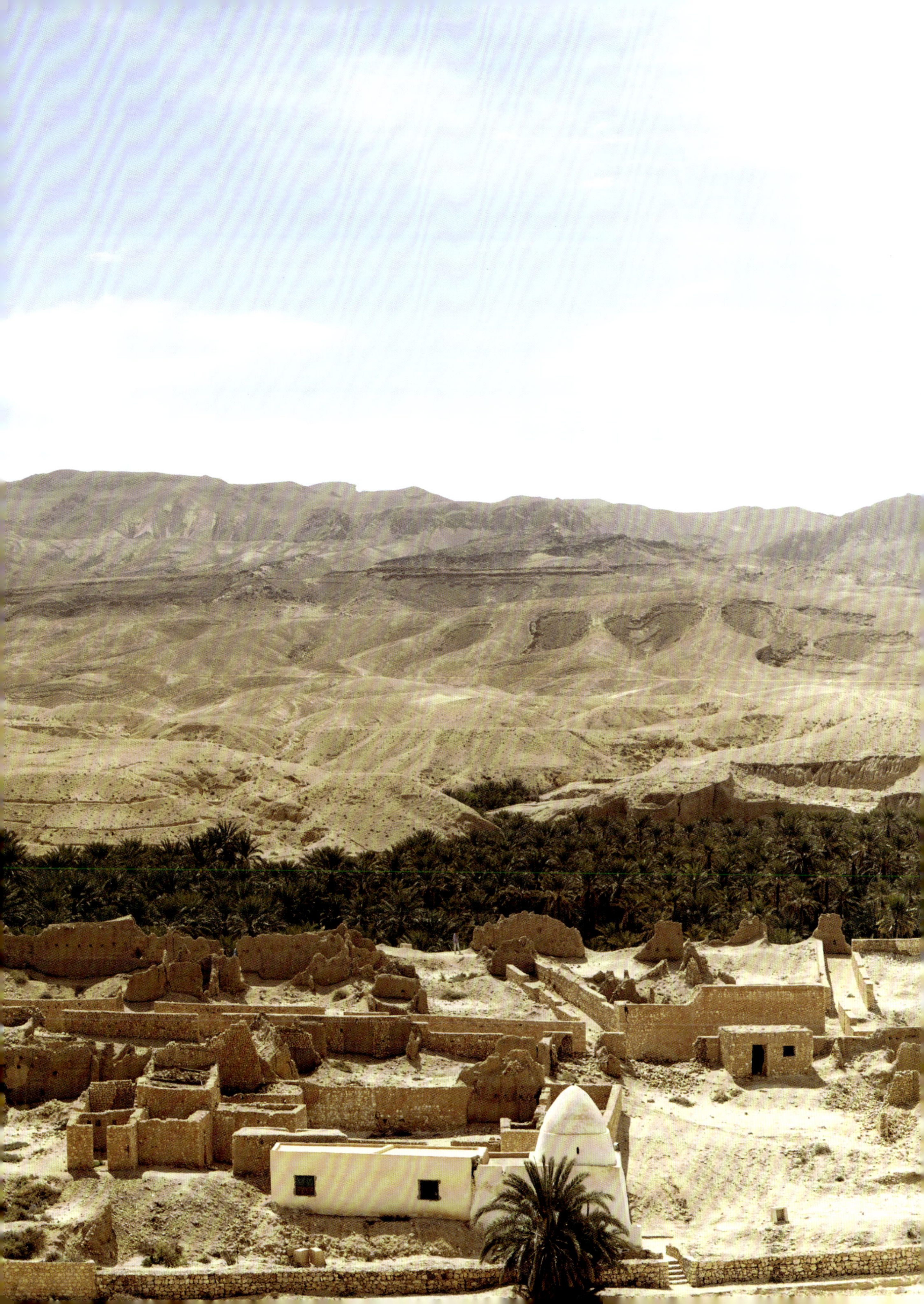

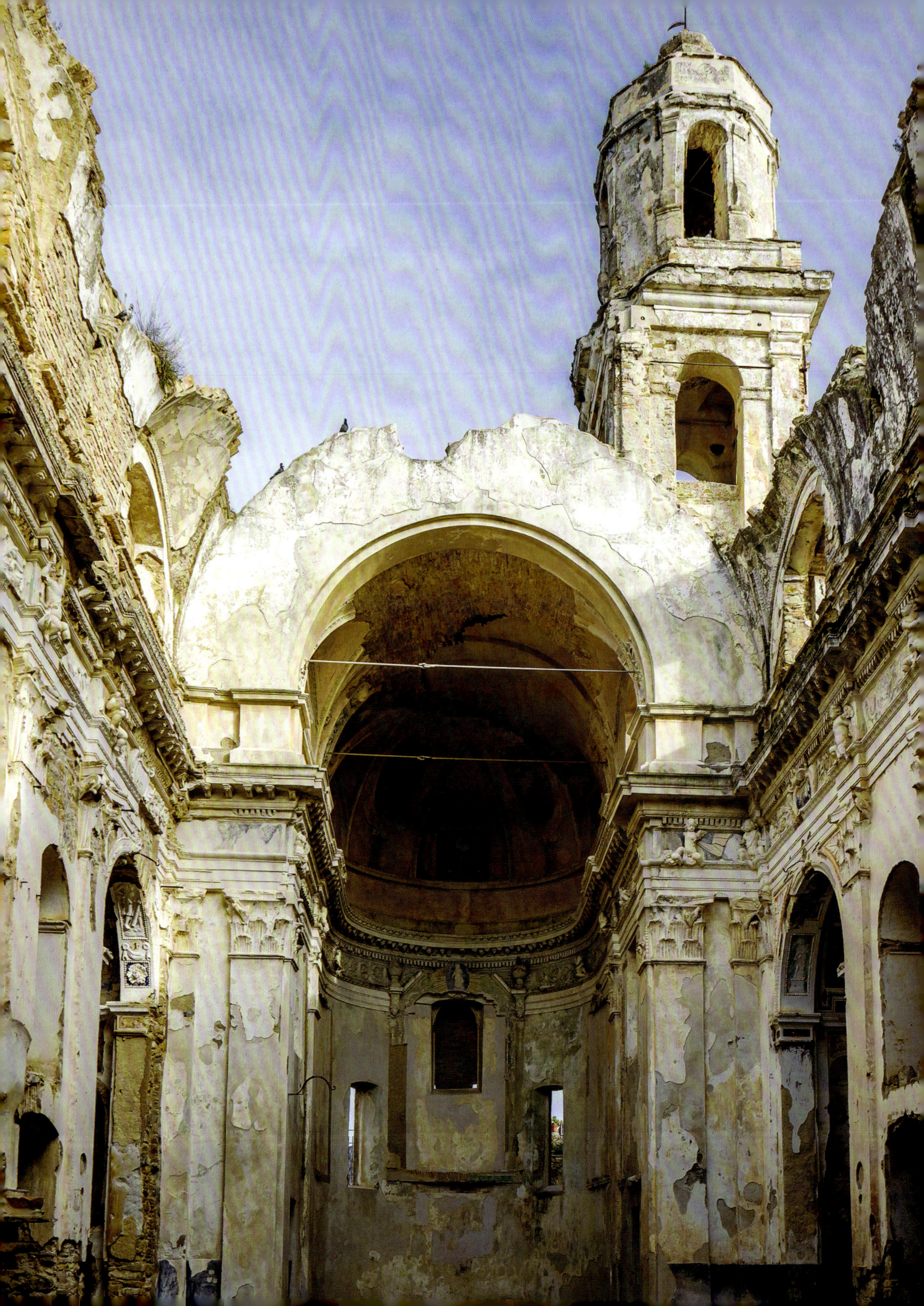

Europe

It is sometimes surprising to discover just how many ghost towns are littered across Europe. The continent of Europe is a very densely populated region of the planet (if we exclude Asiatic Russia), with a population of nearly 750 million people (2015). Space and housing are at a premium in many countries, demand often outstripping supply. Yet Europe is a place of geographical, historical and social diversity, perhaps even more so than the other continents considered in this book – consider, for example, just the climatic differences between arctic Norway and semi-tropical southern Italy or Spain. Diversity produces opportunity, certainly, but it also creates pockets of inequity, exclusion and instability, the conditions upon which ghost towns are built. Thus we have a true spectrum of causes behind the abandonment of the villages, towns and cities in this chapter. Some, like many of those in Italy, are the products of geological instability or gradual depopulation to the big, prosperous cities. Others began their decline when taken over for military purposes, and never subsequently returned to their civilian owners. Yet others – like Chernobyl and its surrounding areas – were emptied of people in a matter of days, the population fleeing in response to an unprecedented nuclear disaster. Despite the apparent wealth of Europe, its ghost towns illustrate how towns and even cities are not ordained to exist.

LEFT:
Bussana Vecchia, Liguria, Italy
Bussana Vecchia was a typically beautiful Italian hill town, founded in the 9th century. Having thrived for more than 500 years, the town was hit by a horrific earthquake on 23 February 1887, which killed 2000 inhabitants and led to the abandonment of the town. Here is the ruined shell of the town's principal church.

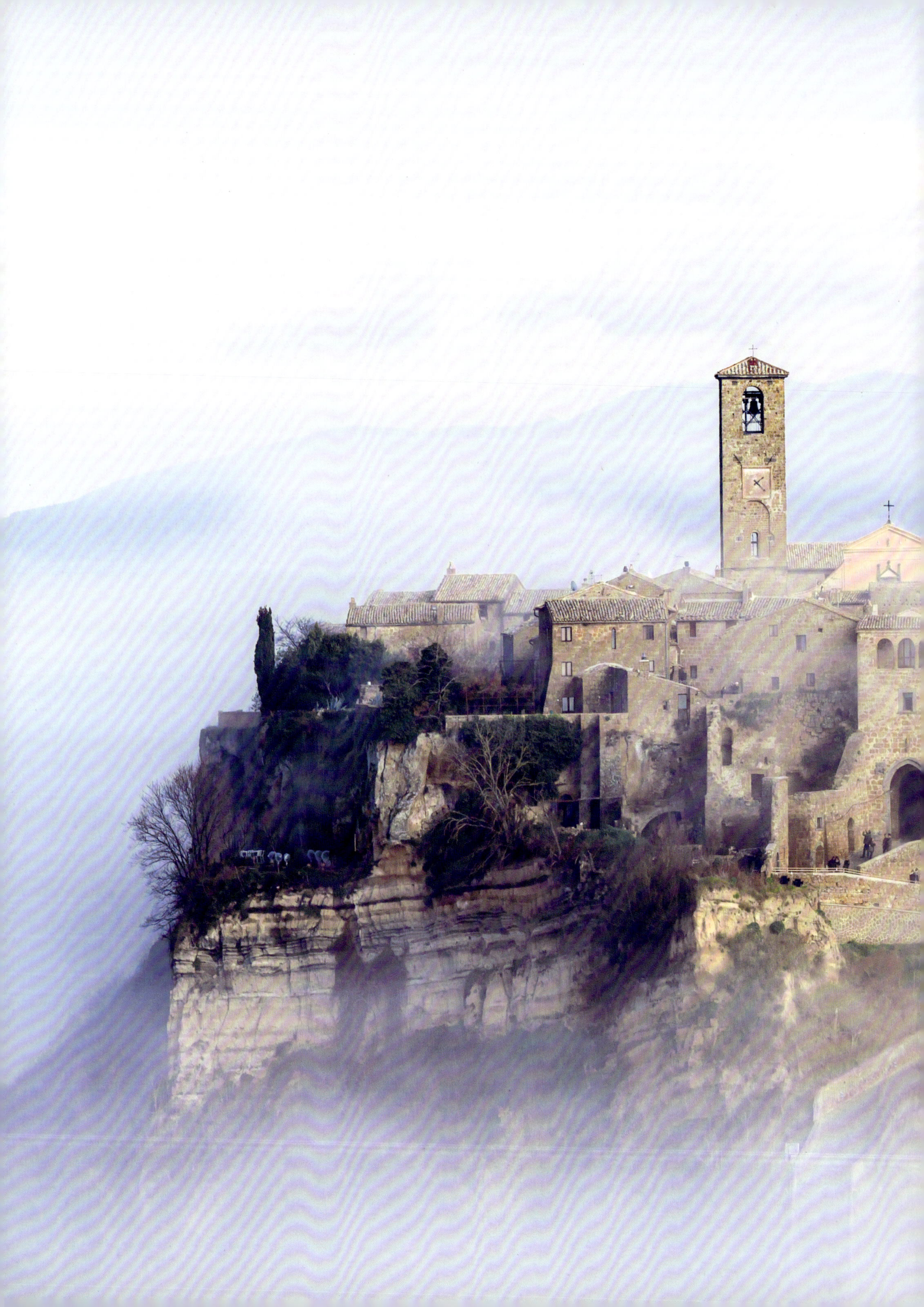

Civita di Bagnoregio, Viterbo, Italy

Given its spectacular location, it seems inconceivable that Civita di Bagnoregio is known locally as *La città che muore* ('The Dying Town'). Yet this 13th-century town, set atop a volcanic outcrop overlooking the Tiber River, went into decline from the 18th century following damage by earthquake and natural erosion. A very small population, sometimes as low as 12, fluctuates in the town throughout the seasons.

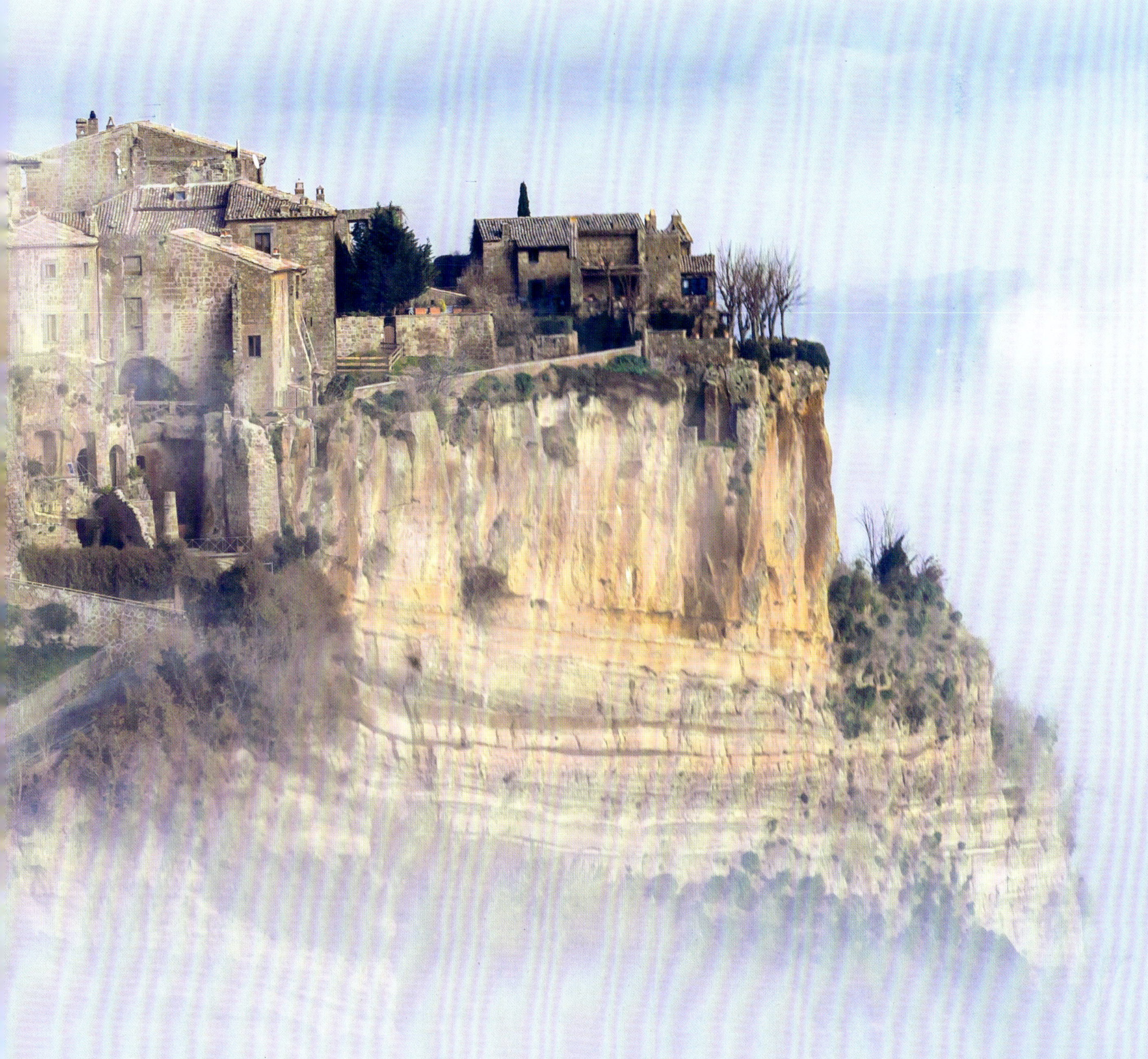

RIGHT:

Argentiera, Sassari, Sardinia

The silver-mining industry lay at the origins of Argentiera back in the Roman era, and defined its existence for much of subsequent history. Only in the 1960s were the seams finally exhausted, and the town abandoned. Unlike many Italian ghost towns, Argentiera has a distinctly industrial feel to it, and it attracts many tourists each year.

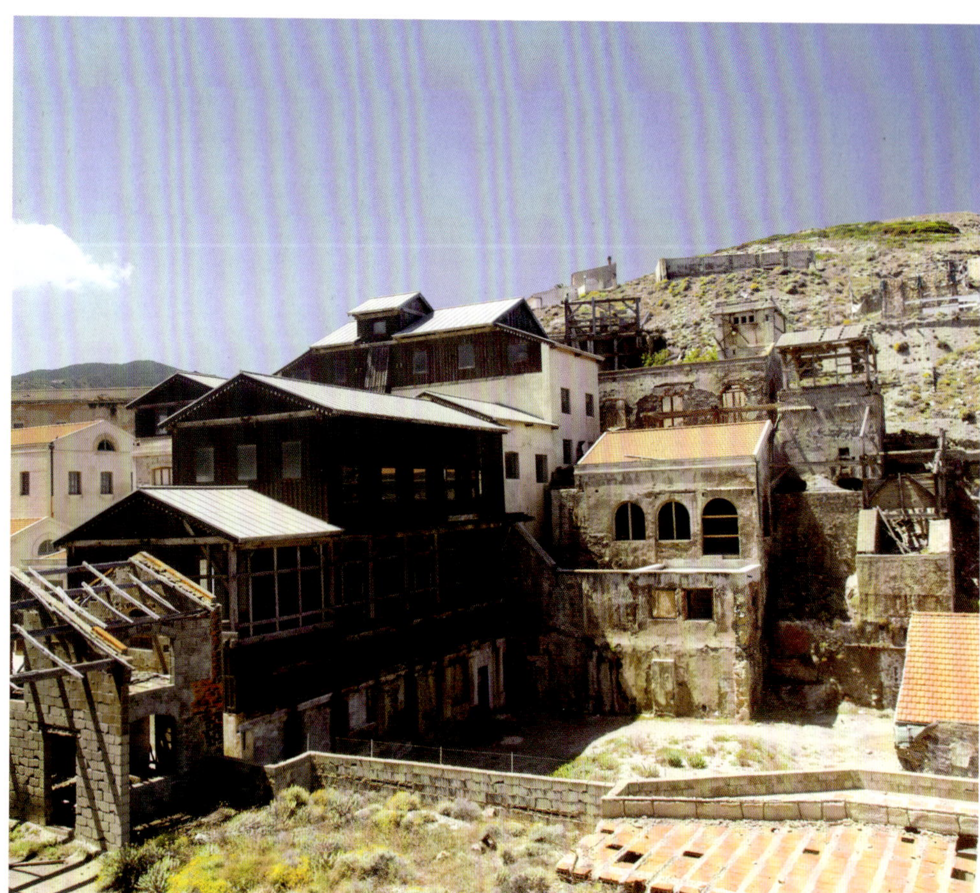

BELOW AND OPPOSITE:

Balestrino, Liguria, Italy

Balestrino is one of the most intriguing ghost towns in Italy. Situated 70km (43 miles) southwest of Genoa, the town dates back to the 11th century, and subsequently had a turbulent political and military history. Its decline began with Italian occupation in the 19th century, but was cemented by earthquakes and hydrogeological instability, with the last residents leaving in 1953. The fact that the town is cordoned off to visitors makes it even more compelling.

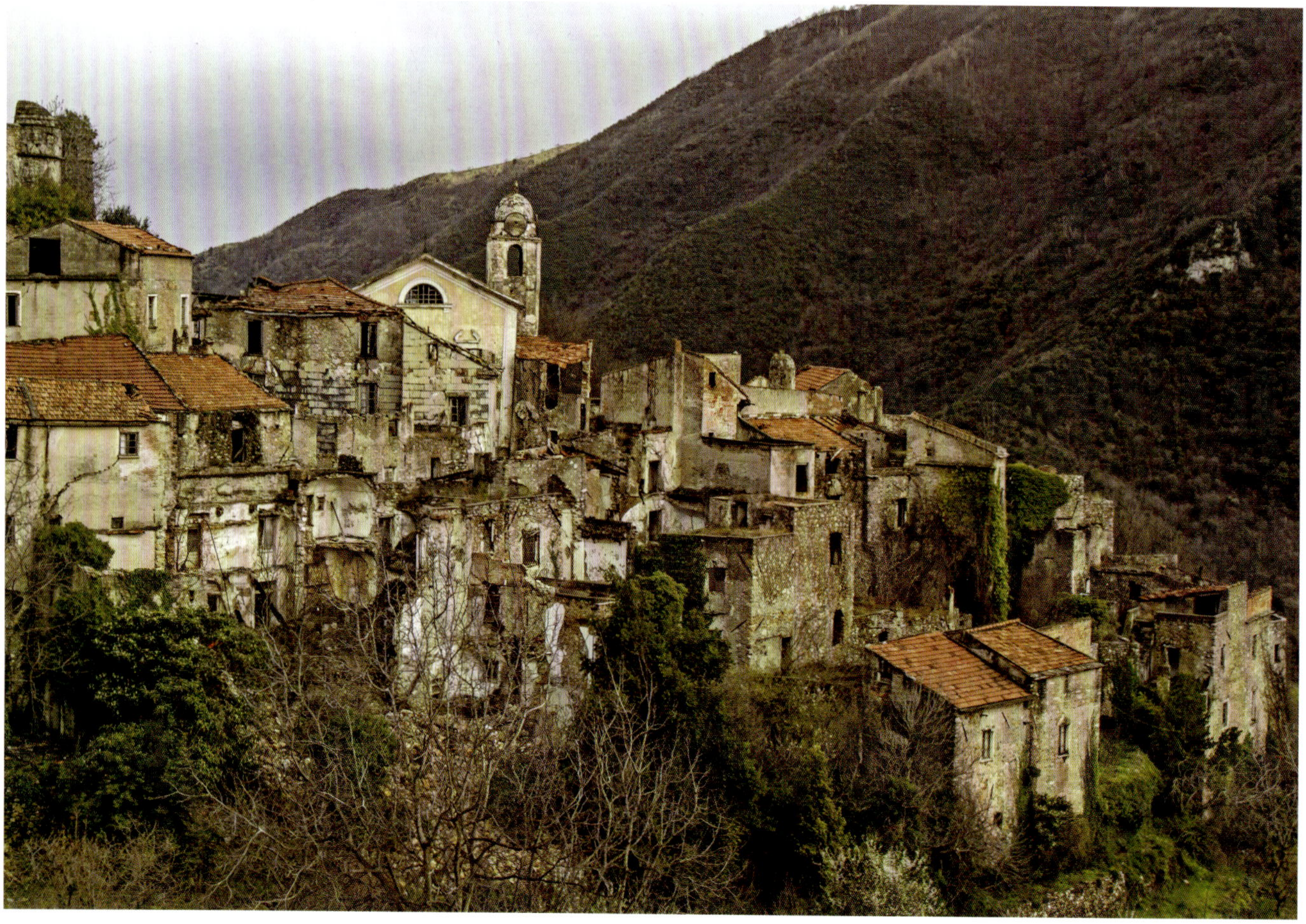

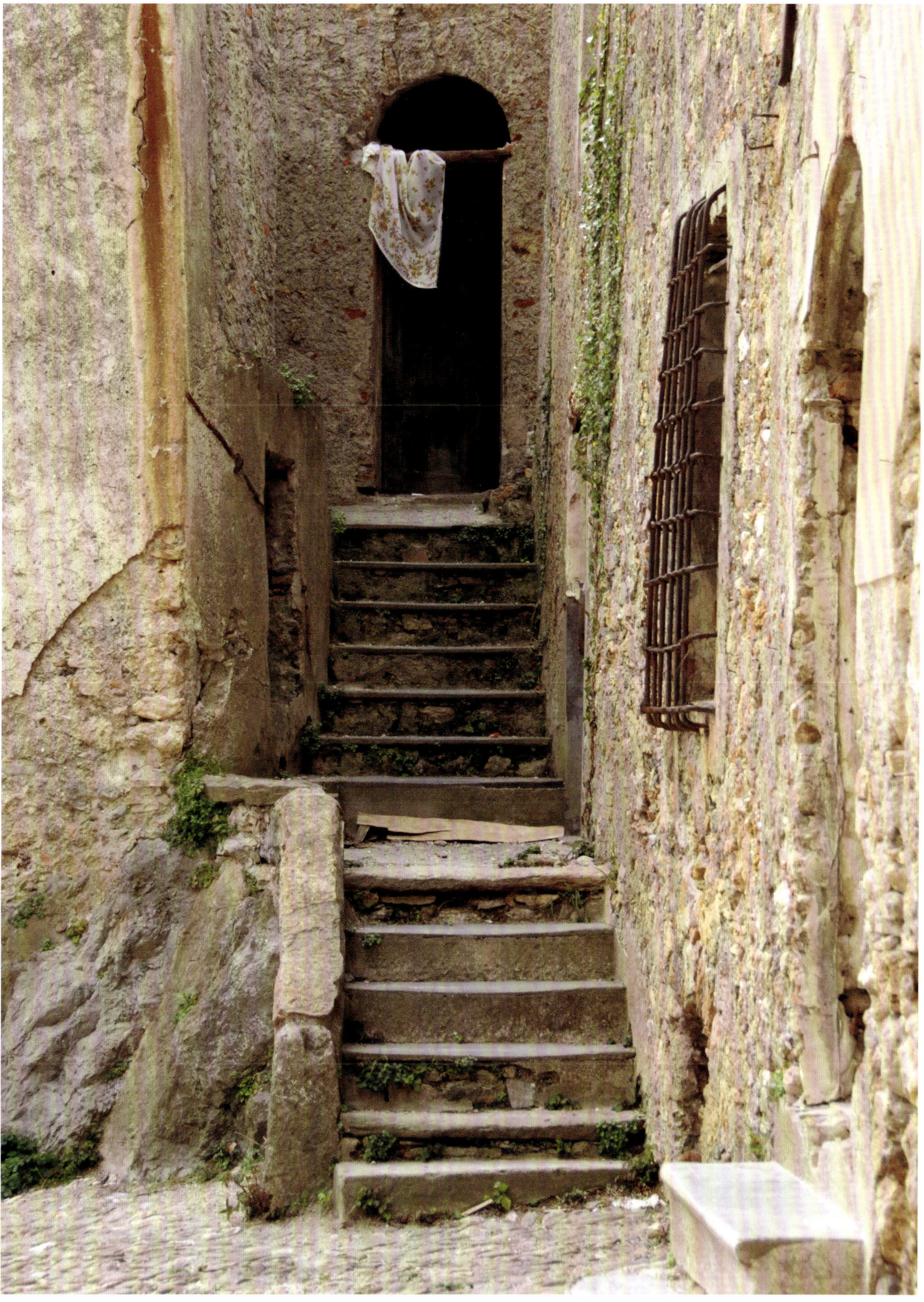

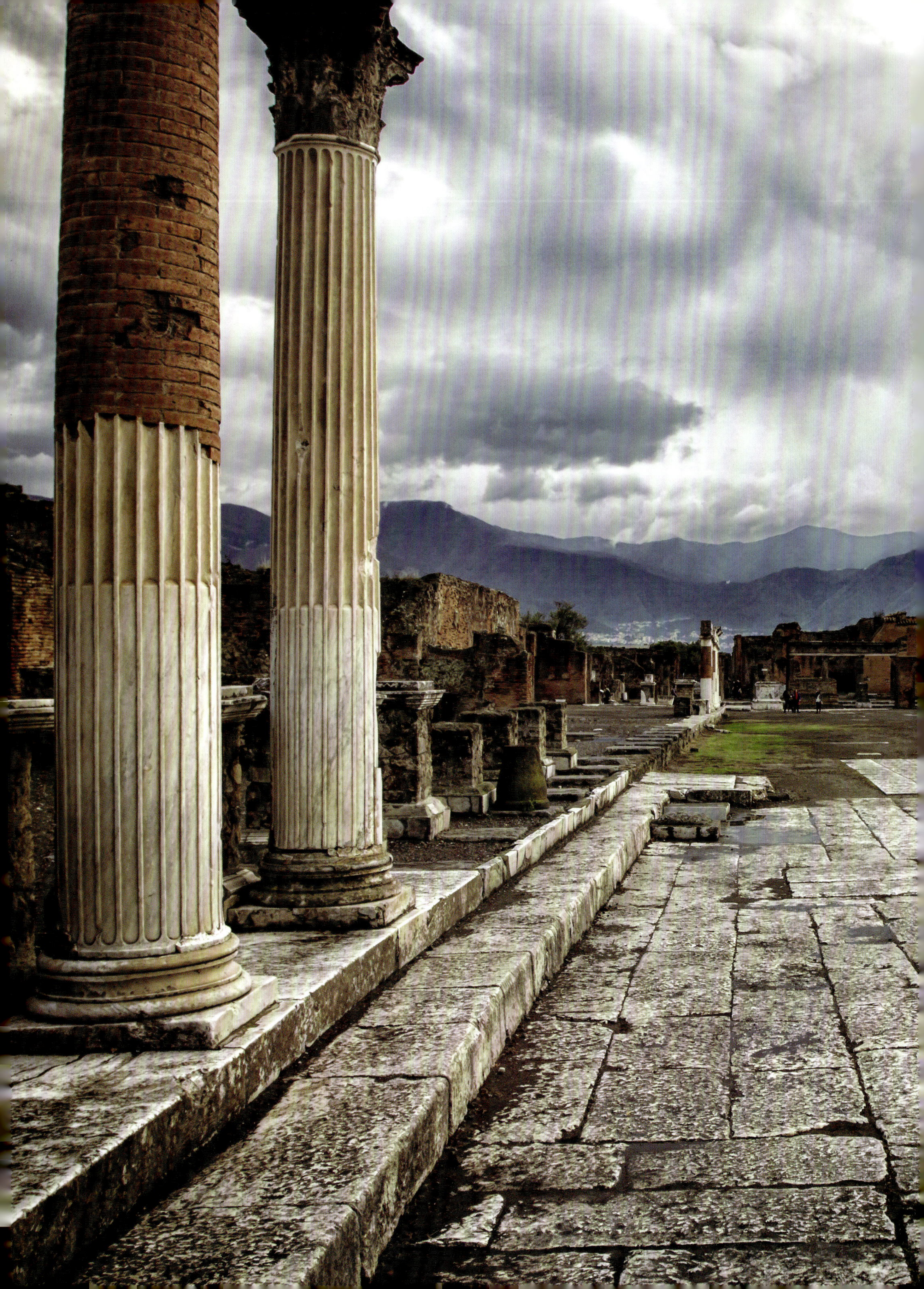

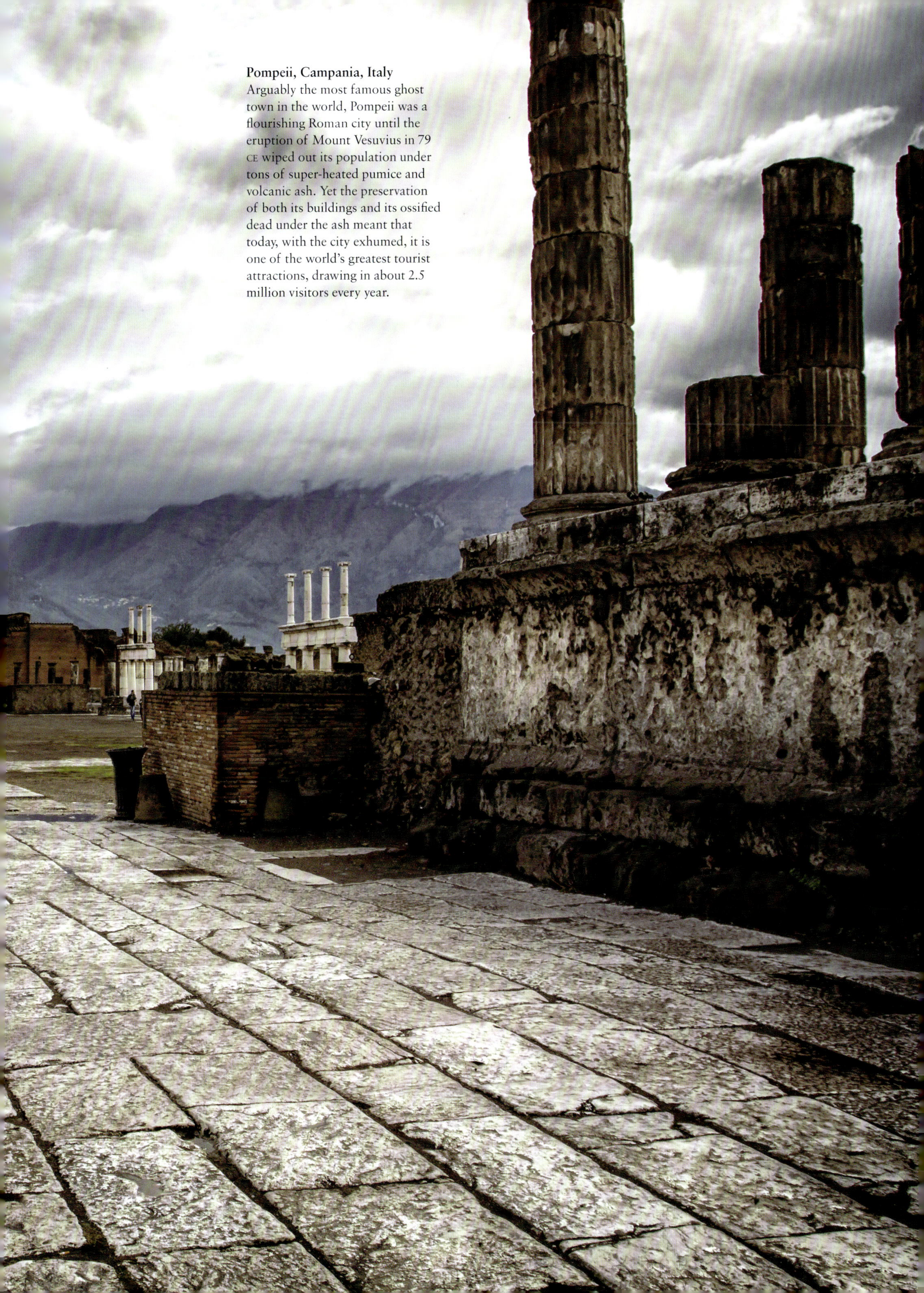

Pompeii, Campania, Italy
Arguably the most famous ghost town in the world, Pompeii was a flourishing Roman city until the eruption of Mount Vesuvius in 79 CE wiped out its population under tons of super-heated pumice and volcanic ash. Yet the preservation of both its buildings and its ossified dead under the ash meant that today, with the city exhumed, it is one of the world's greatest tourist attractions, drawing in about 2.5 million visitors every year.

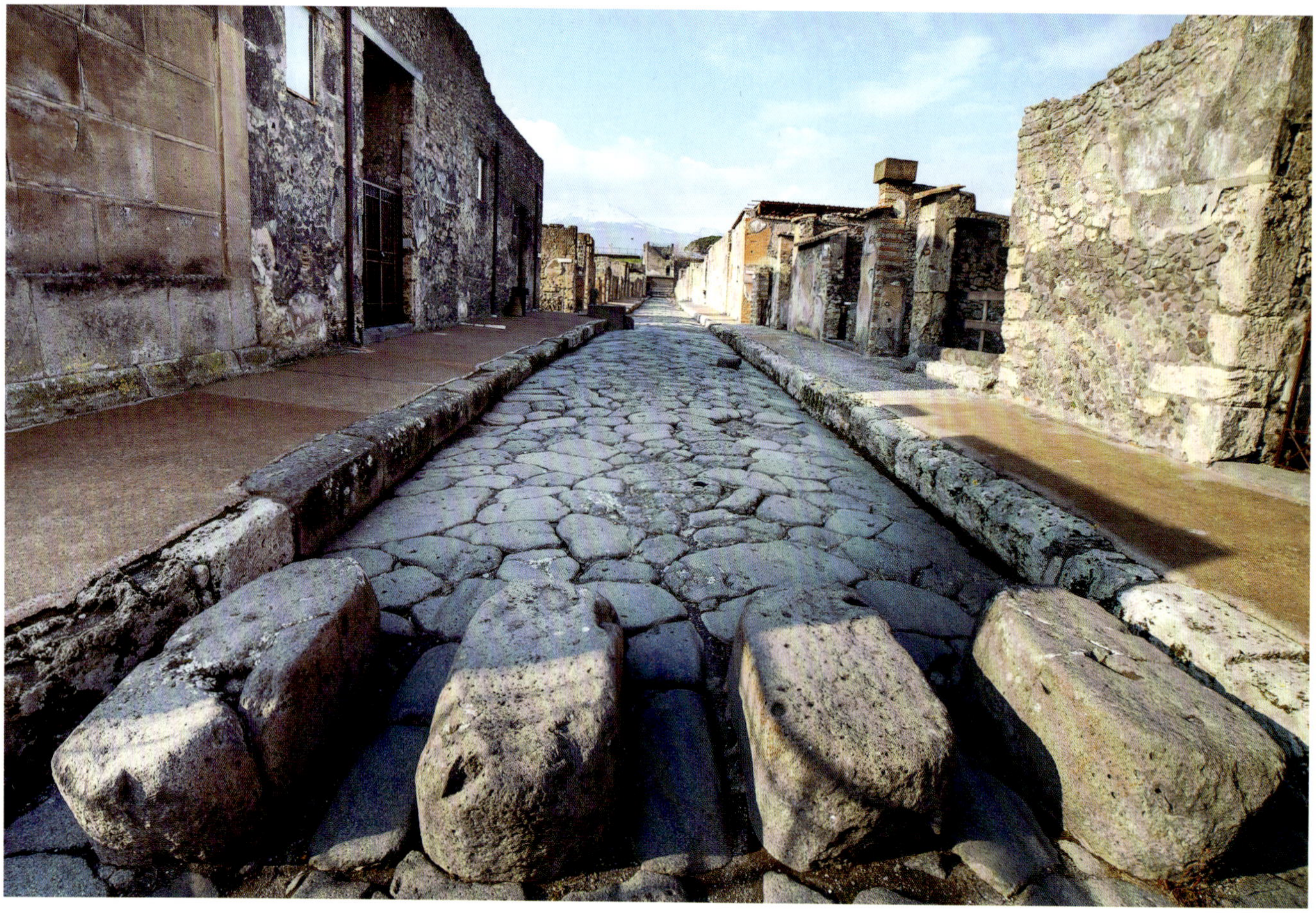

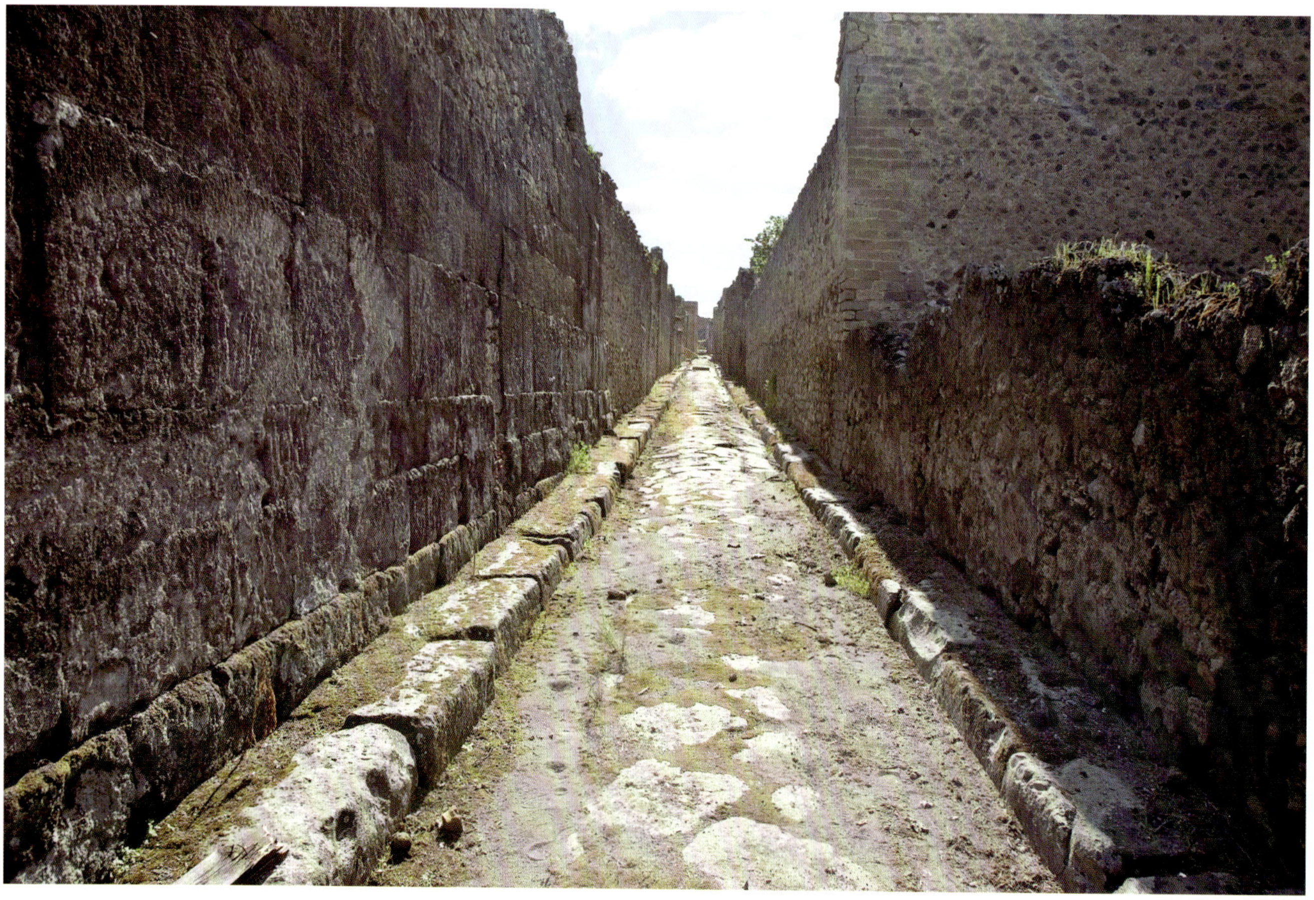

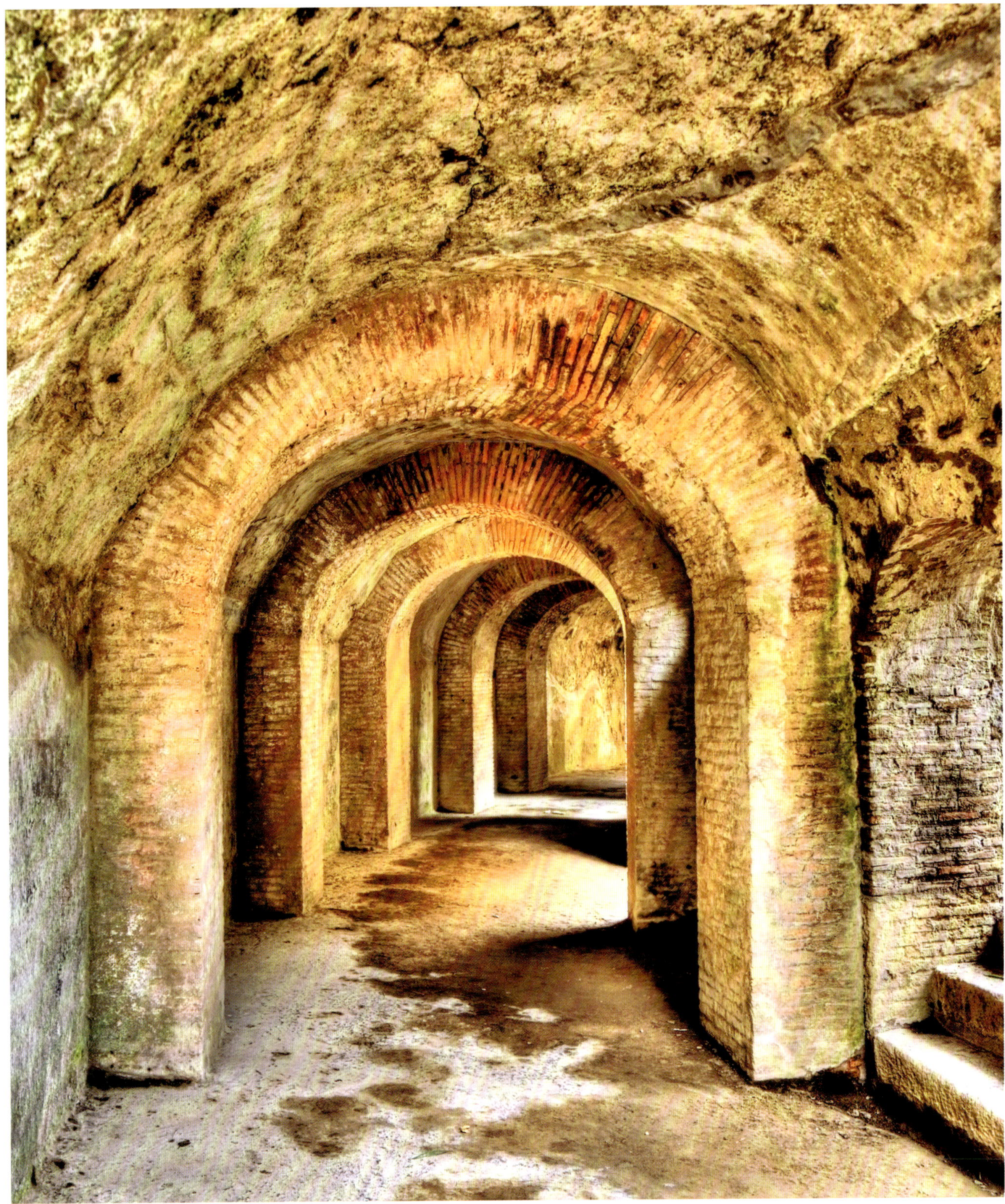

OPPOSITE ABOVE:
Pompeii, Campania, Italy
One of the many cobbled streets lacing ancient Pompeii. The raised stone blocks are stepping stones, which allowed the citizens to cross the street when it was wet or dirty, but permitted cart wheels to pass through the gaps.

OPPOSITE BELOW:
Pompeii, Campania, Italy
A narrow alleyway in one of Pompeii's backstreets. Many of the more developed Roman towns and cities had their streets laid out in a grid pattern, much as we see today in modern town planning in countries such as the United States.

ABOVE:
Pompeii, Campania, Italy
An interior passageway in Pompeii's famous amphitheatre. The building was constructed in 70 BCE, and like other Roman amphitheatres it hosted violent gladiatorial games. Despite the brutality of its events, the amphitheatre was a work of superb architectural sophistication. It was buried in ash during the Mount Vesuvius eruption, but it actually survived the event with surprisingly little damage; hence historians have been able to study the building's design and how it worked in exceptional detail.

Herculaneum, Campania, Italy
Pompeii was not the only victim of Mount Vesuvius in 79 CE. The nearby town of Herculaneum was destroyed yet simultaneously preserved by the pyroclastic avalanche that thundered down from the volcano. Most of the several hundred people who died in and around the town were killed by the extreme heat of the volcanic storm, although by this stage the majority of the inhabitants had already fled.

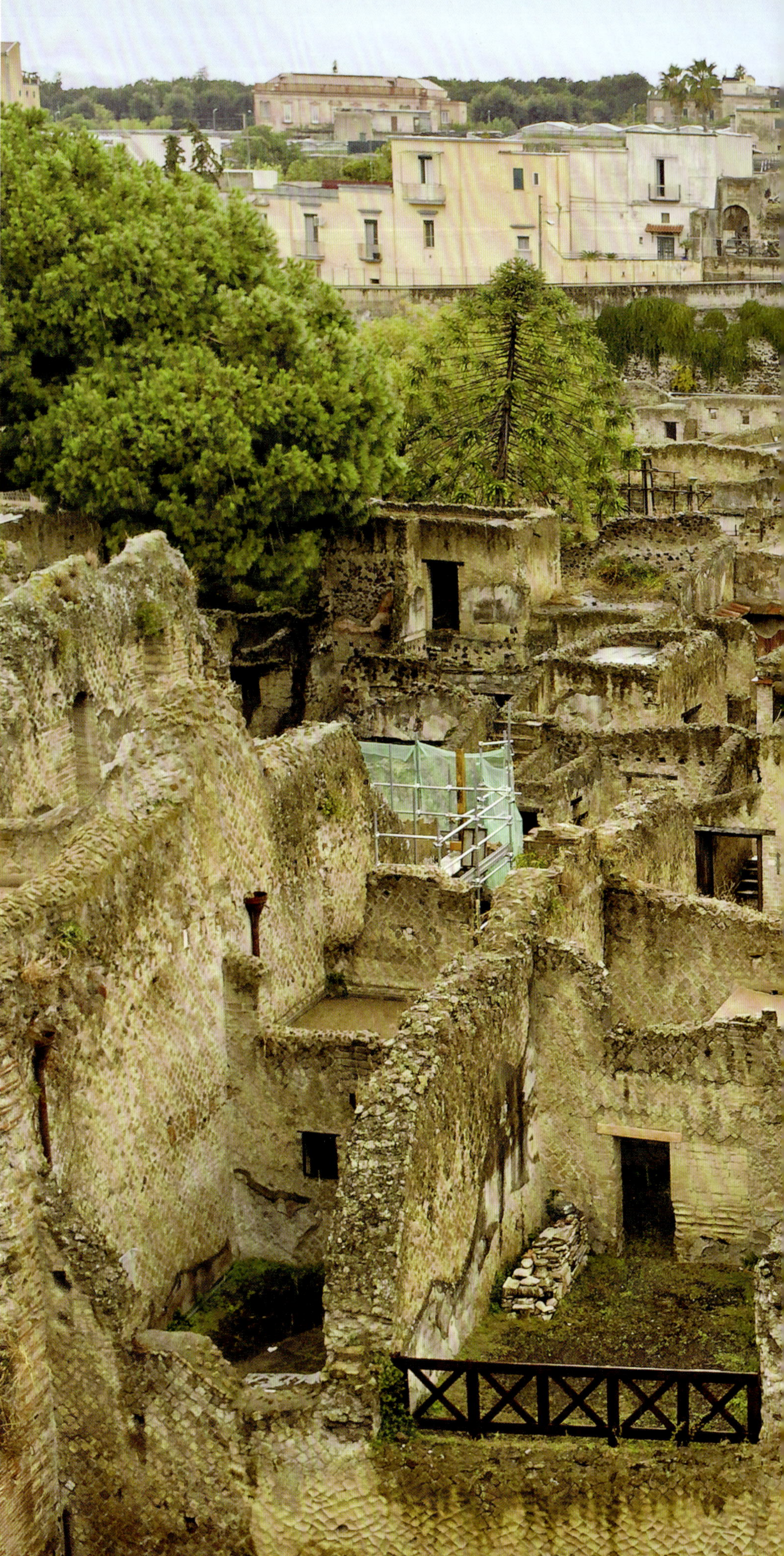

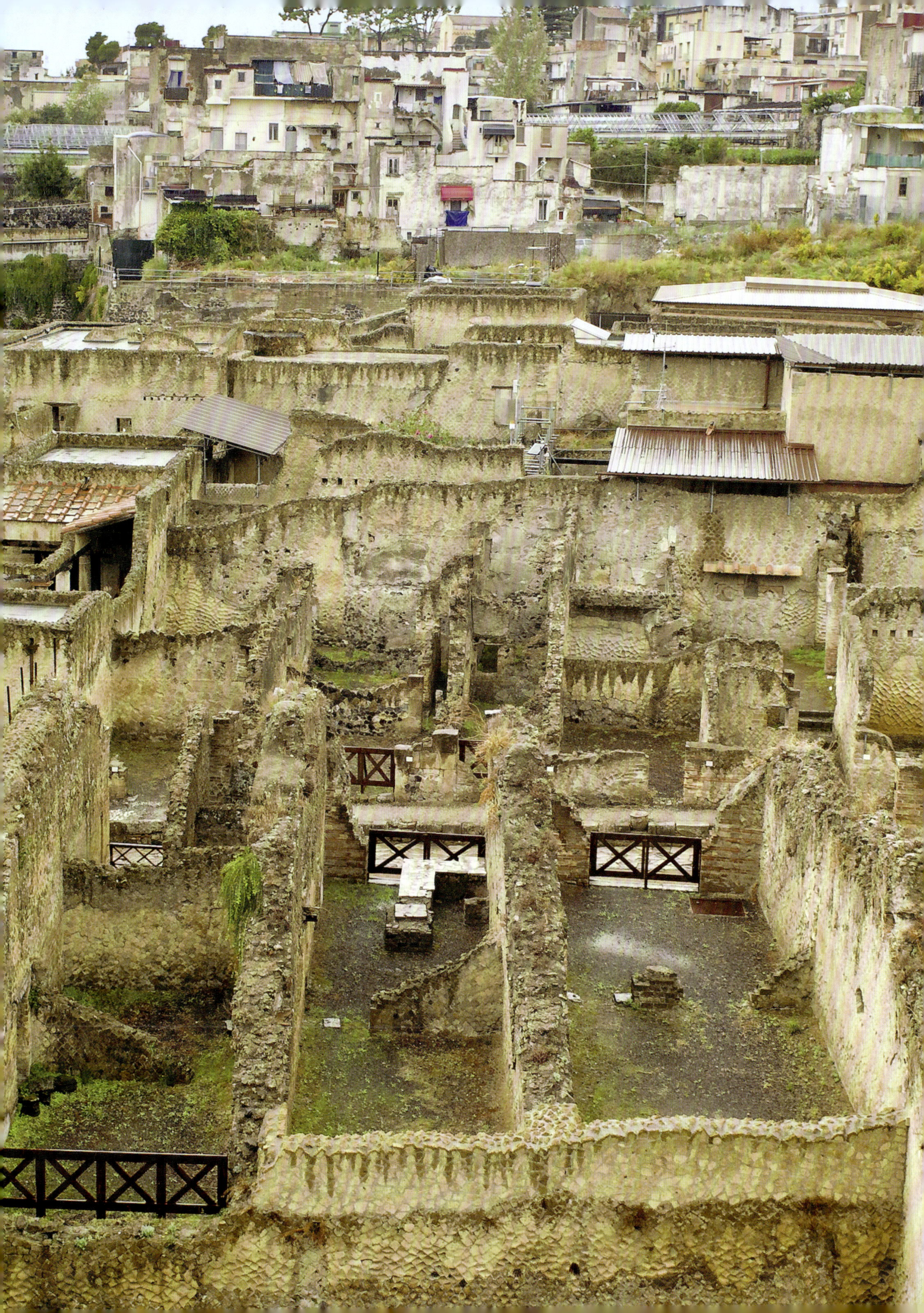

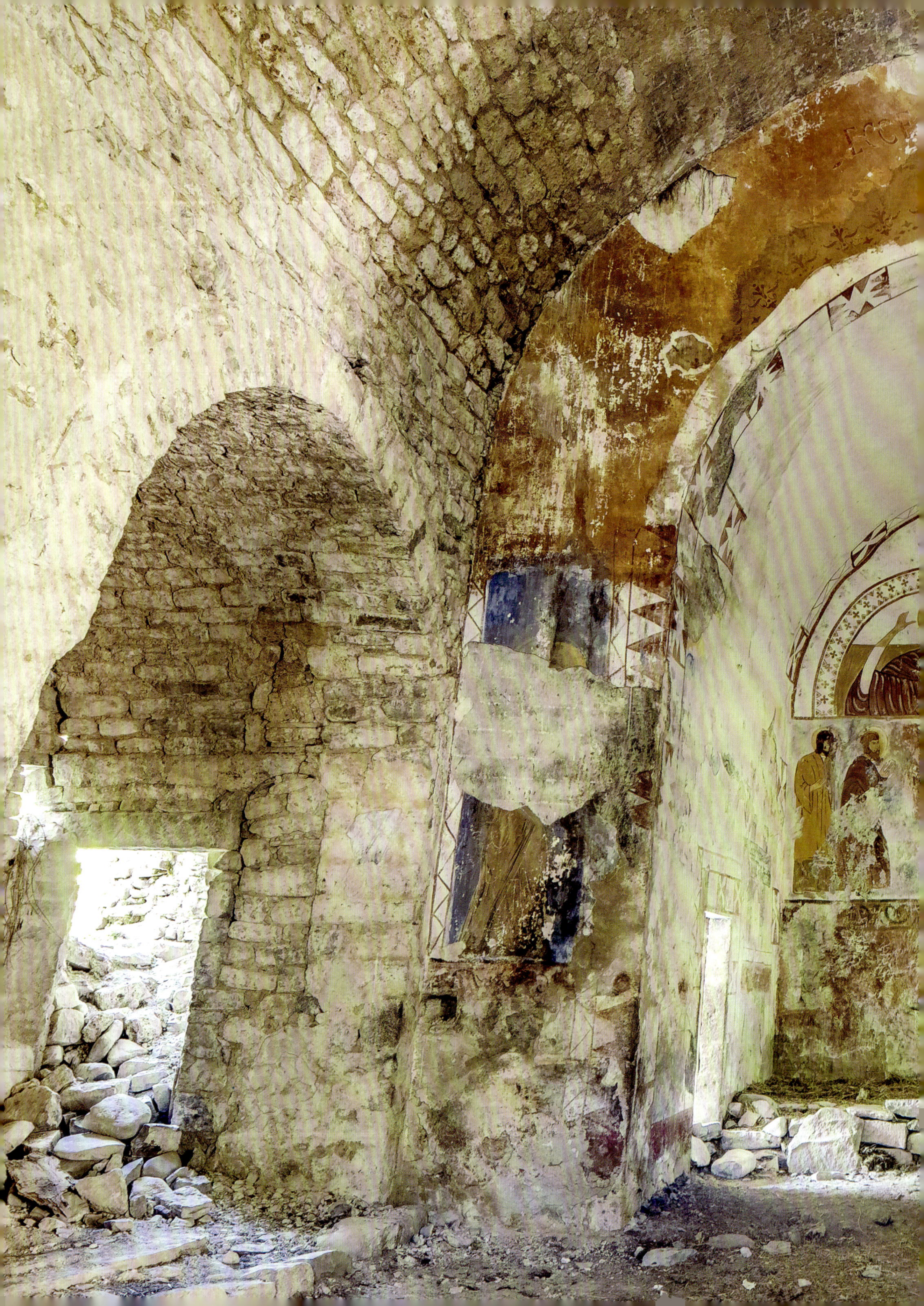

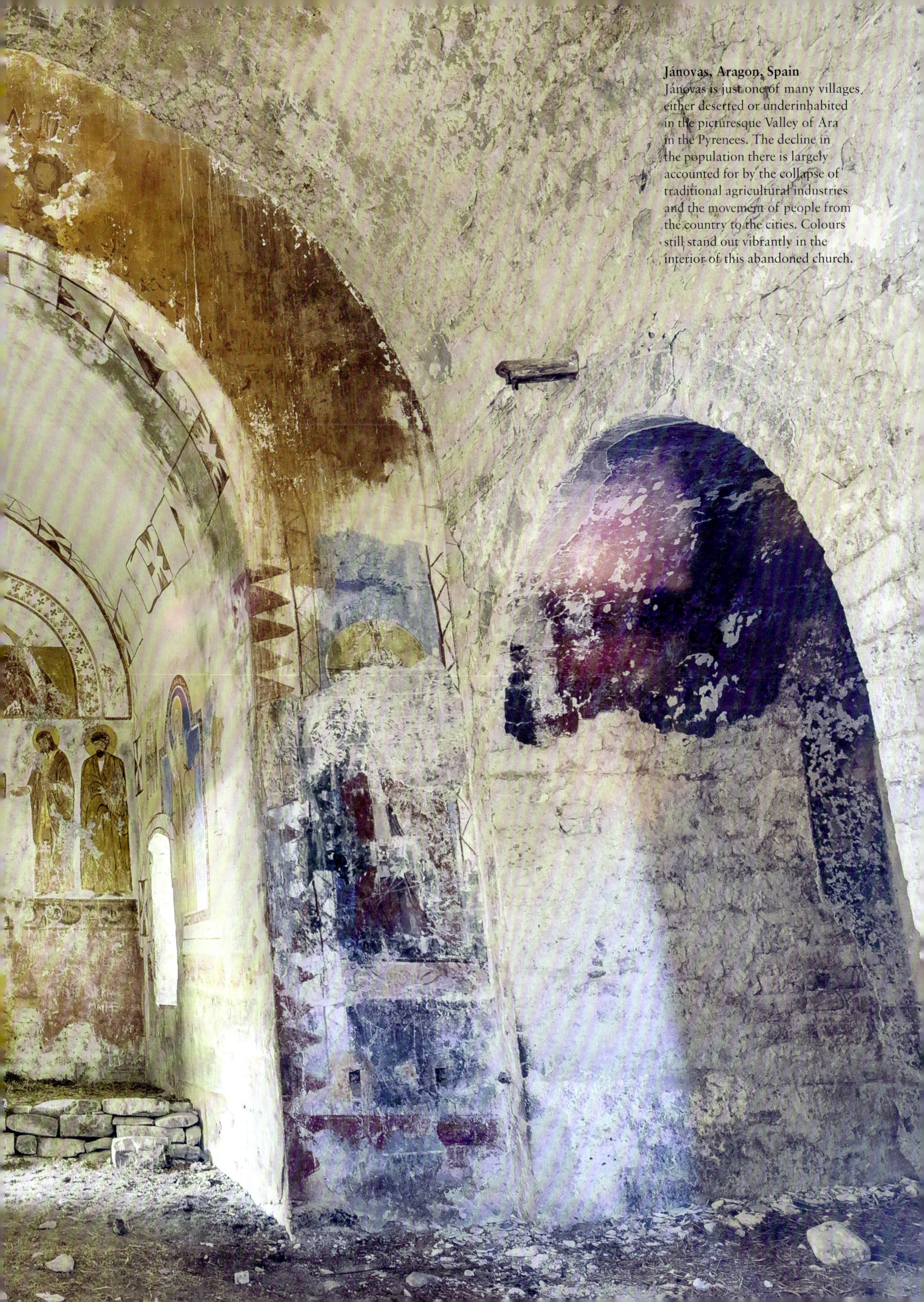

Jánovas, Aragon, Spain
Jánovas is just one of many villages either deserted or underinhabited in the picturesque Valley of Ara in the Pyrenees. The decline in the population there is largely accounted for by the collapse of traditional agricultural industries and the movement of people from the country to the cities. Colours still stand out vibrantly in the interior of this abandoned church.

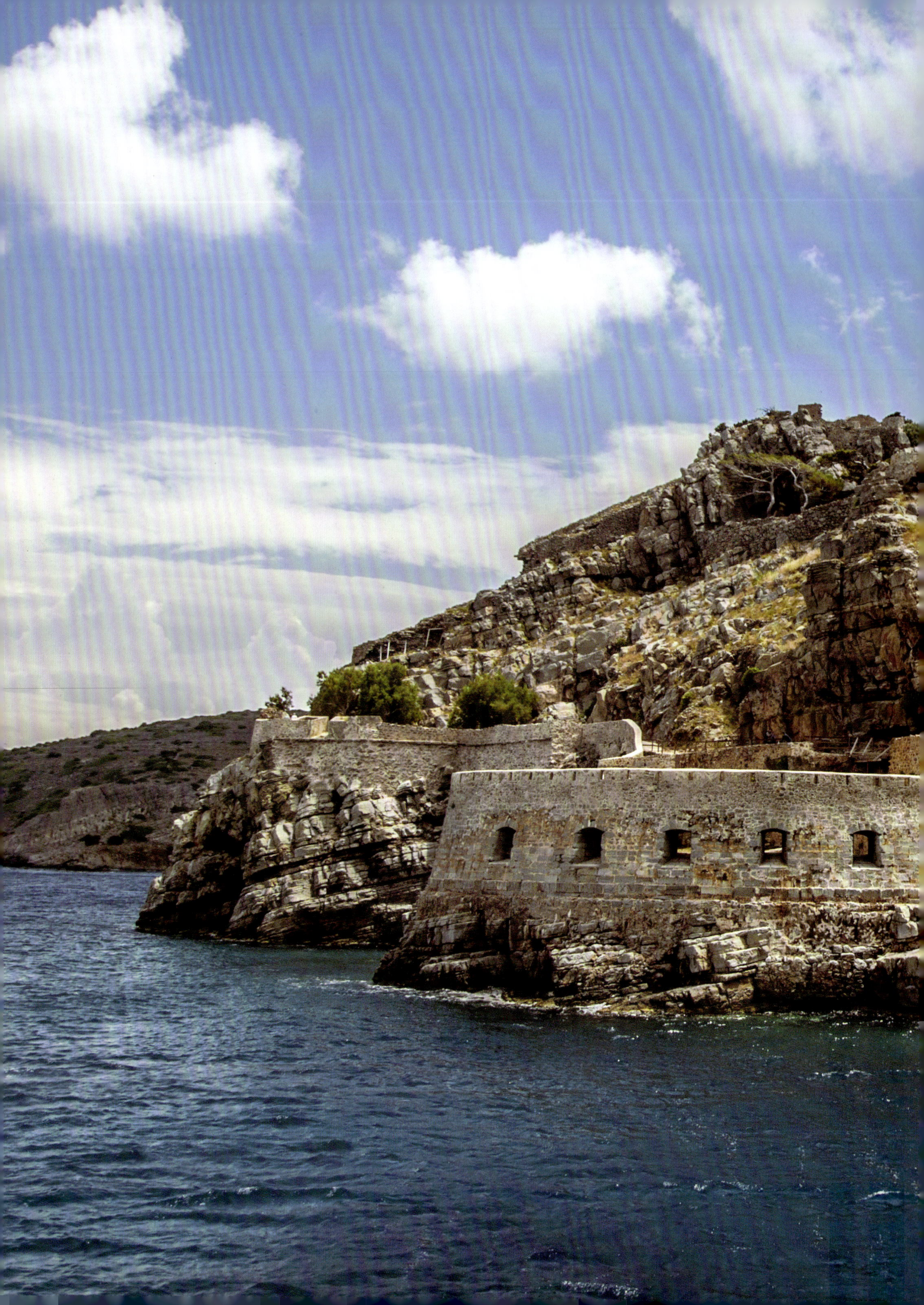

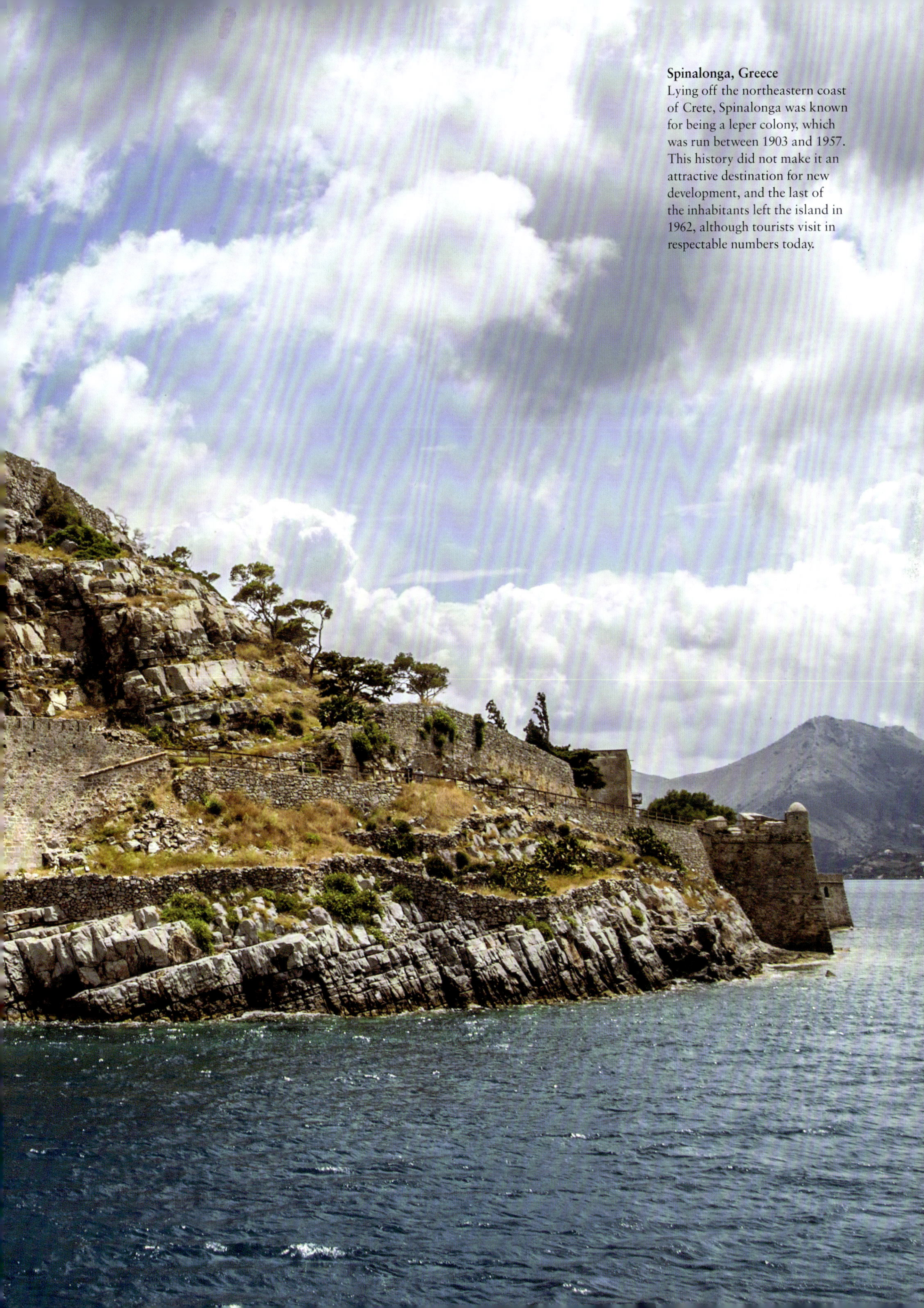

Spinalonga, Greece
Lying off the northeastern coast of Crete, Spinalonga was known for being a leper colony, which was run between 1903 and 1957. This history did not make it an attractive destination for new development, and the last of the inhabitants left the island in 1962, although tourists visit in respectable numbers today.

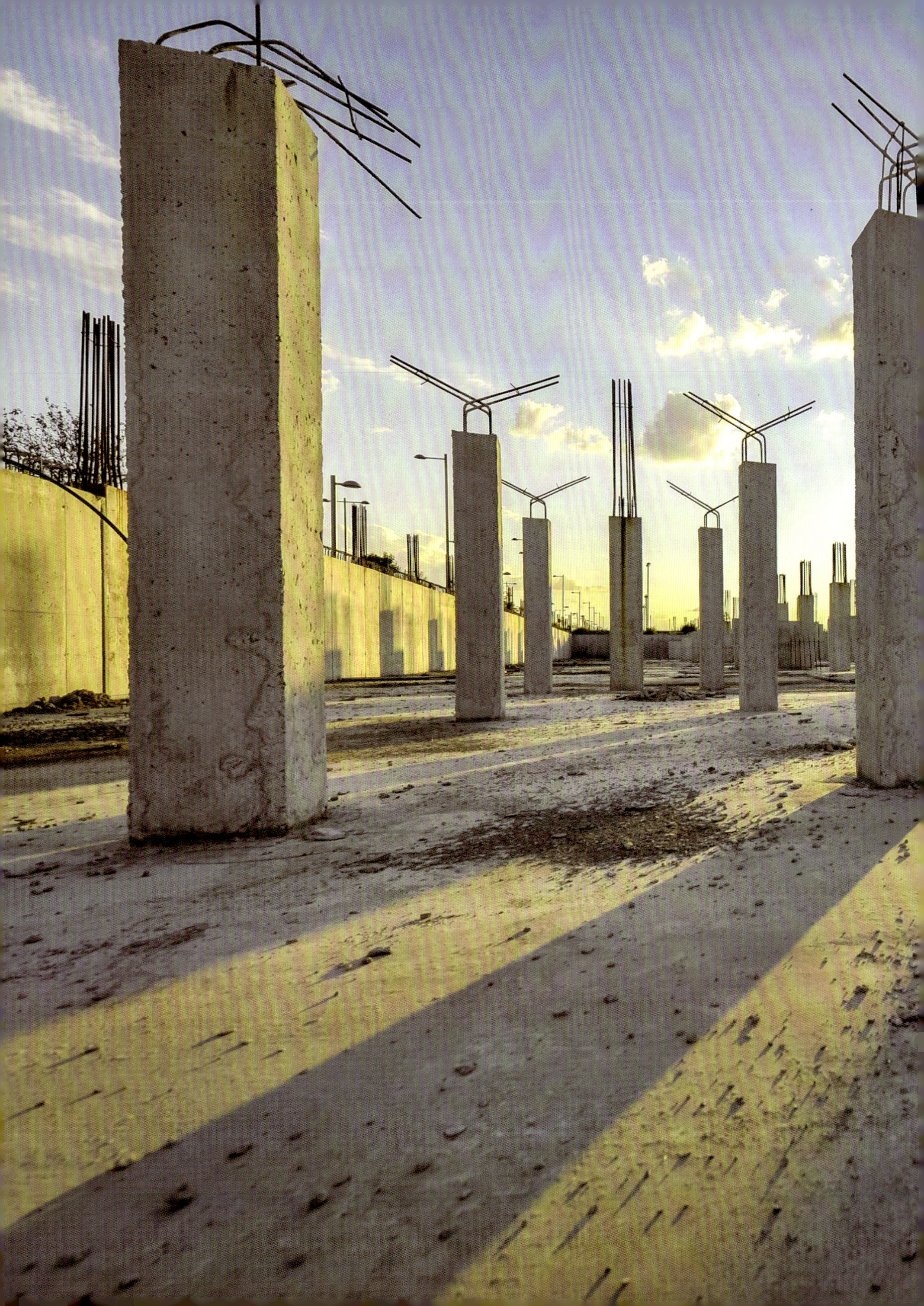

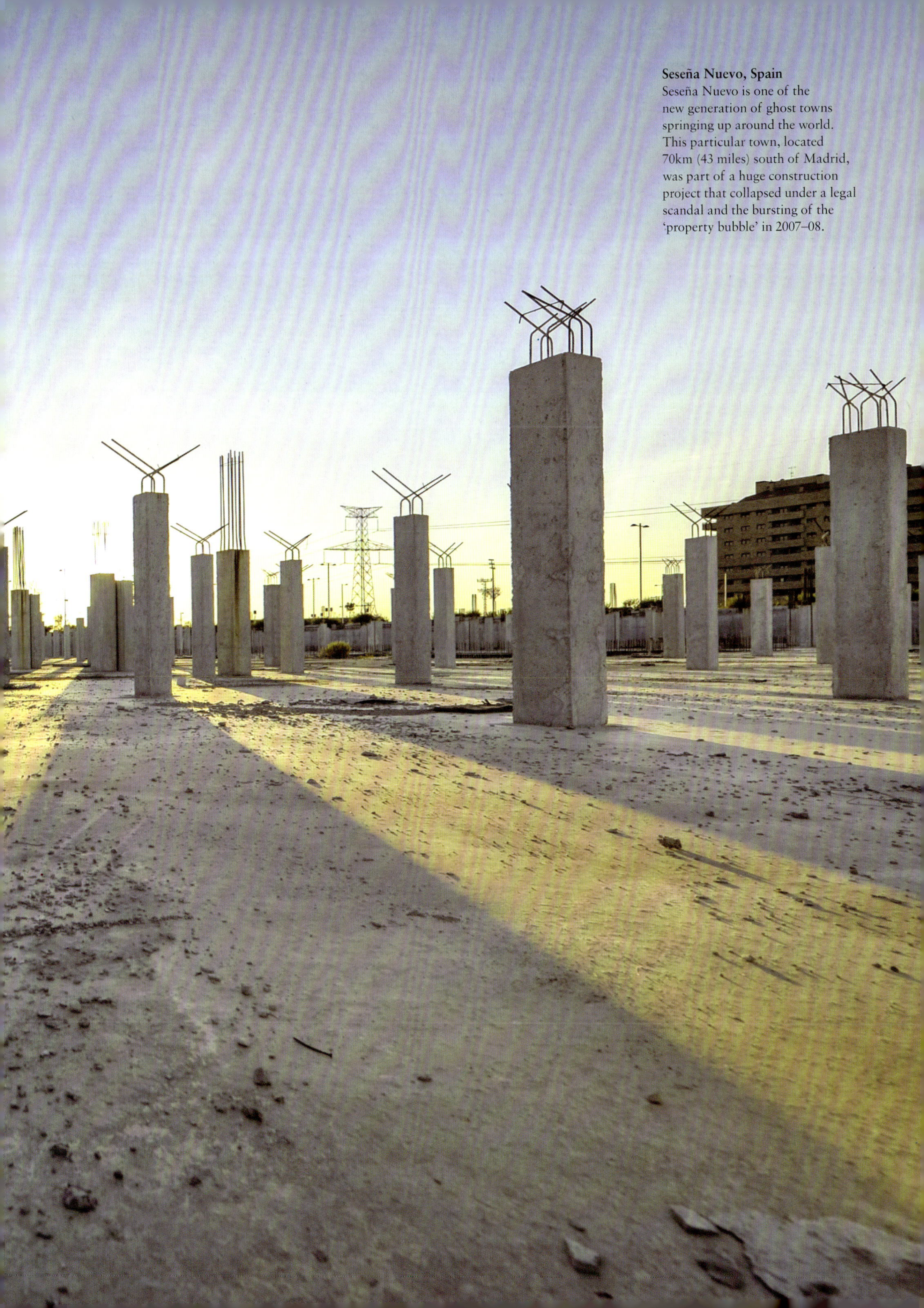

Seseña Nuevo, Spain
Seseña Nuevo is one of the new generation of ghost towns springing up around the world. This particular town, located 70km (43 miles) south of Madrid, was part of a huge construction project that collapsed under a legal scandal and the bursting of the 'property bubble' in 2007–08.

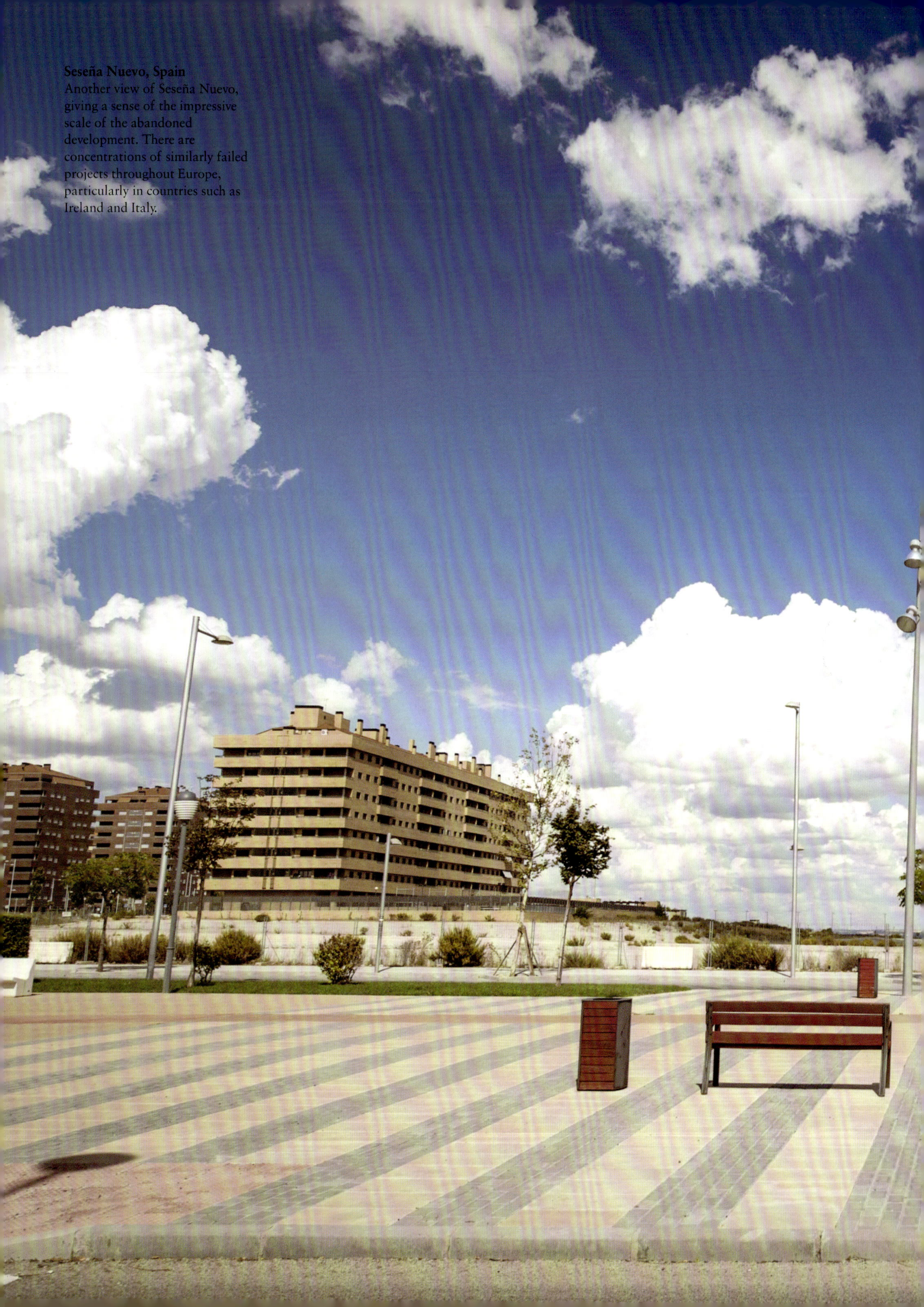

Seseña Nuevo, Spain
Another view of Seseña Nuevo, giving a sense of the impressive scale of the abandoned development. There are concentrations of similarly failed projects throughout Europe, particularly in countries such as Ireland and Italy.

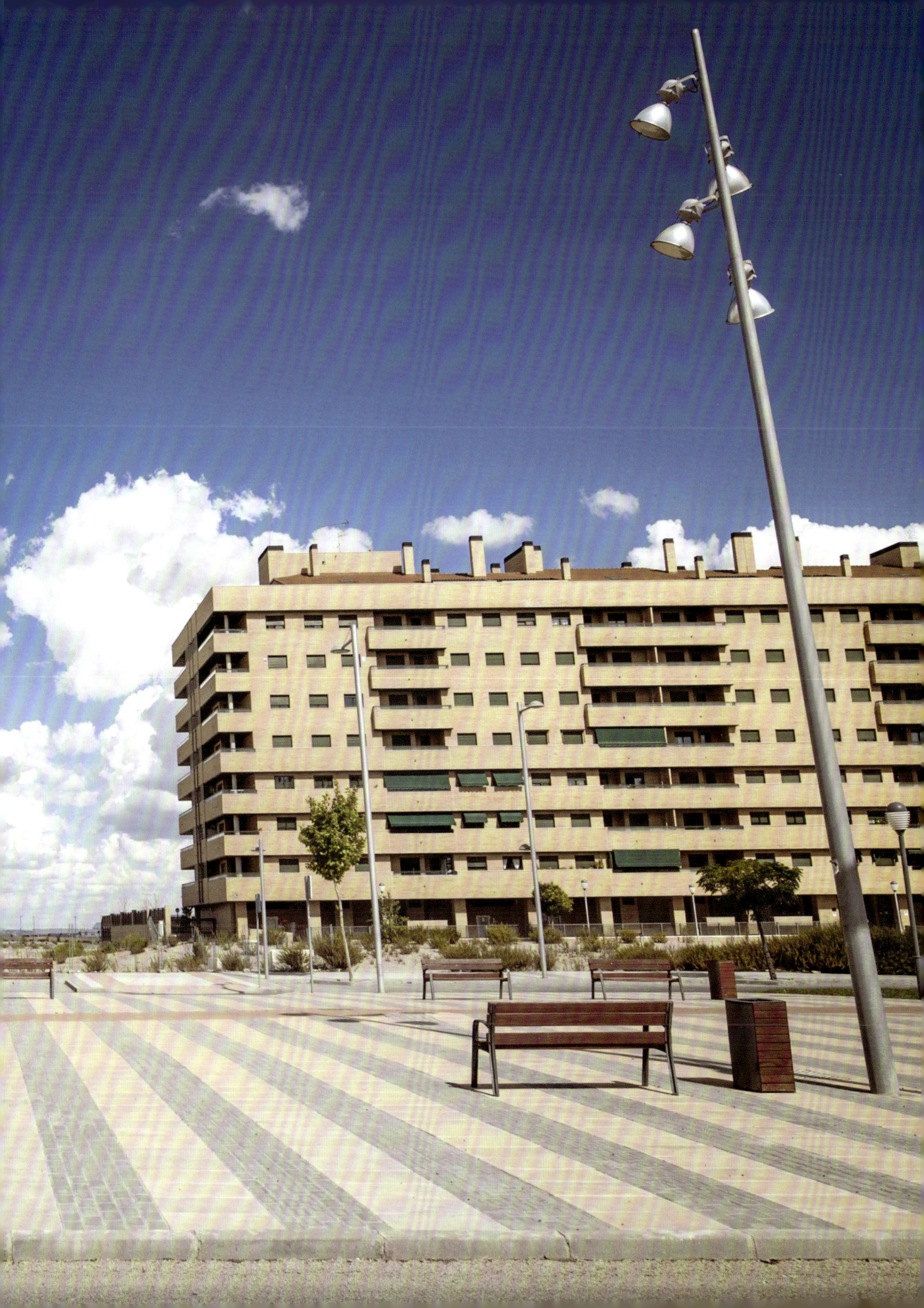

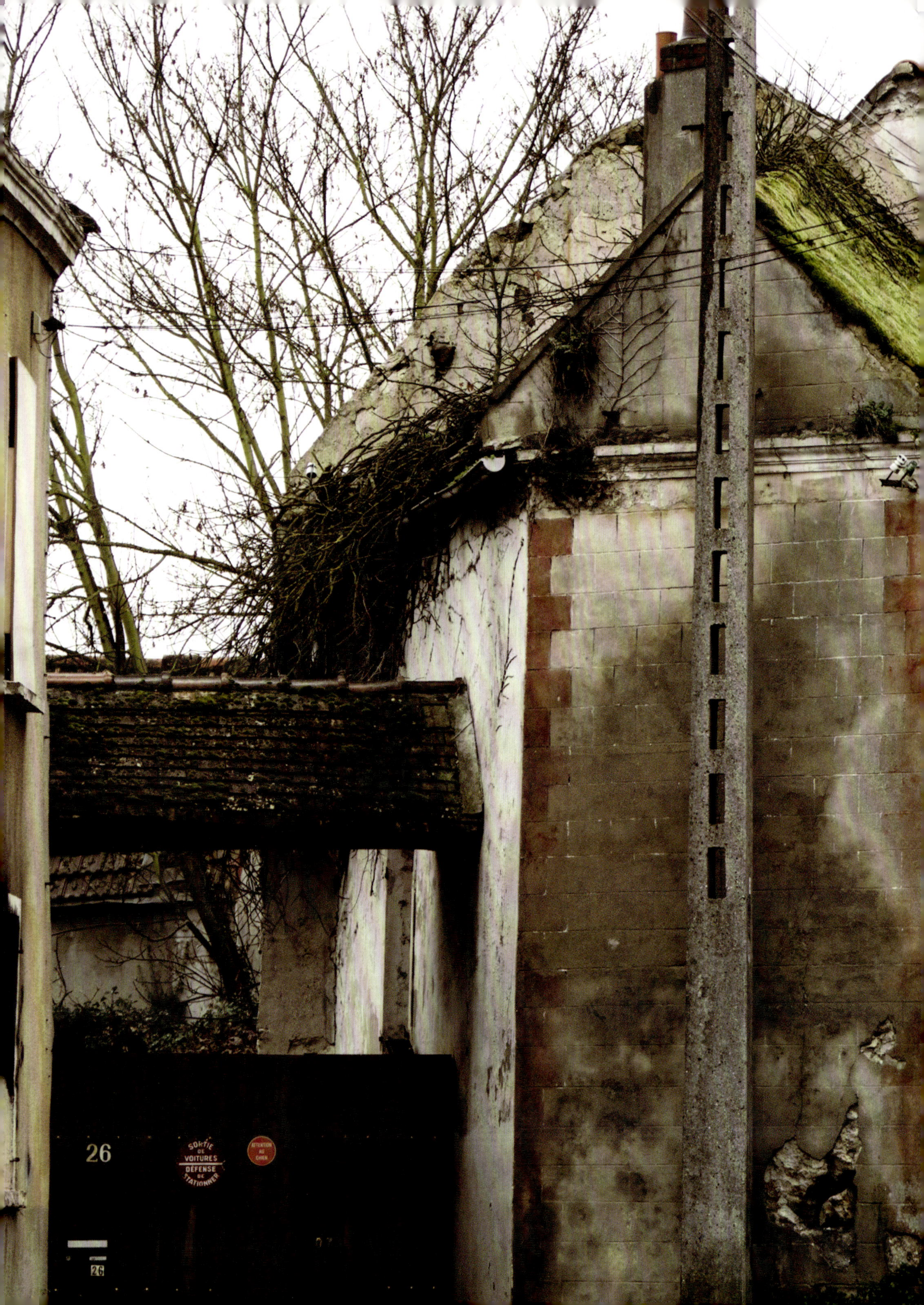
26
SORTIE DE VOITURES
DÉFENSE DE STATIONNER
26

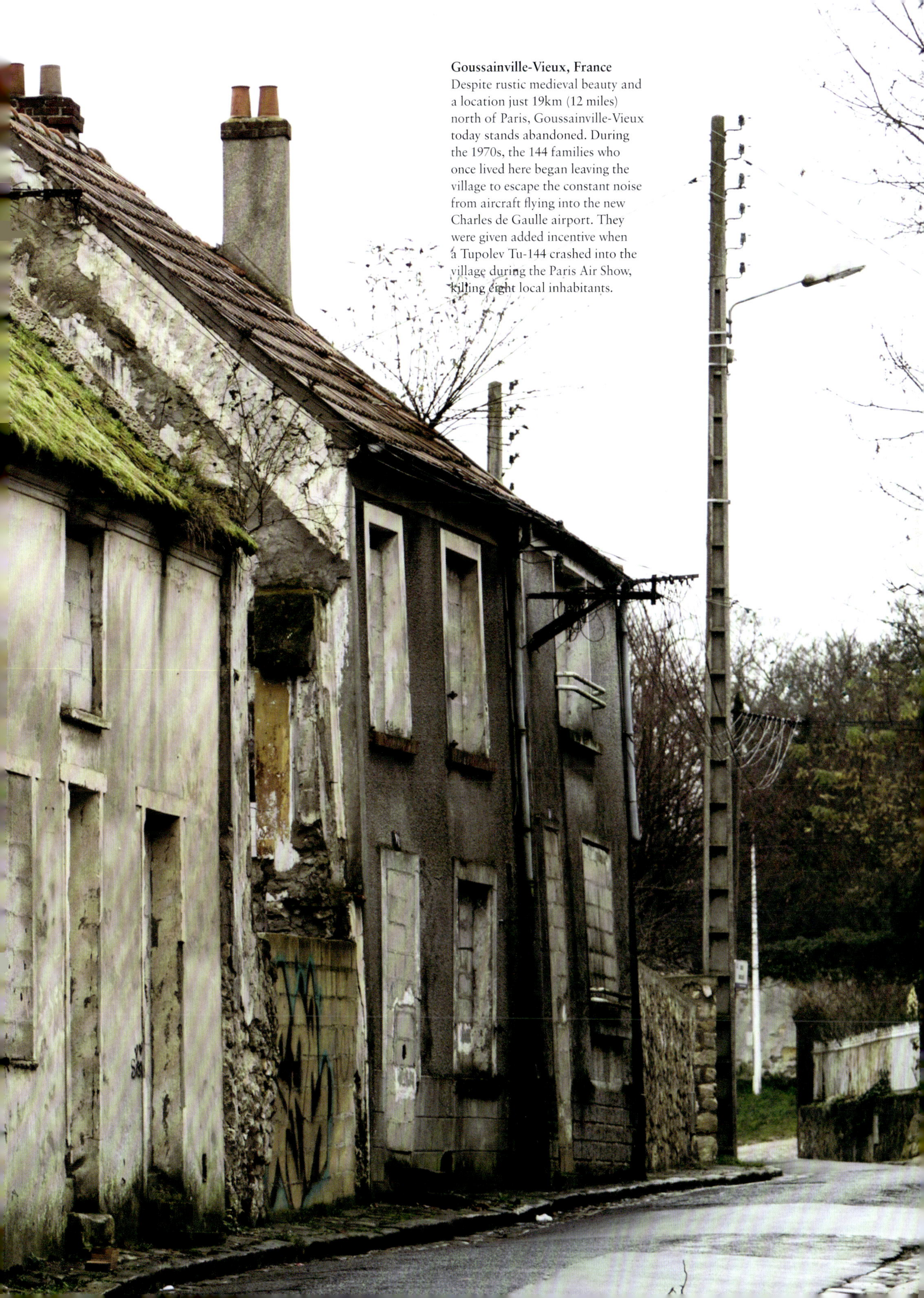

Goussainville-Vieux, France
Despite rustic medieval beauty and a location just 19km (12 miles) north of Paris, Goussainville-Vieux today stands abandoned. During the 1970s, the 144 families who once lived here began leaving the village to escape the constant noise from aircraft flying into the new Charles de Gaulle airport. They were given added incentive when a Tupolev Tu-144 crashed into the village during the Paris Air Show, killing eight local inhabitants.

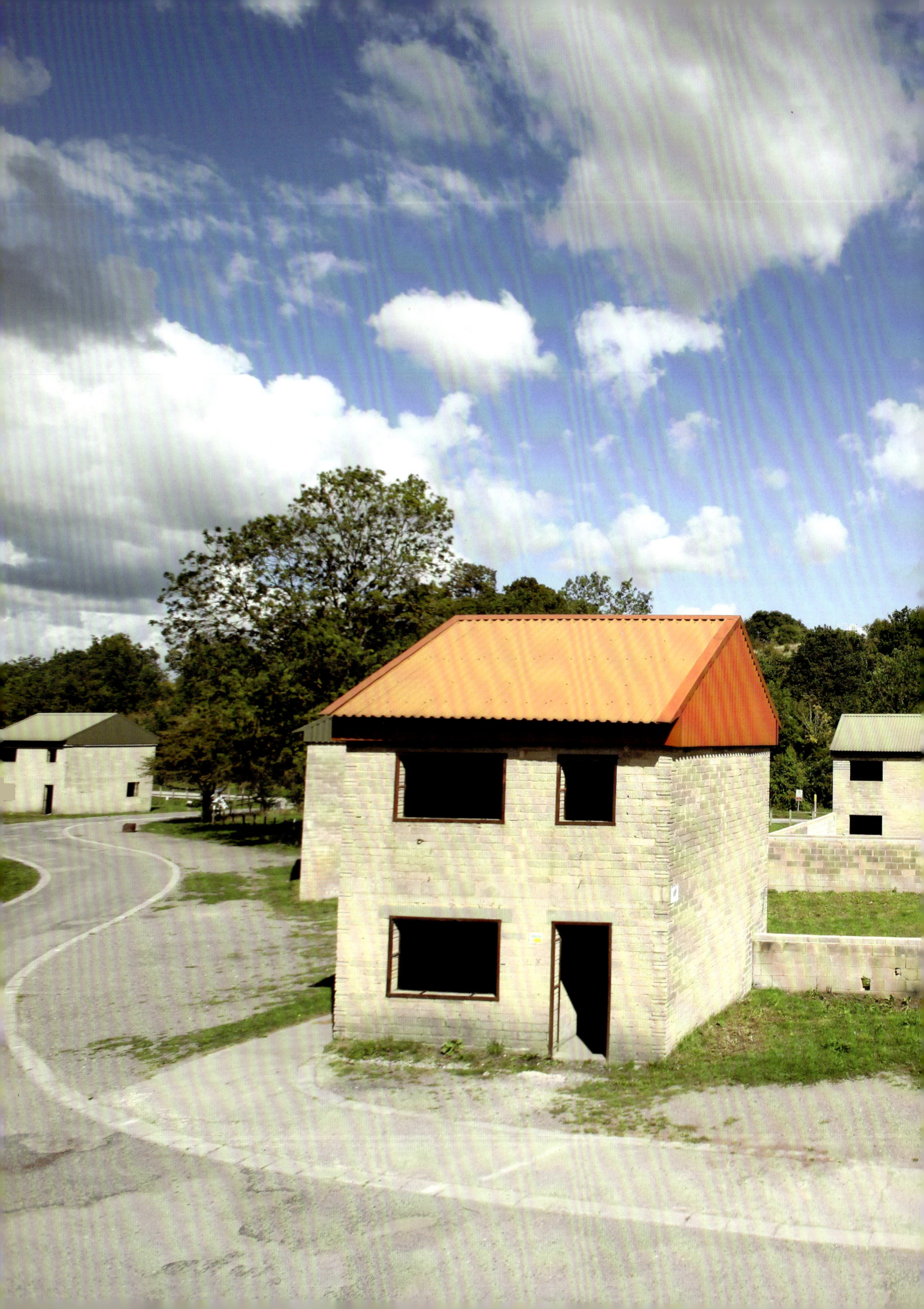

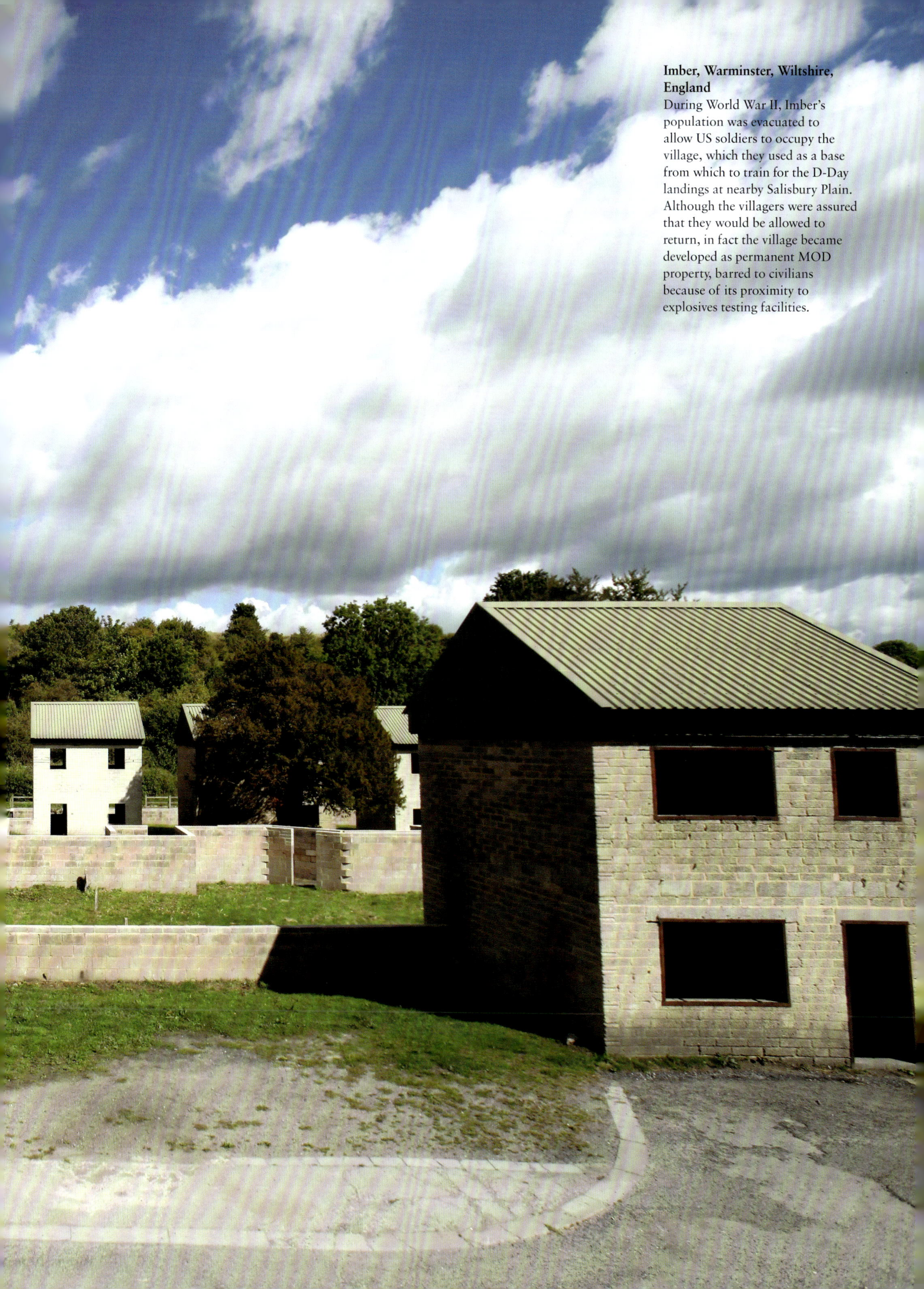

Imber, Warminster, Wiltshire, England
During World War II, Imber's population was evacuated to allow US soldiers to occupy the village, which they used as a base from which to train for the D-Day landings at nearby Salisbury Plain. Although the villagers were assured that they would be allowed to return, in fact the village became developed as permanent MOD property, barred to civilians because of its proximity to explosives testing facilities.

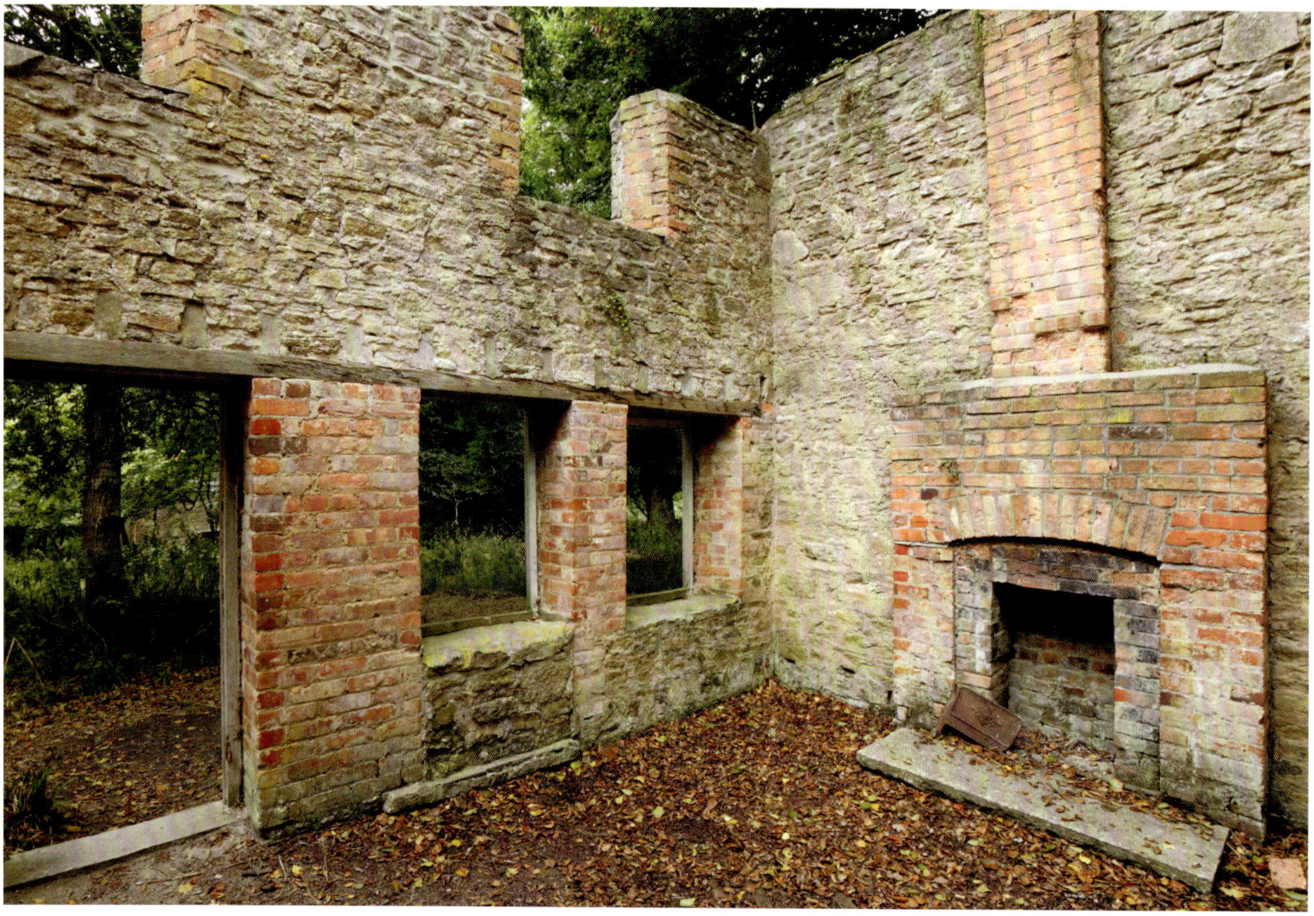

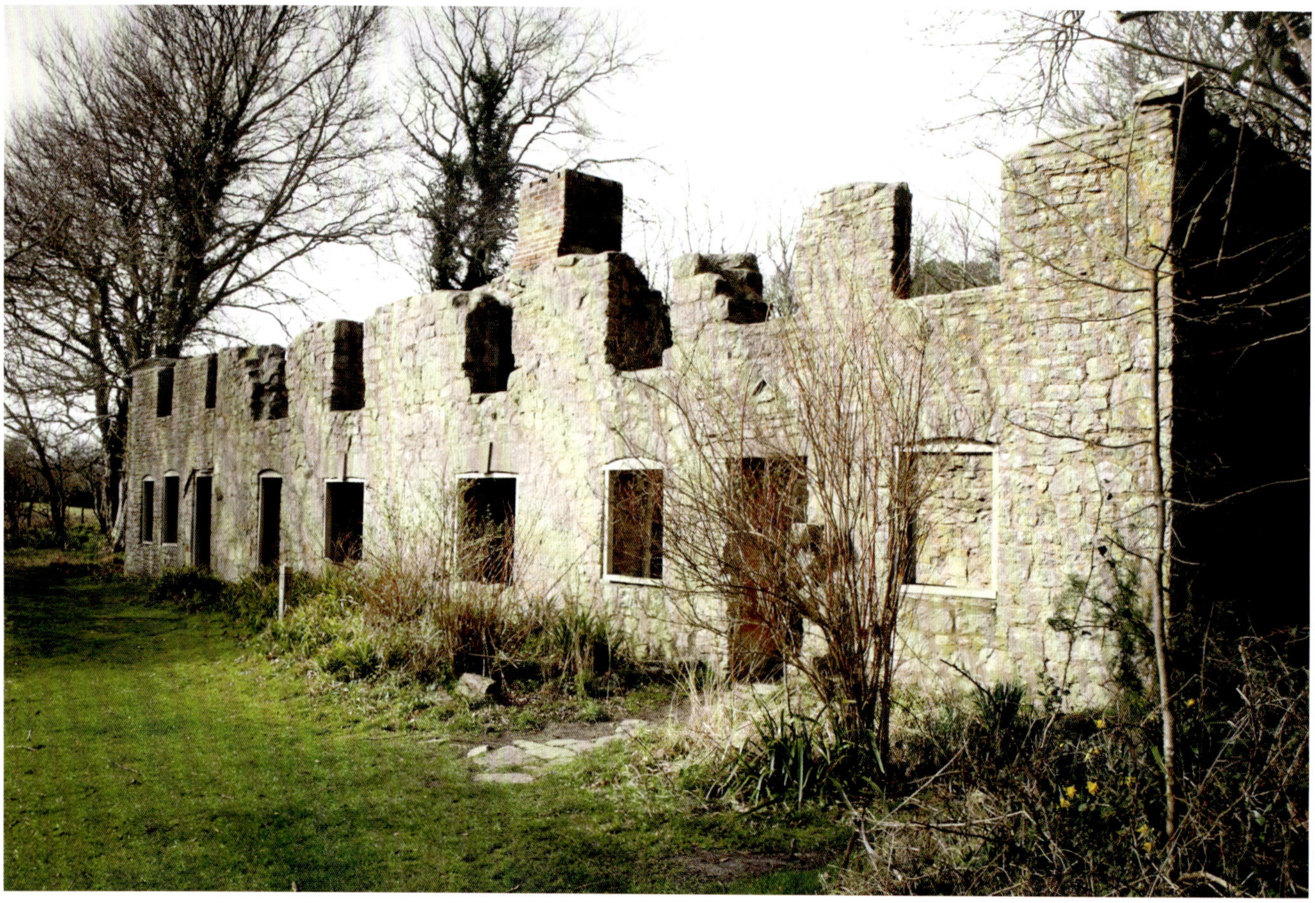

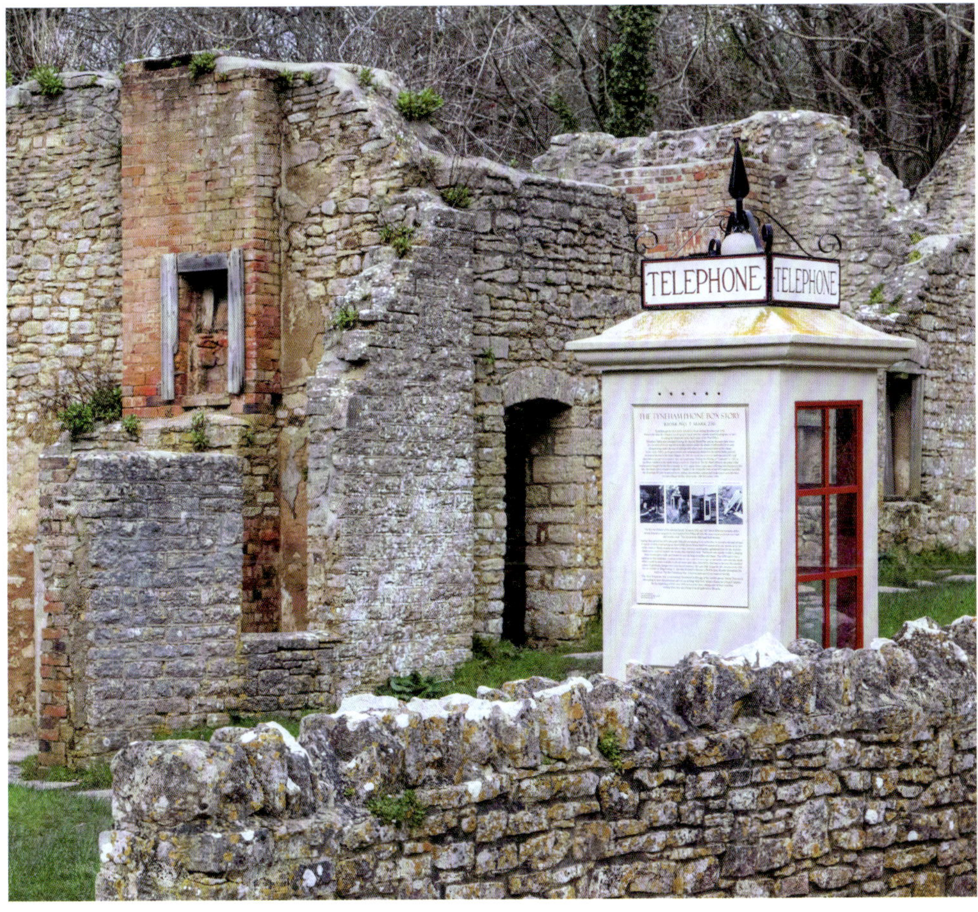

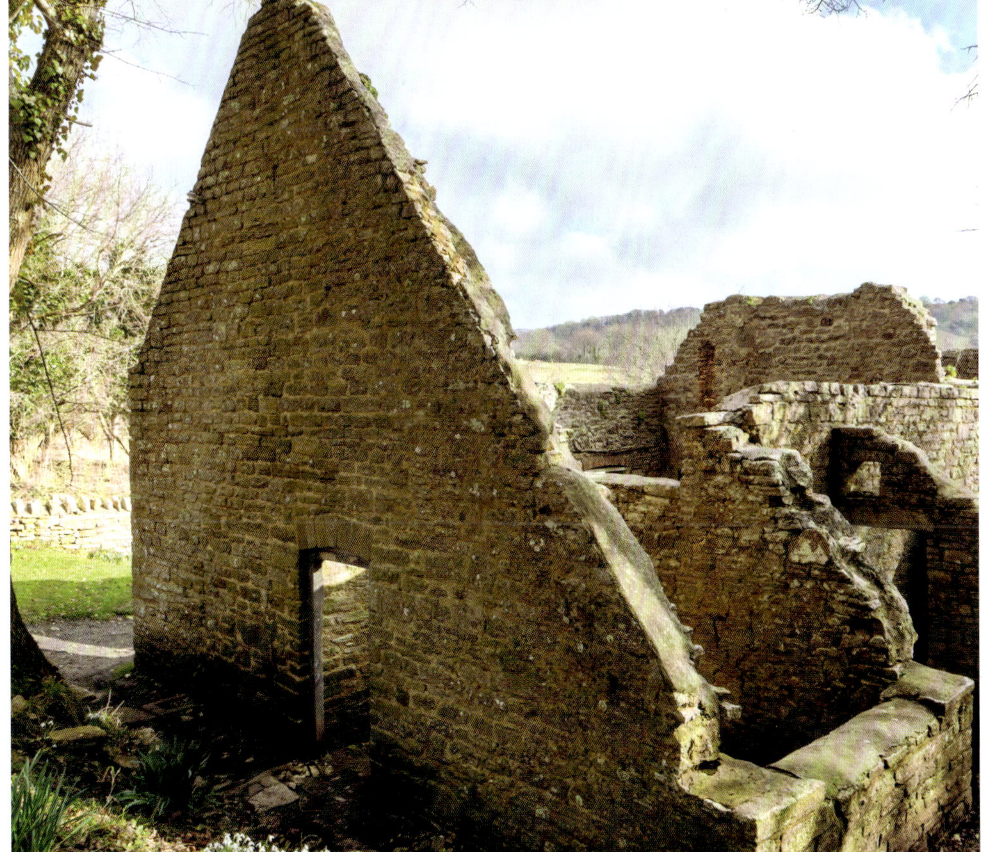

ALL PHOTOGRAPHS:

Tyneham, Dorset, England

Like Imber, the 225 residents of Tyneham had their village requisitioned for military service in 1943, in the run-up to the D-Day landings. Similarly, the village was never returned to civilian ownership following the end of the war, instead becoming a training base for infantry and armour. Here we see aspects of the village cottages, plus some particular features trapped in a time warp – note the now-antiquated telephone box. At the time of their eviction in 1943, Tyneham's residents were given just one month to transplant their lives to other parts of the country. The official government letter to the residents stated that: 'The Government appreciate that this is no small sacrifice which you are asked to make, but they are sure that you will give this further help towards winning the war with a good heart.' The occupants did go, but with every intention of returning. One resident, Helen Taylor, pinned a note to the door of the village church, asking that the new occupants 'Please treat the church and houses with care. We have given up our homes, where many of us have lived for generations, to help win the war to keep men free. We will return one day and thank you for treating the village kindly.' An eventual return was not to be, even after pleas made to the government as late as 1974. The MOD did, however, grant more permissive walking rights and weekend access. Tyneham is now part of the British Army's Armoured Fighting Vehicles Gunnery School.

OVERLEAF:

Pyramiden, Svalbard, Spitsbergen, Norway

Pyramiden was a coal-mining settlement established on the remote arctic archipelago of Svalbard by Sweden in 1910. It was subsequently sold to the Soviets in 1927, and at the height of its productivity the settlement had a population of about 1000 people. By the 1990s, however, the mining there was in decline, and the very last resident left in October 1998.

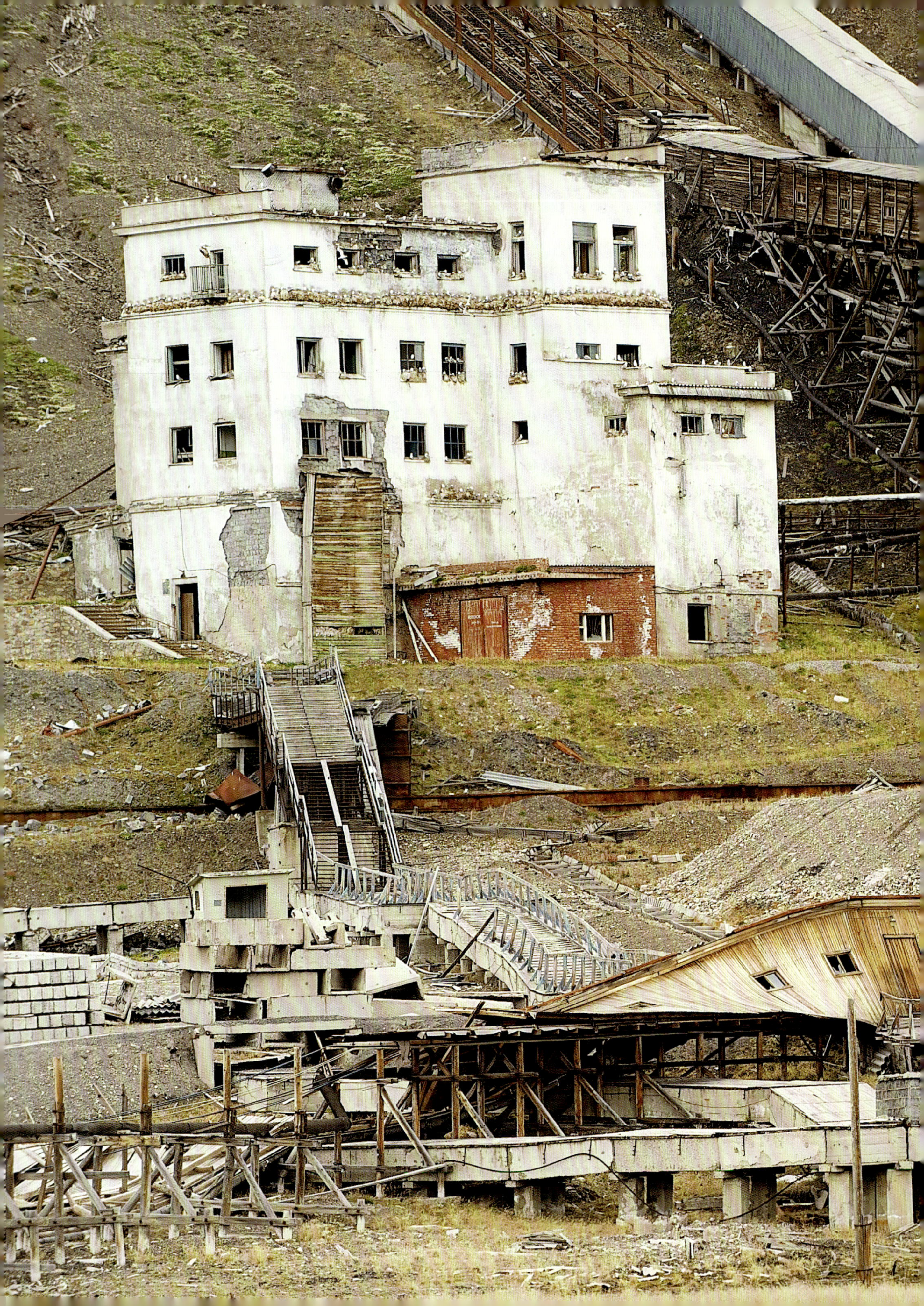

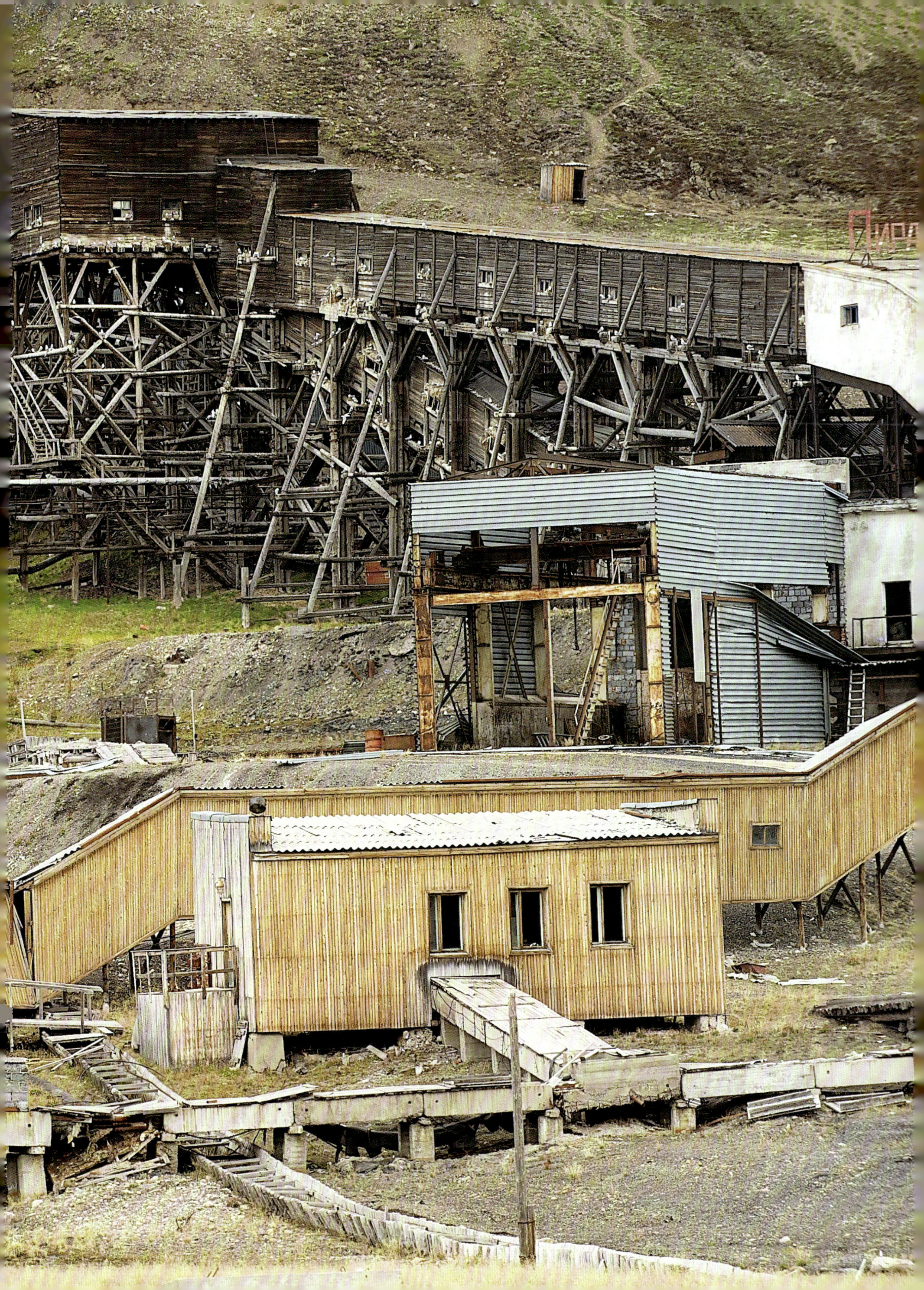

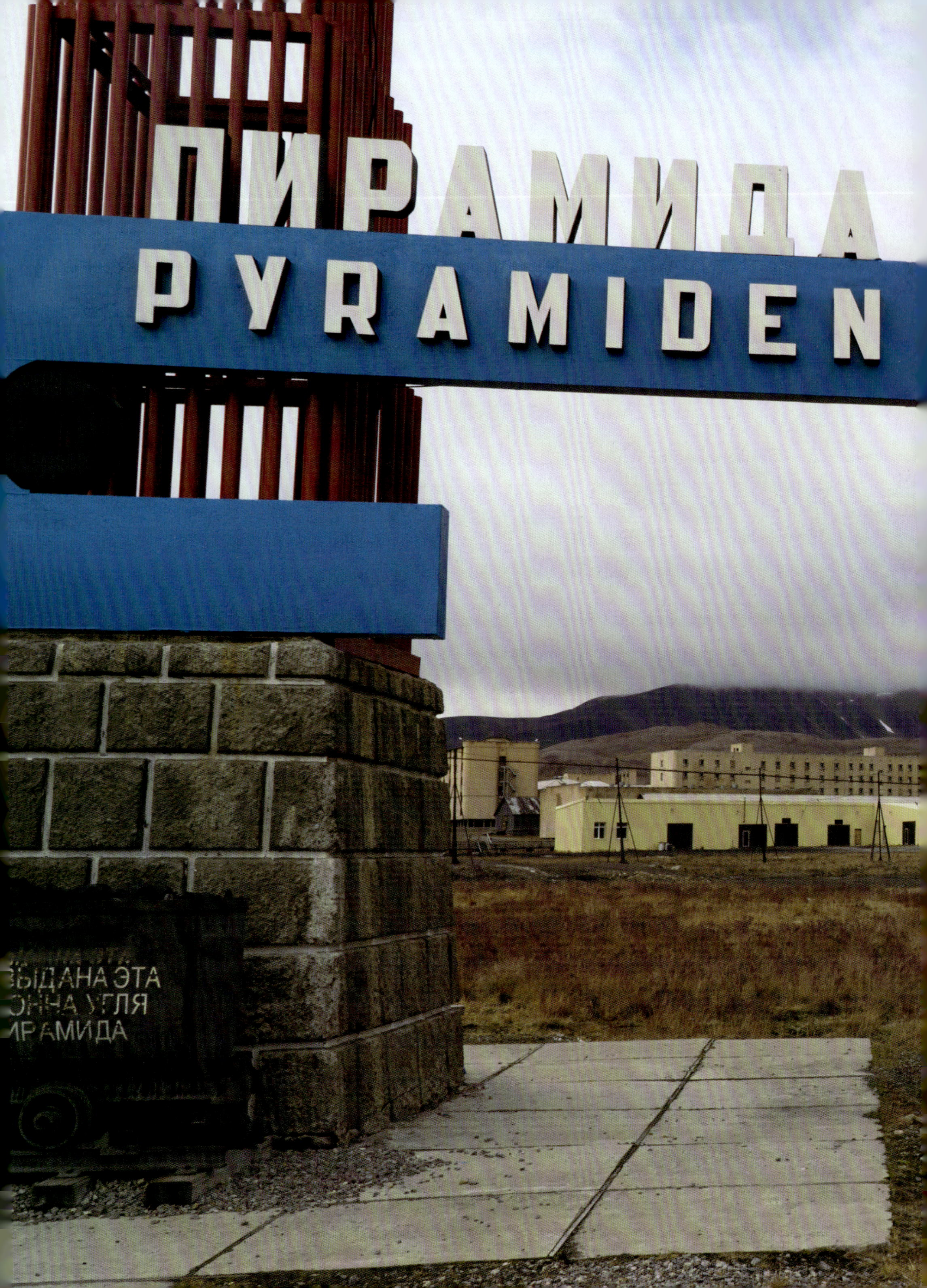
ПИРАМИДА
PYRAMIDEN
ЫДАНА ЭТА
ОННА УГЛЯ
ИРАМИДА

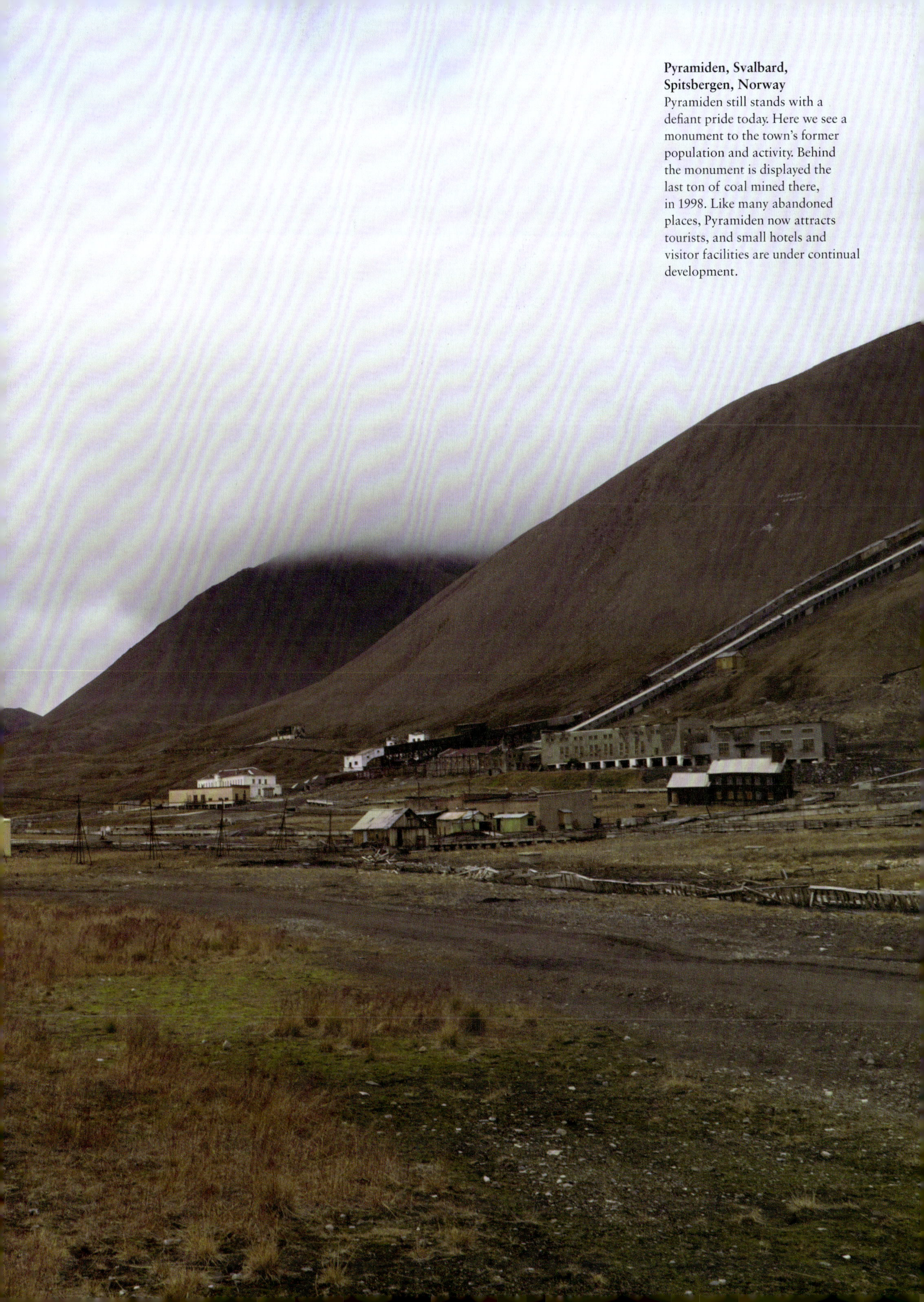

Pyramiden, Svalbard, Spitsbergen, Norway
Pyramiden still stands with a defiant pride today. Here we see a monument to the town's former population and activity. Behind the monument is displayed the last ton of coal mined there, in 1998. Like many abandoned places, Pyramiden now attracts tourists, and small hotels and visitor facilities are under continual development.

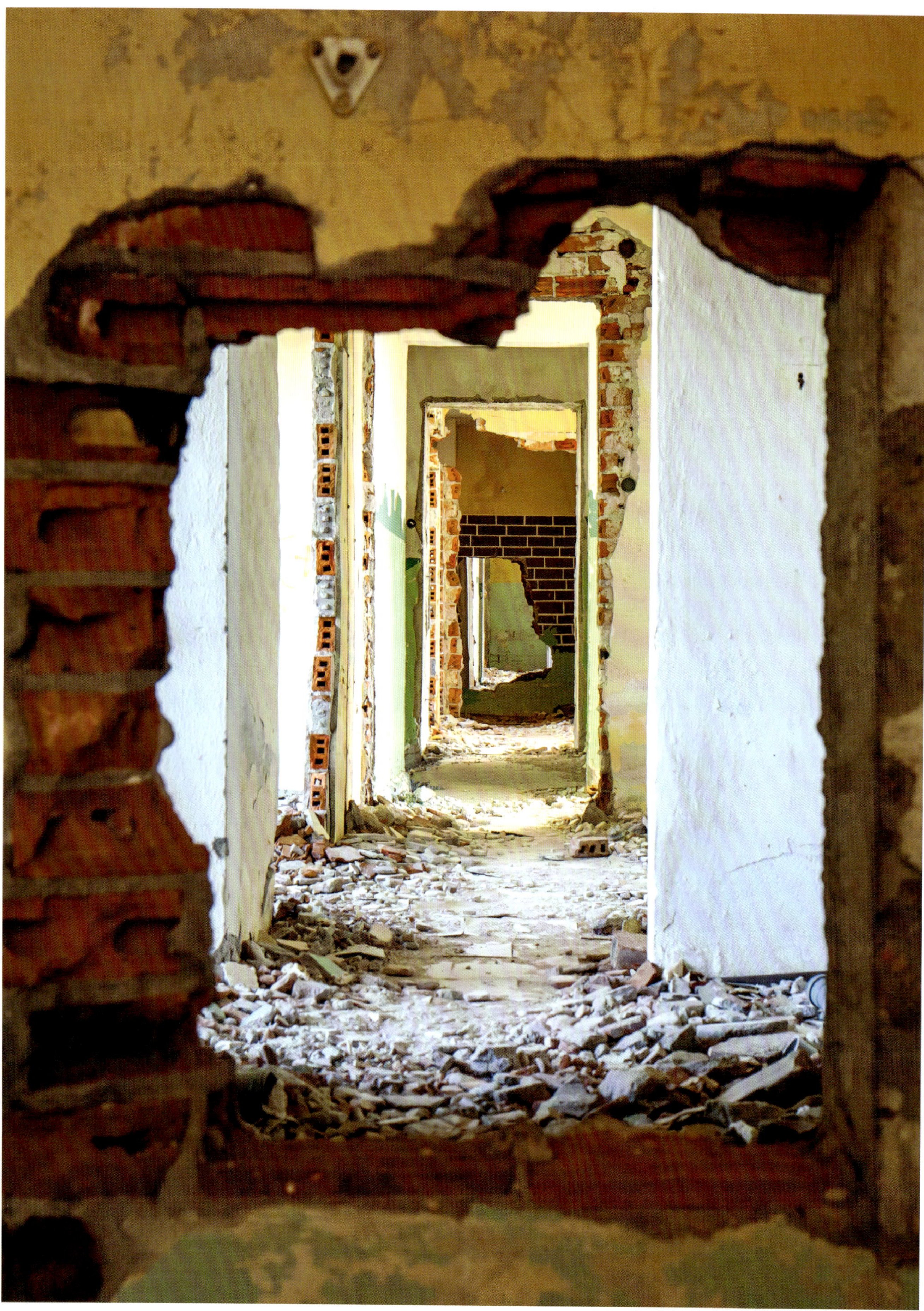

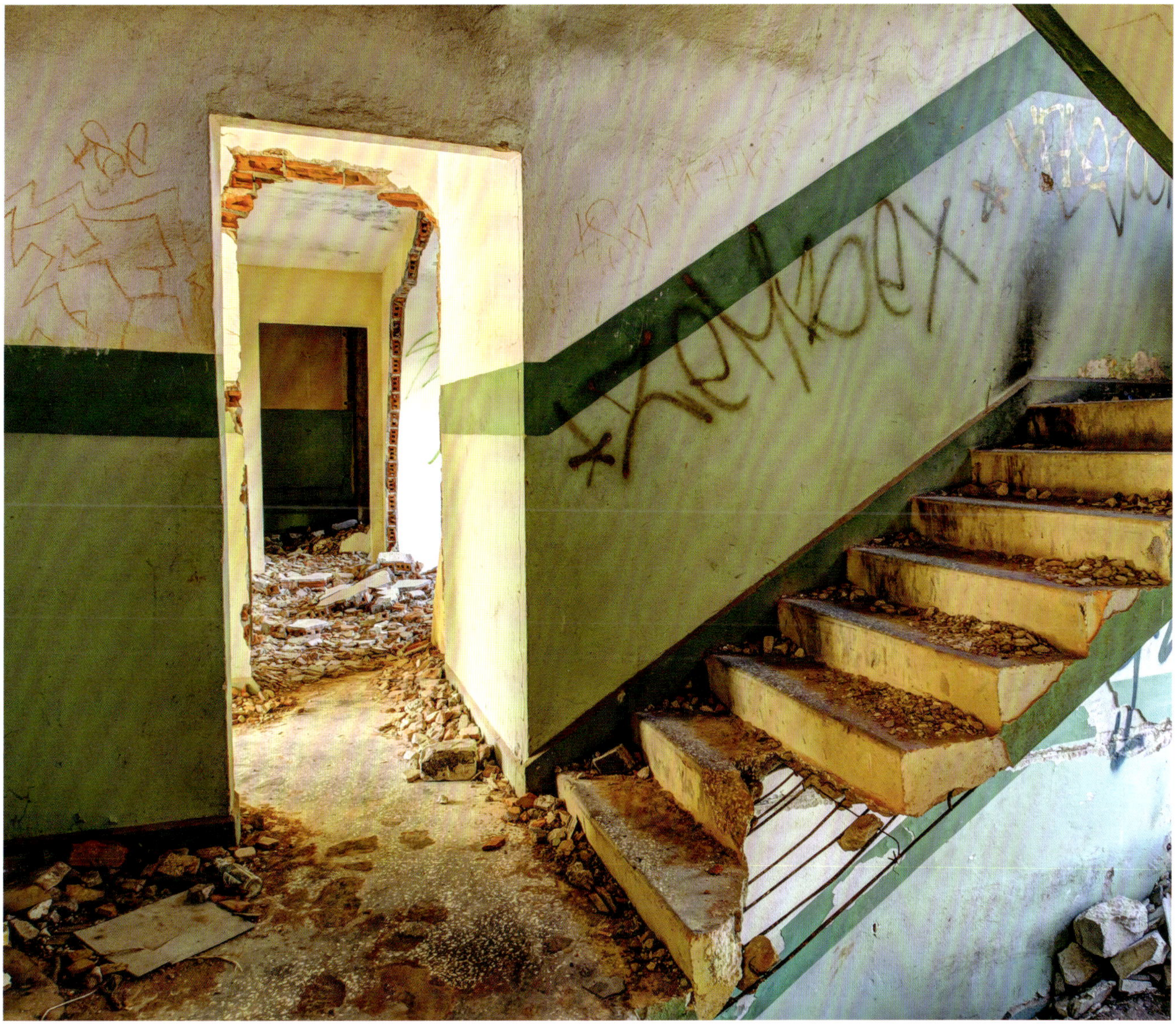

ALL PHOTOGRAPHS:

Kłomino, Poland

Located near Szczecinek in north-western Poland, Kłomino acts as another ghostly monument to Poland's harrowing past in World War II and the communist era. During the war, it was occupied by the Germans, who called it Westfalenhof and who used it both as a garrison town and as the location for a POW camp for Polish and French prisoners. Following the town's liberation by the Soviets in 1945, it became an official Red Army base, but was finally abandoned by the military in 1993. The Polish government's attempts to bring in new buyers and developers have so far proved to be unfruitful.

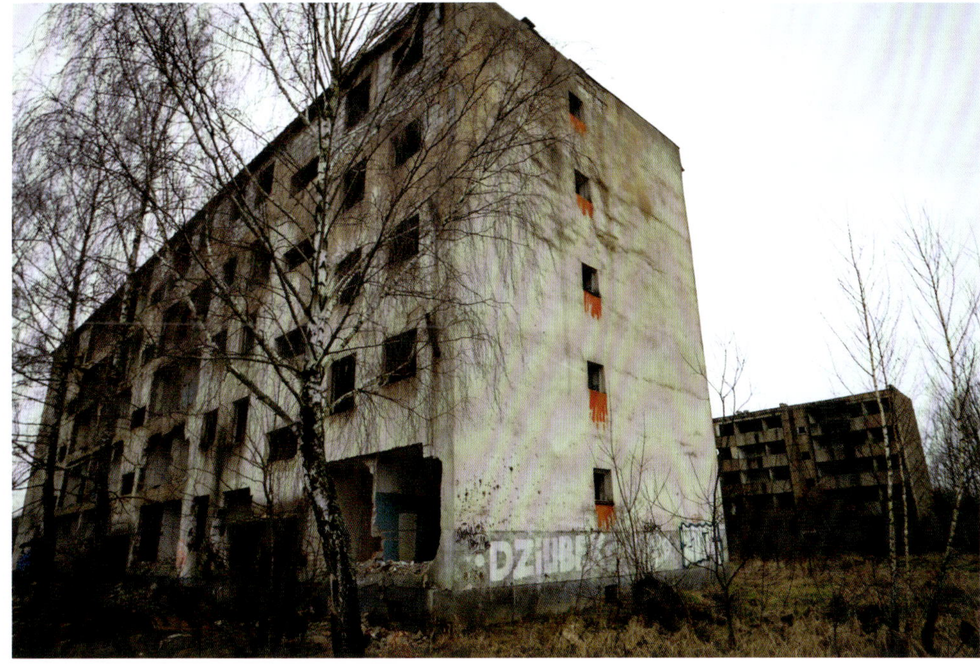

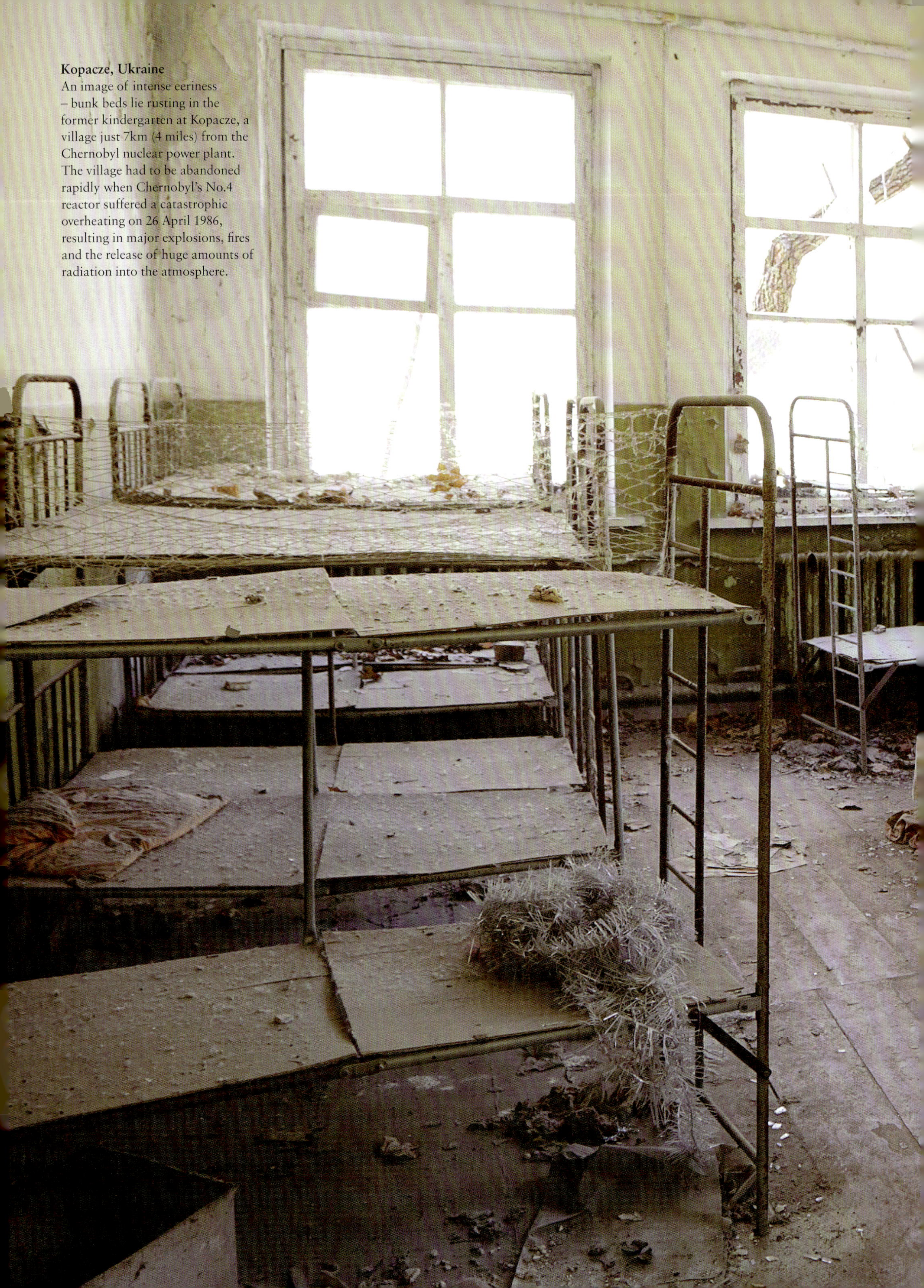

Kopacze, Ukraine
An image of intense eeriness – bunk beds lie rusting in the former kindergarten at Kopacze, a village just 7km (4 miles) from the Chernobyl nuclear power plant. The village had to be abandoned rapidly when Chernobyl's No.4 reactor suffered a catastrophic overheating on 26 April 1986, resulting in major explosions, fires and the release of huge amounts of radiation into the atmosphere.

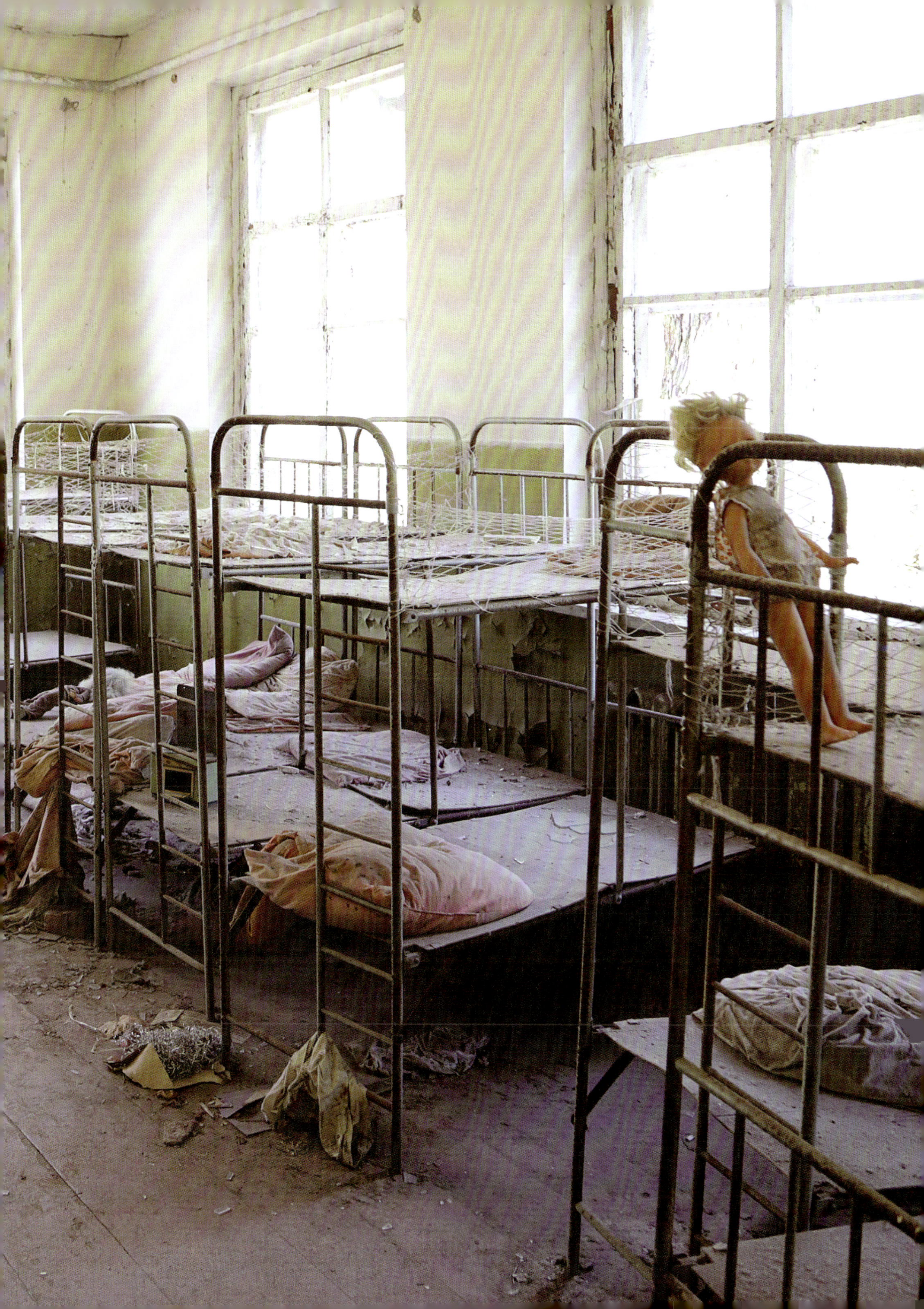

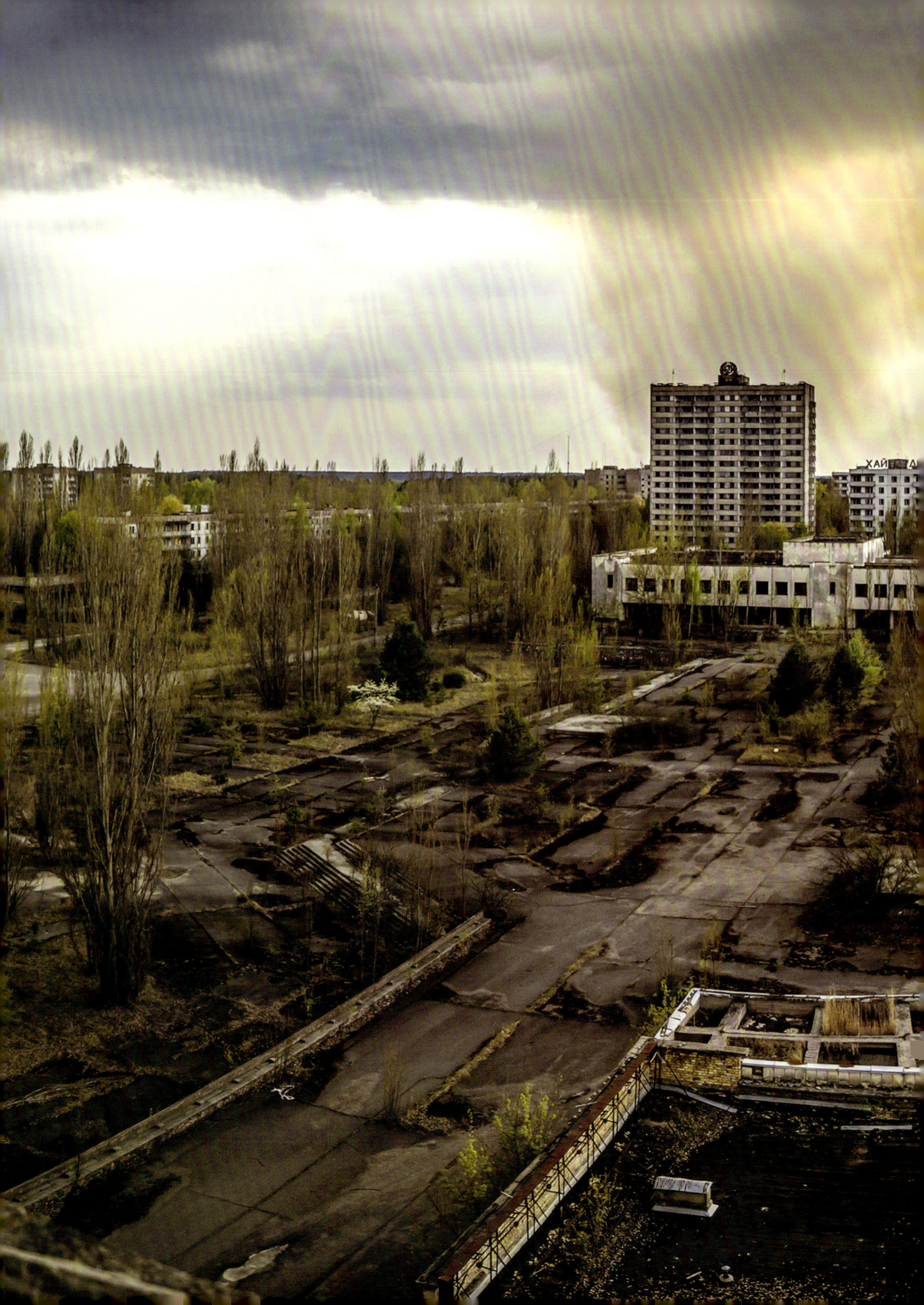

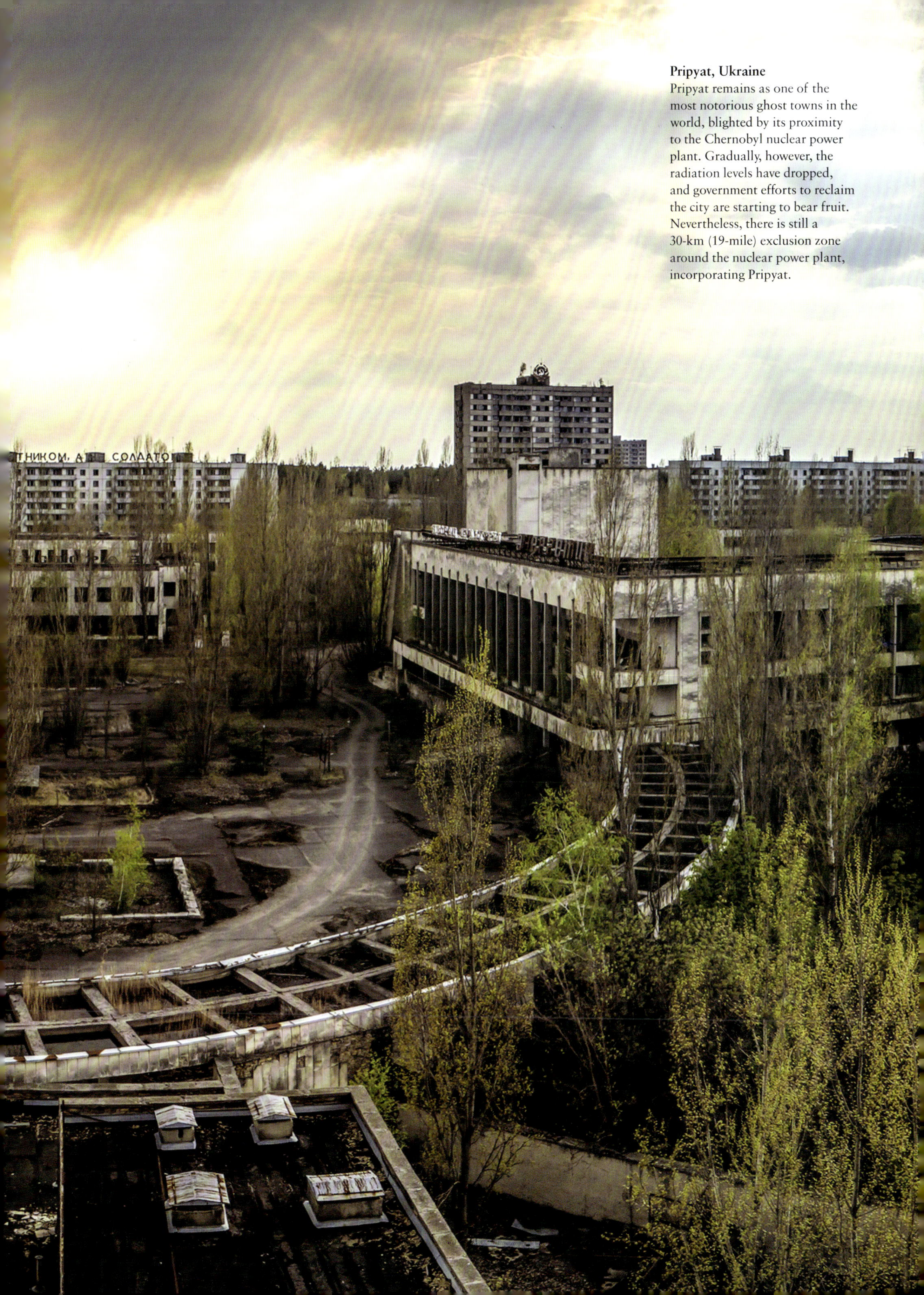

Pripyat, Ukraine
Pripyat remains as one of the most notorious ghost towns in the world, blighted by its proximity to the Chernobyl nuclear power plant. Gradually, however, the radiation levels have dropped, and government efforts to reclaim the city are starting to bear fruit. Nevertheless, there is still a 30-km (19-mile) exclusion zone around the nuclear power plant, incorporating Pripyat.

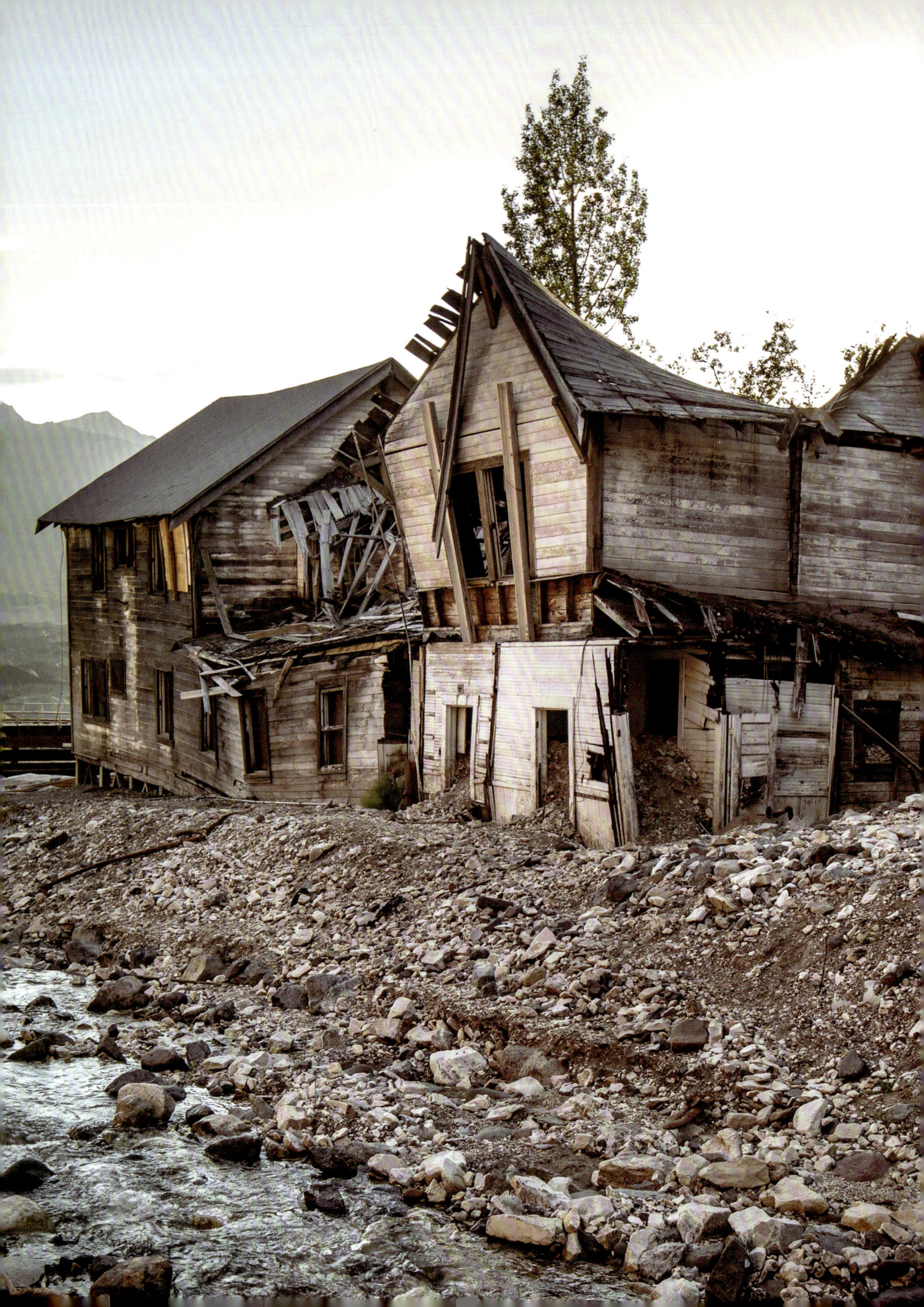

North America

The ghost towns featured in this chapter seem to attest to both the reality of what we call the 'American Dream', but also the fragility and temporal nature of that vision. Many of the habitations explored here were born in a sudden frenzy of commercial activity and self-belief, either through the discovery of gold or silver or via the arrival of the great railroad network connecting the continent. For a brief period, usually measured in less than a century, these communities burned hot and bright in a beautiful but unforgiving wilderness. Fortunes were made by some, livings by most others, but then the reckoning came. The gold and silver deposits were mined out; natural disasters – slow or sudden – forced weary rebuilding; rail and road routes were diverted, and sheer hard living made inhabitants seek easier days elsewhere. Living towns thus became ghost towns. Yet today's ghost towns still speak a powerful message. On one level they act as a cautionary tale, showing that while economic vitality might seem permanent for those living through it, in reality time keeps working away underneath, changing fortunes for better and for worse. Particularly in North America, however, the ghost towns also seem to show how this is a continent forged by commercial drive and optimism. For in the most difficult and unpromising locations, people built lives and homes, and so demonstrated the product of sheer will power.

LEFT:
Kennecott Mines, Valdez-Cordova, Alaska, USA
Kennecott Mines was a remote copper-mining outpost in Alaska, with a total of five mines run by the Kennecott Mining Corporation. Established in 1903, the settlement was populated by miners and mill operators, attracted by higher-than-average wages. By the late 1930s, however, the area was mined out and the town was abandoned.

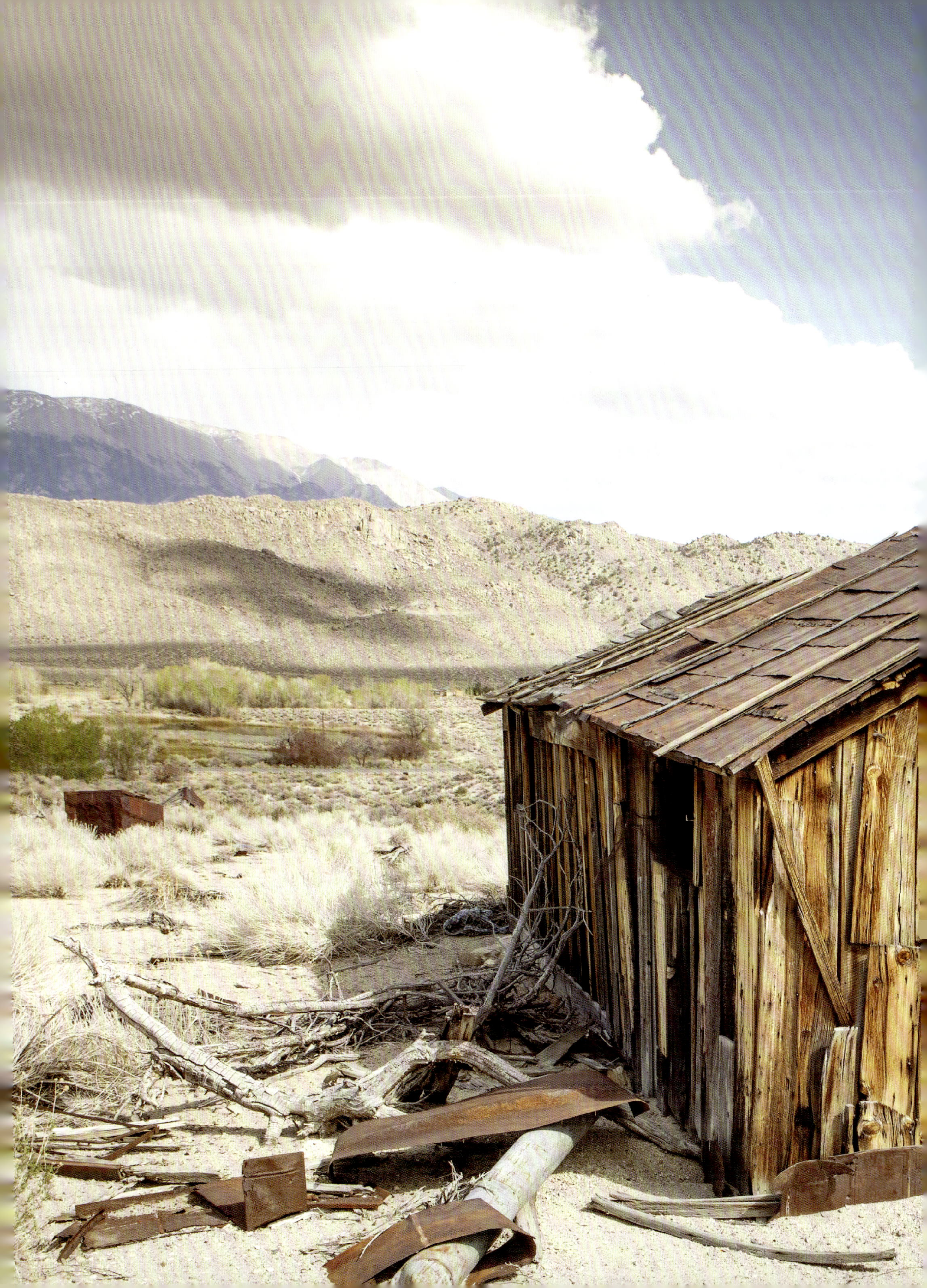

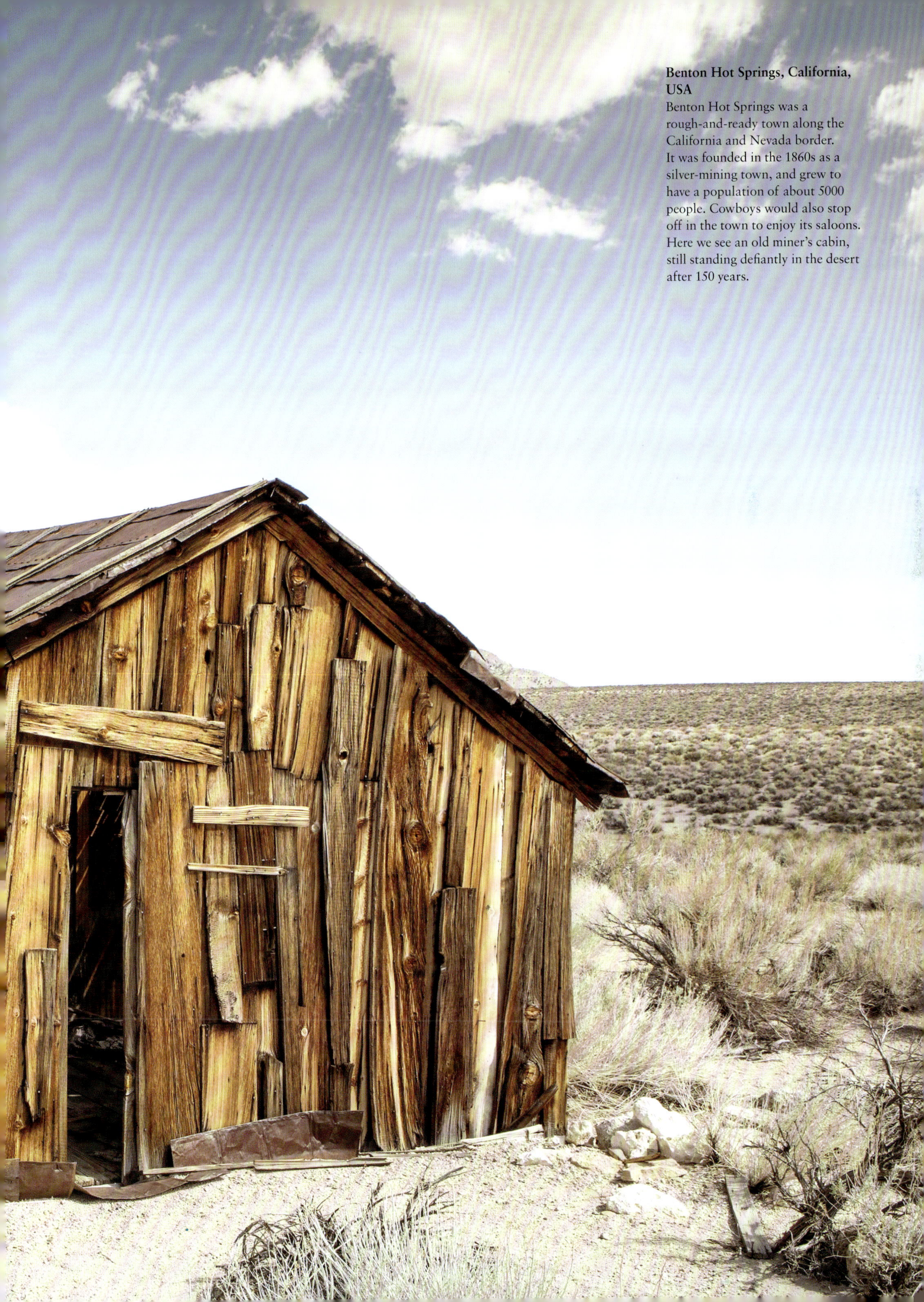

Benton Hot Springs, California, USA

Benton Hot Springs was a rough-and-ready town along the California and Nevada border. It was founded in the 1860s as a silver-mining town, and grew to have a population of about 5000 people. Cowboys would also stop off in the town to enjoy its saloons. Here we see an old miner's cabin, still standing defiantly in the desert after 150 years.

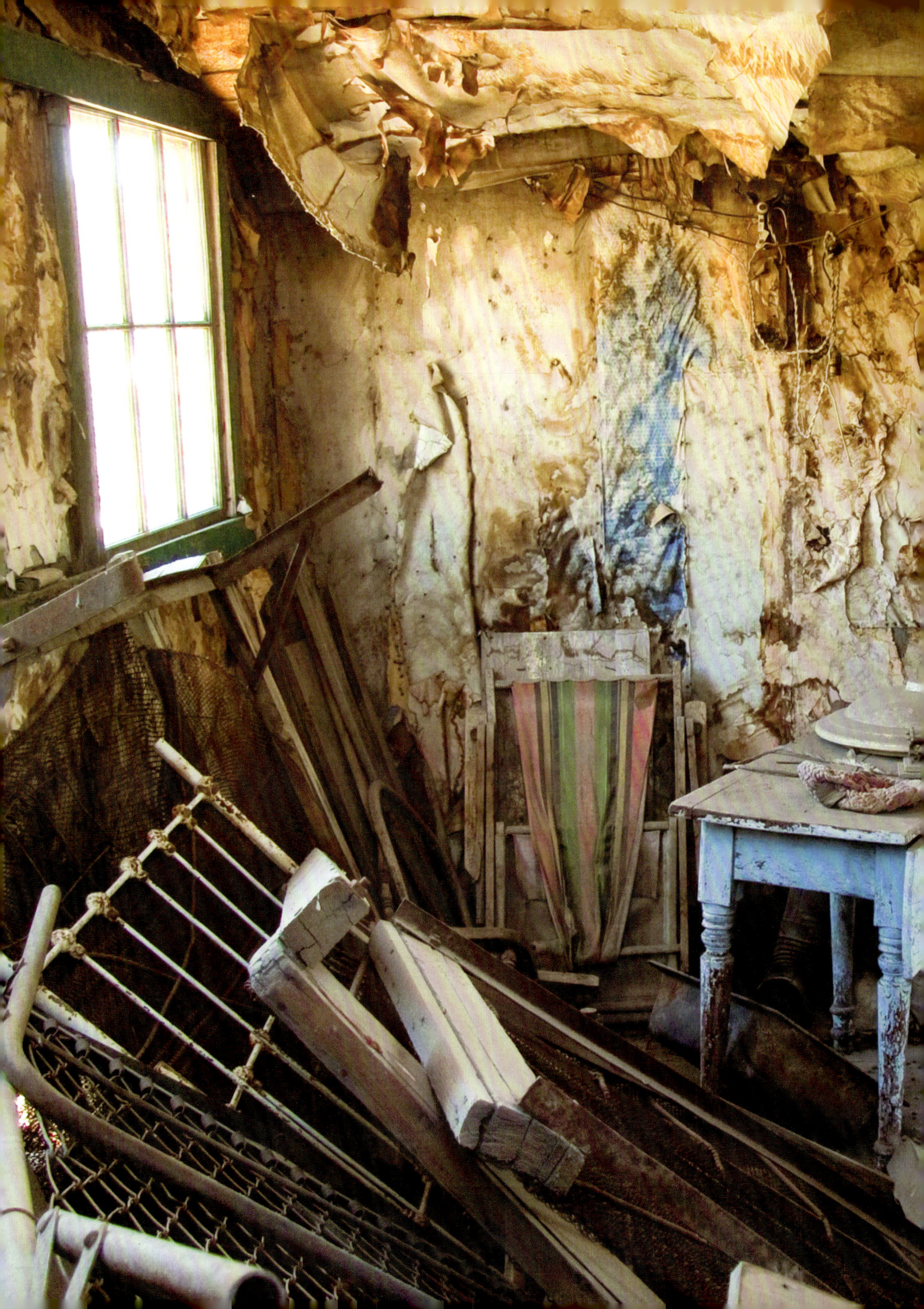

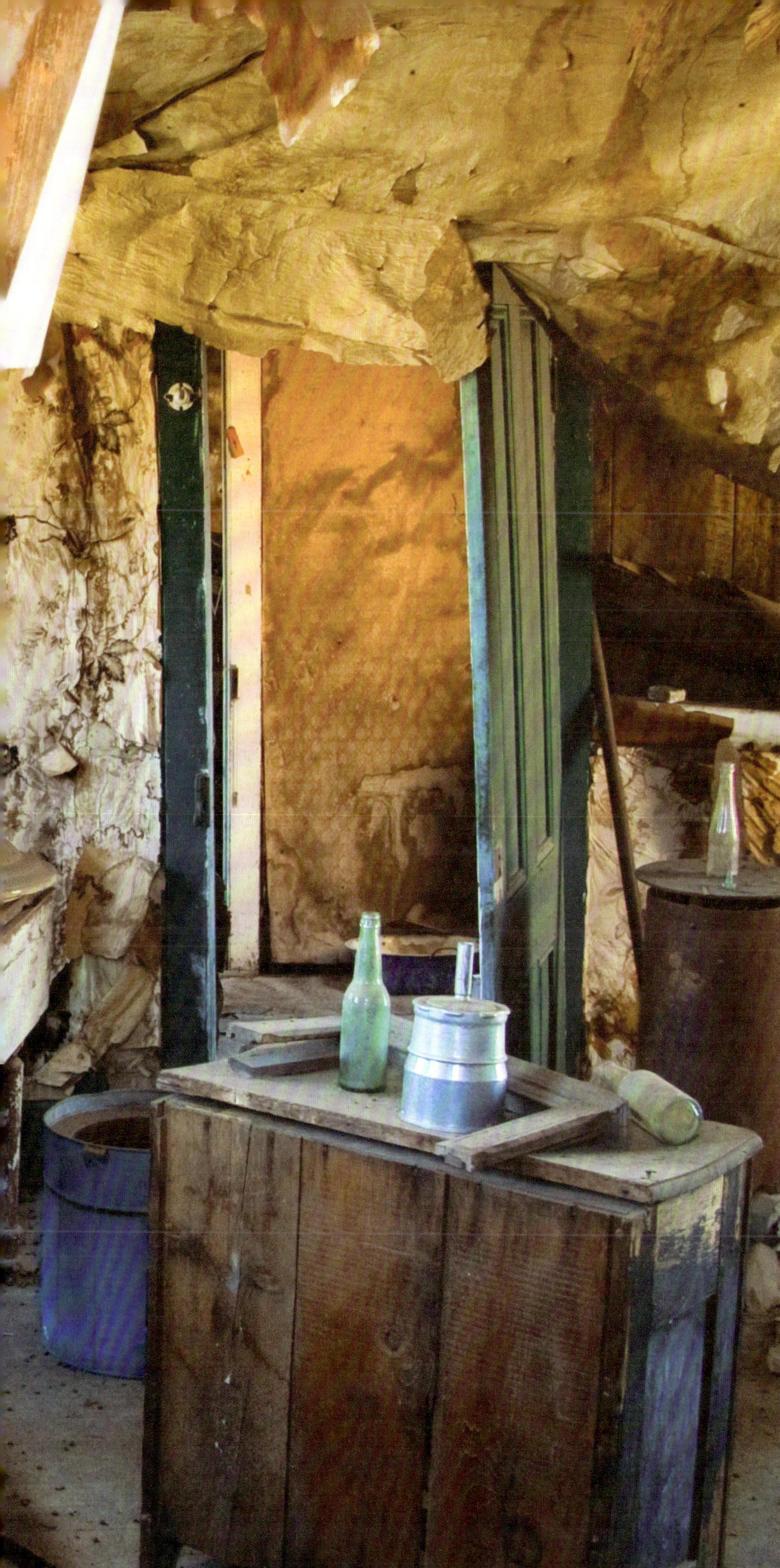

Drawbridge, San Francisco Bay, California, USA
Drawbridge was one of the numerous towns that sprang up along North America's spreading railroad network during the 19th century. This particular town was founded in 1876 by the South Pacific Coast Railroad on Station Island in southern San Francisco Bay. Drawbridge had a lawless feel for much of its history, home to brothels, speakeasies (in defiance of the Prohibition era) and heavily armed citizens.

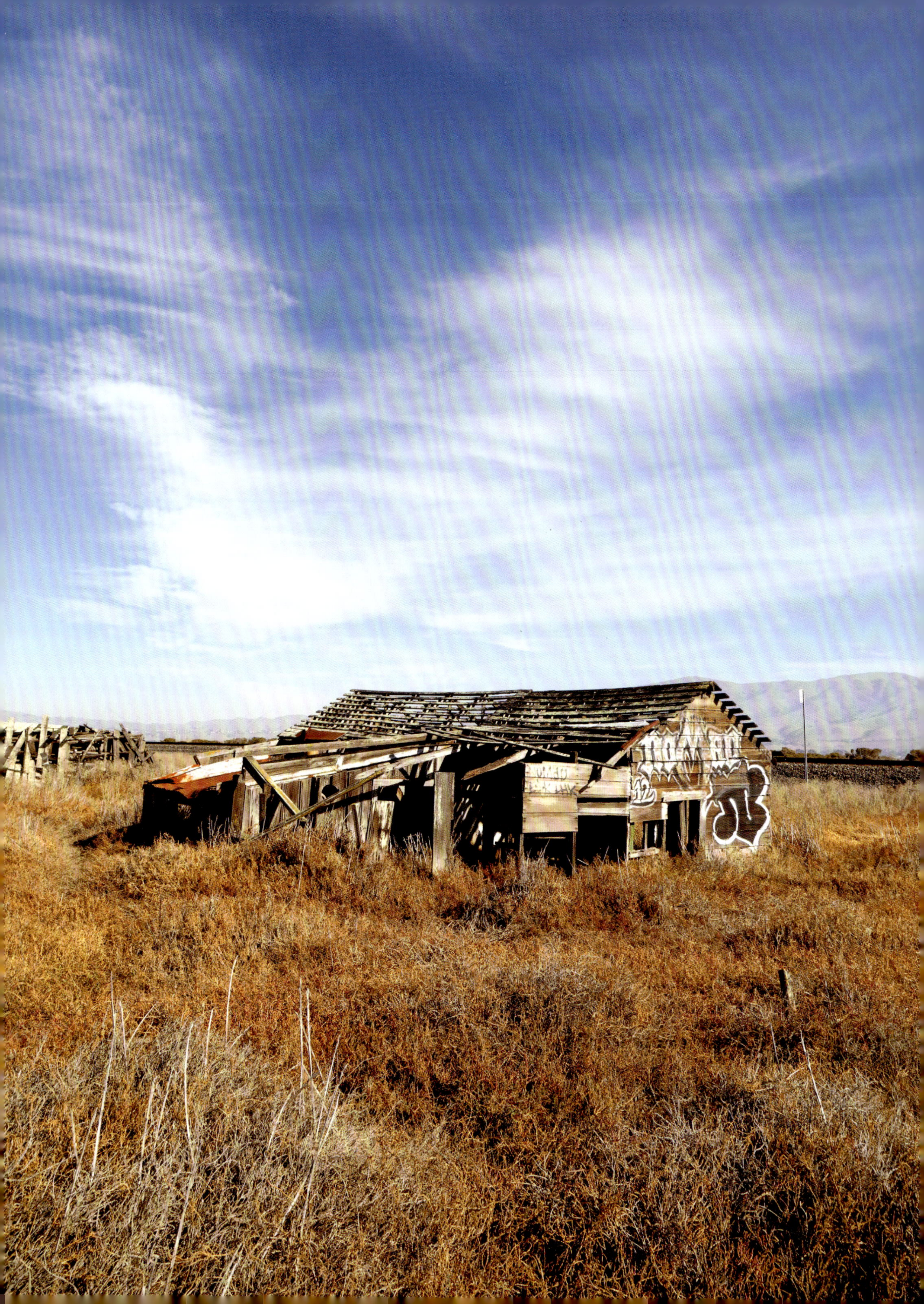

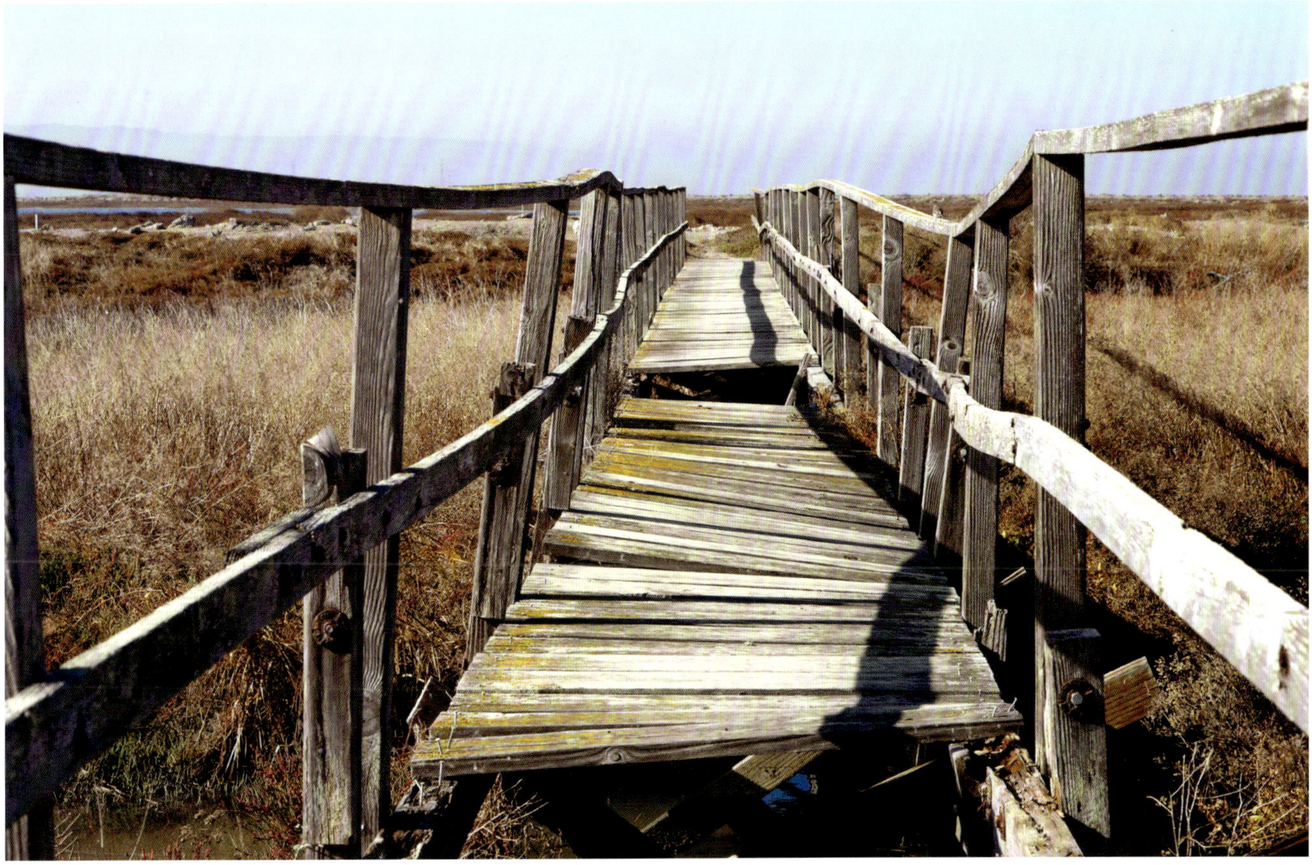

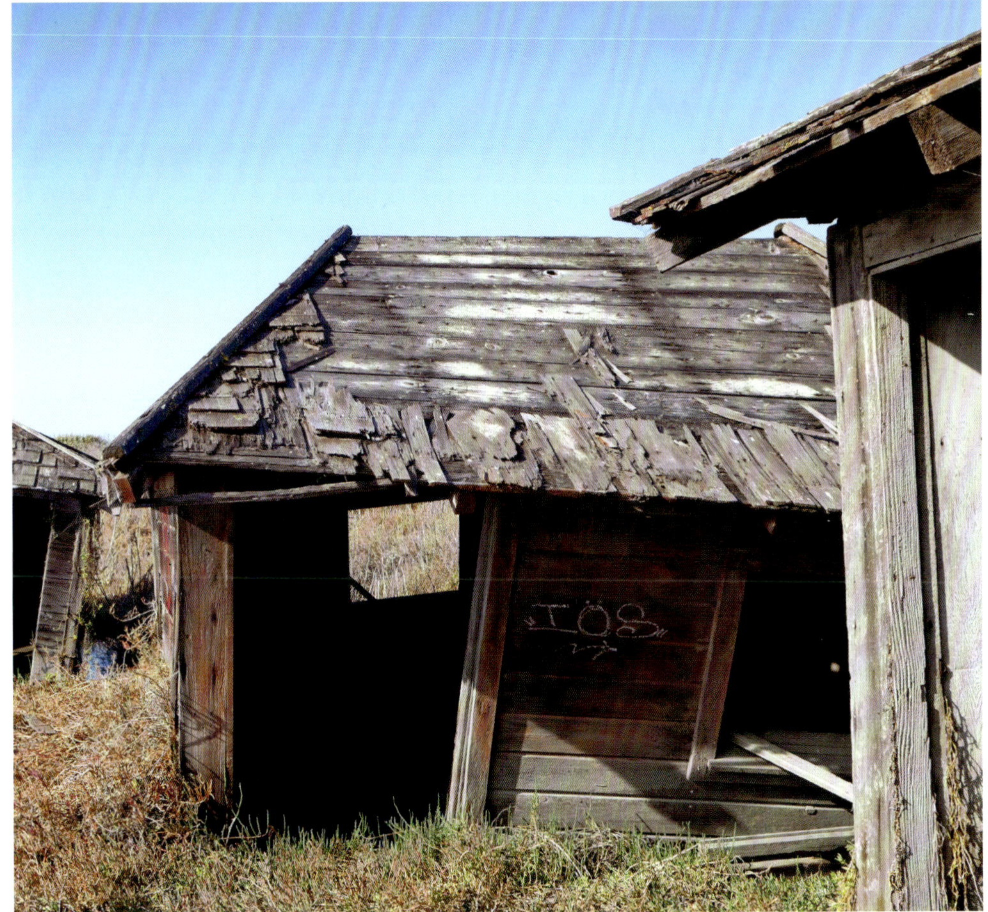

OPPOSITE:

Drawbridge, San Francisco Bay, California, USA

An abandoned shack in Drawbridge. With the end of Prohibition, the town was robbed of much of its appeal and its population steadily declined to nothing. The marshland on which the town was built is gradually absorbing the buildings.

ABOVE:

Drawbridge, San Francisco Bay, California, USA

A ramshackle footbridge ambles across the marshland at Drawbridge. To this day, the only route in and out of Drawbridge is along the railroad tracks.

LEFT:

Drawbridge, San Francisco Bay, California, USA

Another of the abandoned shacks at Drawbridge. It is difficult today to see the former vitality of this settlement. At the peak of its energy in the 1880s, the trains would bring about 1000 people into the town every weekend, giving the settlement a reputation for partying.

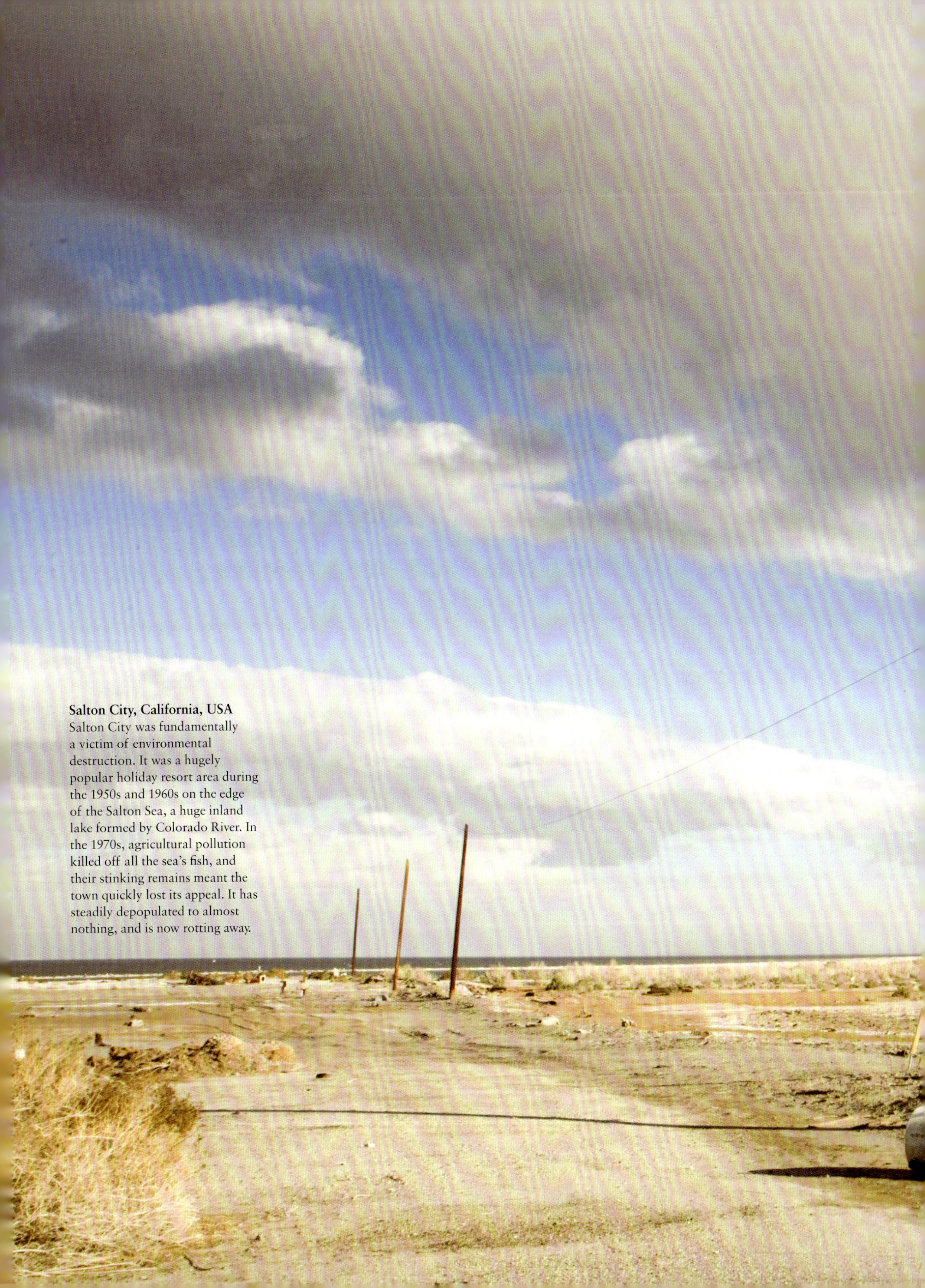

Salton City, California, USA
Salton City was fundamentally a victim of environmental destruction. It was a hugely popular holiday resort area during the 1950s and 1960s on the edge of the Salton Sea, a huge inland lake formed by Colorado River. In the 1970s, agricultural pollution killed off all the sea's fish, and their stinking remains meant the town quickly lost its appeal. It has steadily depopulated to almost nothing, and is now rotting away.

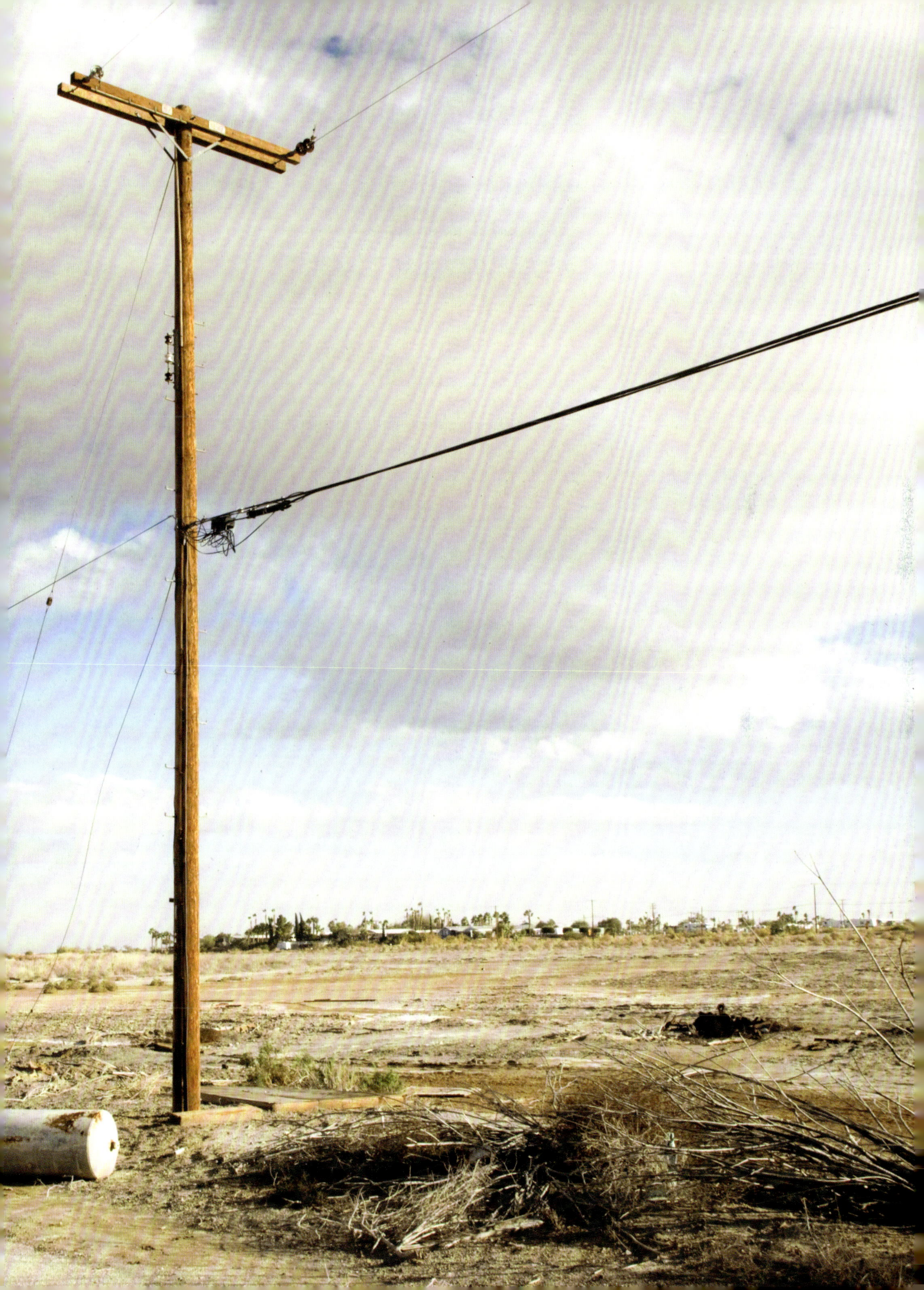

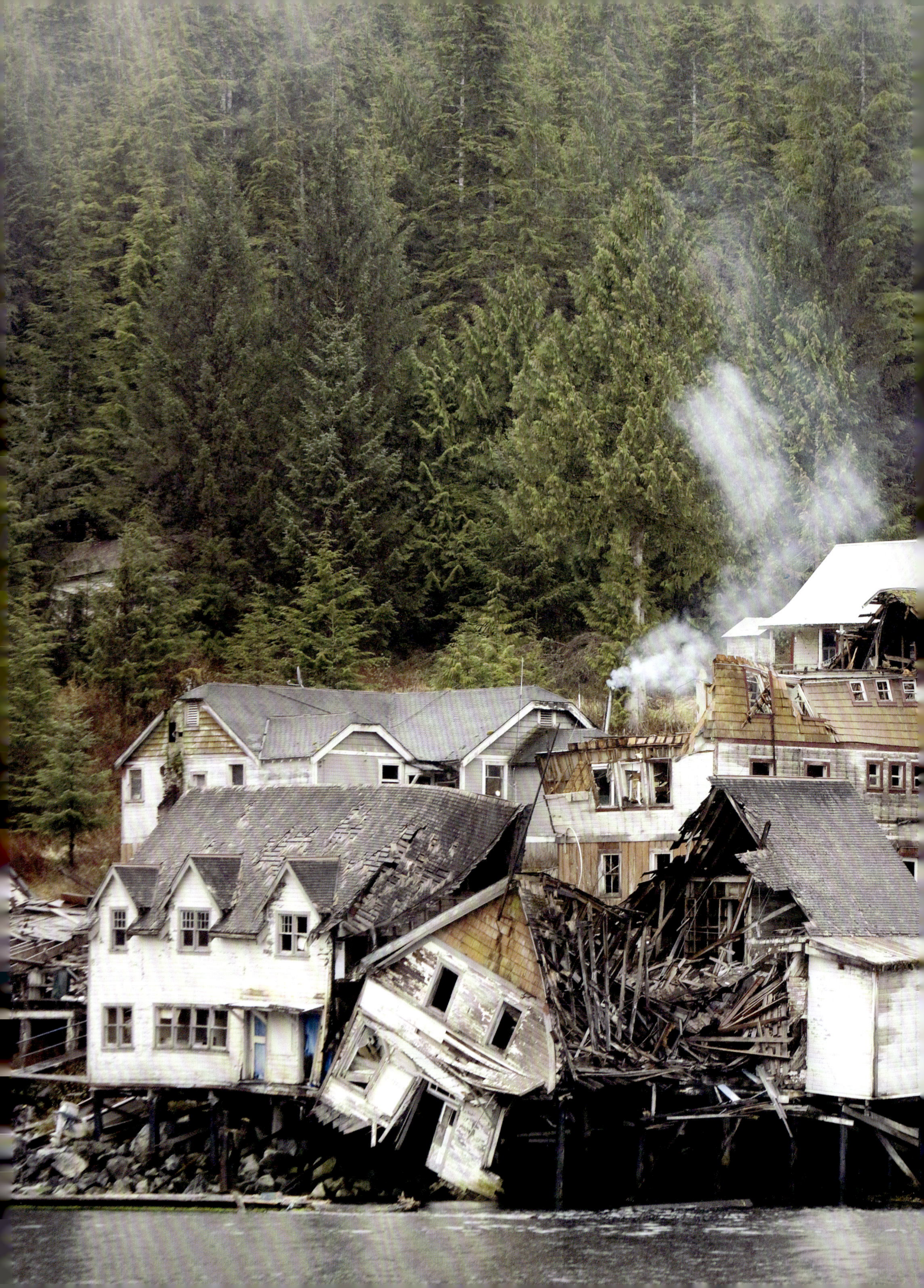

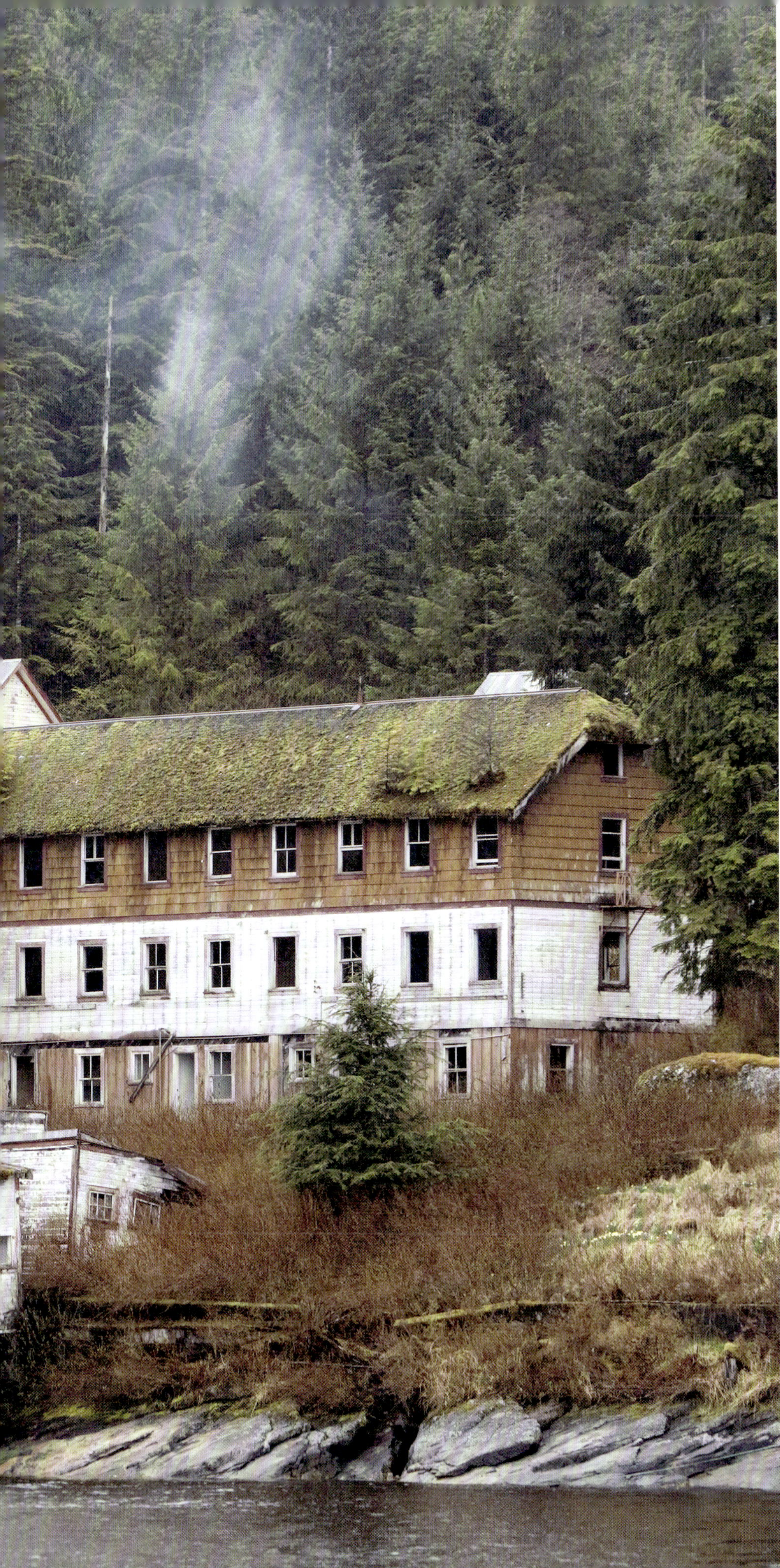

Butedale, Princess Royal Island, British Columbia, Canada
Although picturesque, this salmon cannery is now virtually deserted, home to just a few self-sufficient squatters. Many of the ghost towns throughout Canada and the United States testify to the industrial depletion of natural resources, to the extent that they can no longer support a particular town or facility.

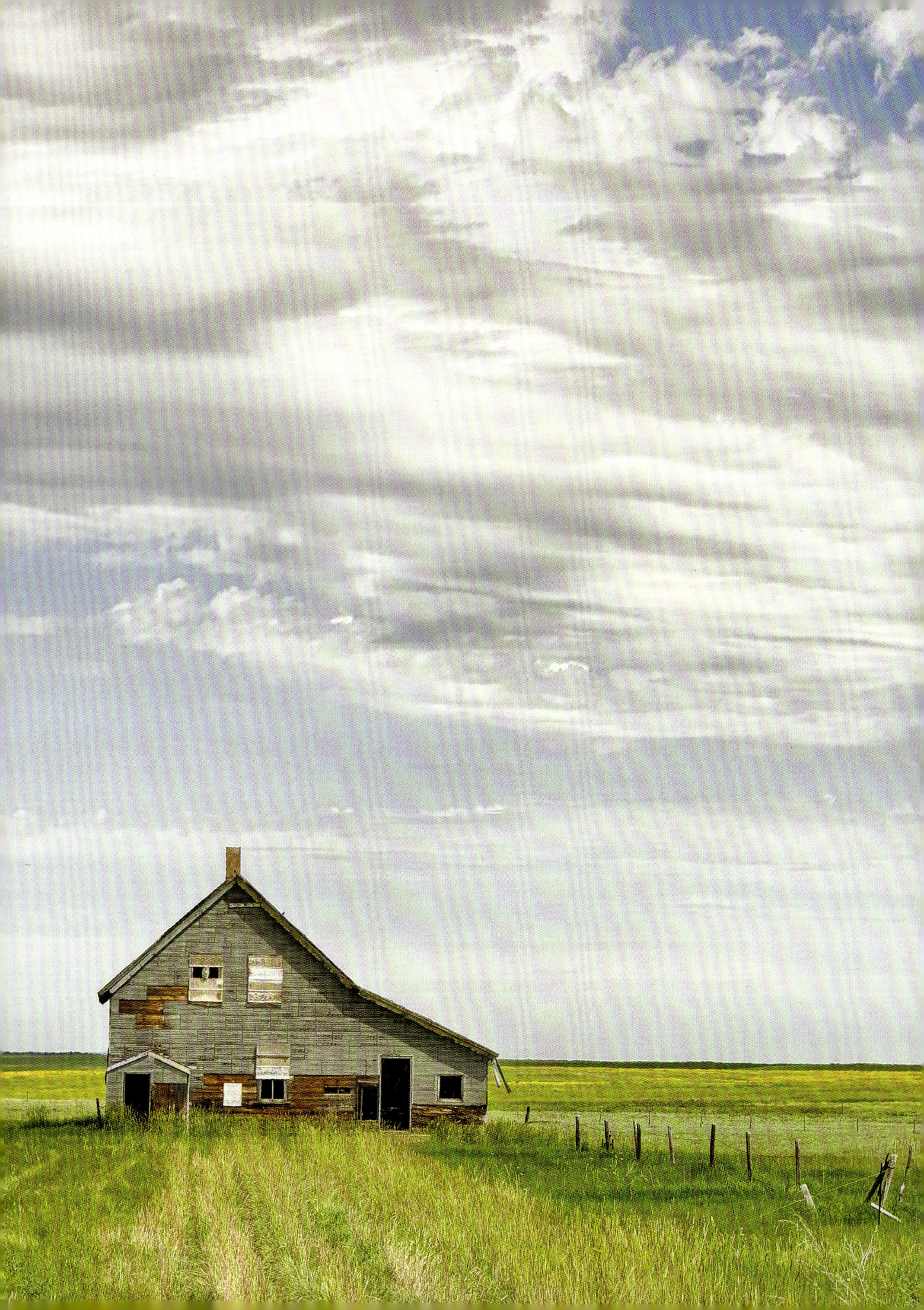

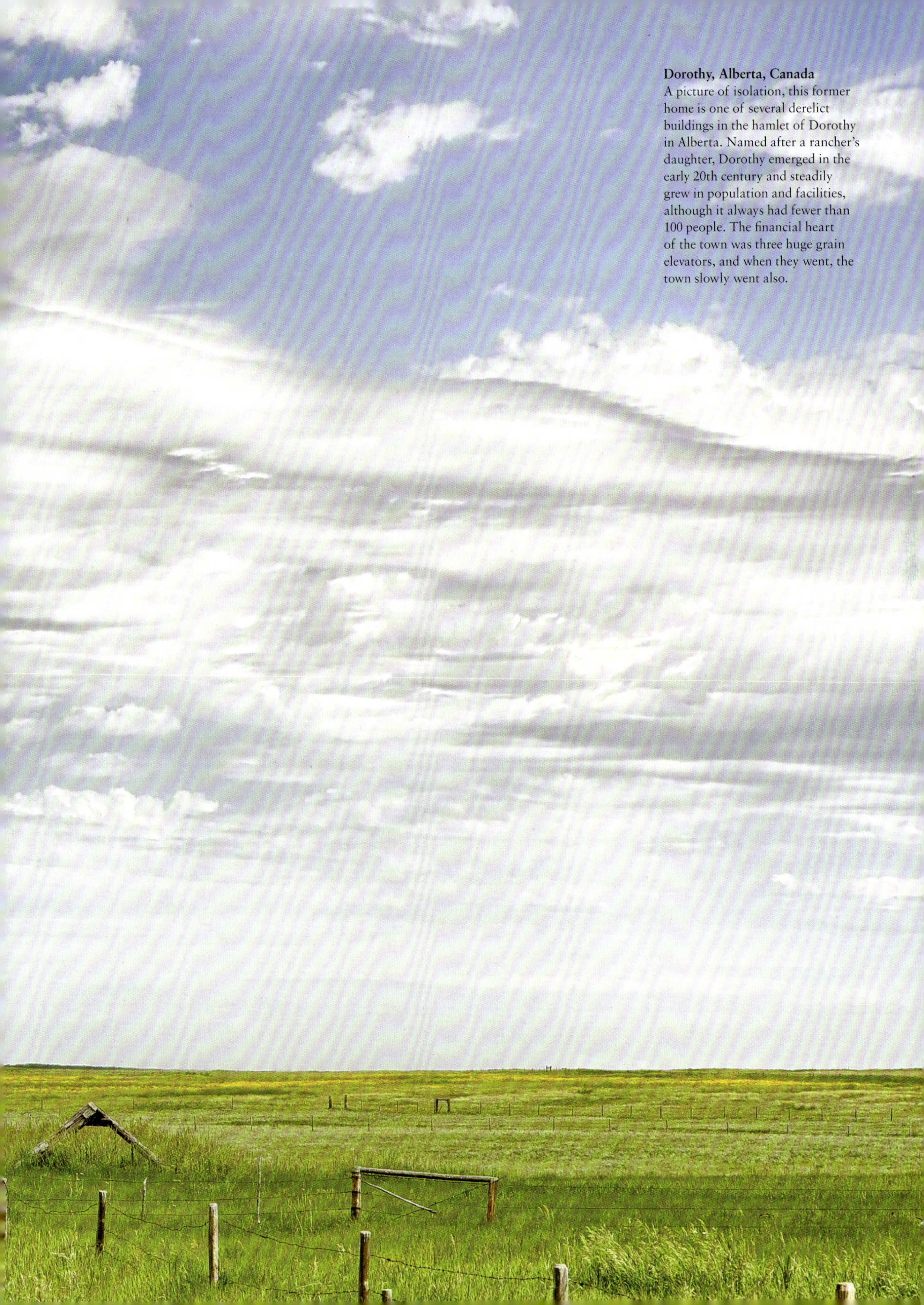

Dorothy, Alberta, Canada
A picture of isolation, this former home is one of several derelict buildings in the hamlet of Dorothy in Alberta. Named after a rancher's daughter, Dorothy emerged in the early 20th century and steadily grew in population and facilities, although it always had fewer than 100 people. The financial heart of the town was three huge grain elevators, and when they went, the town slowly went also.

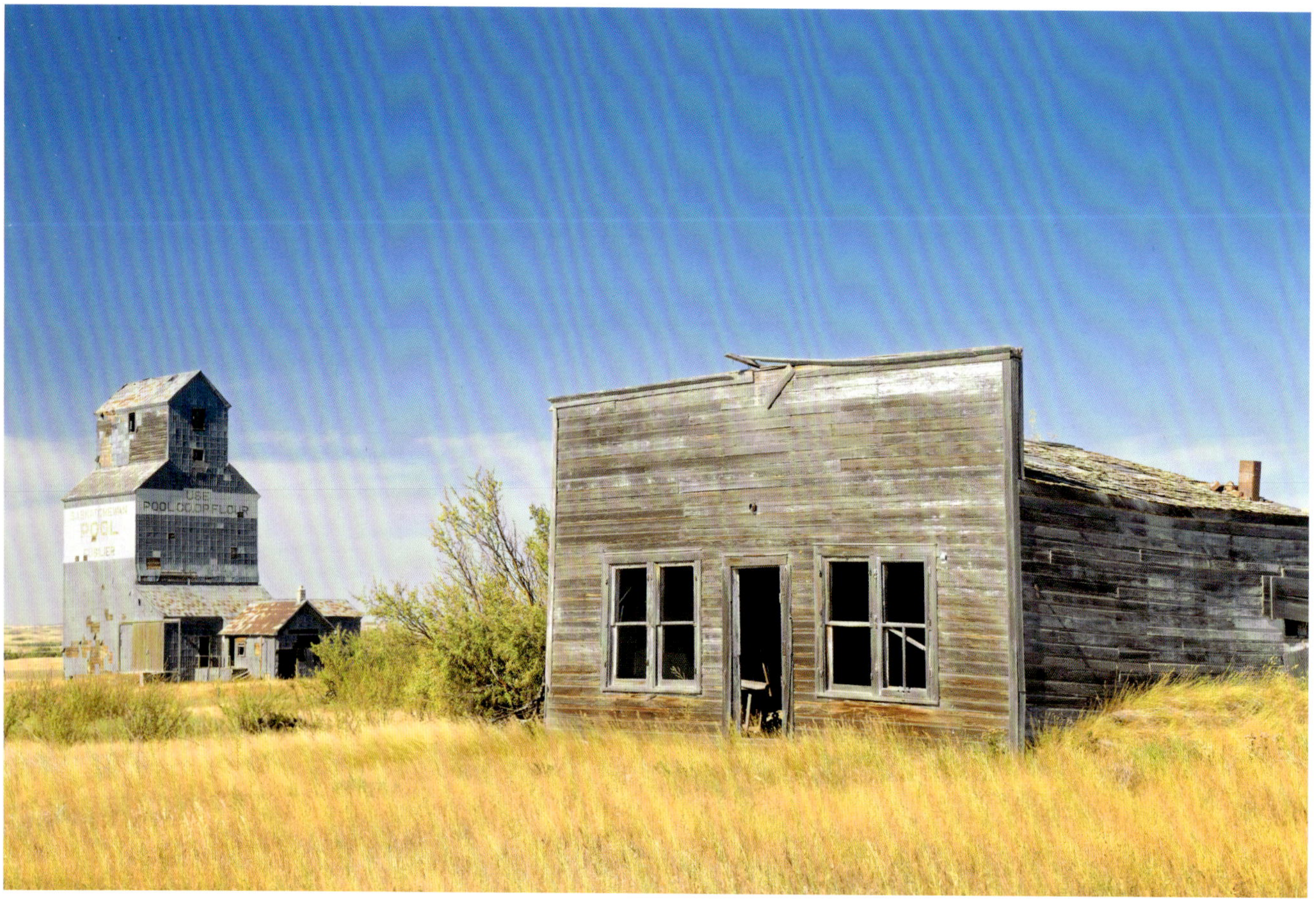

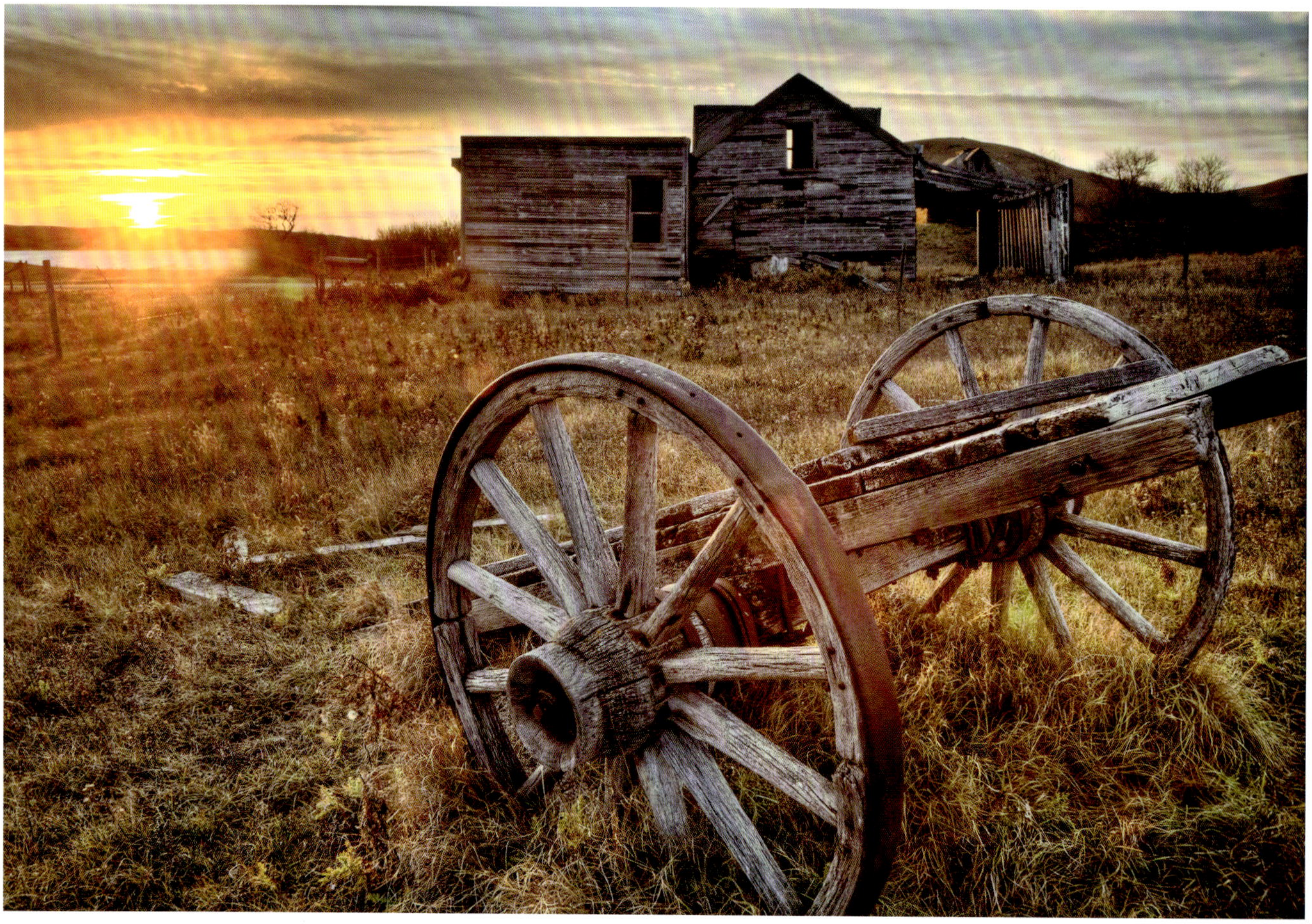

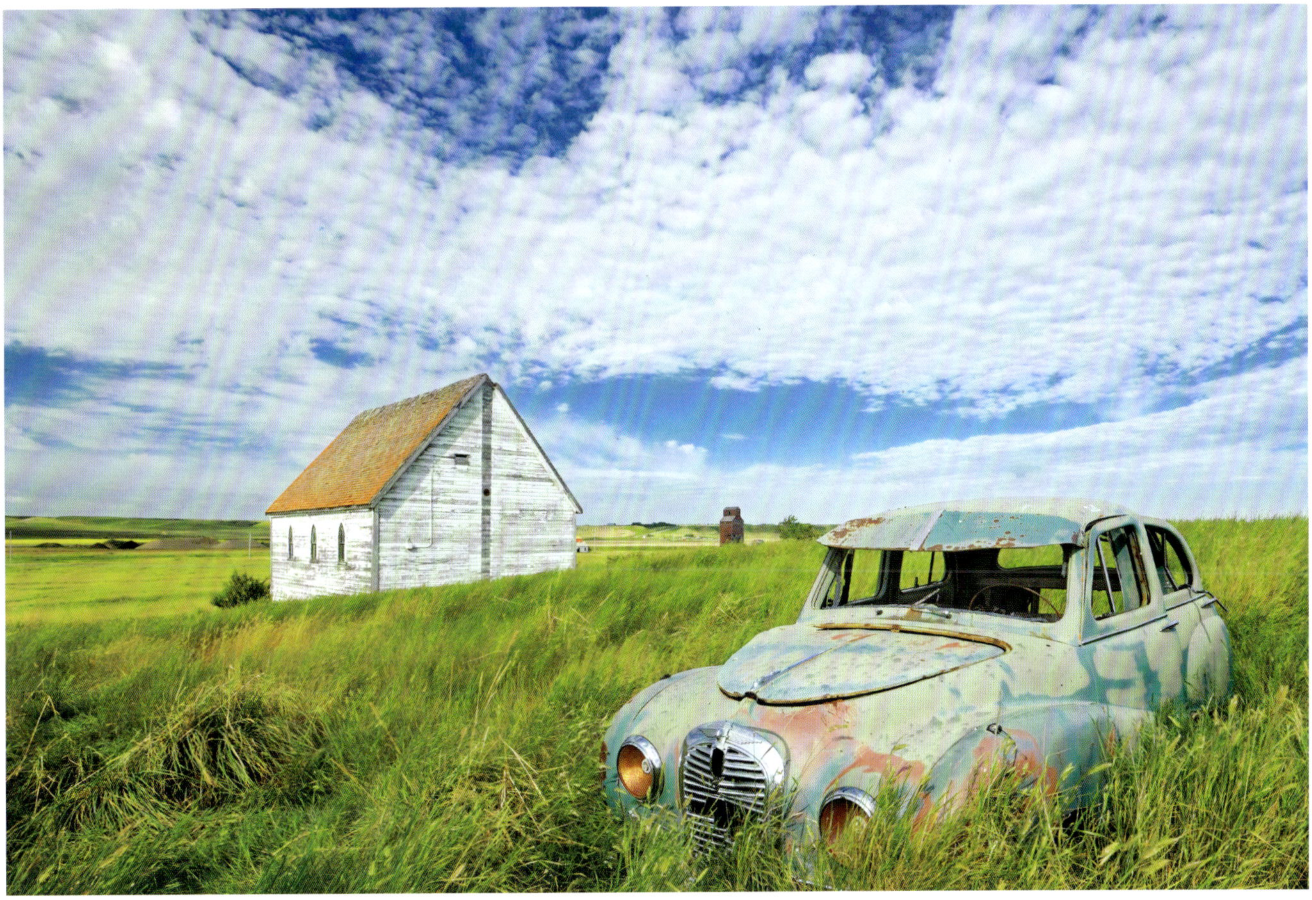

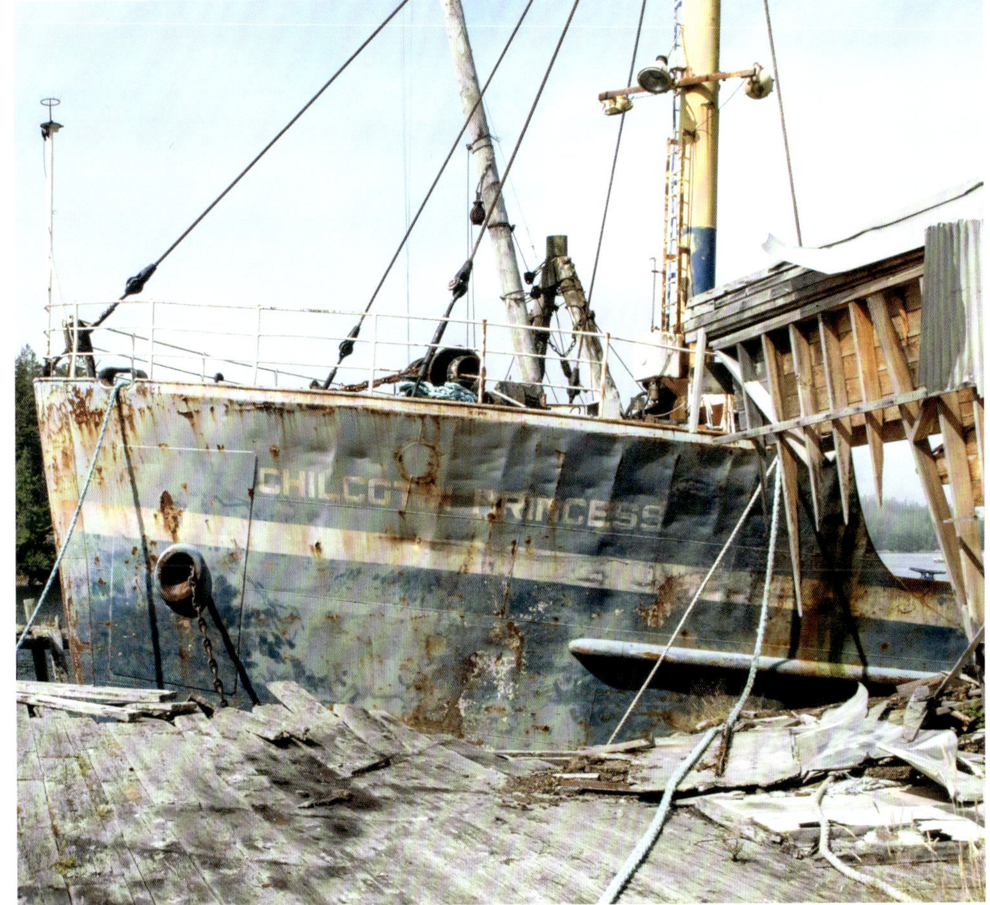

OPPOSITE ABOVE:
Fusilier, Saskatchewan, Canada
A house and one of the three grain elevators at Fusilier. The town started to be abandoned when its sodium sulphate plant closed in 1938, and Depression hit the town.

OPPOSITE BELOW:
Galilee, Saskatchewan, Canada
Galilee, like many other abandoned villages in Saskatchewan, rose and fell over a period of about 50 years, from its founding in 1913 to the closure of its facilities in the 1950s and 1960s.

ABOVE:
Neidpath, Saskatchewan, Canada
The village of Neidpath was actually named after Neidpath Castle, near Peebles, Scotland. In the background we see the former church and a grain elevator.

LEFT:
Namu, British Columbia, Canada
Set in the Great Bear Rainforest, on the British Columbia coast, Namu was a cannery and fishing community founded in 1893, but shut down in the 1970s. The oil in the rusting ships has presented a serious environmental hazard.

RIGHT:
Ashcroft, Castle Creek Valley, Aspen, Colorado, USA
Established in the 19th century as a silver-mining settlement, Ashcroft was later used by the US 10th Mountain Division as a winter training base.

OPPOSITE:
St Elmo, Colorado, USA
Superbly preserved in its mountainous environment, St Elmo is another former mining settlement (gold and silver), which once was home to 2000 people.

BELOW:
Animas Forks, Colorado, USA
Set high up in the San Juan Mountains, Animas Forks was a 19th-century mining town, abandoned by the 1920s. The settlement's name was originally Three Forks of the Animas, describing its location at the nearby meeting place of three rivers, one of them being the Animas. Many people left to escape the vicious winter conditions, especially once the mines had ceased to deliver a good profit.

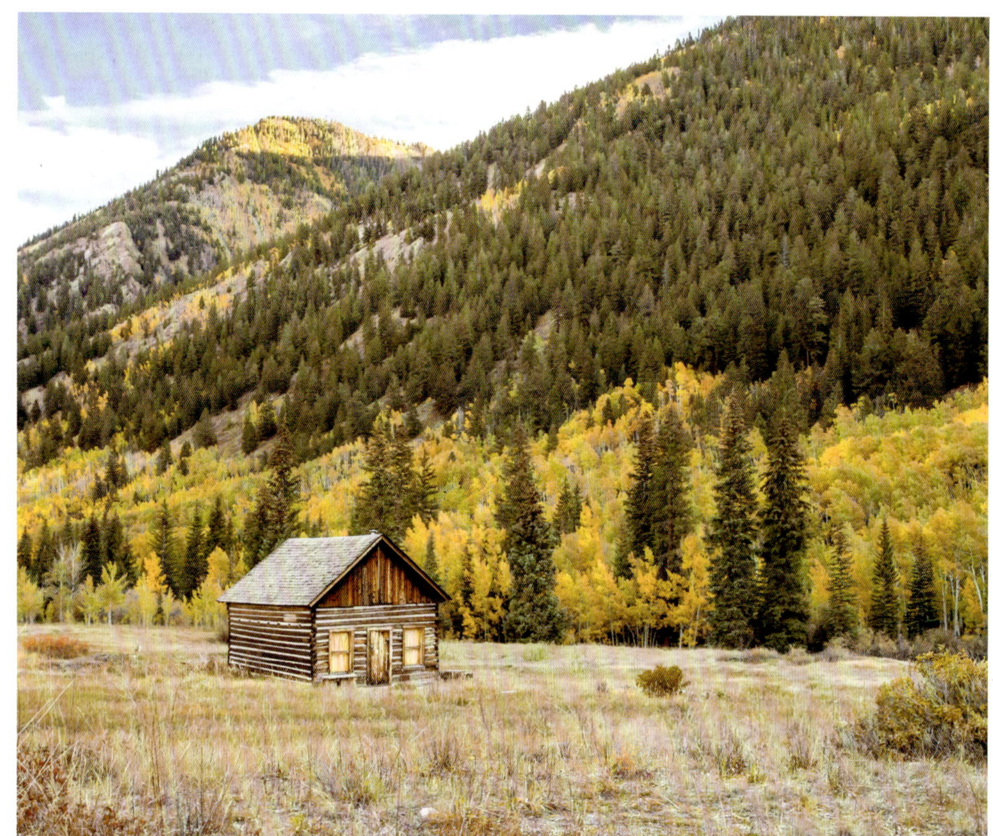

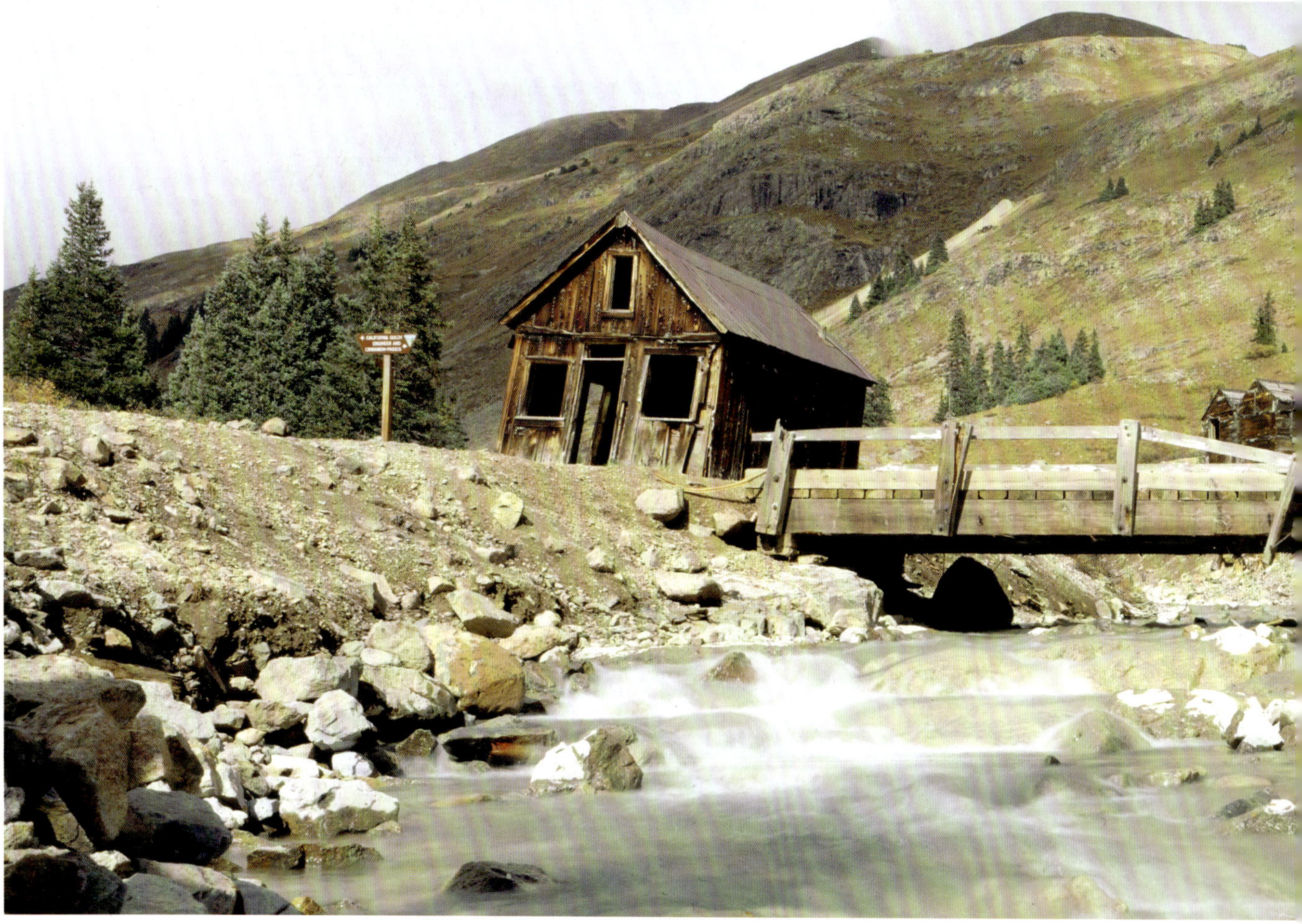

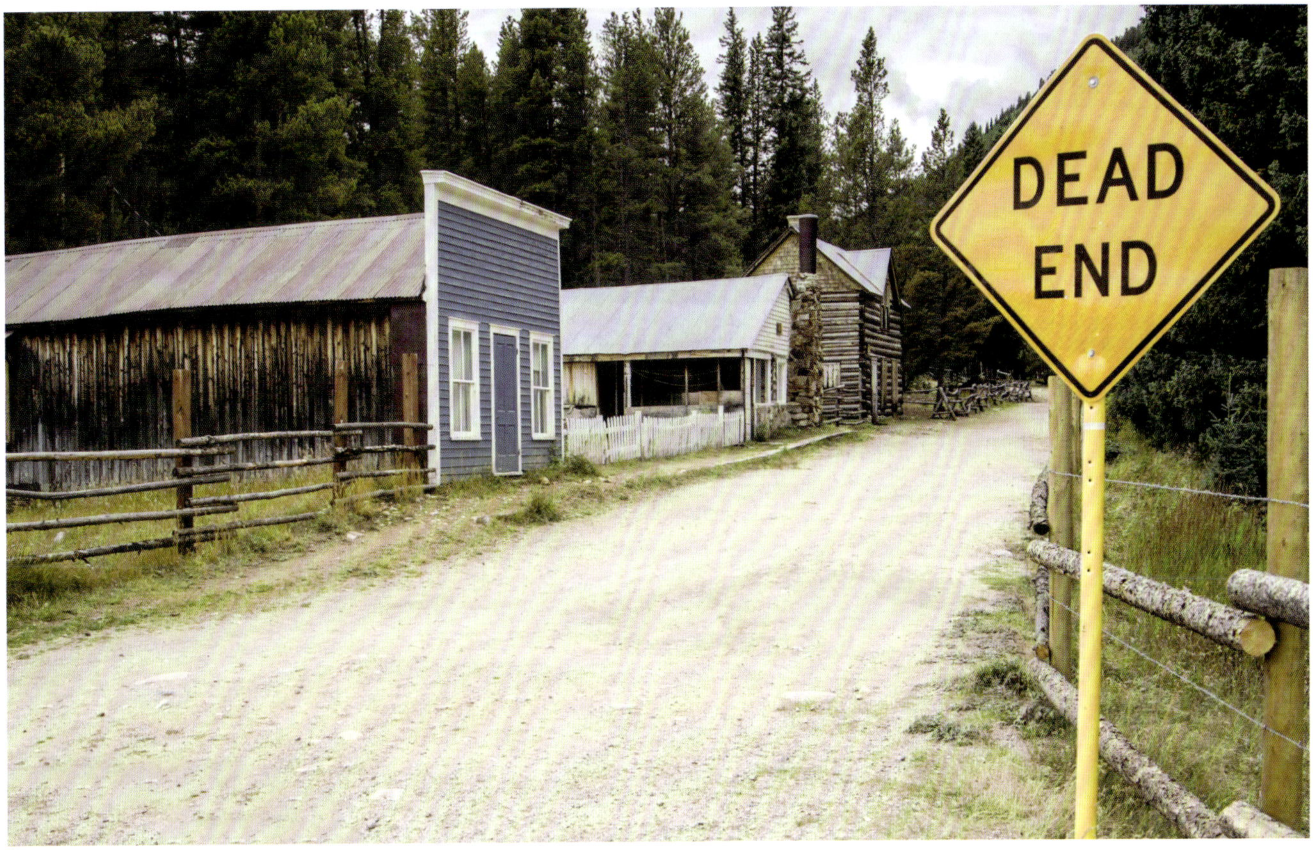

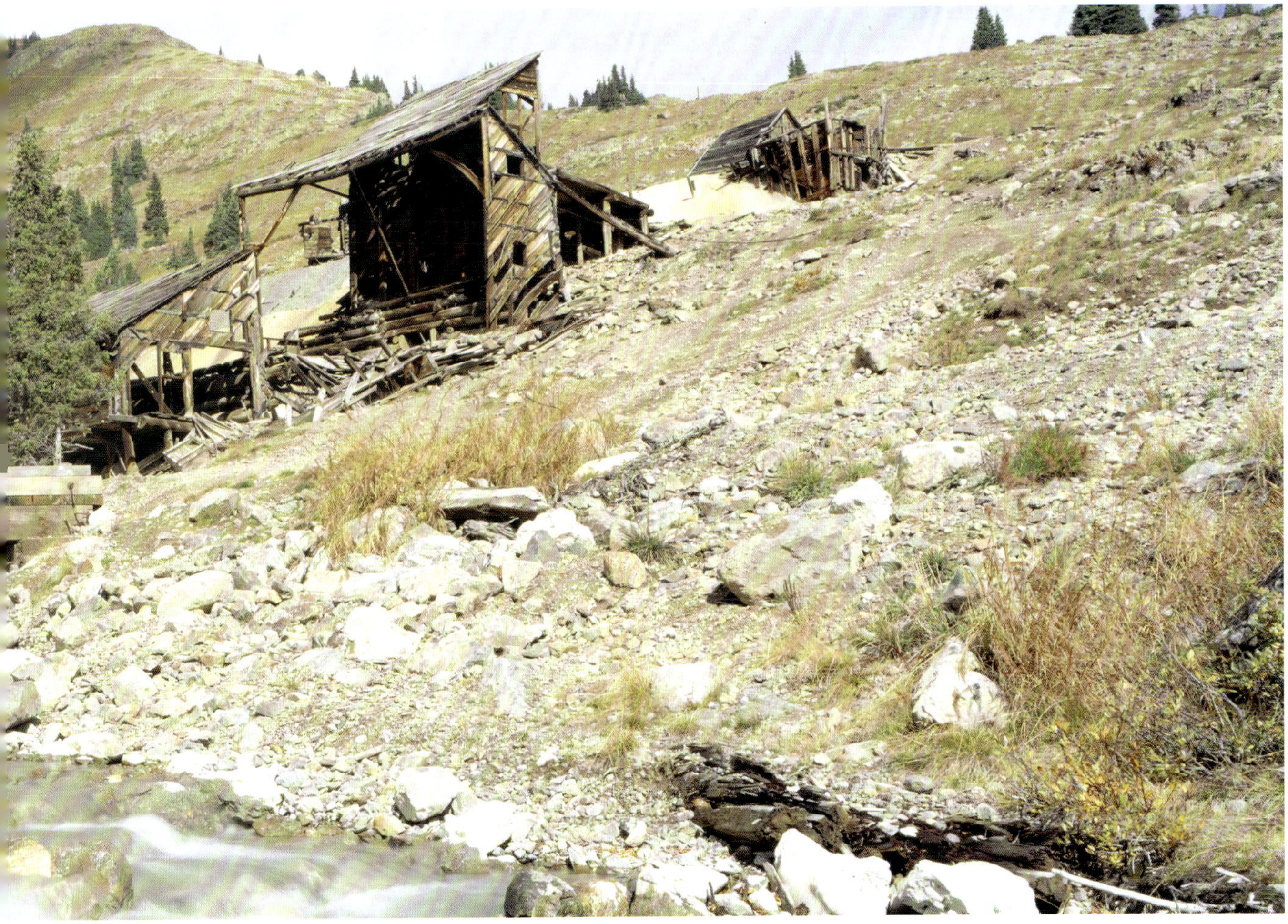

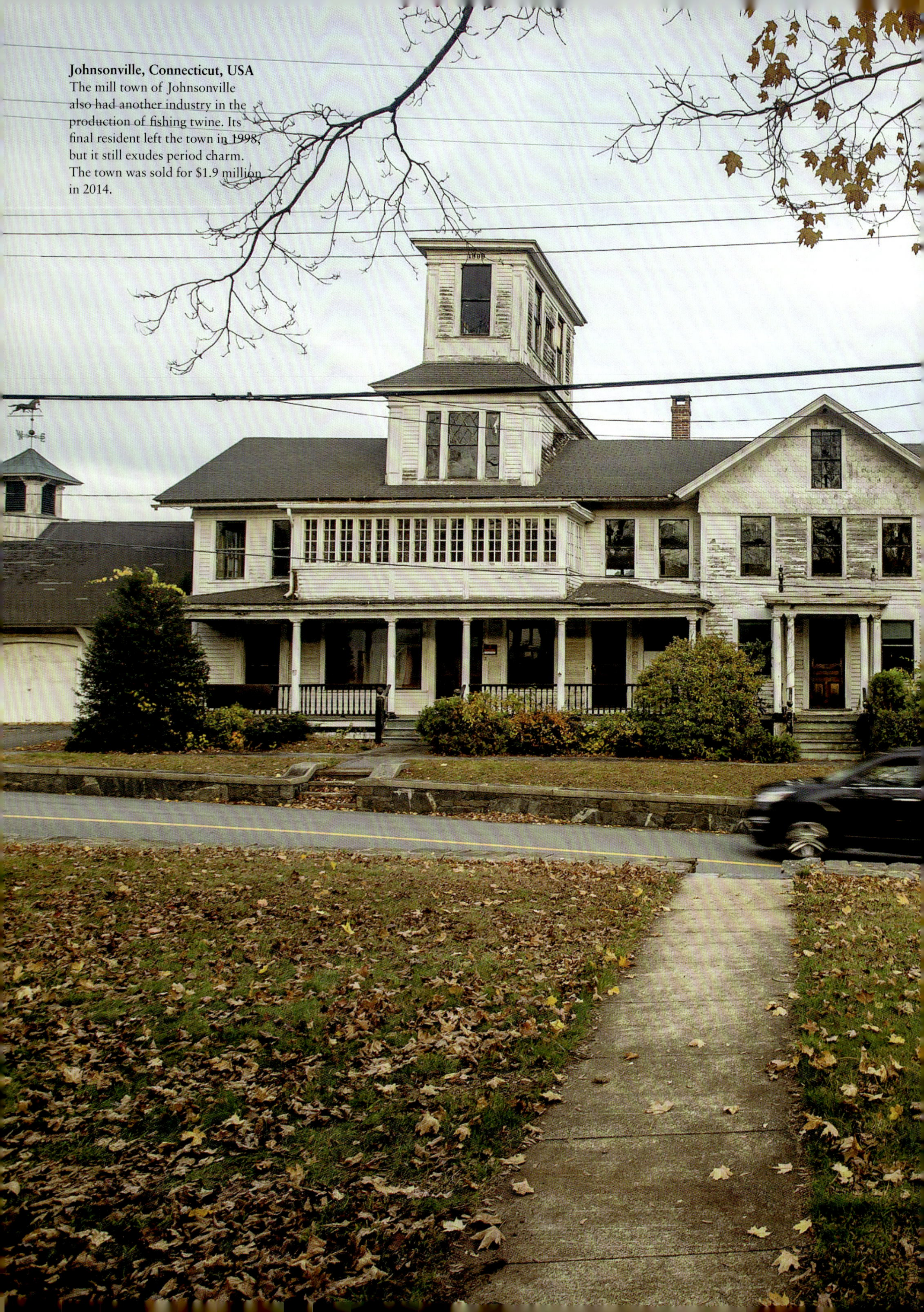

Johnsonville, Connecticut, USA
The mill town of Johnsonville also had another industry in the production of fishing twine. Its final resident left the town in 1998, but it still exudes period charm. The town was sold for $1.9 million in 2014.

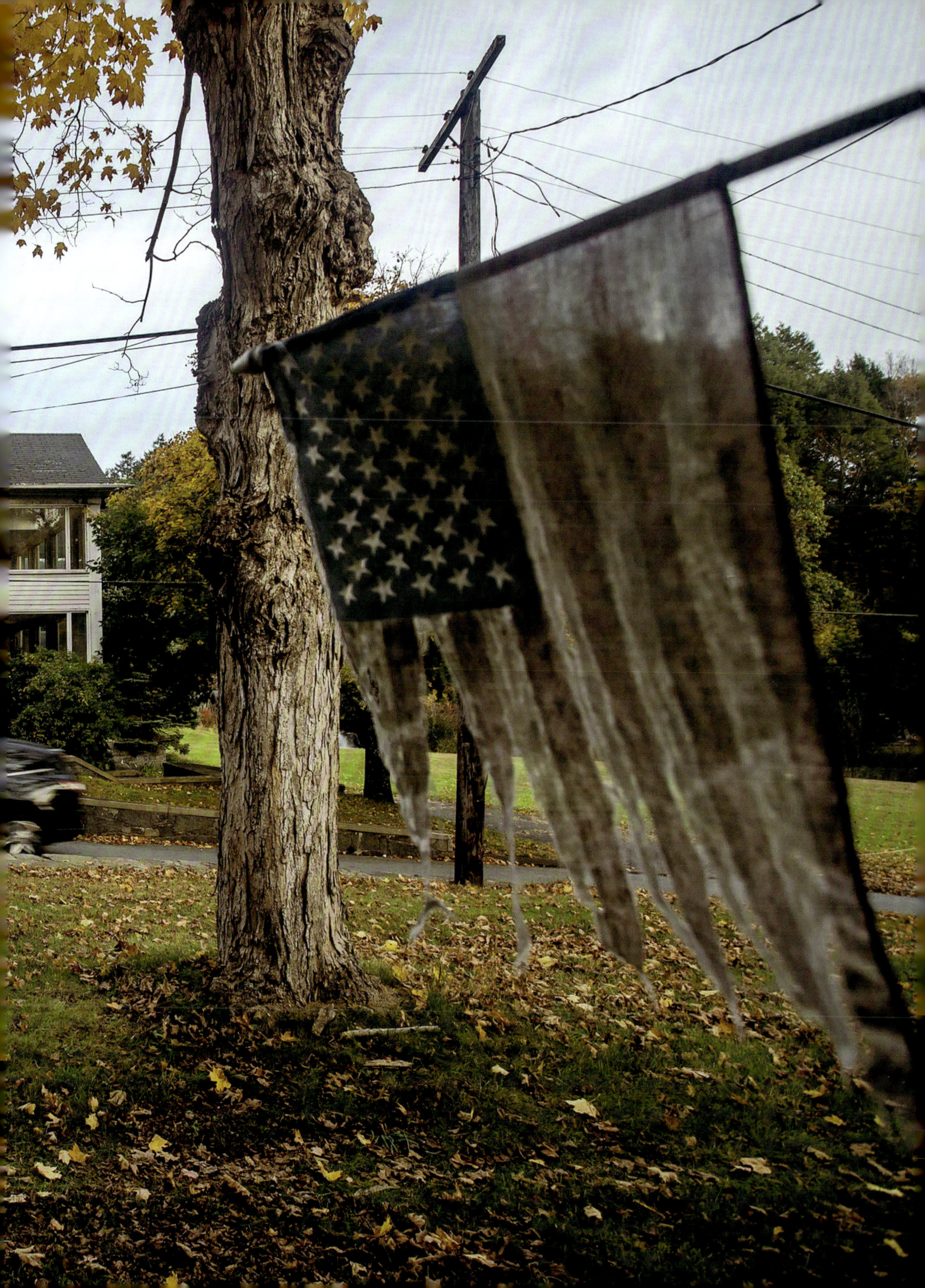

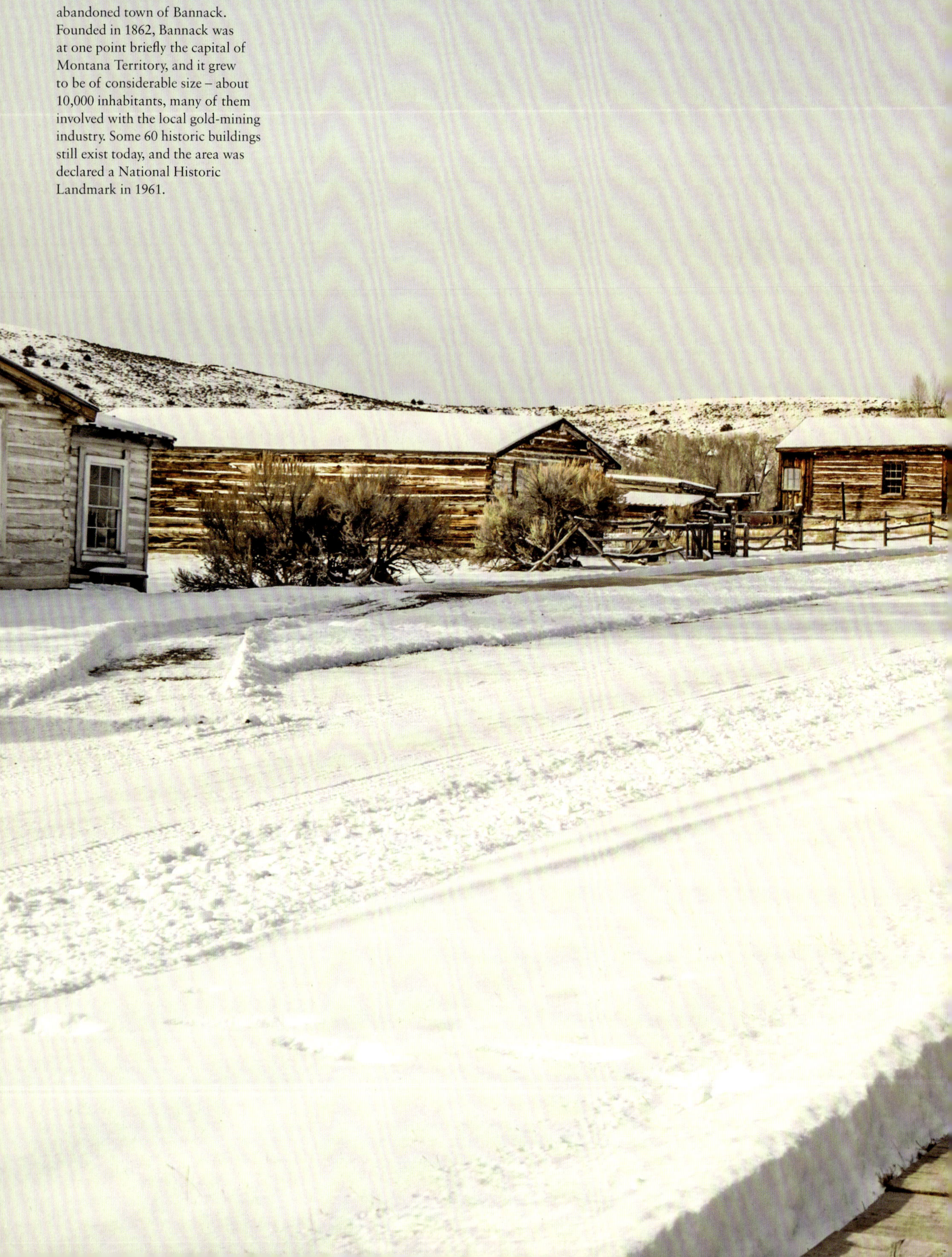

Bannack, Montana, USA
Winter snow blankets the abandoned town of Bannack. Founded in 1862, Bannack was at one point briefly the capital of Montana Territory, and it grew to be of considerable size – about 10,000 inhabitants, many of them involved with the local gold-mining industry. Some 60 historic buildings still exist today, and the area was declared a National Historic Landmark in 1961.

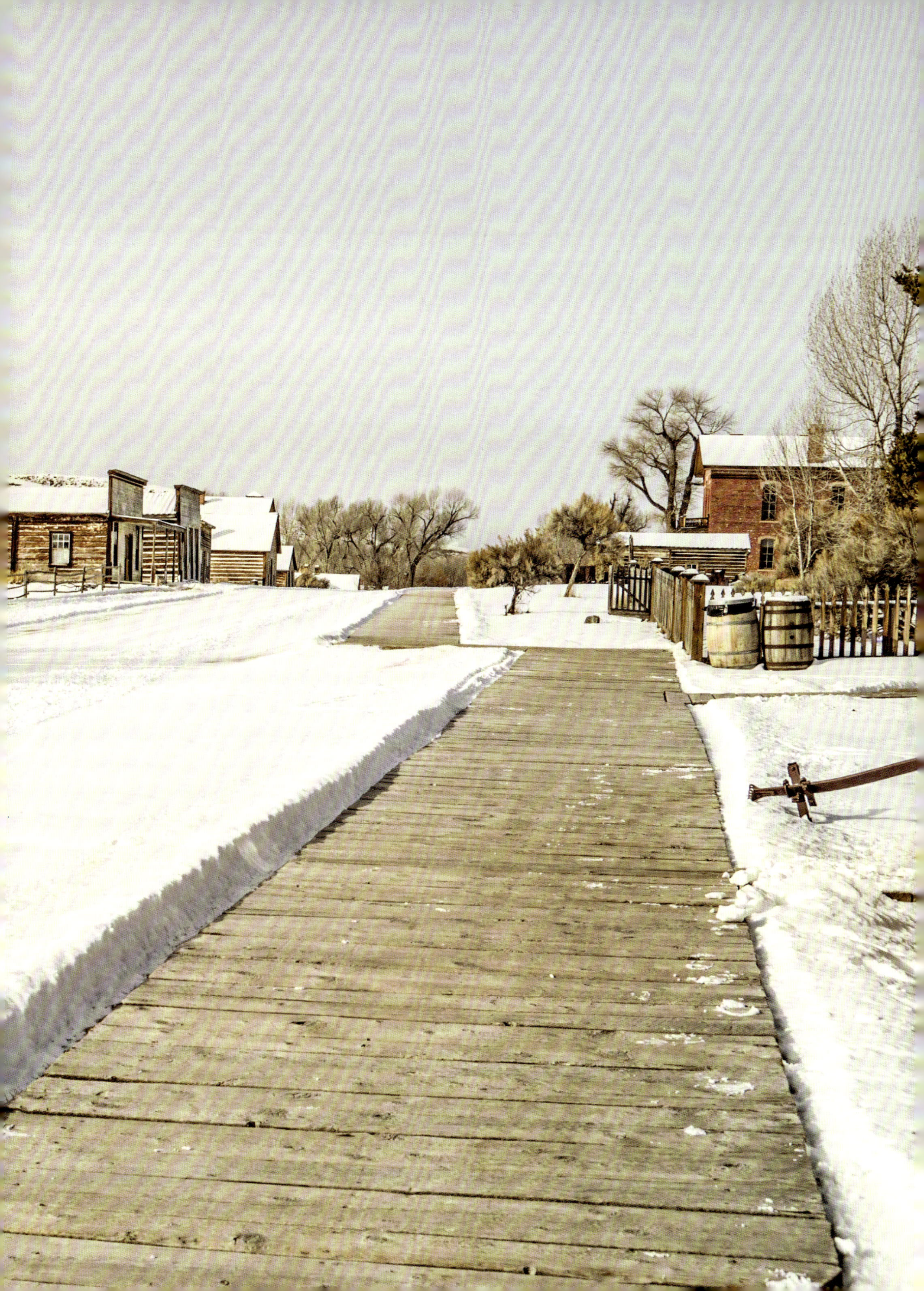

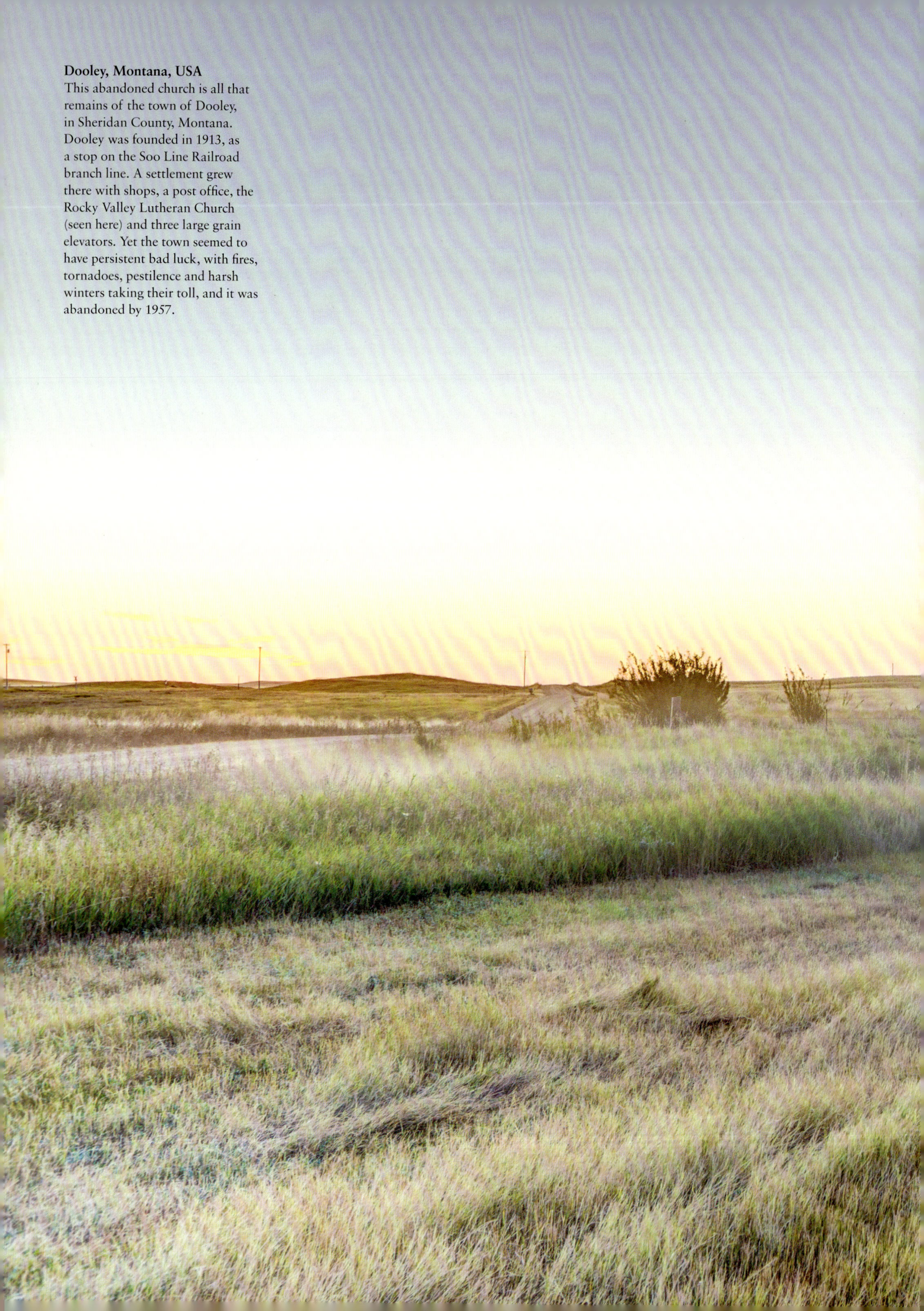

Dooley, Montana, USA

This abandoned church is all that remains of the town of Dooley, in Sheridan County, Montana. Dooley was founded in 1913, as a stop on the Soo Line Railroad branch line. A settlement grew there with shops, a post office, the Rocky Valley Lutheran Church (seen here) and three large grain elevators. Yet the town seemed to have persistent bad luck, with fires, tornadoes, pestilence and harsh winters taking their toll, and it was abandoned by 1957.

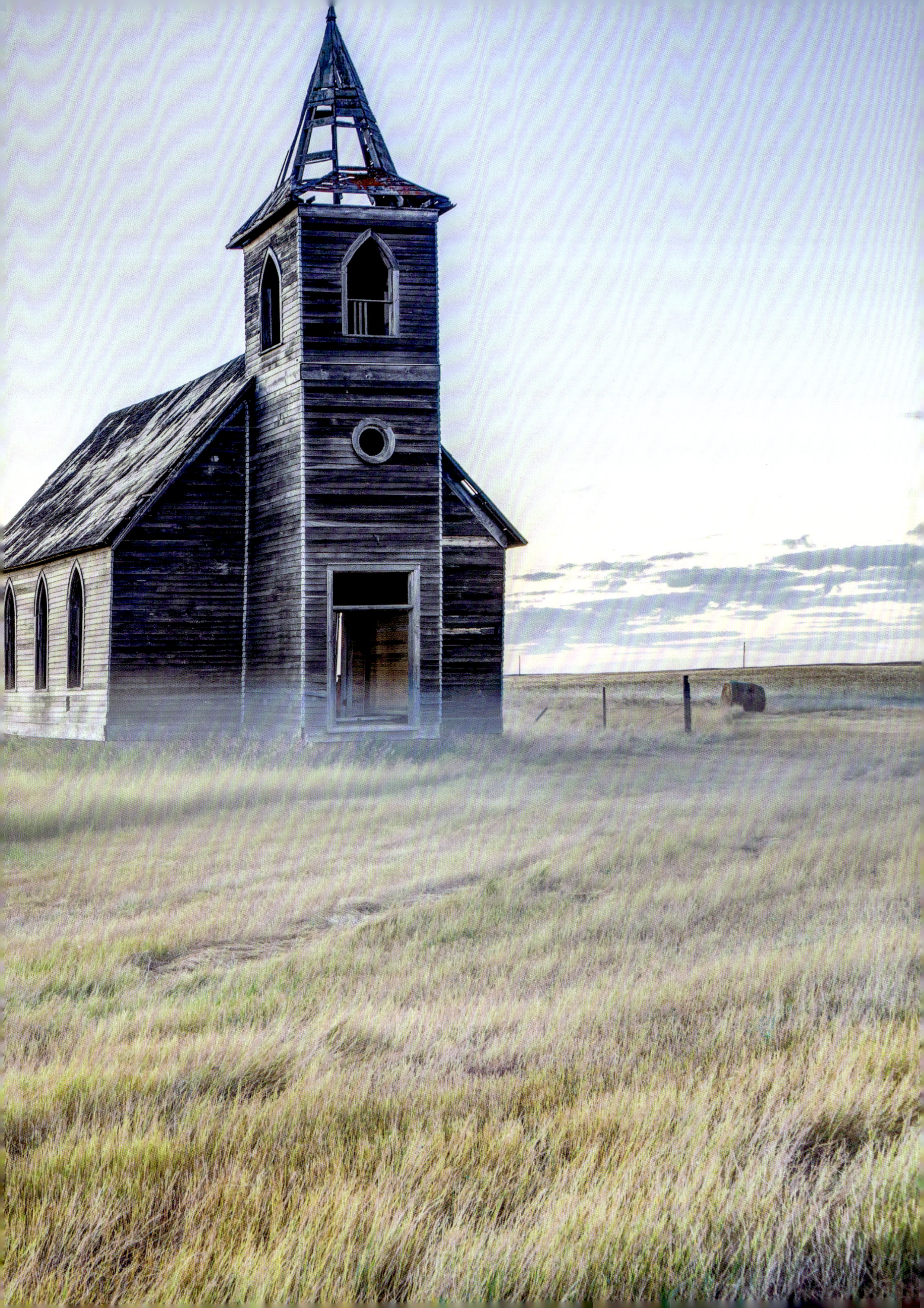

Goldfield, Nevada, USA
Goldfield is not entirely uninhabited, but comparing its present-day population of c. 250 with the 30,000 people living there in 1913 shows the extent of its decline. The town was founded in 1903 following the discovery of gold nearby, which brought the expanding population enormous profits – $11 million of gold was mined in 1906. But the gold seemed to run out as quickly as it was found, and population and profits began their downward spiral.

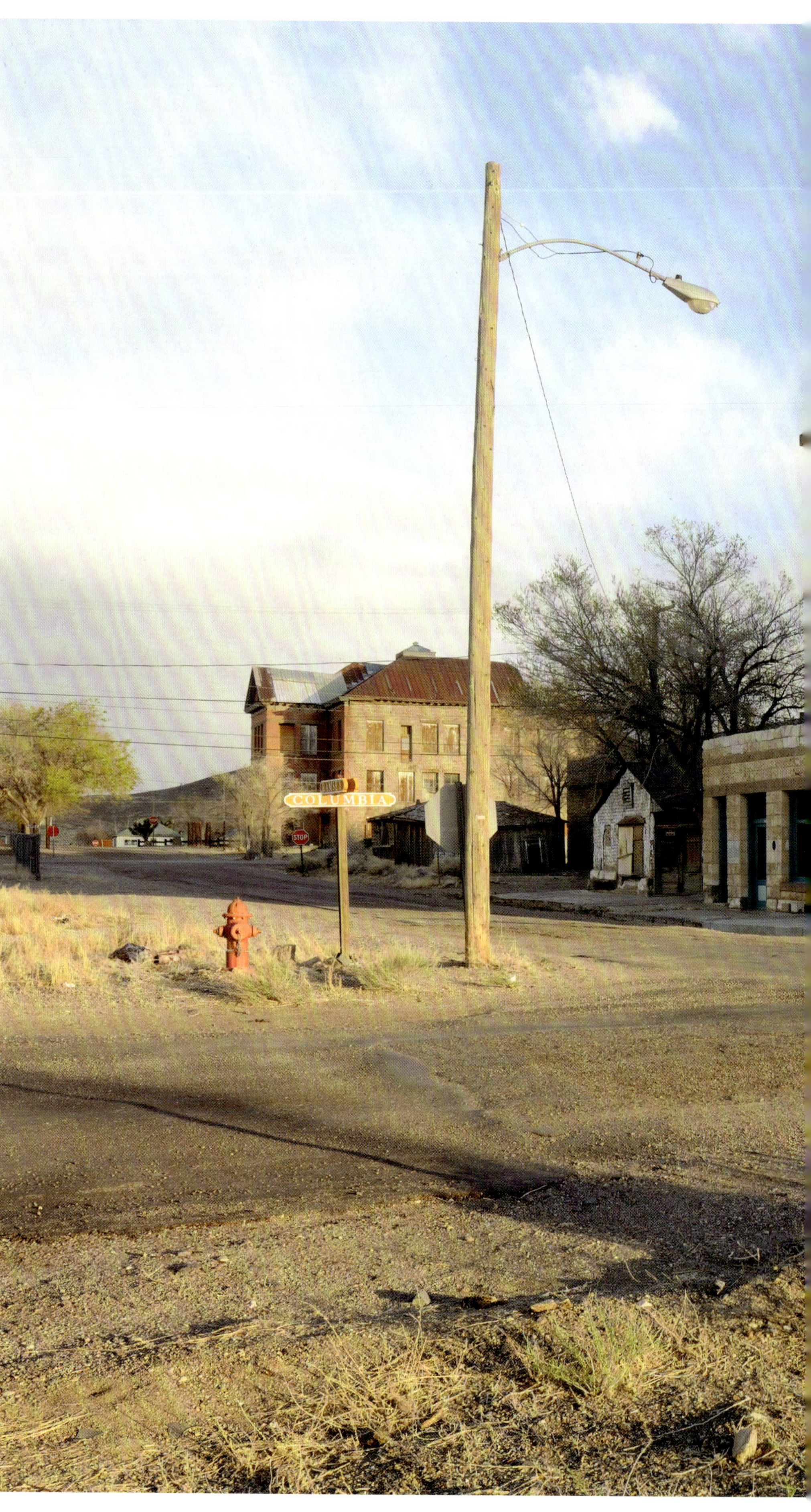

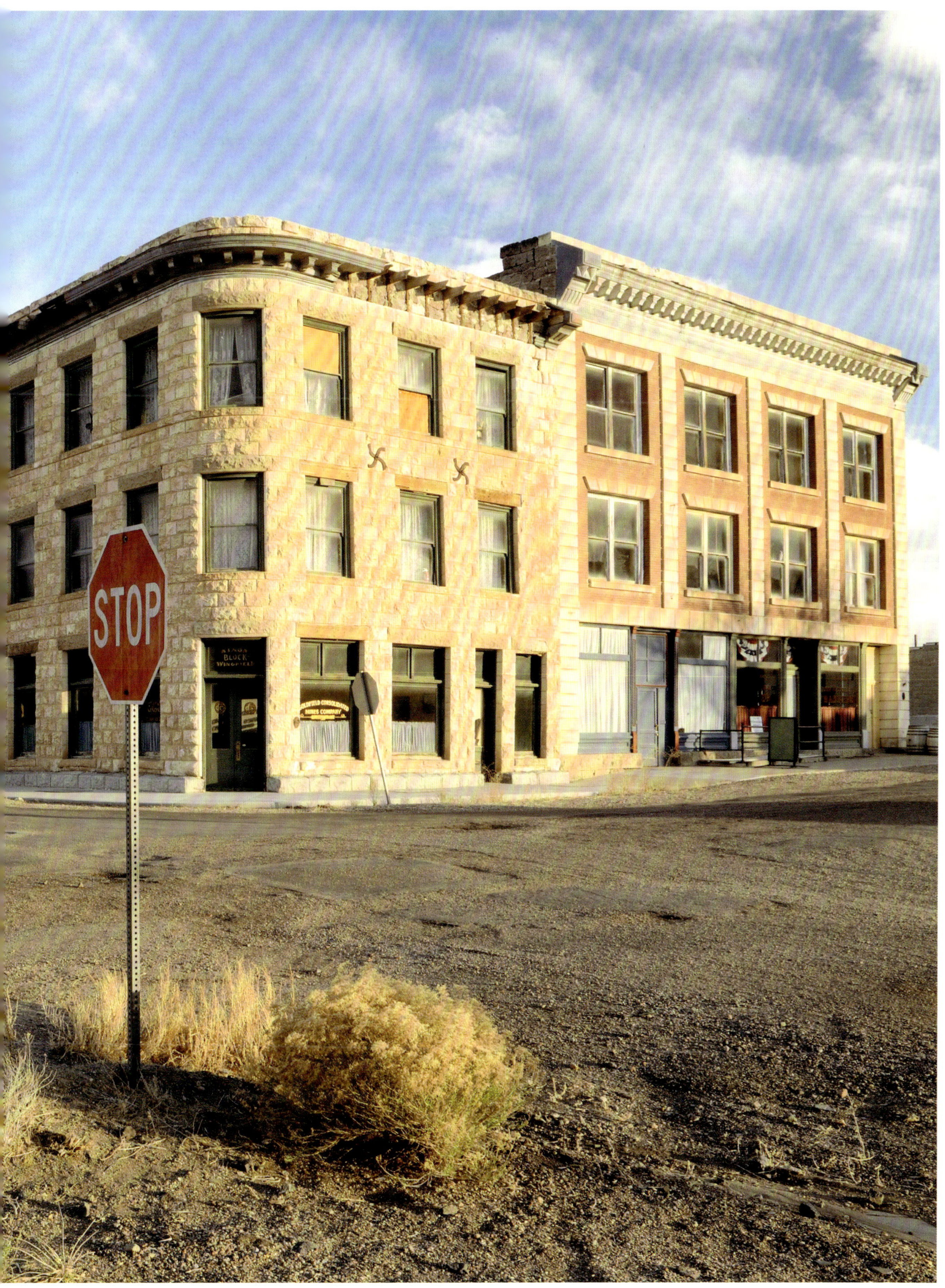
STOP
BLOCK
MINES COMPANY

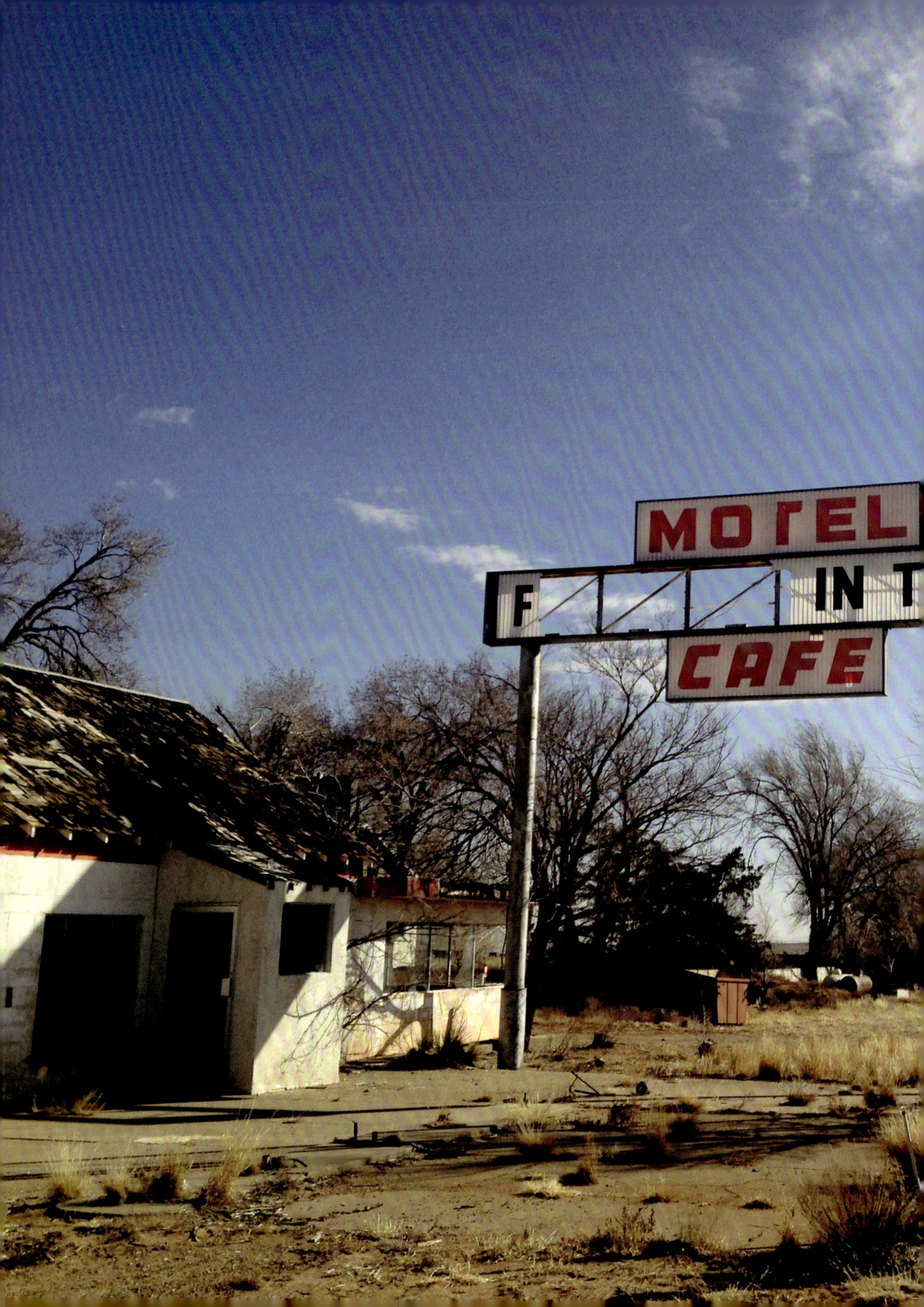

MOTEL
F
INT
CAFE

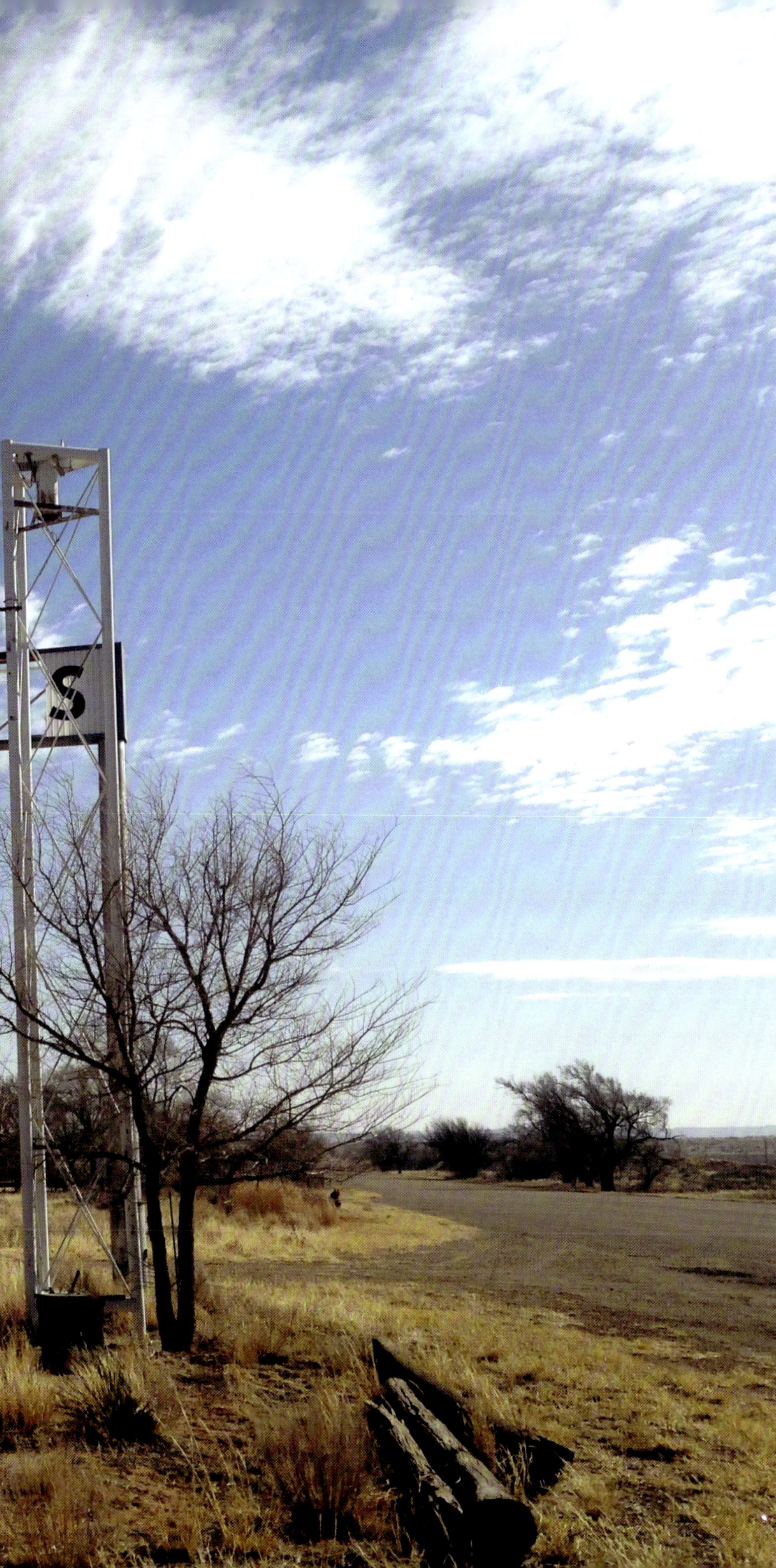

Glenrio, New Mexico/Texas, USA

Glenrio sits precisely on the border of New Mexico and Texas, so much so that the town's gas stations variously reclassified their locations to provide petrol at either New Mexico or Texas prices. This remote outpost was originally a stop point on the Rock Island and Pacific Railroad and on the motorists' Ozark Trail and Route 66. Eventually the transportation networks were reconfigured and no longer included Glenrio as a stop; hence the town withered on the vine, abandoned by the 1980s.

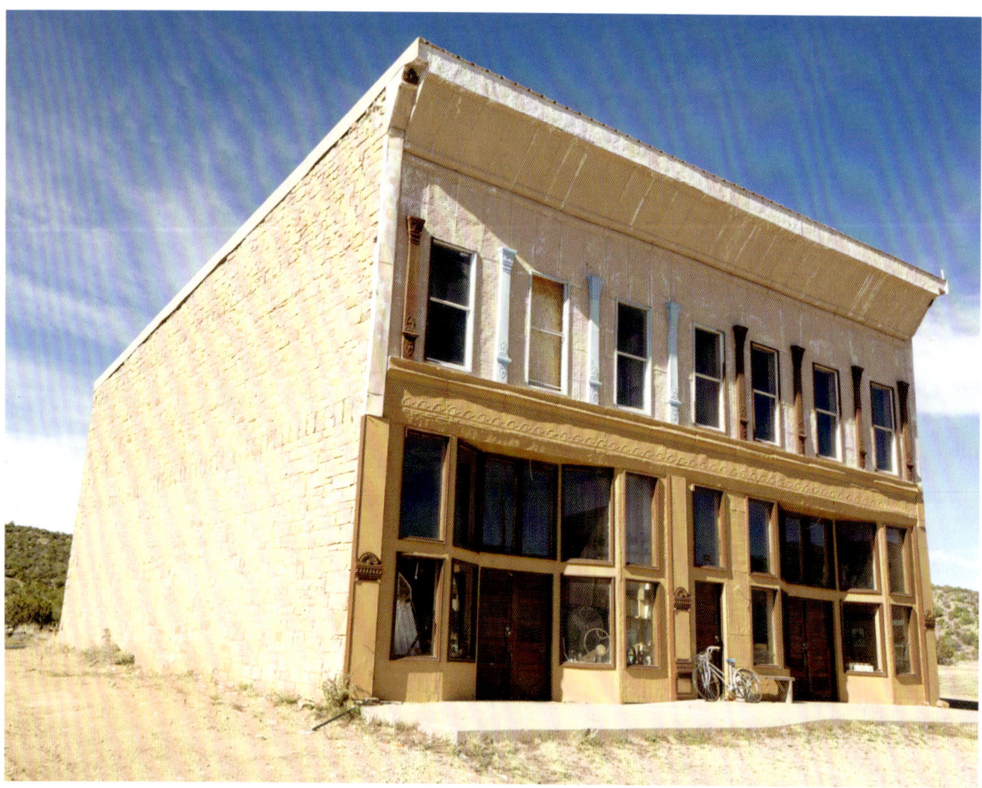

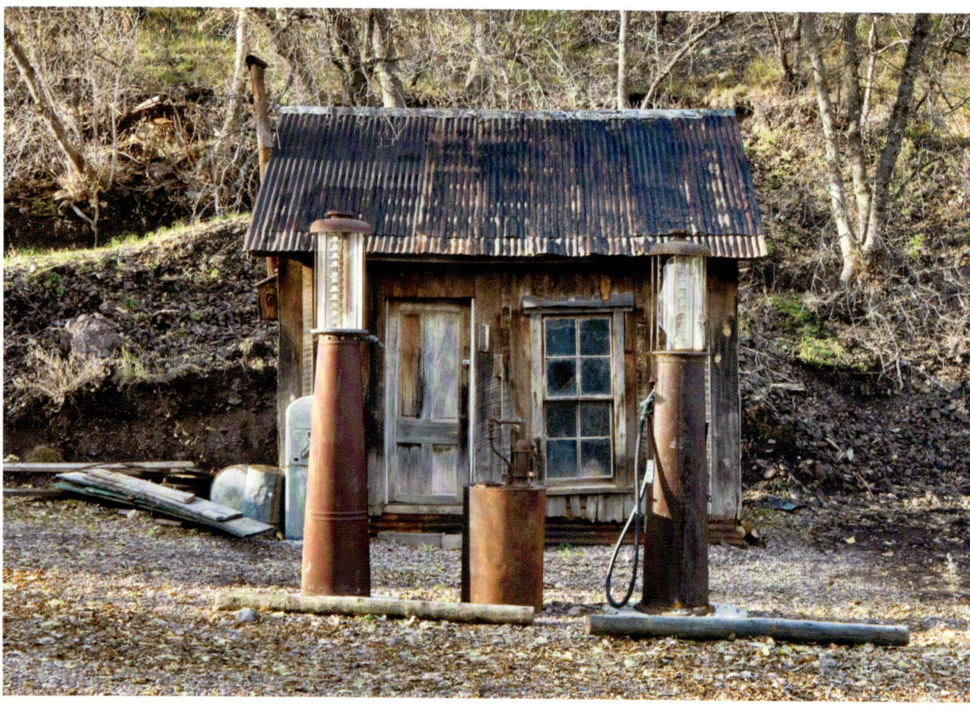

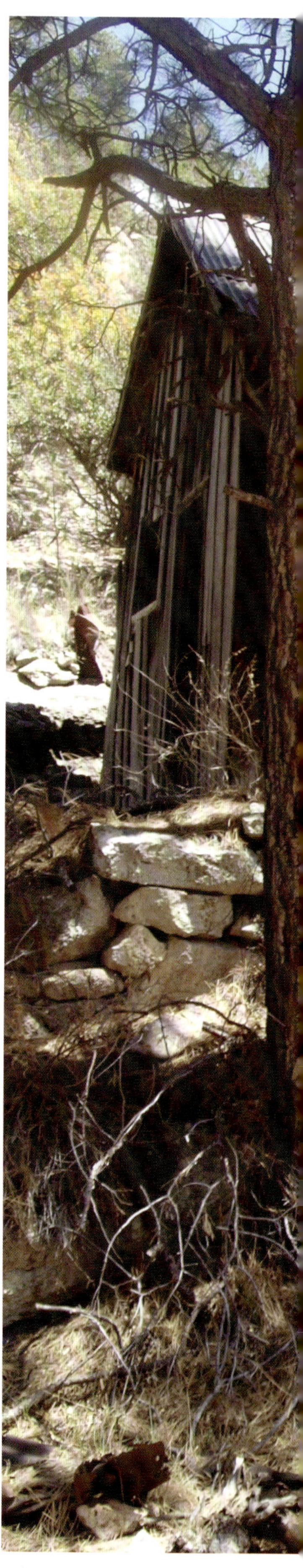

TOP:
White Oaks, New Mexico, USA
Built in 1885, Brown Store is one of the buildings that comprised historic White Oaks, New Mexico. Like so many towns in the southern United States, White Oaks was born in the 19th century on the back of the gold rush. The town was a lively place (Billy the Kid was a visitor), yet it failed when the gold ran out and the railroads bypassed it.

ABOVE:
Mogollon, New Mexico, USA
At 2702m (6800ft) elevation in the Gila National Forest, Mogollon enjoys commanding views over the Silver Creek Canyon. The surrounding mountains yielded the gold and silver that made the foundation of Mogollon possible, around 1870, but the contraction of those industries brought decline in the first half of the 20th century.

RIGHT:
Mogollon, New Mexico, USA
Another of the abandoned buildings in Mogollon. Although this photograph, taken in the summer sunlight, has a picturesque quality about it, life in Mogollon was extremely hard for most of its inhabitants. The miners suffered from respiratory illnesses, and flooding and fire periodically wrecked parts of the town.

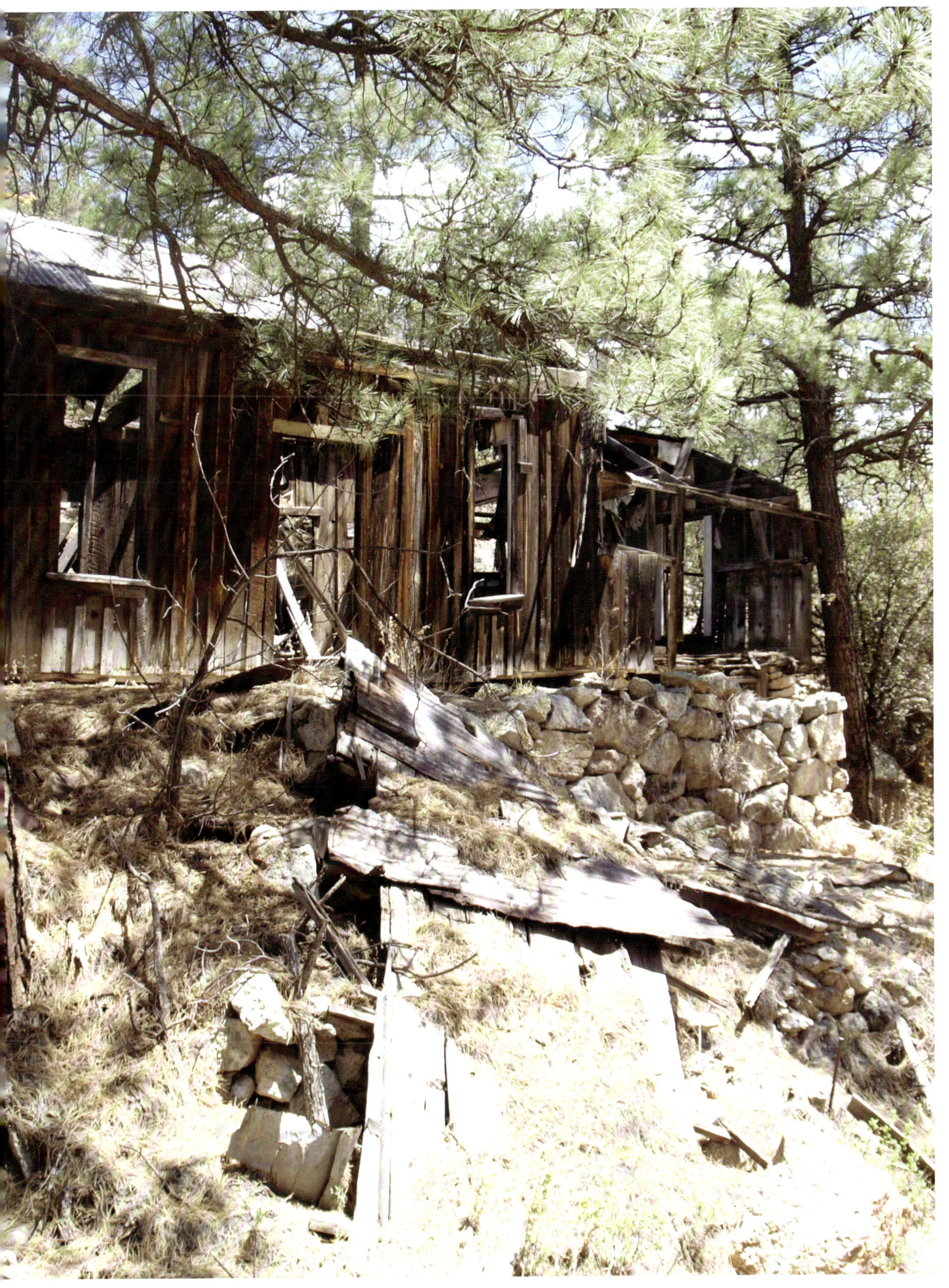

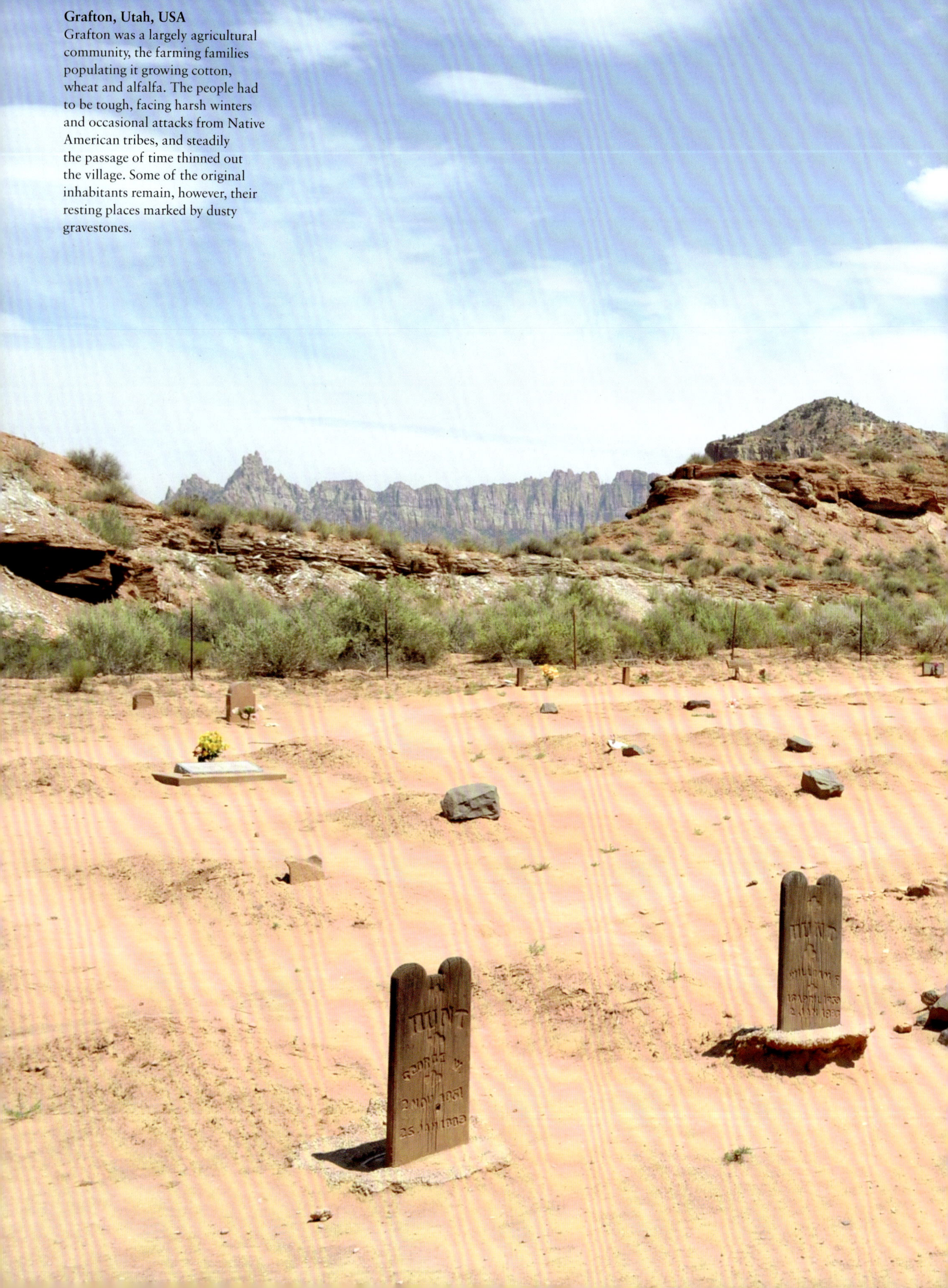

Grafton, Utah, USA
Grafton was a largely agricultural community, the farming families populating it growing cotton, wheat and alfalfa. The people had to be tough, facing harsh winters and occasional attacks from Native American tribes, and steadily the passage of time thinned out the village. Some of the original inhabitants remain, however, their resting places marked by dusty gravestones.

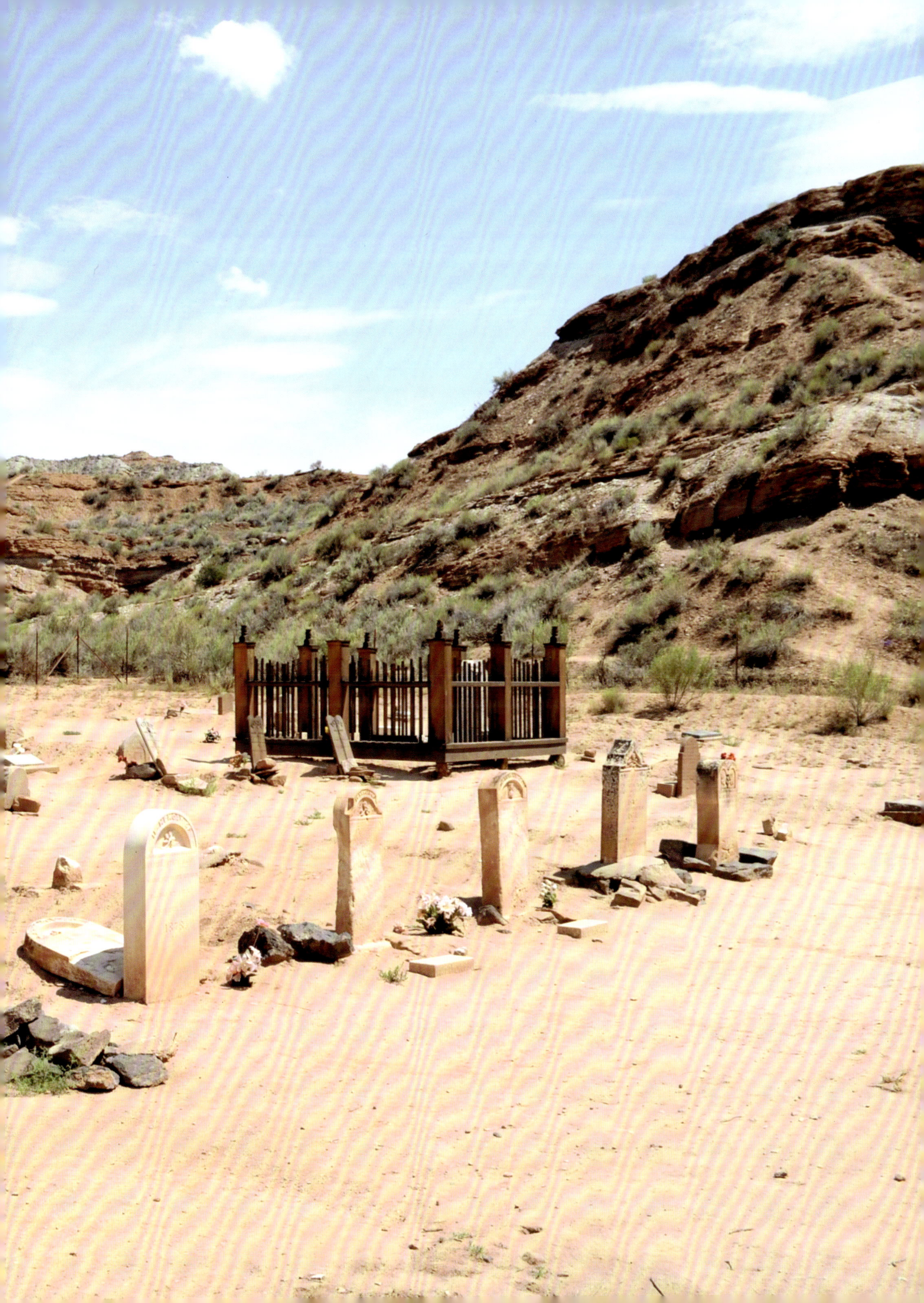

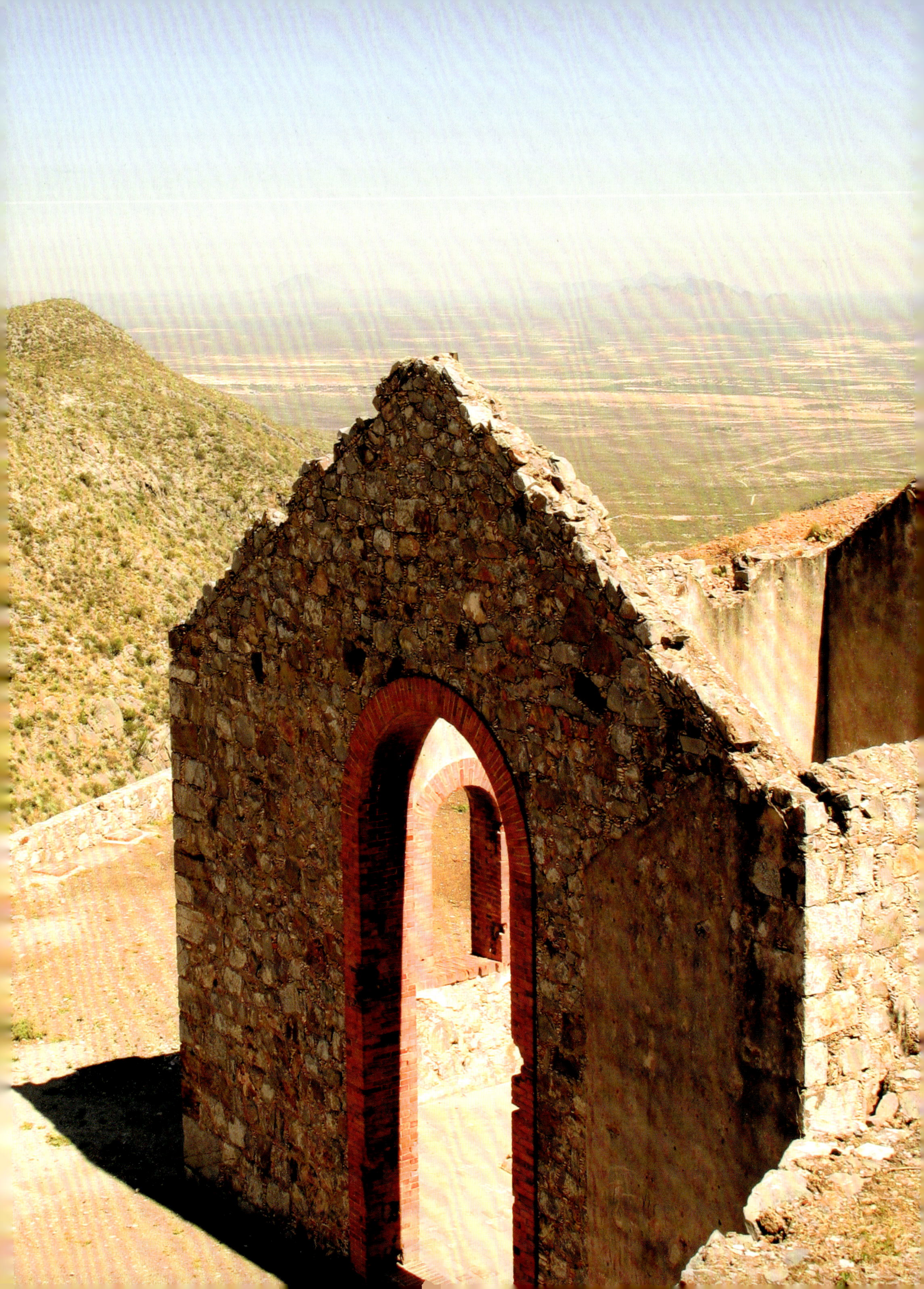

South & Central America

It is the location that often grabs your attention first. Many of the ghost towns in this chapter are set in places of unparalleled beauty, sat high atop Andean plateaus or within the depths of the Amazonian rainforest. These natural settings are spectacular and picturesque, setting the ruins of the ghost town against a majestic backdrop, and adding to their aura of romanticism. But we should always remind ourselves that there is all the difference in the world between viewing a place through traveller's eyes, and through those of someone who actually lived there. Workers labouring in South and Central America's remote or high-altitude locations would have had little time or energy to think about the beauty of their surroundings. Indeed, notwithstanding the exhaustion and industrial diseases that often accompanied their labours, the workers would also have to endure everything that nature could throw at them, from sub-zero winters in thin atmospheres to cloying tropical humidity. Then there was also the fact of what happened to the inhabitants of the ghost town once their mine closed or their community dispersed. Taking on board these reflections reminds us that the ghost towns of the southern Americas have a human history worthy of respect. Often in the face of much adversity, thrown at them by both nature and other human beings, entire communities managed to forge livings in the most demanding of contexts.

LEFT:
Ojuela, Coahuila, Mexico
As this old church attests, faith remained important to the gold and silver miners of Ojuela in northern Mexico. Mining in the territory began back in the 16th century, but it was during the 19th that the settlement flourished. The ore deposits ran out in the early 20th century.

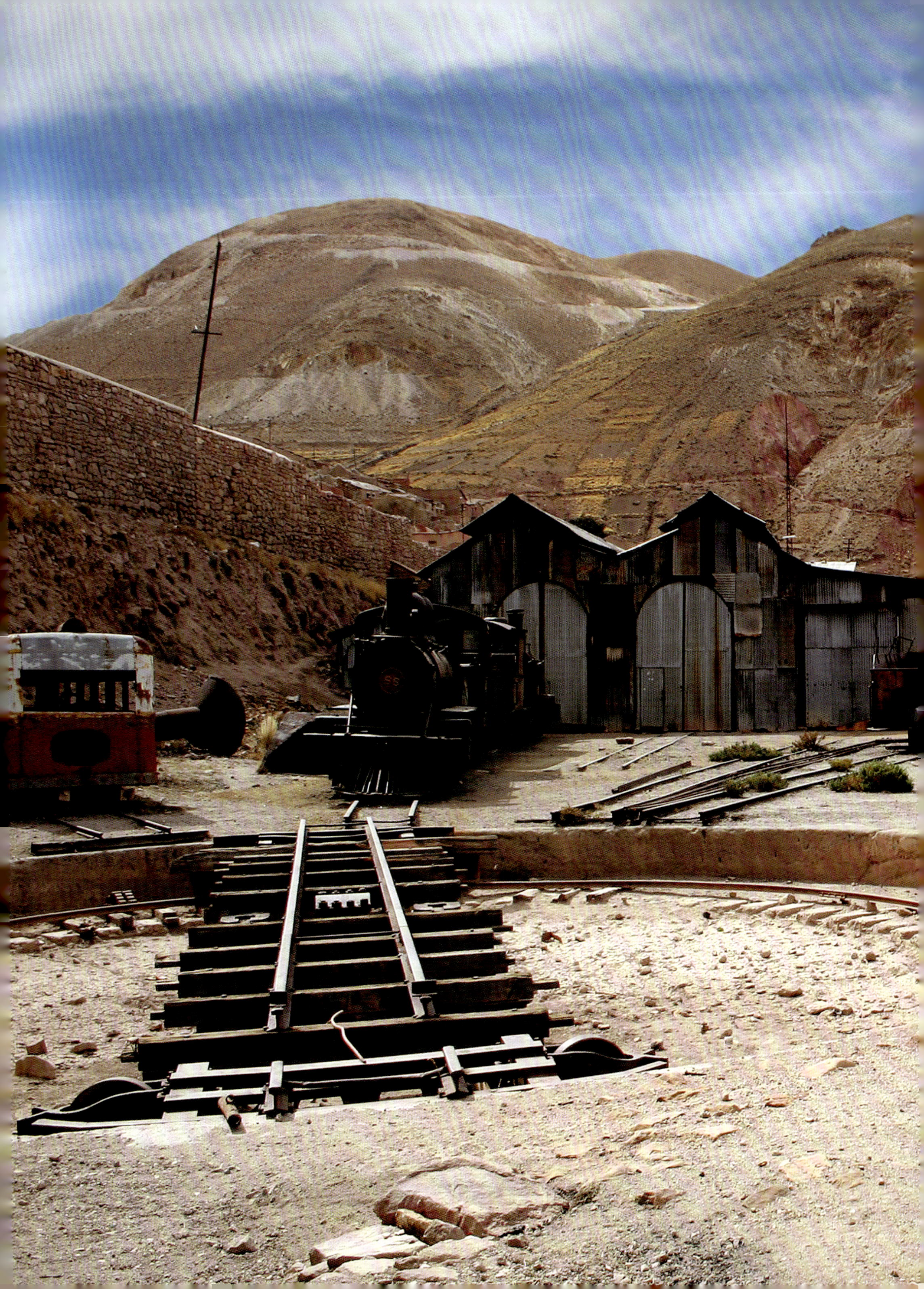

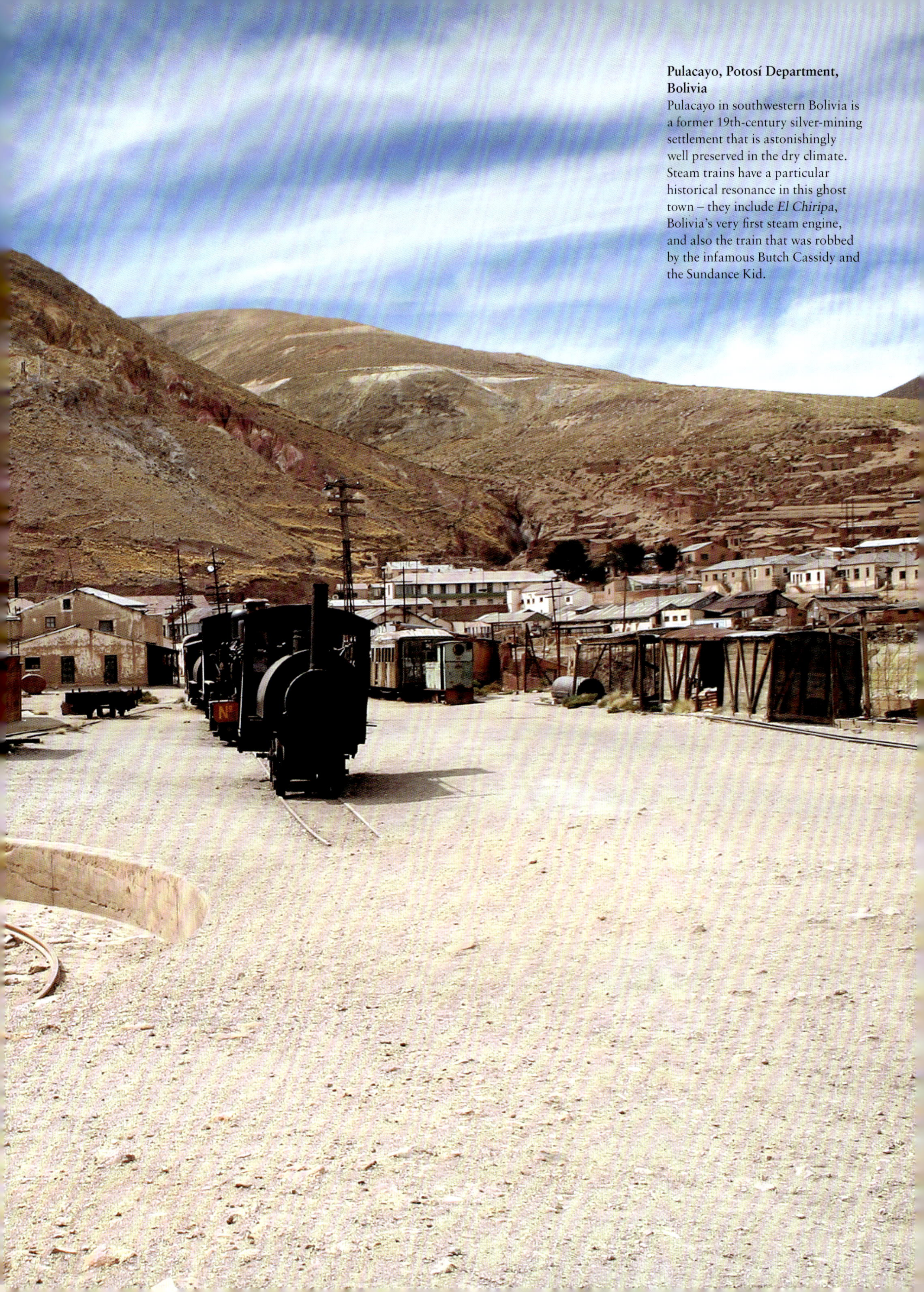

Pulacayo, Potosí Department, Bolivia
Pulacayo in southwestern Bolivia is a former 19th-century silver-mining settlement that is astonishingly well preserved in the dry climate. Steam trains have a particular historical resonance in this ghost town – they include *El Chiripa*, Bolivia's very first steam engine, and also the train that was robbed by the infamous Butch Cassidy and the Sundance Kid.

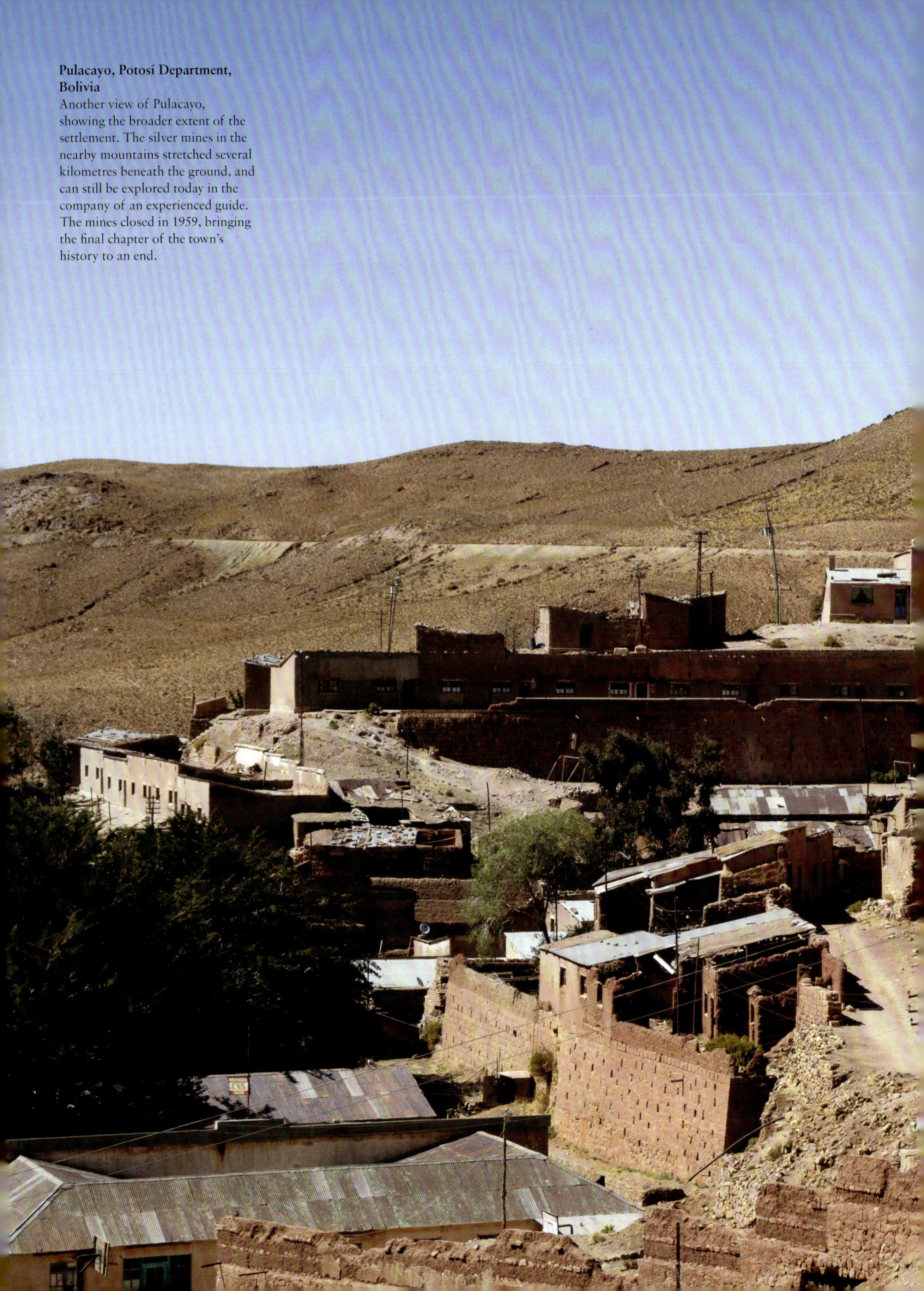

Pulacayo, Potosí Department, Bolivia
Another view of Pulacayo, showing the broader extent of the settlement. The silver mines in the nearby mountains stretched several kilometres beneath the ground, and can still be explored today in the company of an experienced guide. The mines closed in 1959, bringing the final chapter of the town's history to an end.

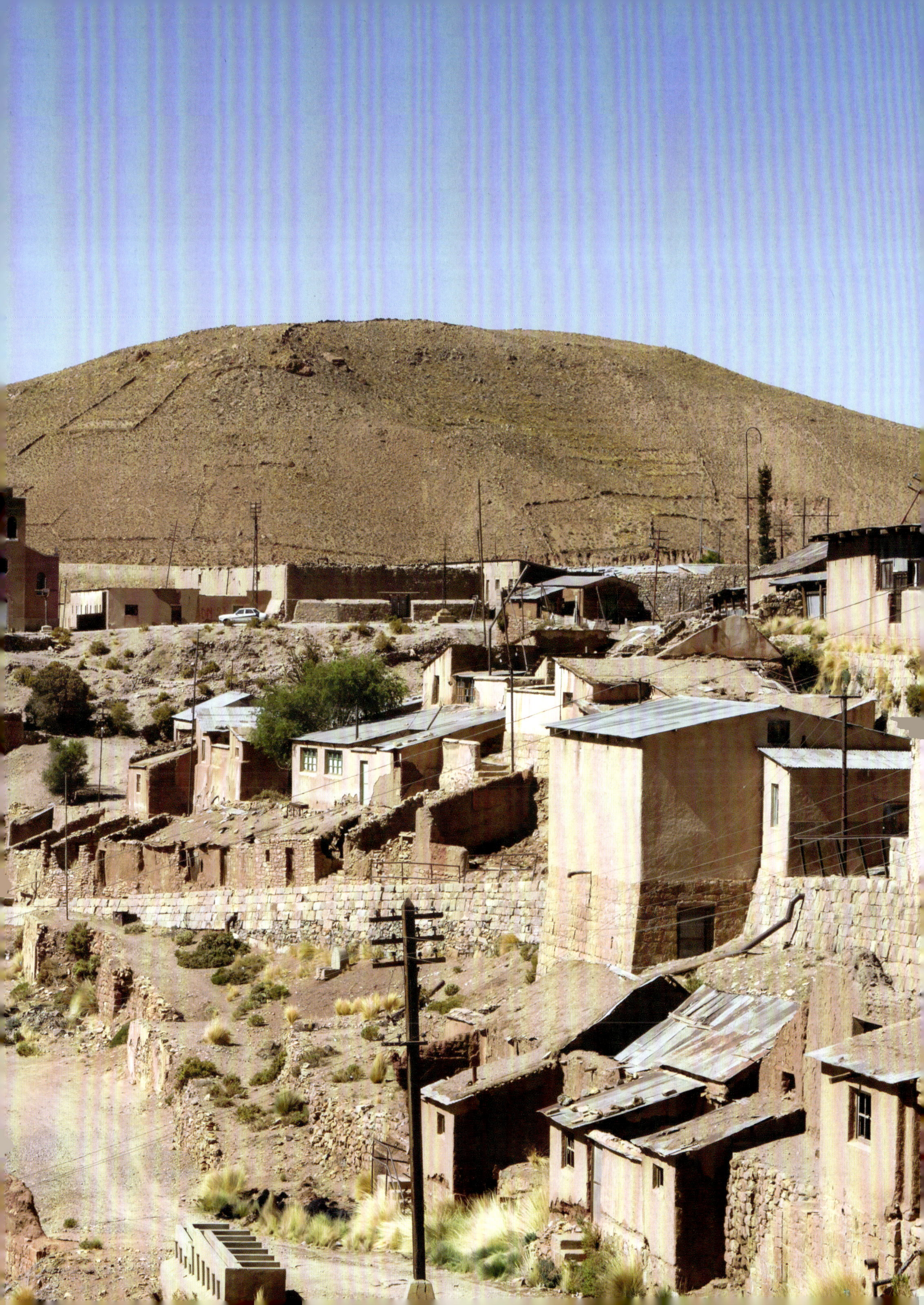

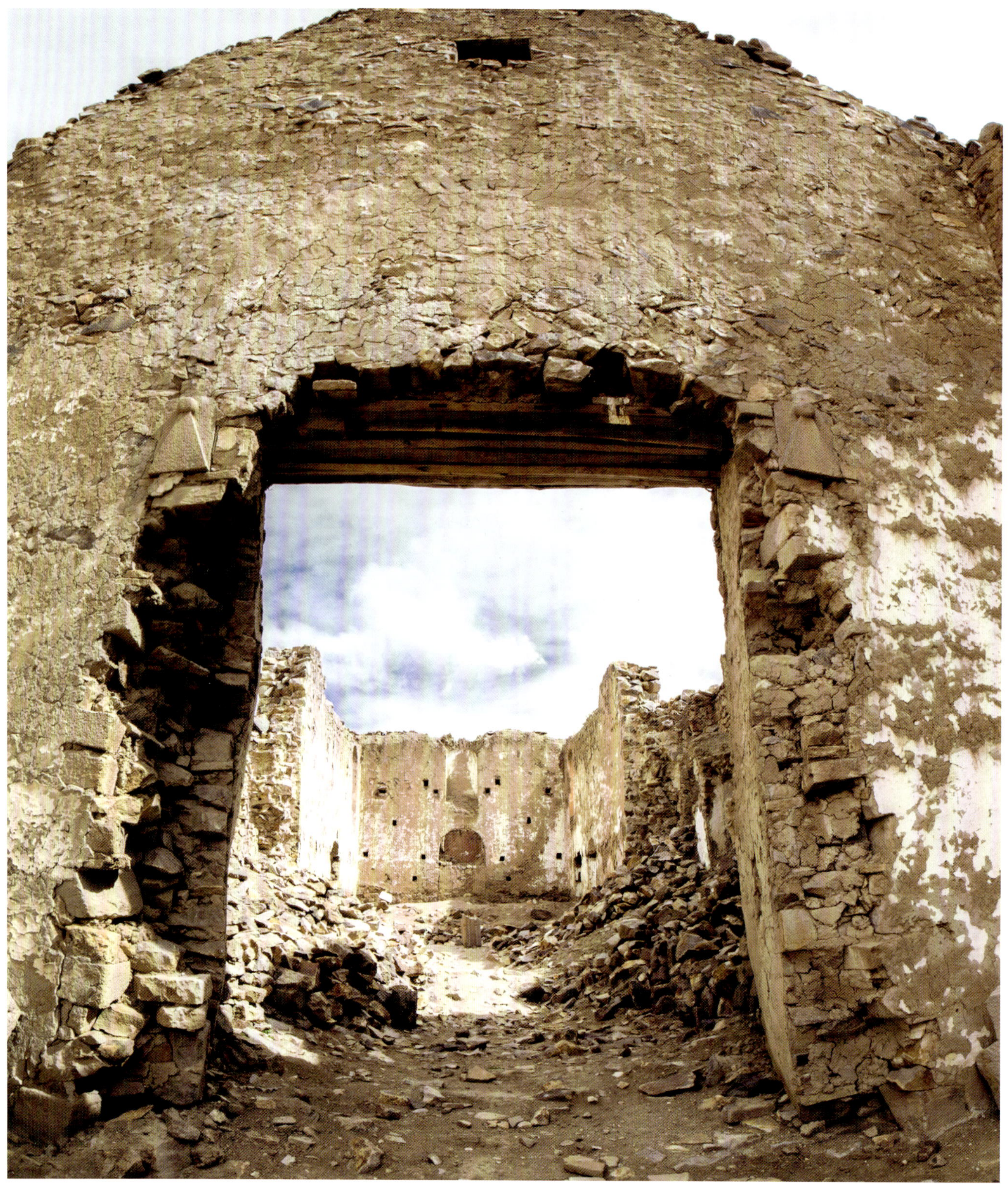

ABOVE:
San Antonio de Lipez, Uyuni, Bolivia
The history of this gold-mining settlement stretches back to the 16th century. Today the only industries in the immediate area are related to agriculture, particularly to livestock (sheep and llamas), potatoes and quinoa.

OPPOSITE ABOVE:
San Antonio de Lipez, Uyuni, Bolivia
Another crumbling building from San Antonio de Lipez. The scale of the mining activity has now been virtually erased by time, but at one point some 150,000 people might have been living in the vicinity of the local mines.

OPPOSITE BELOW:
San Antonio de Lipez, Uyuni, Bolivia
Dark legends surround the abandoned site of San Antonio de Lipez. Some tales speak of the mine workers making a pact with the Devil to bring wealth, but breaking the pact and thus bringing a curse down upon them.

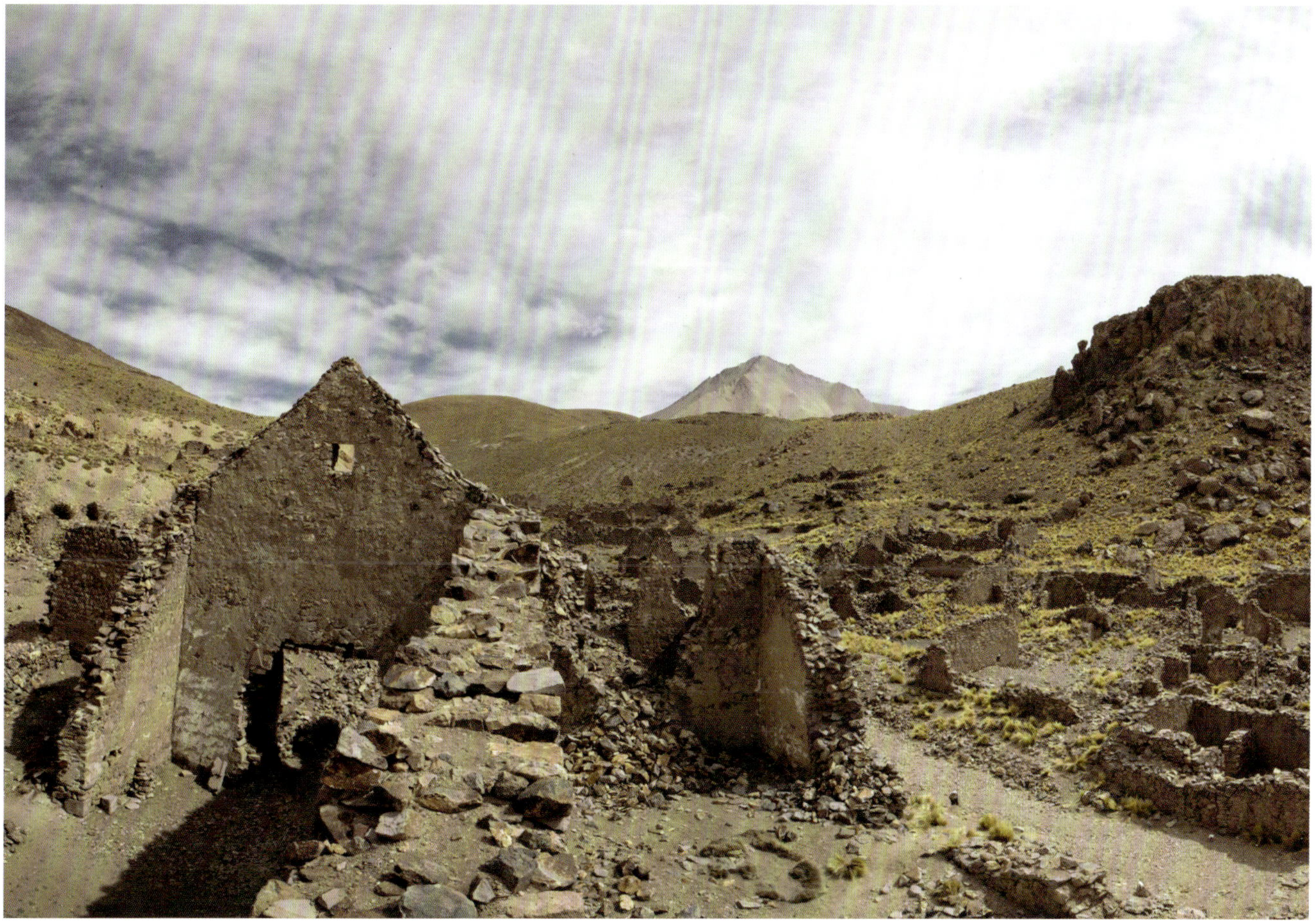

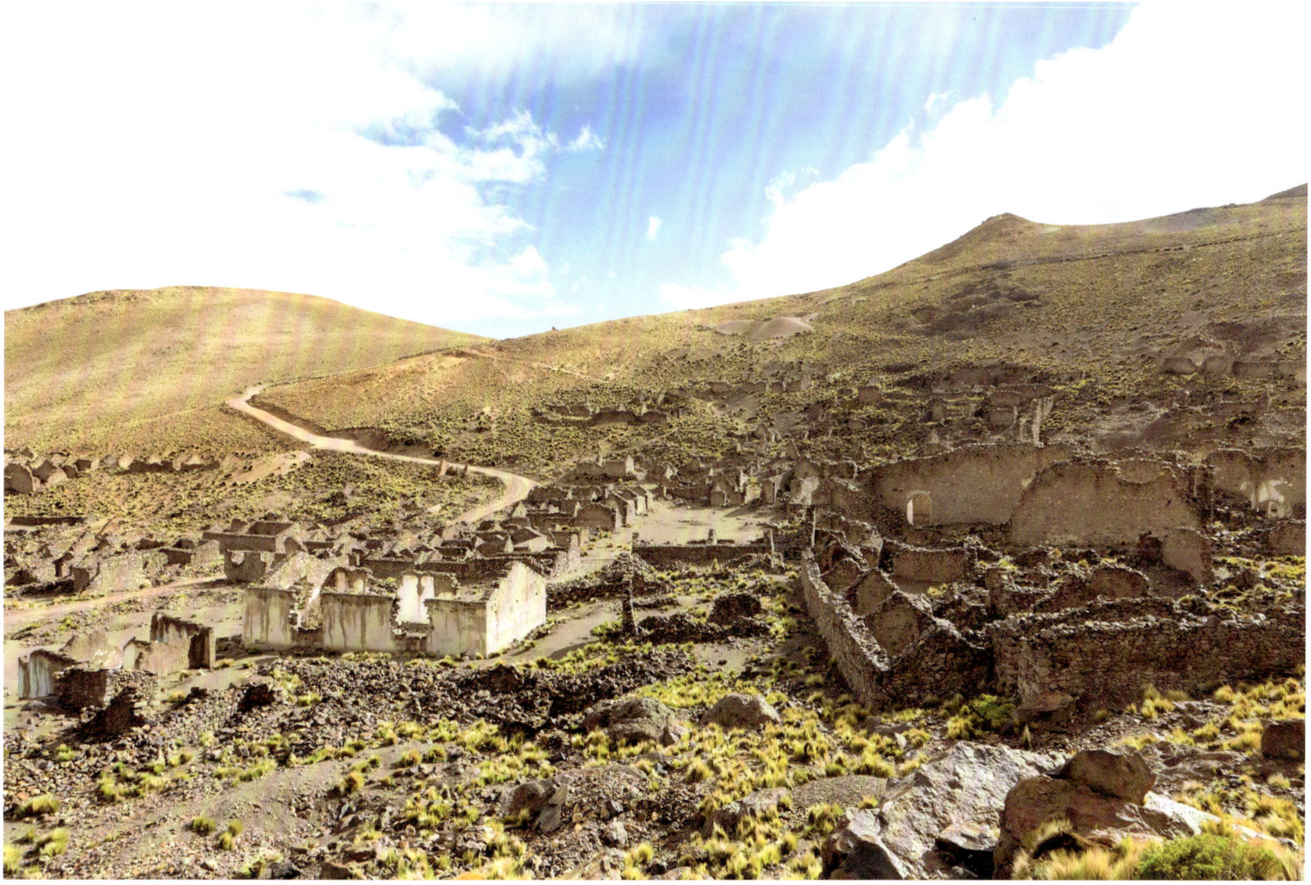

ALL PHOTOGRAPHS:

Fordlândia, Pará, Brazil

Fordlândia was an extraordinary commercial and social experiment by none other than the automative industrialist Henry T. Ford. He acquired the land in the mid-1920s, his ambition being to create a huge facility for the production of rubber (thus circumventing the British monopoly on the product) and also to create something of a utopian society for the plant's estimated 10,000 workers. Building work began in 1929, and when completed the complex had many modern facilities, including a hospital, schools, a library, a golf course, swimming pool and dance halls. Yet a utopia it was not. The work of rubber tapping was arduous, and very strict social rules were imposed on the population. The American managers had little idea of how to manage either their workers or the tropical plantations, and the factories produced little of value. Riots and violence broke out in 1930, and in 1934 Ford abandoned the project.

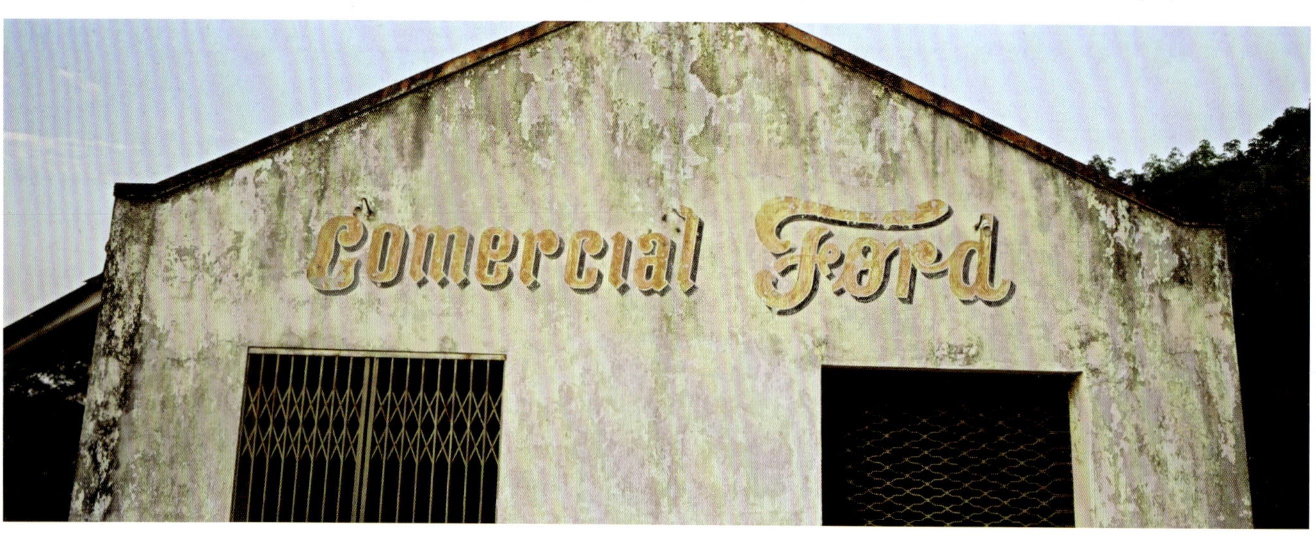

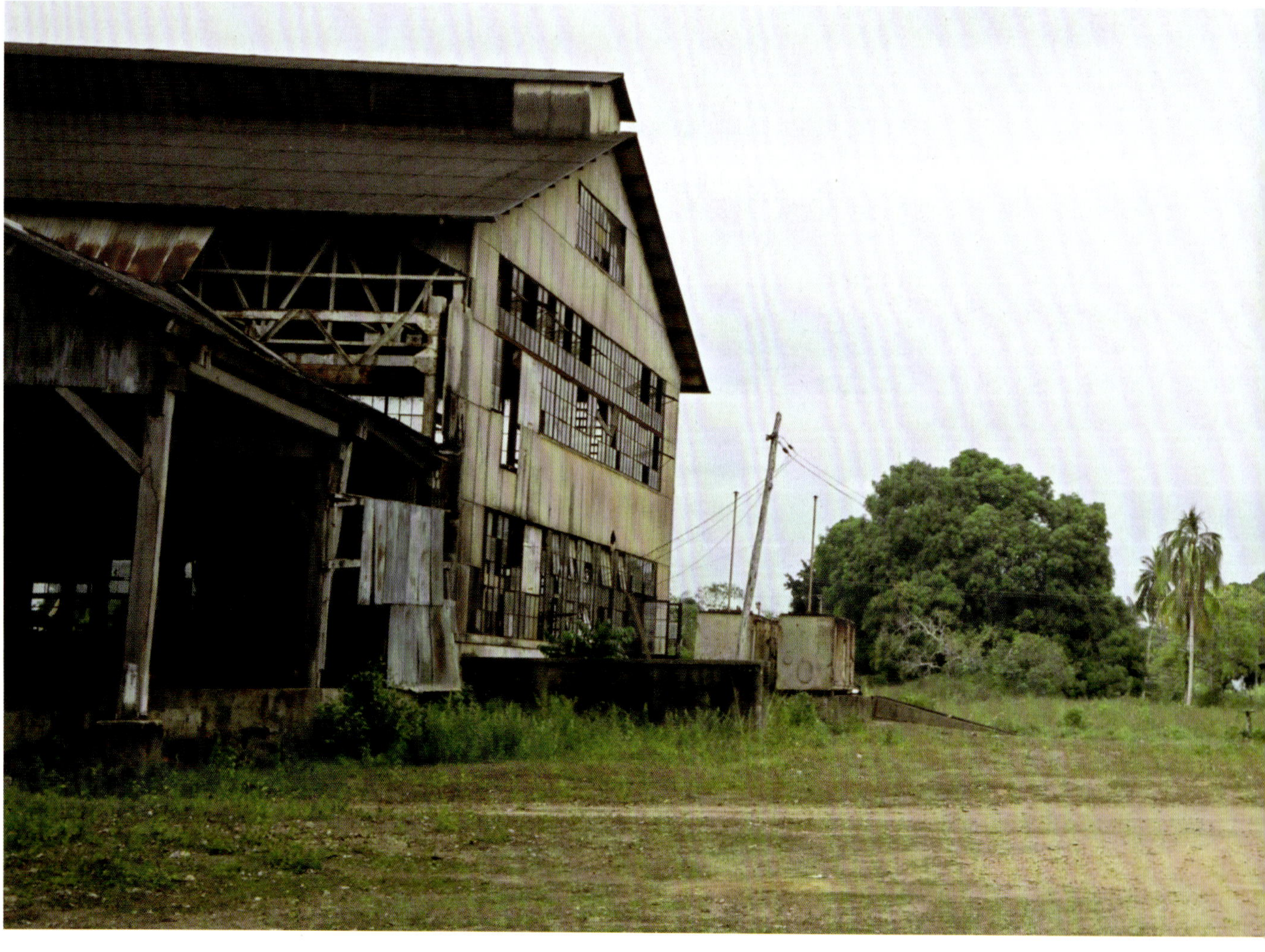

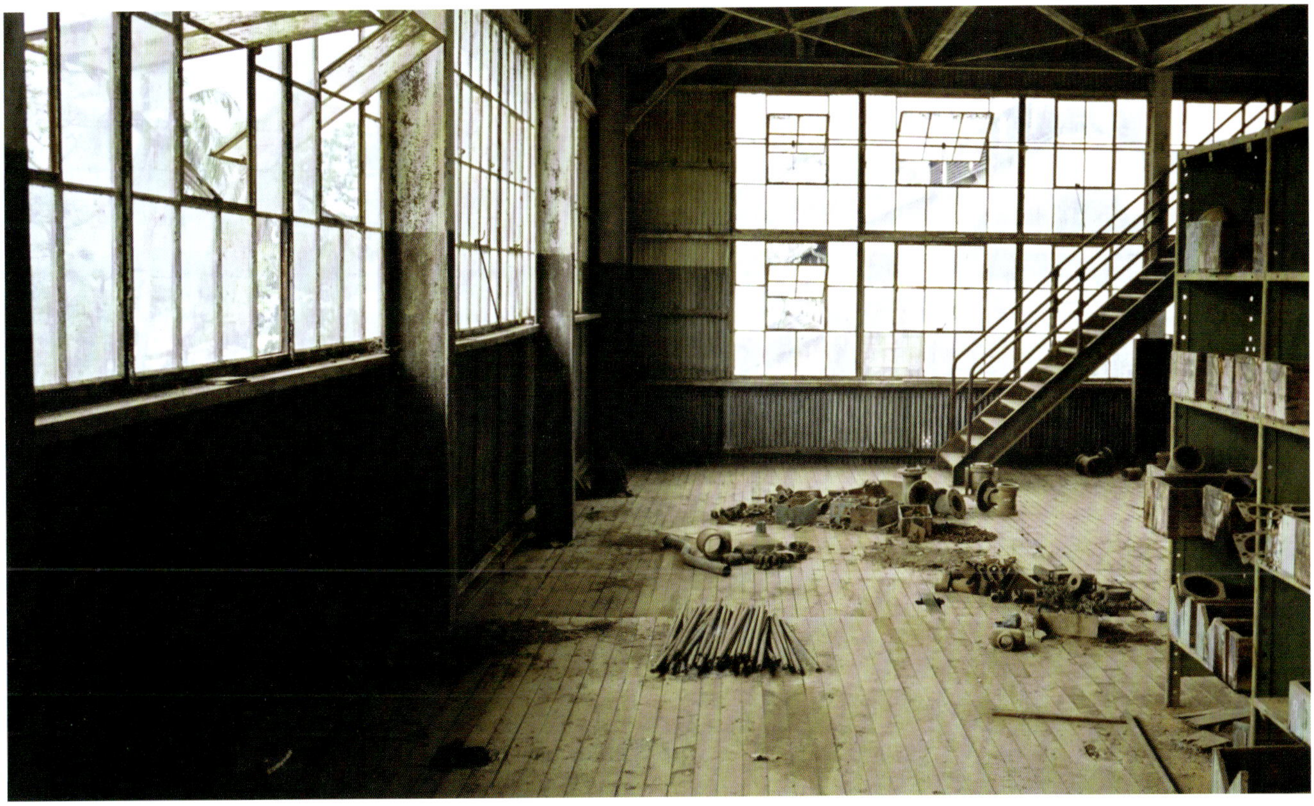

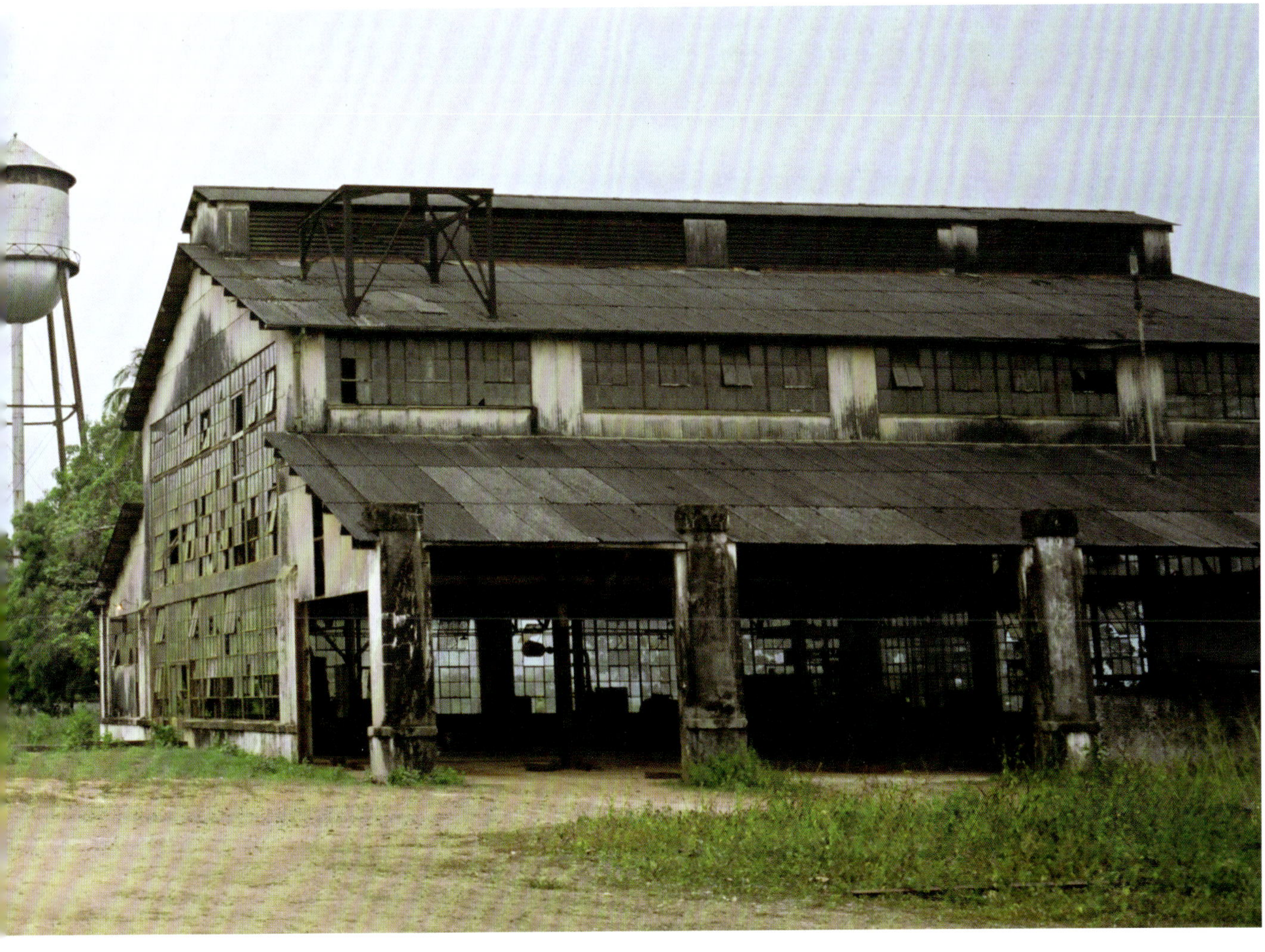

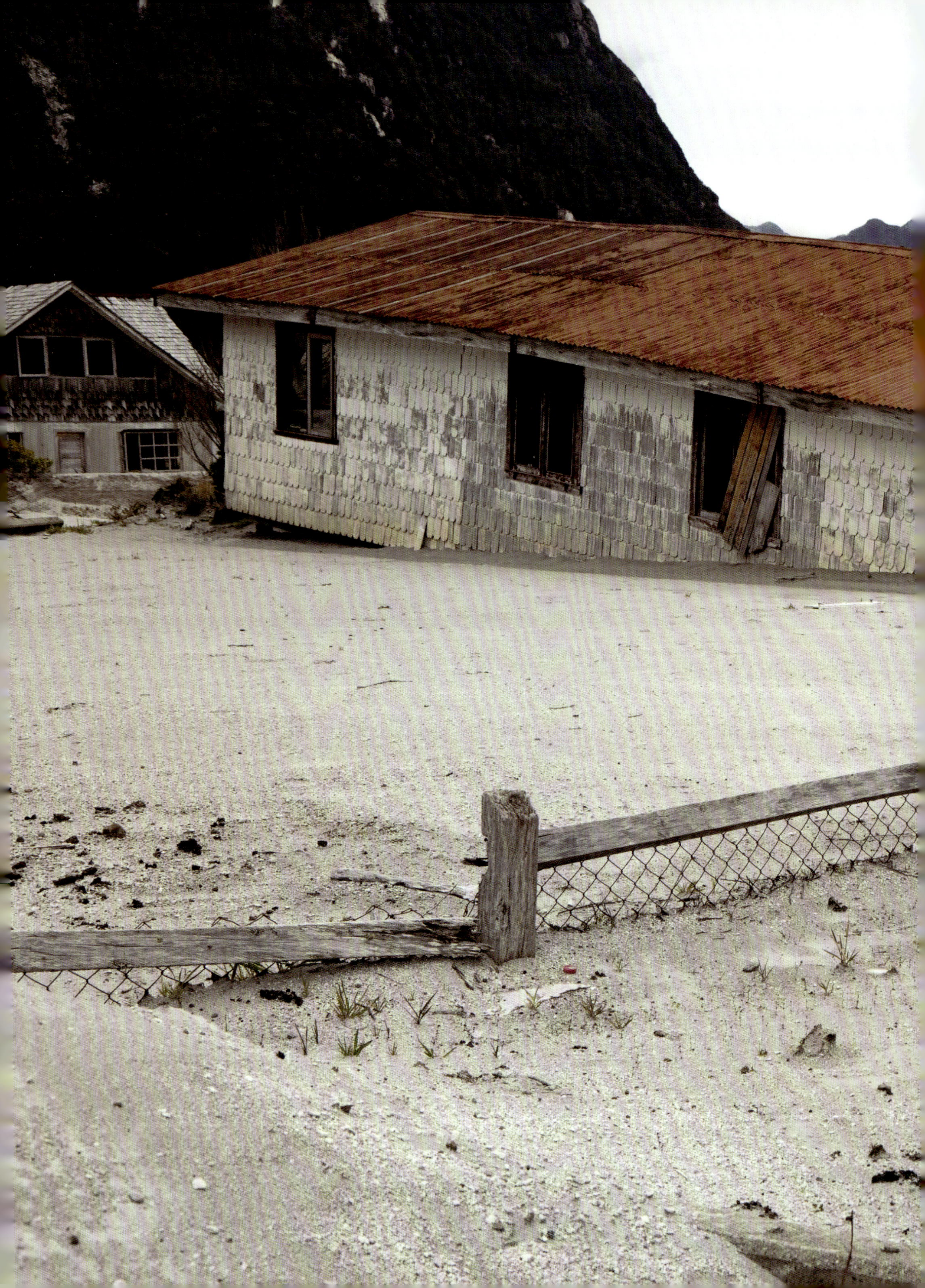

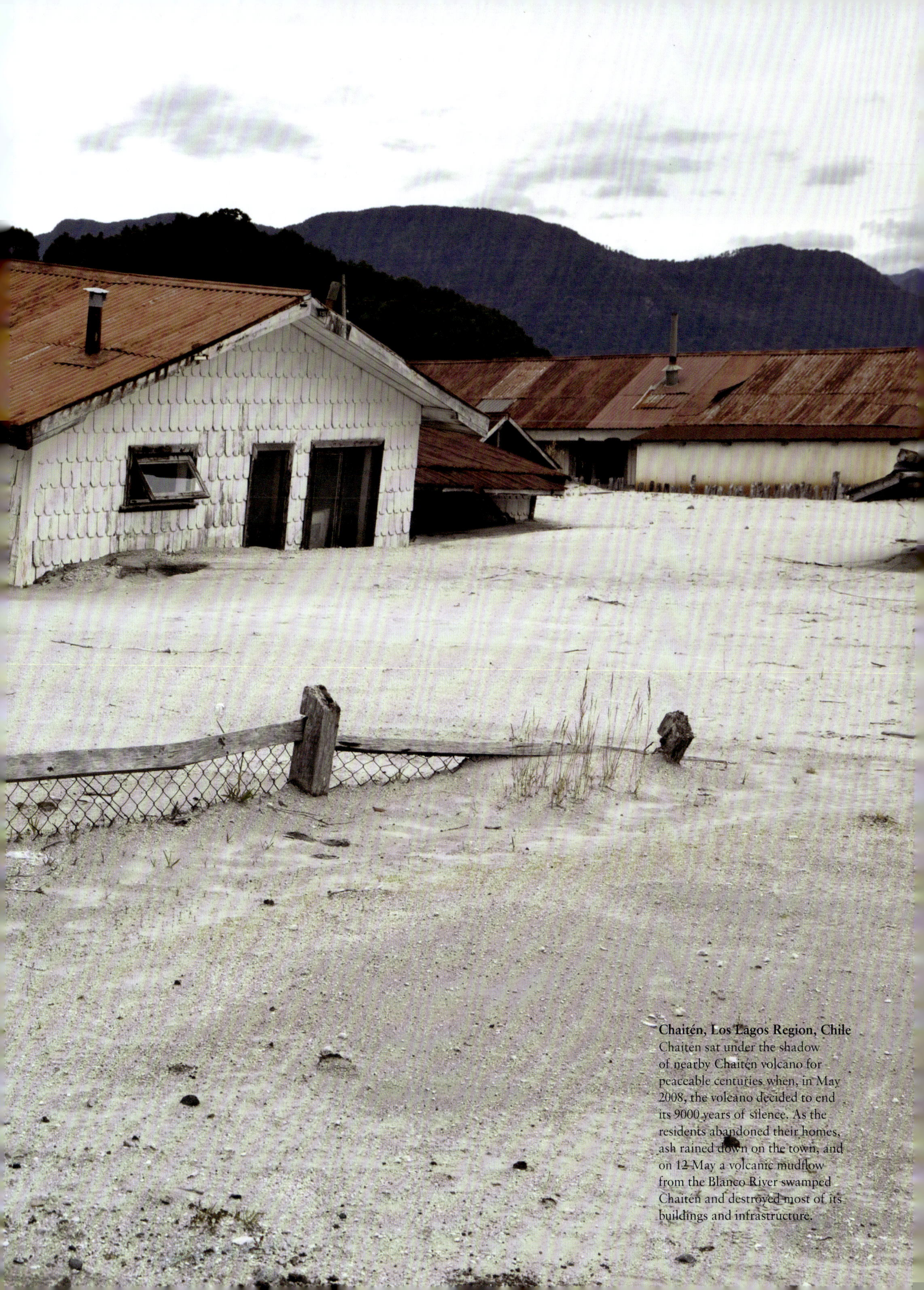

Chaitén, Los Lagos Region, Chile
Chaitén sat under the shadow of nearby Chaitén volcano for peaceable centuries when, in May 2008, the volcano decided to end its 9000 years of silence. As the residents abandoned their homes, ash rained down on the town, and on 12 May a volcanic mudflow from the Blanco River swamped Chaitén and destroyed most of its buildings and infrastructure.

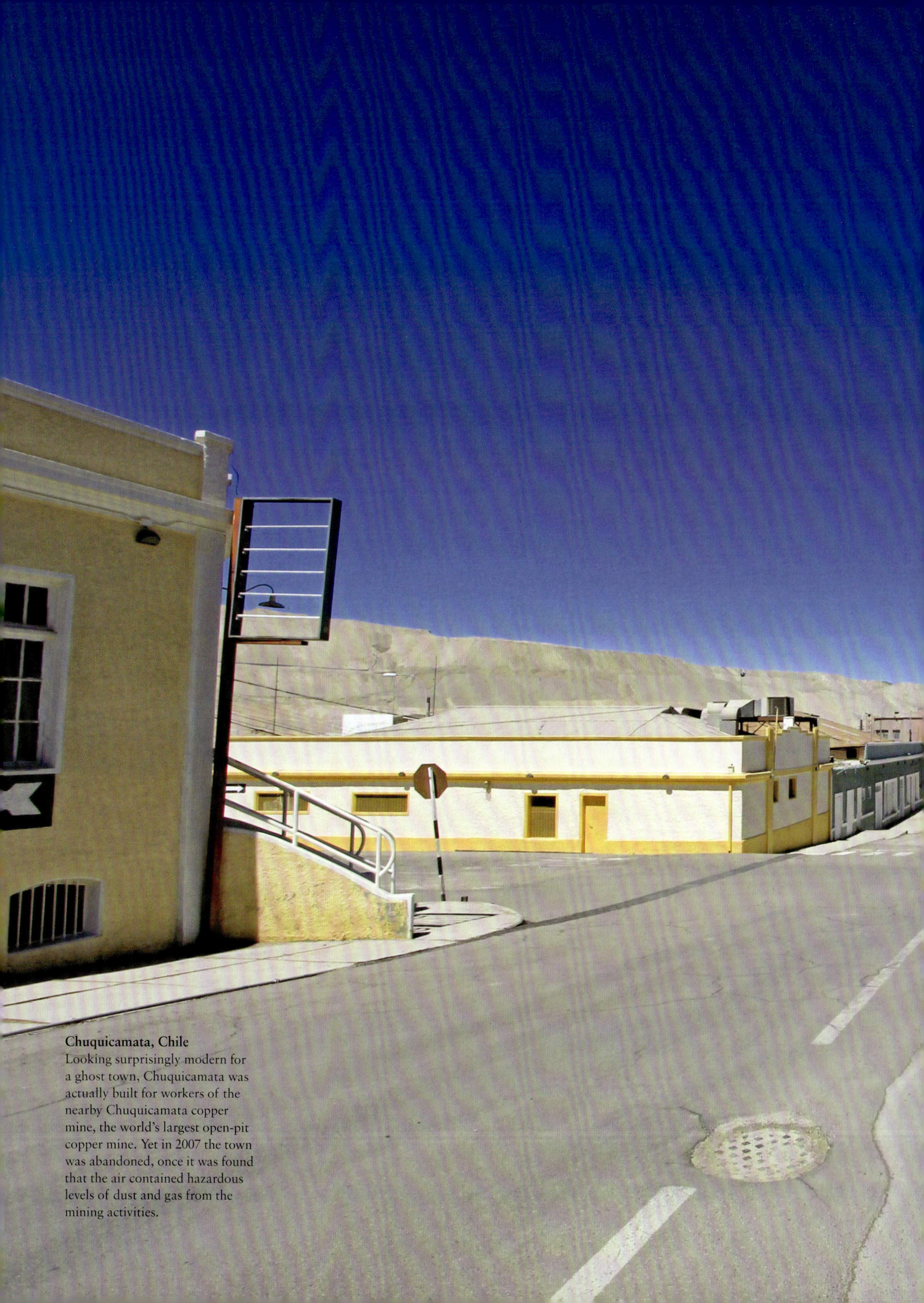

Chuquicamata, Chile
Looking surprisingly modern for a ghost town, Chuquicamata was actually built for workers of the nearby Chuquicamata copper mine, the world's largest open-pit copper mine. Yet in 2007 the town was abandoned, once it was found that the air contained hazardous levels of dust and gas from the mining activities.

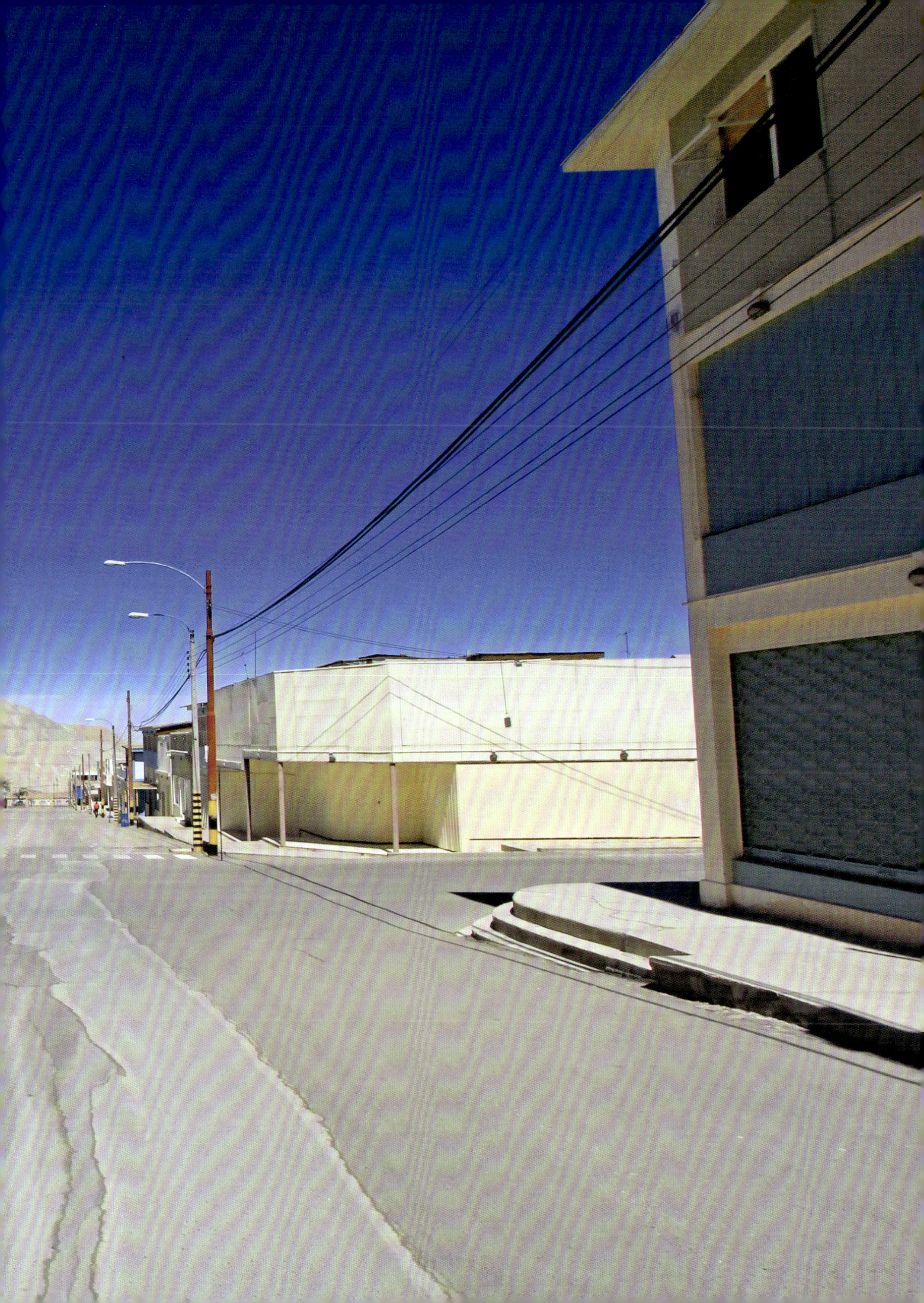

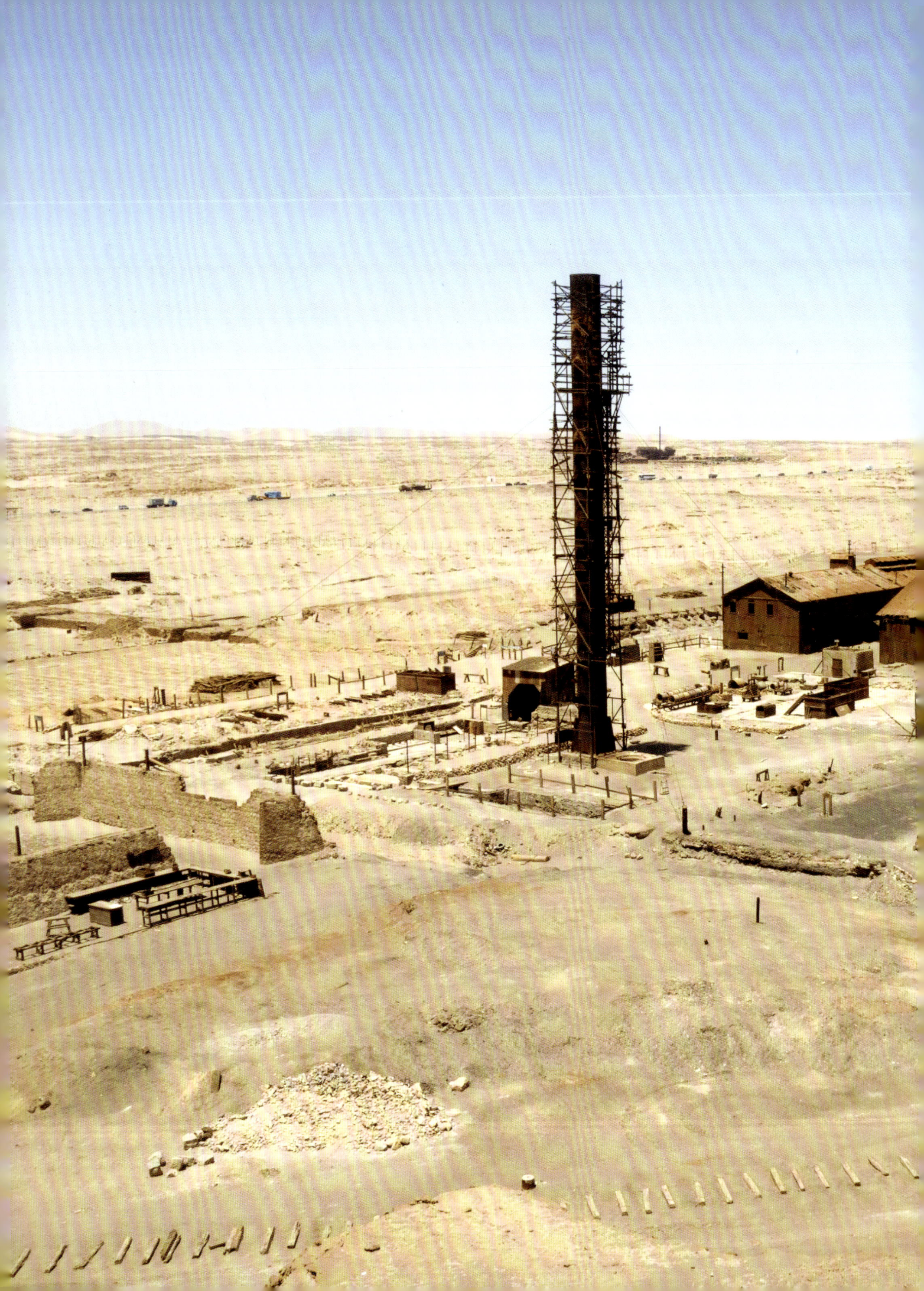

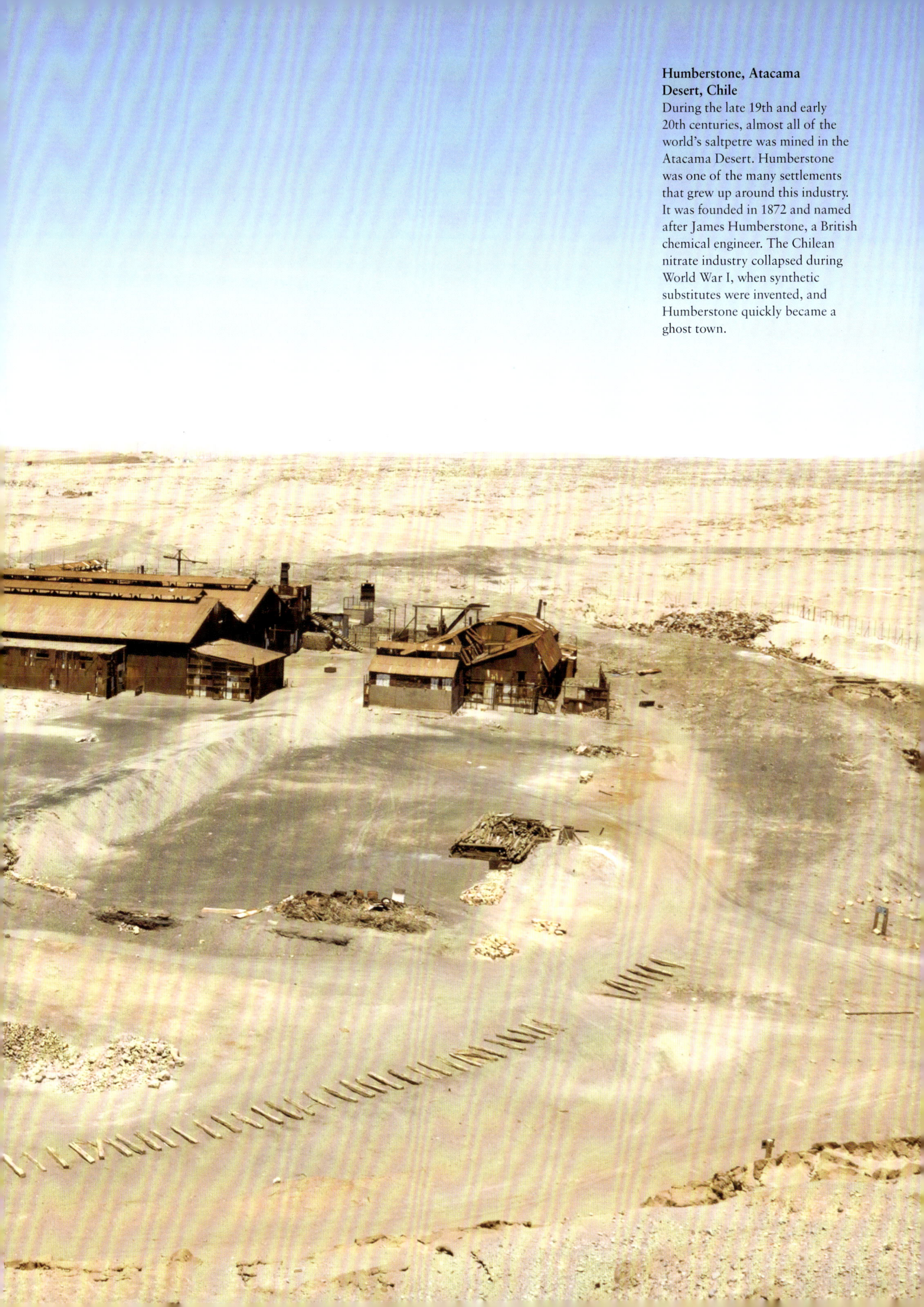

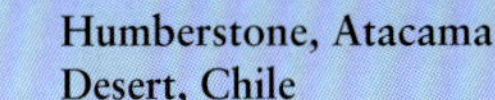

Humberstone, Atacama Desert, Chile

During the late 19th and early 20th centuries, almost all of the world's saltpetre was mined in the Atacama Desert. Humberstone was one of the many settlements that grew up around this industry. It was founded in 1872 and named after James Humberstone, a British chemical engineer. The Chilean nitrate industry collapsed during World War I, when synthetic substitutes were invented, and Humberstone quickly became a ghost town.

Sewell Mining Town, Andes, Chile

This extraordinary mining town, built 2000m (6562ft) up in the Andes in 1905 by the Braden Copper Company, was yet another workers' housing settlement, this one used for employees of the world's largest underground copper mine, El Teniente. Logistical difficulties accessing the town, plus changes in the mine's commercial ownership, led to abandonment in the 1970s.

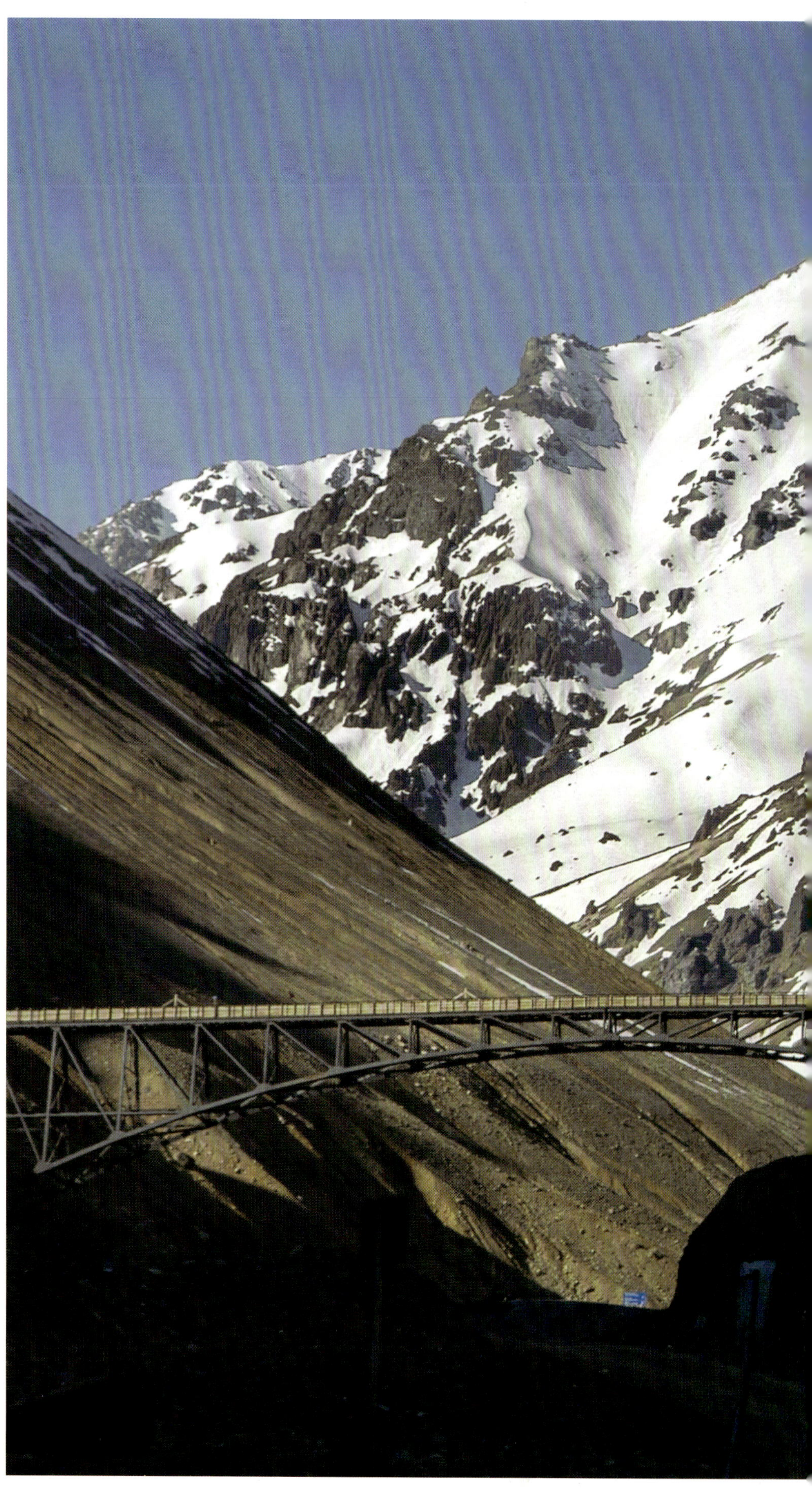

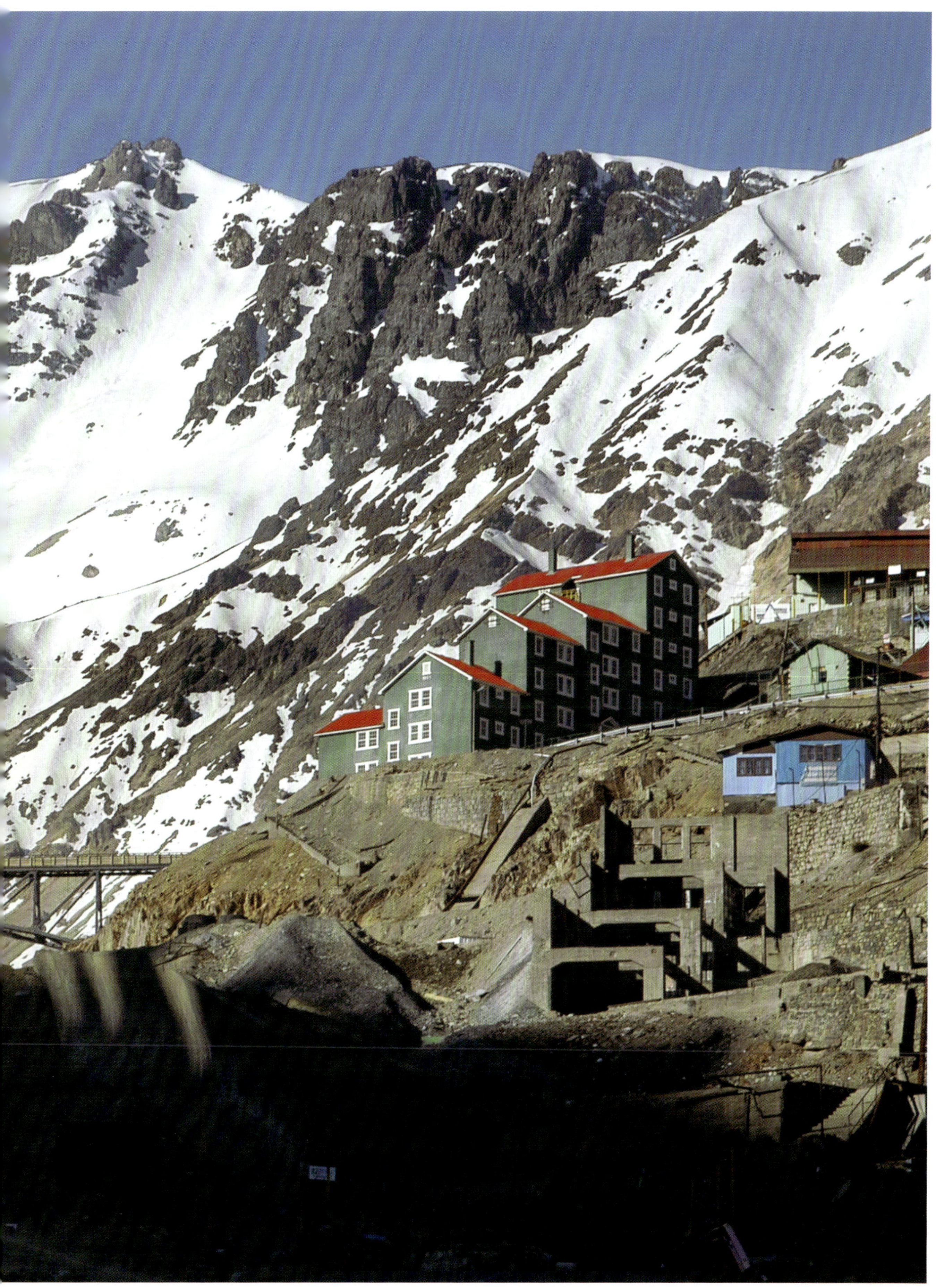

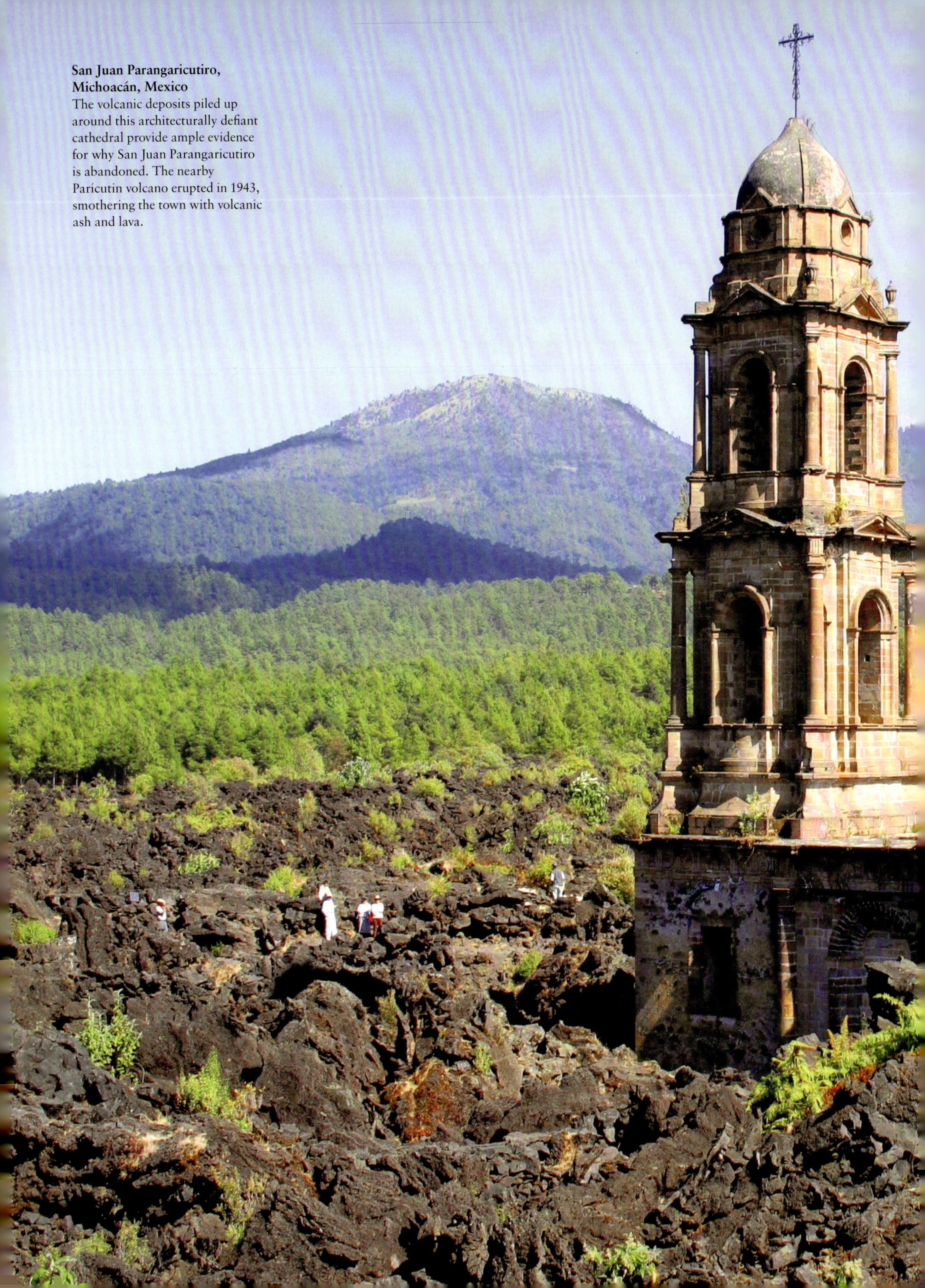

San Juan Parangaricutiro, Michoacán, Mexico
The volcanic deposits piled up around this architecturally defiant cathedral provide ample evidence for why San Juan Parangaricutiro is abandoned. The nearby Parícutin volcano erupted in 1943, smothering the town with volcanic ash and lava.

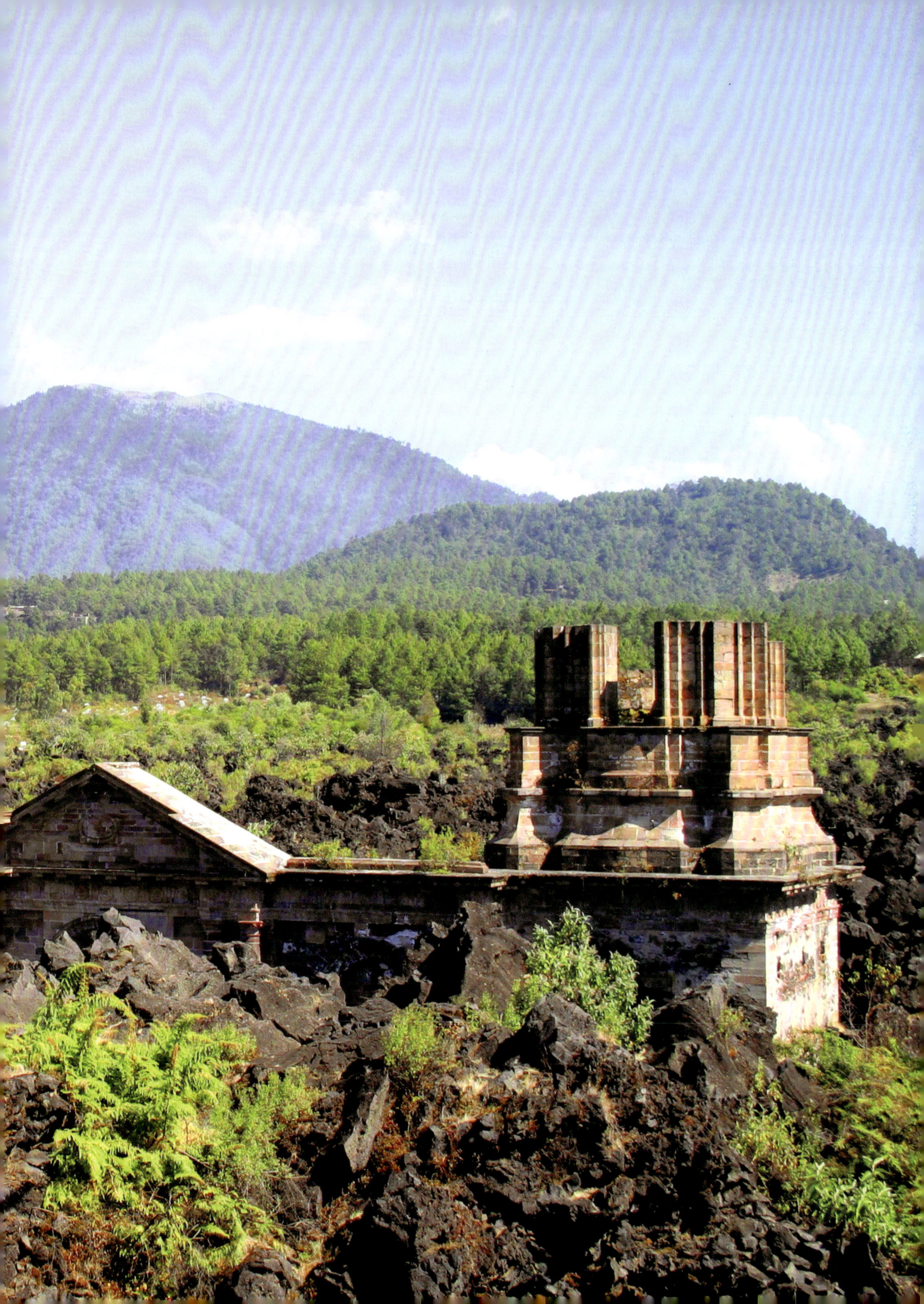

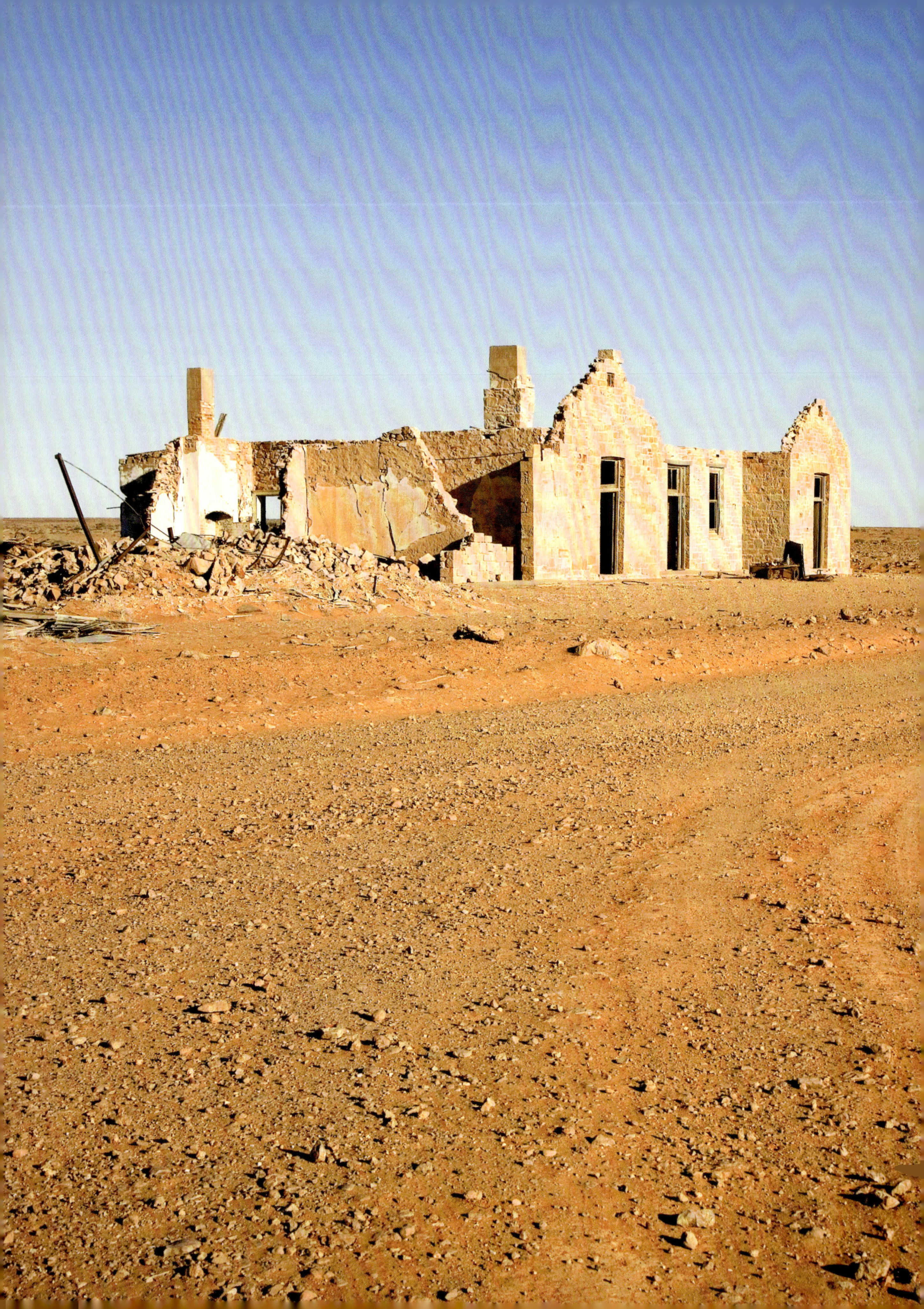

Australasia

The defining characteristic of the ghost towns in this chapter is remoteness. Australia is a truly vast continent – it is the sixth largest country in the world – but most (89 per cent) of its current 25 million inhabitants cluster in a thin ring of cities around Australia's coastline. Bearing in mind that Australia's landmass totals 7.7 million square kilometres (3 million square miles), and we start to get a sense of how sparsely populated this nation really is. Indeed, Australia has the global second lowest population density, beaten only by Mongolia. A full 90 per cent of the territory is officially classed as 'uninhabitable', based particularly on a lack of water and on the ground being unsuitable for agriculture. Yet the ghost towns featured here often did attempt, even for just a few short decades, to survive in this most inhospitable of wildernesses. Typically they clustered around a mine or a railroad, sometimes with explosive increases in the population – Kiandra, for example, went from having almost no inhabitants to being a settlement of more than 10,000 people in less than a year. But once the mining ceased to be profitable for either individuals or companies, the towns emptied rapidly. The scarcity of water in Australia's inland areas, plus the outback's dangerous wildlife, lack of vegetation and tropical temperatures, meant that only the hardiest, or most foolhardy, individuals chose to stay.

LEFT:
Farina, Lyndhurst Marree Road, Australia
Here stand the remains of the Transcontinental Hotel in Farina, an outback settlement some 650km (400 miles) to the north of Adelaide. This agricultural community was founded in 1878, and its peak population was 600 souls, but the cruelty of the climate led to the town's steady abandonment.

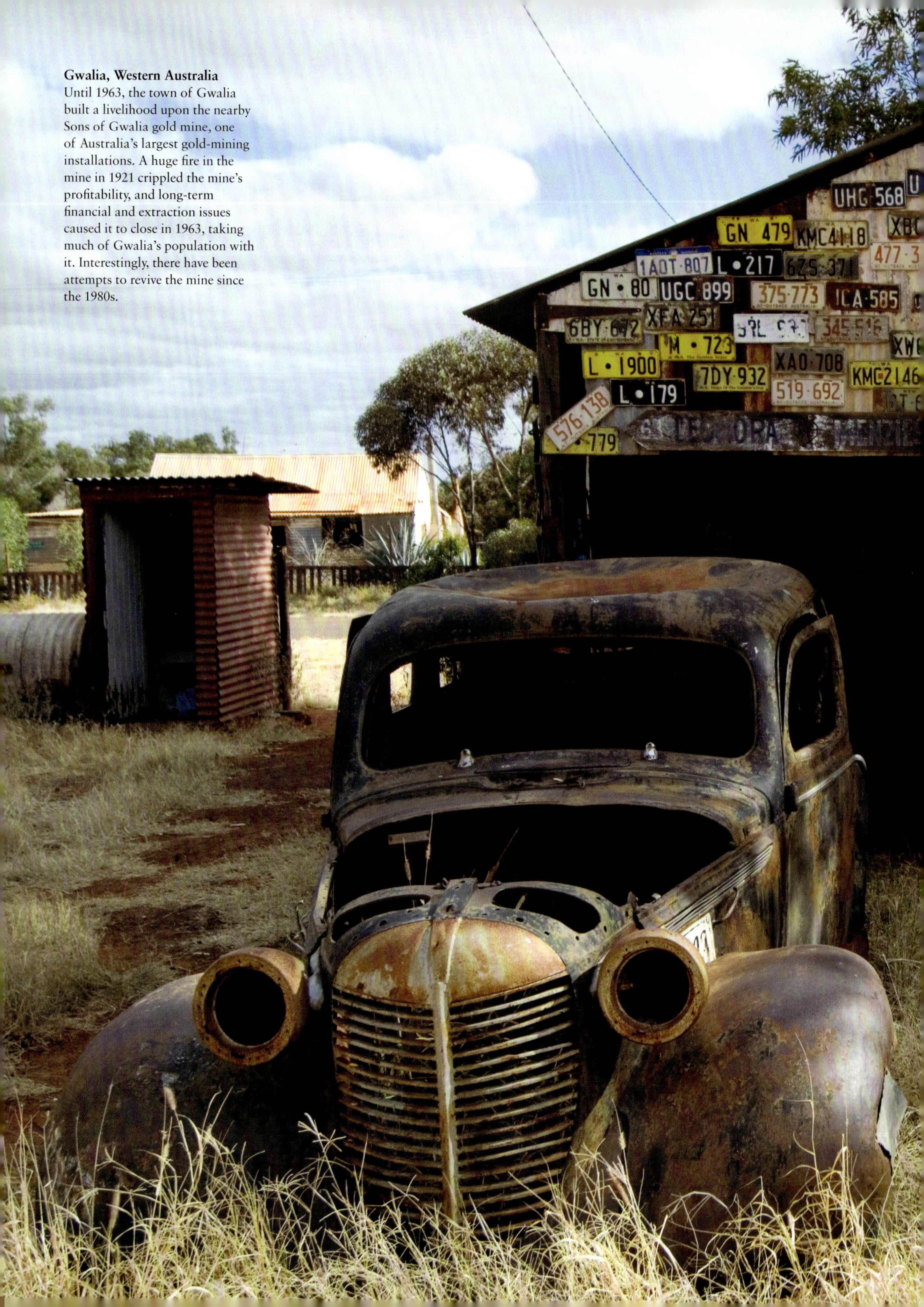

Gwalia, Western Australia

Until 1963, the town of Gwalia built a livelihood upon the nearby Sons of Gwalia gold mine, one of Australia's largest gold-mining installations. A huge fire in the mine in 1921 crippled the mine's profitability, and long-term financial and extraction issues caused it to close in 1963, taking much of Gwalia's population with it. Interestingly, there have been attempts to revive the mine since the 1980s.

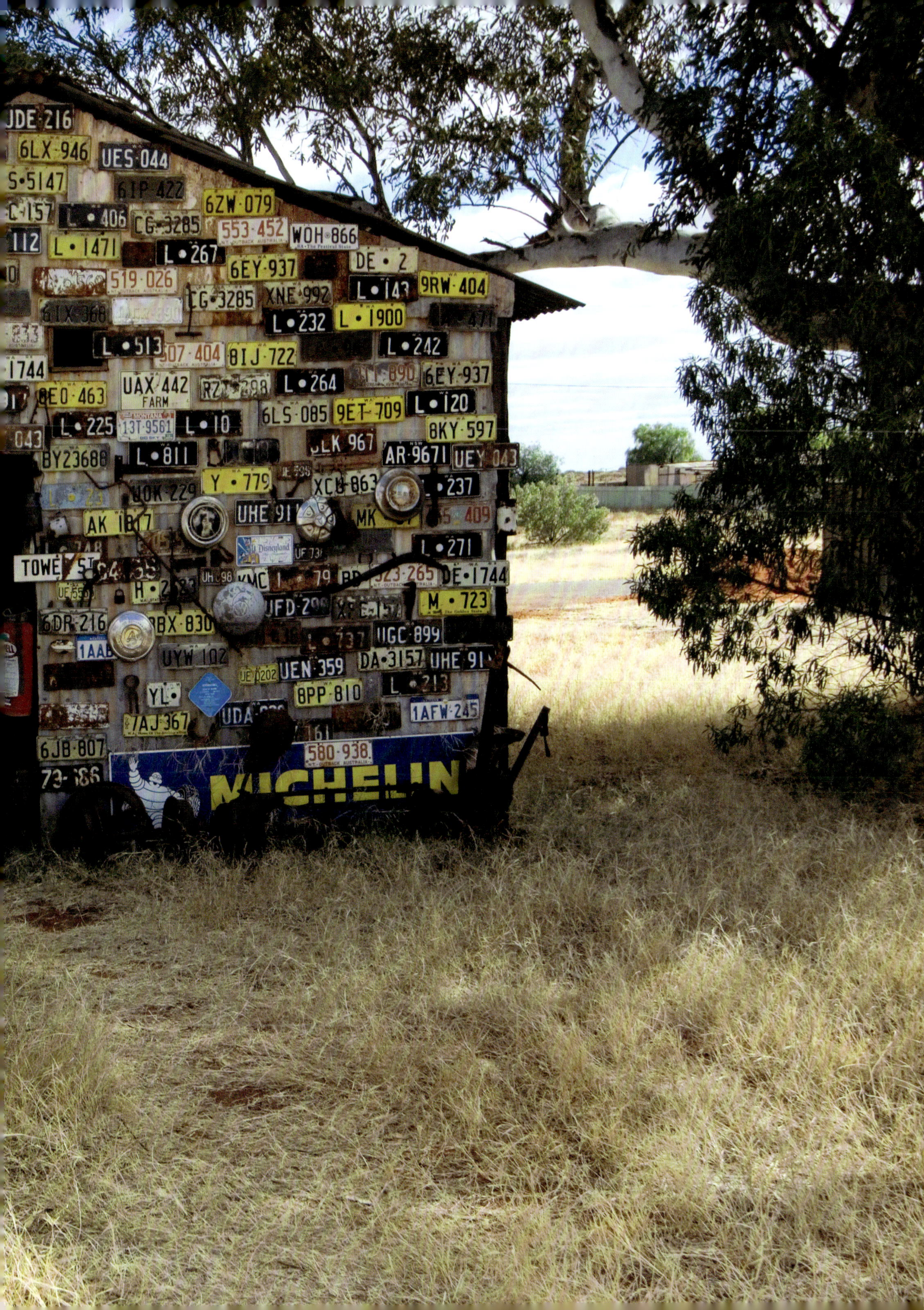
JDE 216
6LX 946
UES 044
S•5147
6ZW 079
553 452
WOH 866
L•1471
L•267
6EY 937
DE•2
519 026
XNE 992
L•143
9RW 404
L•232
L•1900
L•242
L•513
8IJ 722
UAX 442
FARM
L•264
6EY 937
8EO 463
6LS 085
9ET 709
L•120
L•225
L•10
8KY 597
BY23688
L•811
AR•9671
Y•779
UHE 91
L•271
TOWE
DE•1744
M•723
6DR 216
UGC 899
UYW 102
UEN 359
DA•3157
8PP 810
1AFW 245
6JB 807
580 938
MICHELIN

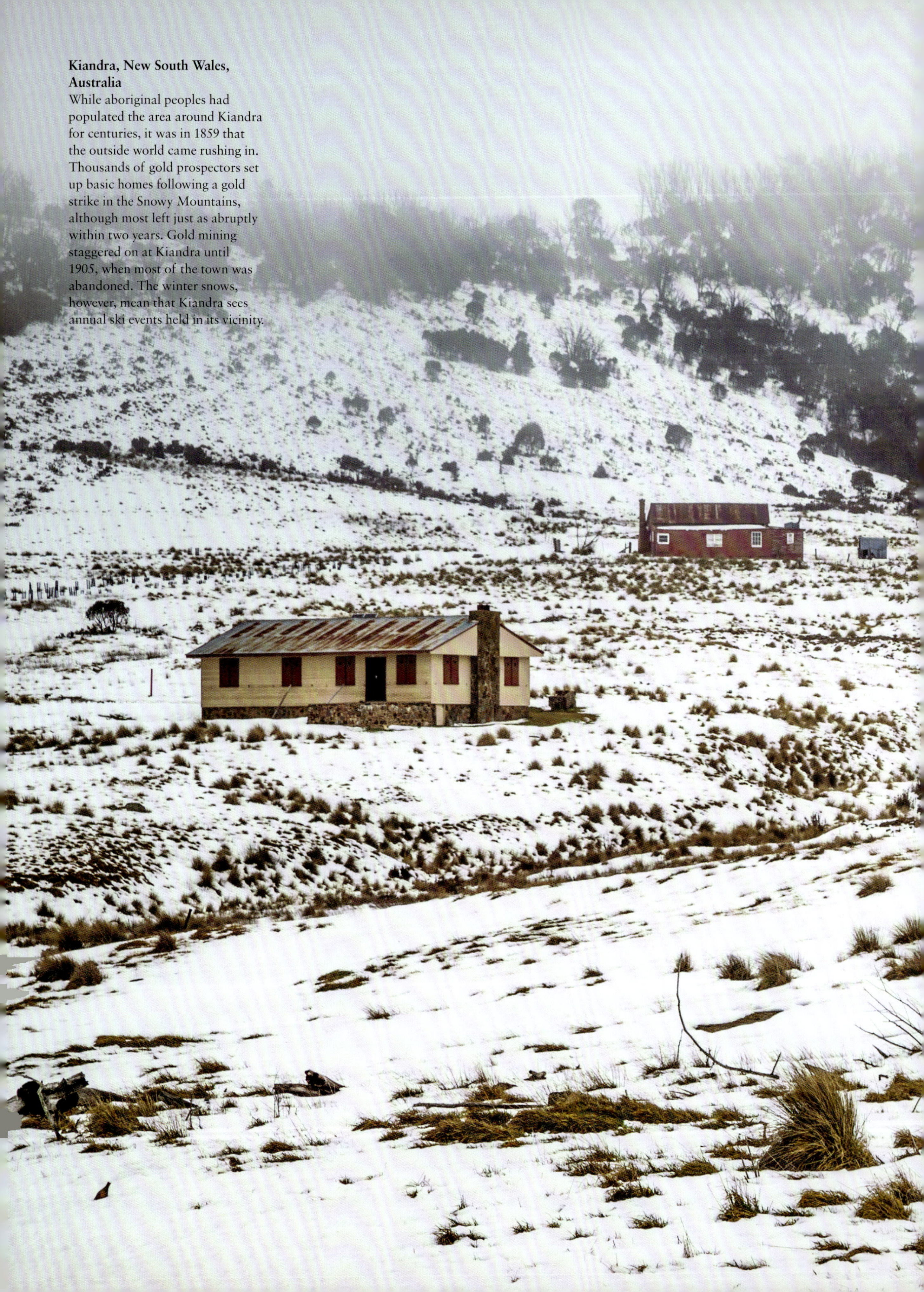

Kiandra, New South Wales, Australia
While aboriginal peoples had populated the area around Kiandra for centuries, it was in 1859 that the outside world came rushing in. Thousands of gold prospectors set up basic homes following a gold strike in the Snowy Mountains, although most left just as abruptly within two years. Gold mining staggered on at Kiandra until 1905, when most of the town was abandoned. The winter snows, however, mean that Kiandra sees annual ski events held in its vicinity.

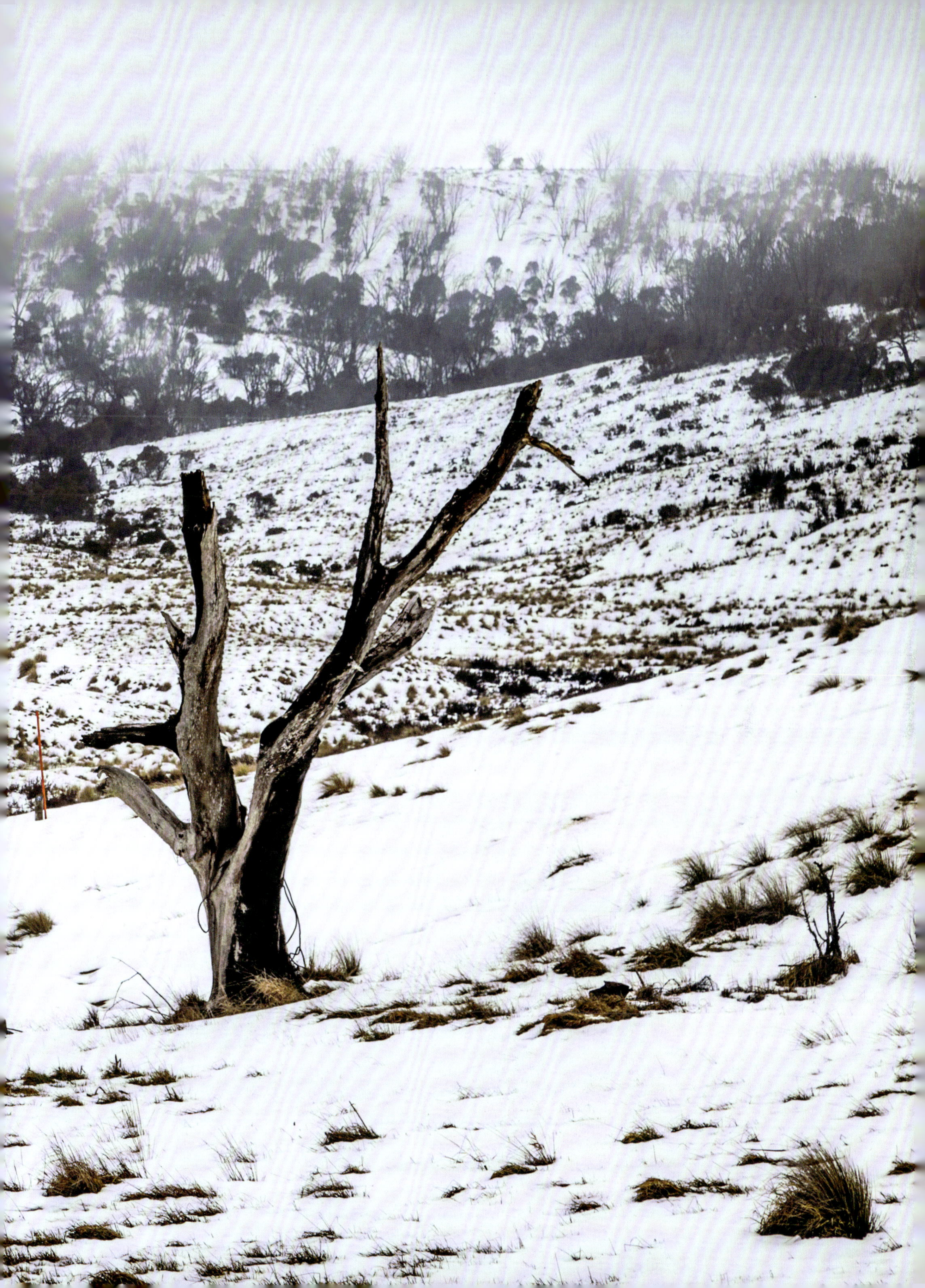

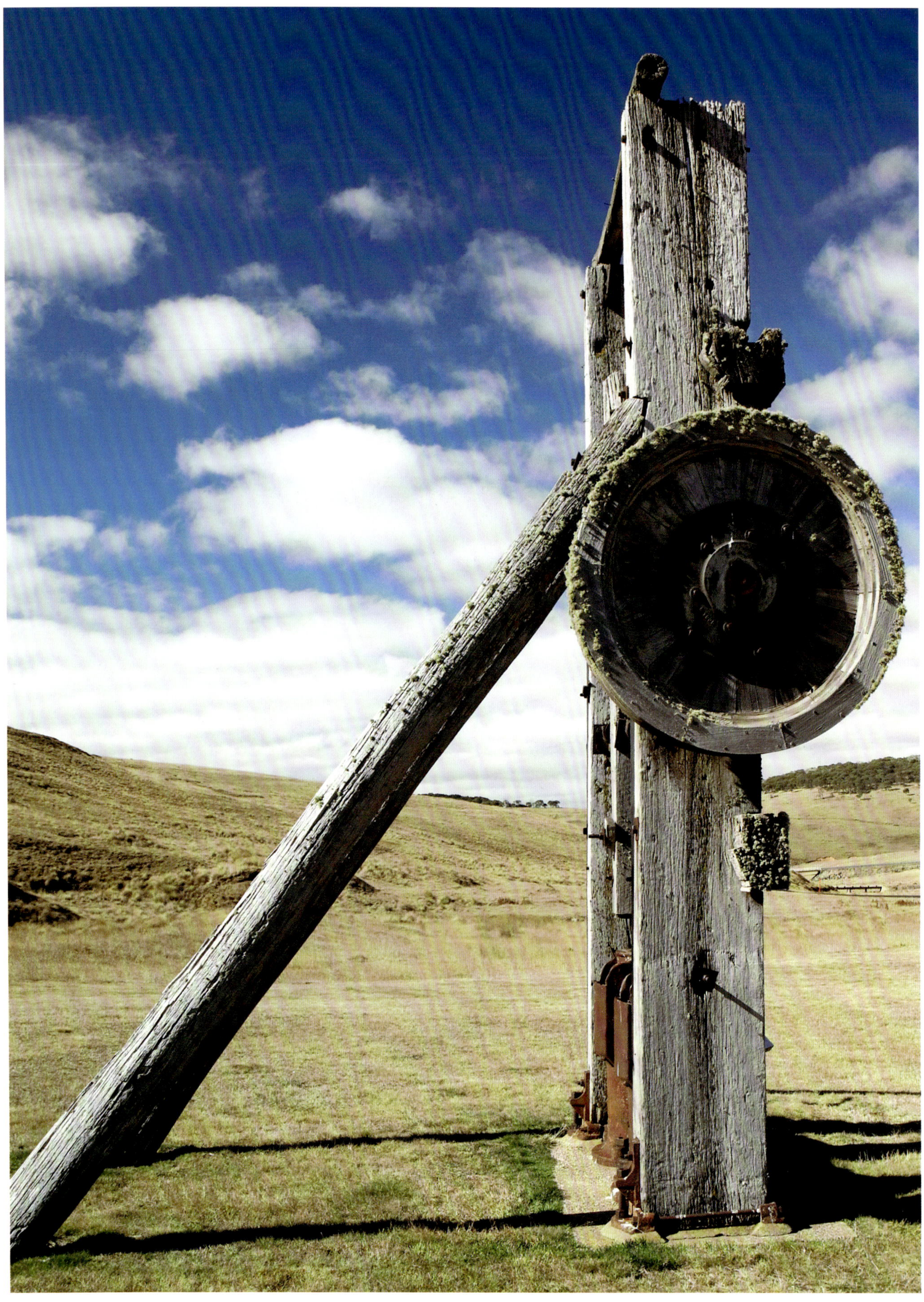

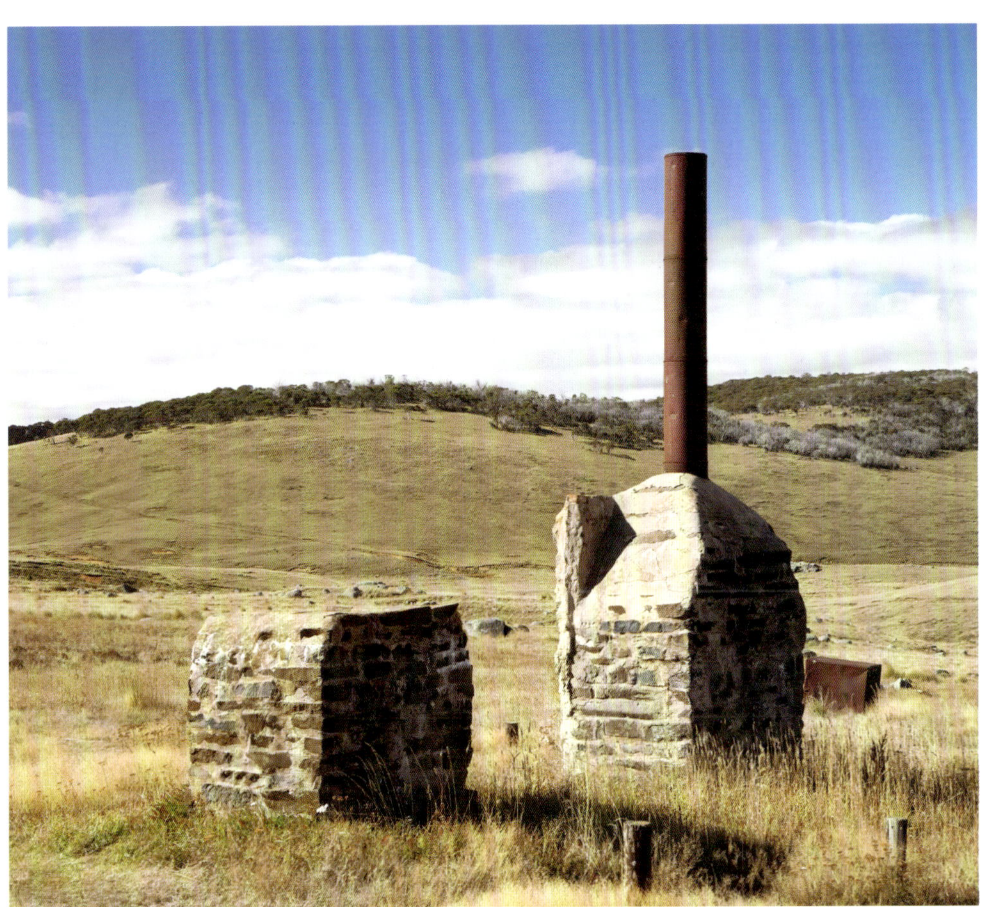

OPPOSITE & LEFT:
Kiandra, New South Wales, Australia
Images of Kiandra during the more congenial months of the year. The scant remnants left today don't give the full impression of the settlement at its peak – the town had a population of c. 15,000 and no fewer than 14 pubs and 54 stores of assorted kinds. Many of the people living in Kiandra were actually Chinese immigrant labourers.

BELOW:
Newnes, New South Wales Australia
Located 189km (117 miles) northwest of Sydney, Newnes is the site of a former oil shale mine – here we see the ruins of some of the brick storage tanks – built by the Commonwealth Oil Corporation in the early 20th century. The settlement was short-lived, and by 1940 only four families lived around the works. Nevertheless, there were inhabitants, and a hotel, at Newnes until the 1980s.

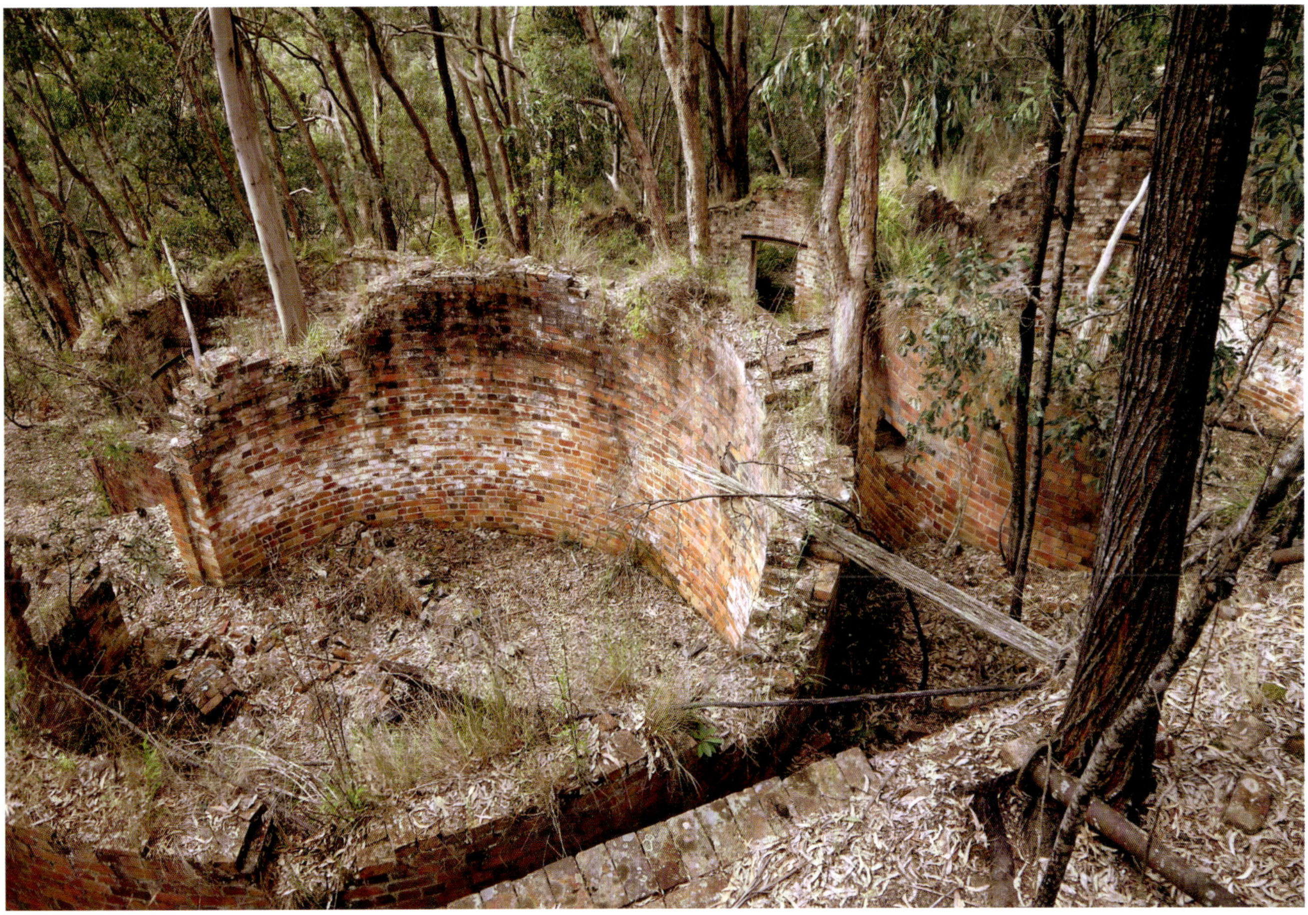

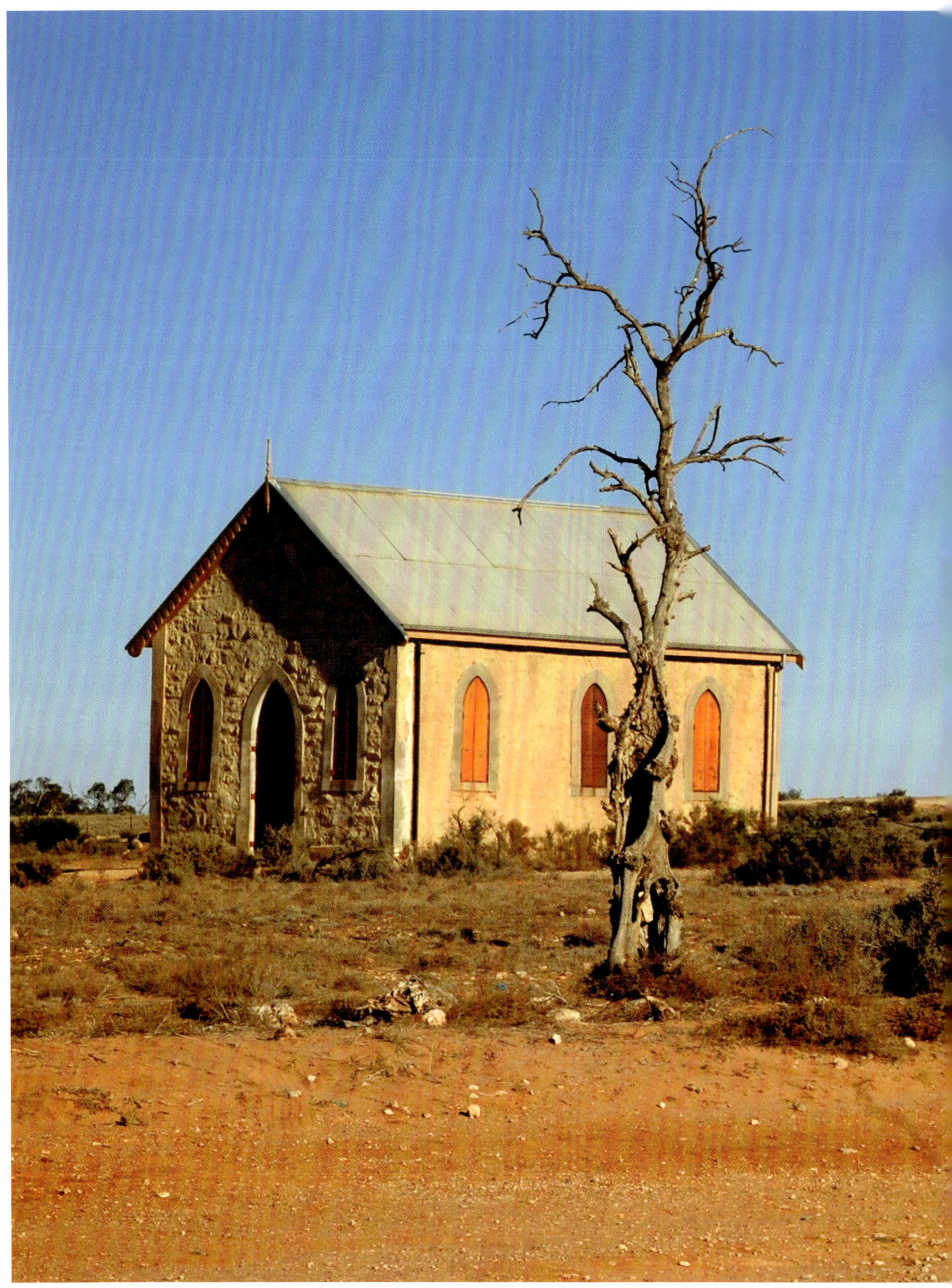

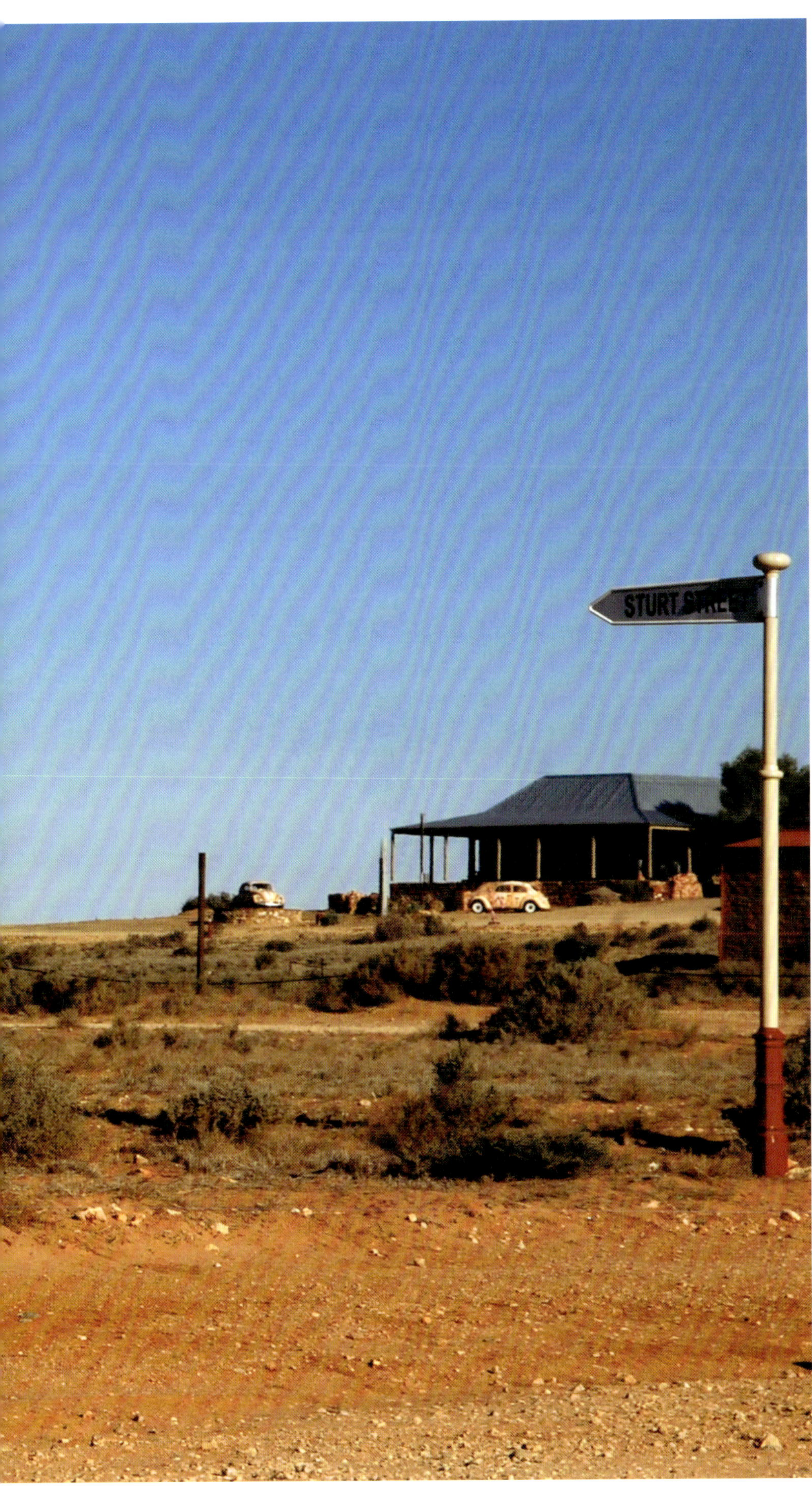

Silverton, New South Wales, Australia

Silverton sprang up in the 1880s as another remote mining settlement, making its money from the extraction of silver, lead and zinc. By the end of the decade it was a fully fledged township, with its own council, numerous businesses, sports teams and a railway line connecting it with the outside world. Yet the discovery of even larger ore deposits at nearby Broken Hill triggered the town's decline; many of Silverton's buildings were actually taken down and reassembled at Broken Hill. A very small population – fewer than 40 – still lives at Silverton.

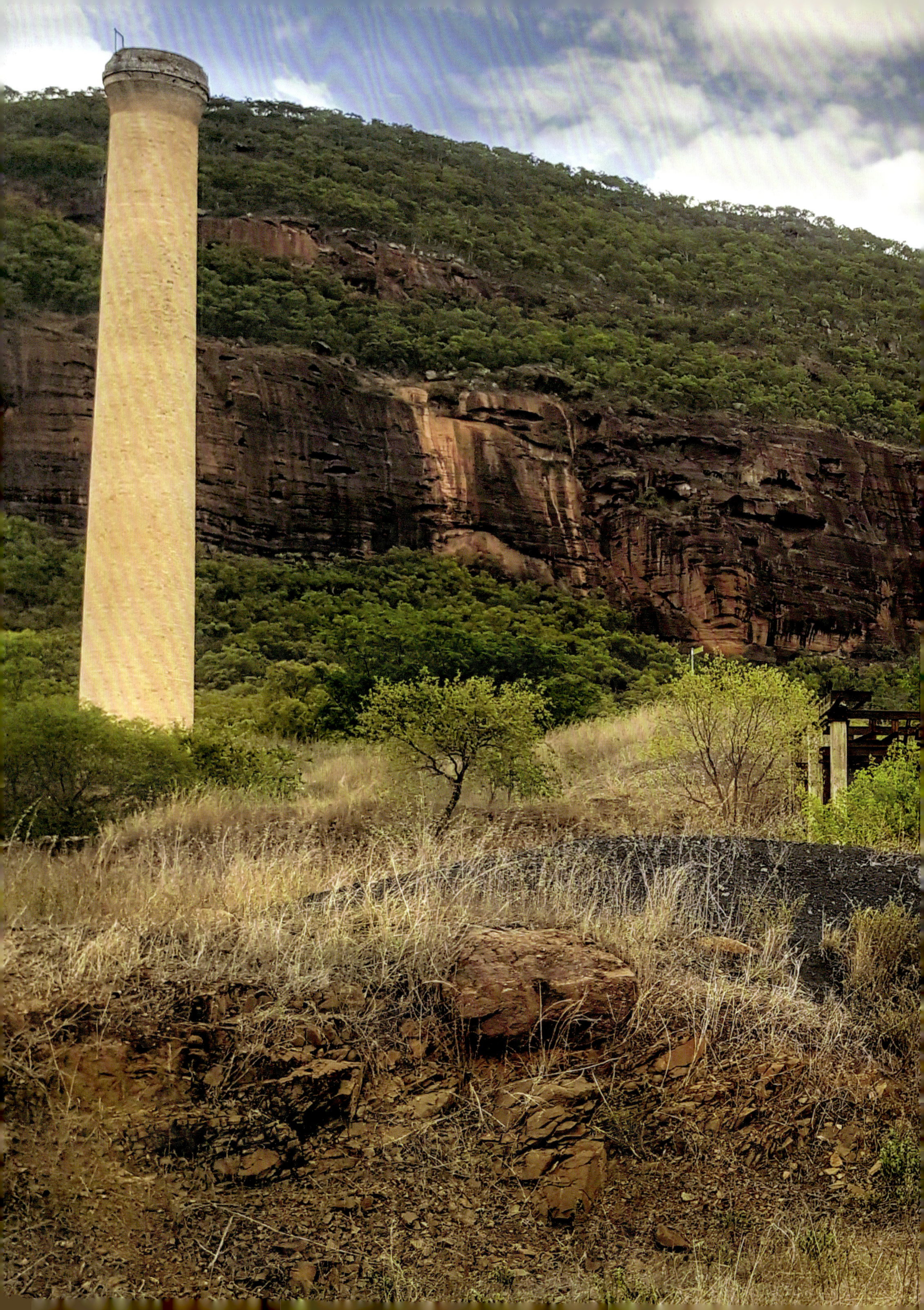

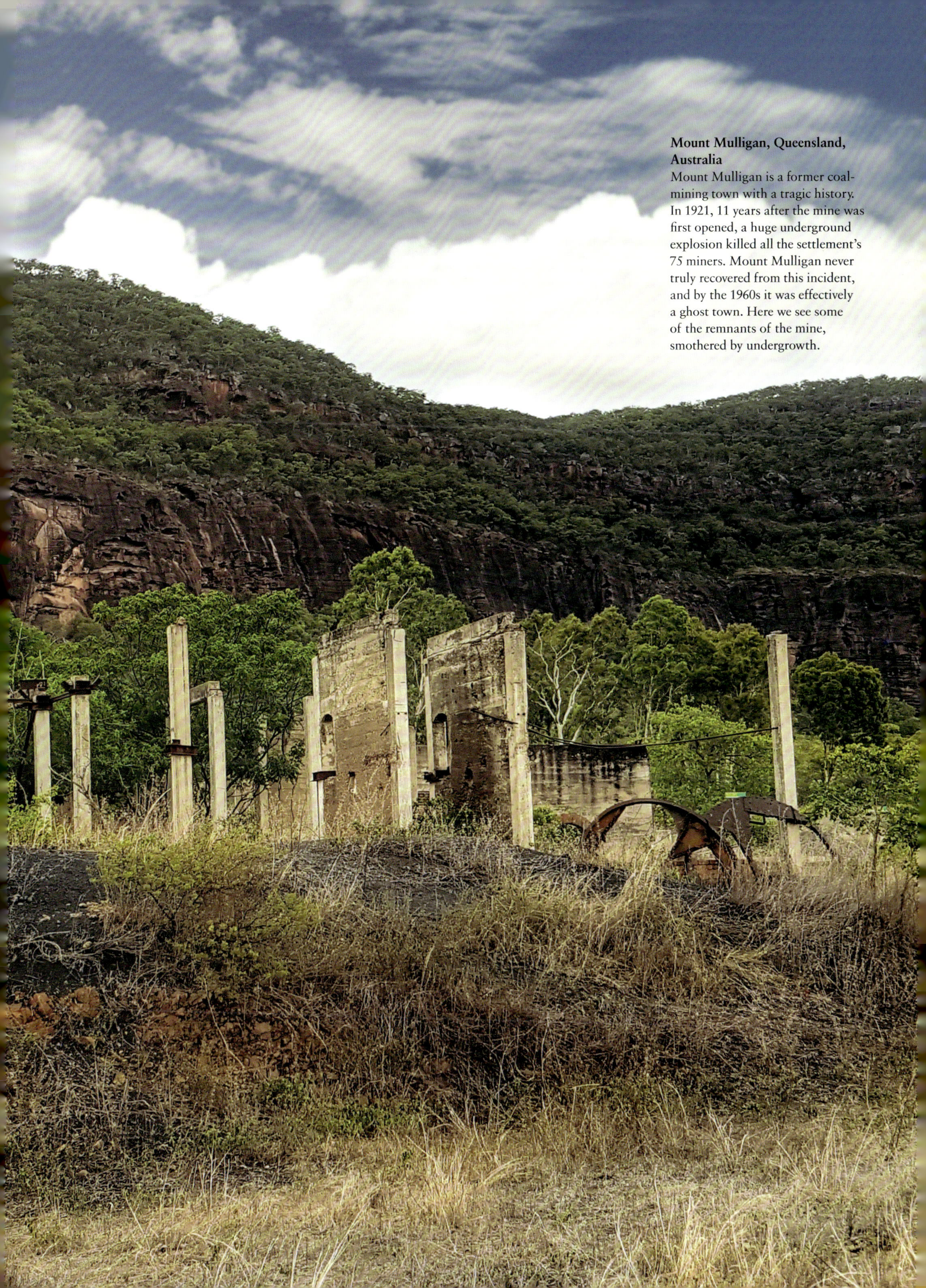

Mount Mulligan, Queensland, Australia
Mount Mulligan is a former coal-mining town with a tragic history. In 1921, 11 years after the mine was first opened, a huge underground explosion killed all the settlement's 75 miners. Mount Mulligan never truly recovered from this incident, and by the 1960s it was effectively a ghost town. Here we see some of the remnants of the mine, smothered by undergrowth.

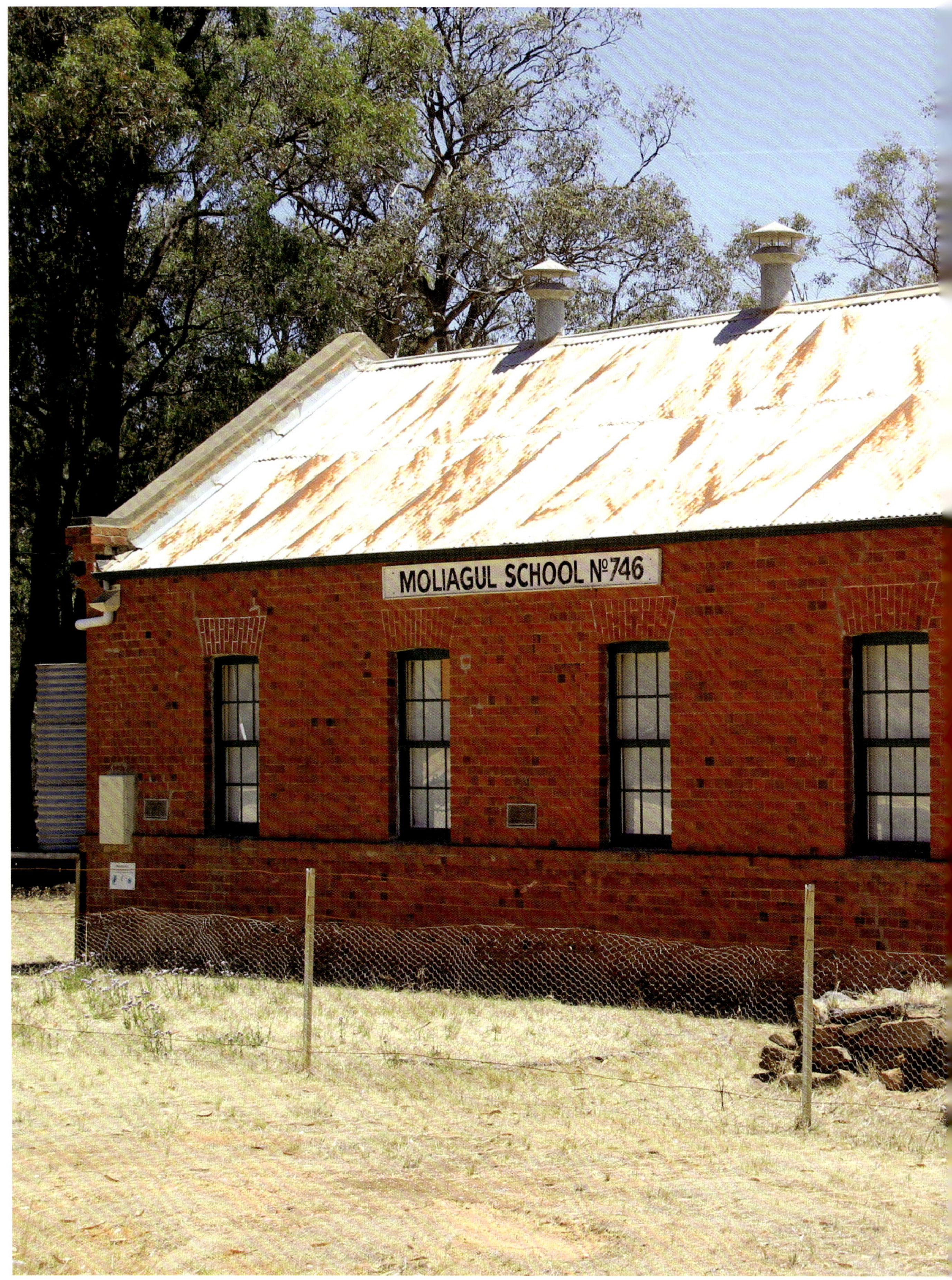
MOLIAGUL SCHOOL №746

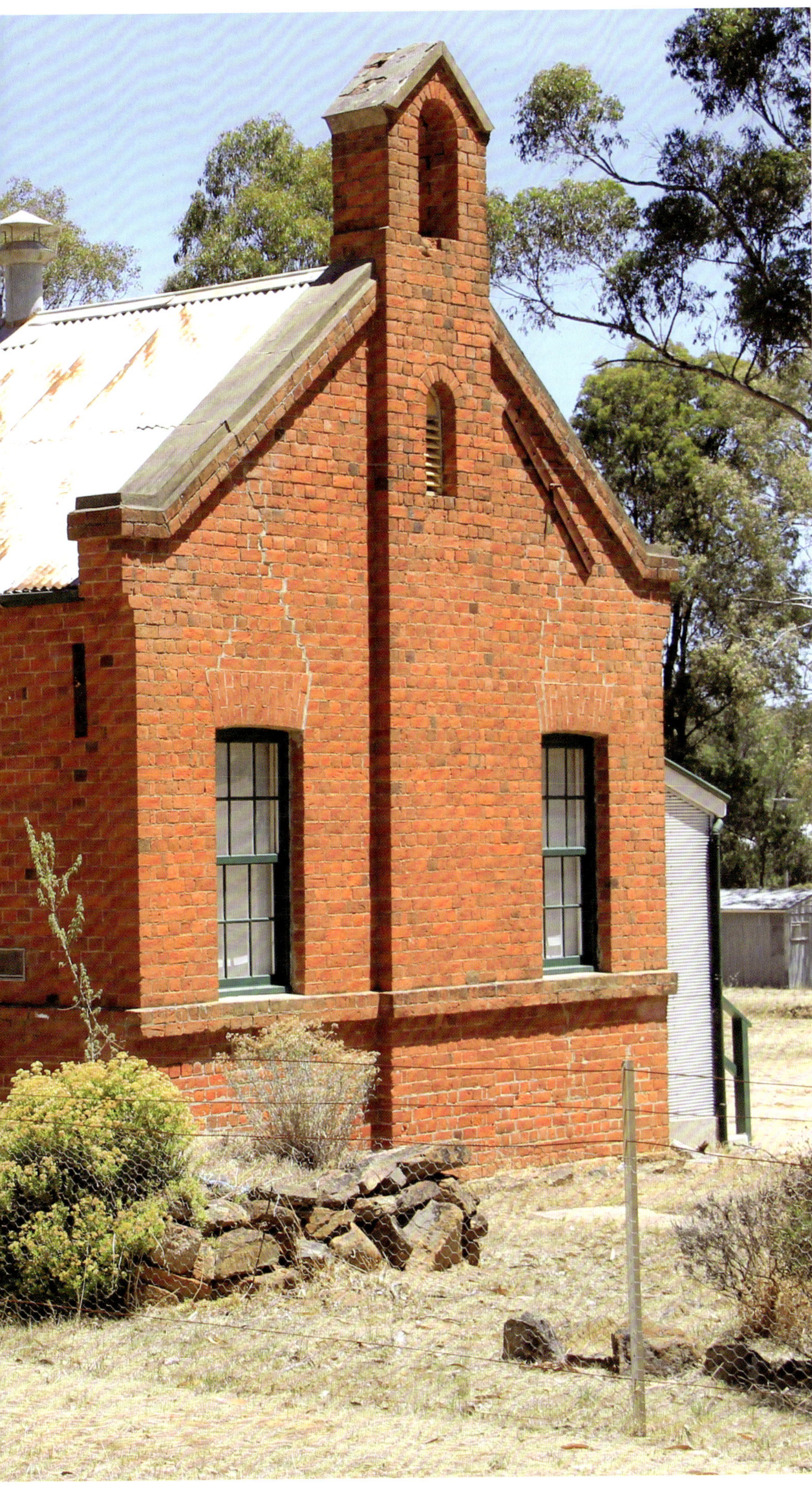

Moliagul, Victoria, Australia
Some 202km (126 miles) northwest of Melbourne, Moliagul was a small gold-mining town with a particular claim to fame. On 5 February 1869, prospectors John Deason and Richard Oates found the world's biggest alluvial gold nugget. Nicknamed the 'Welcome Stranger Nugget', it weighed 2315.5 troy ounces (72.02kg/158lb). Like many Australian gold-mining towns, however, Moliagul peaked quickly and then made an irreversible slow decline, becoming a ghost town by the 1970s.

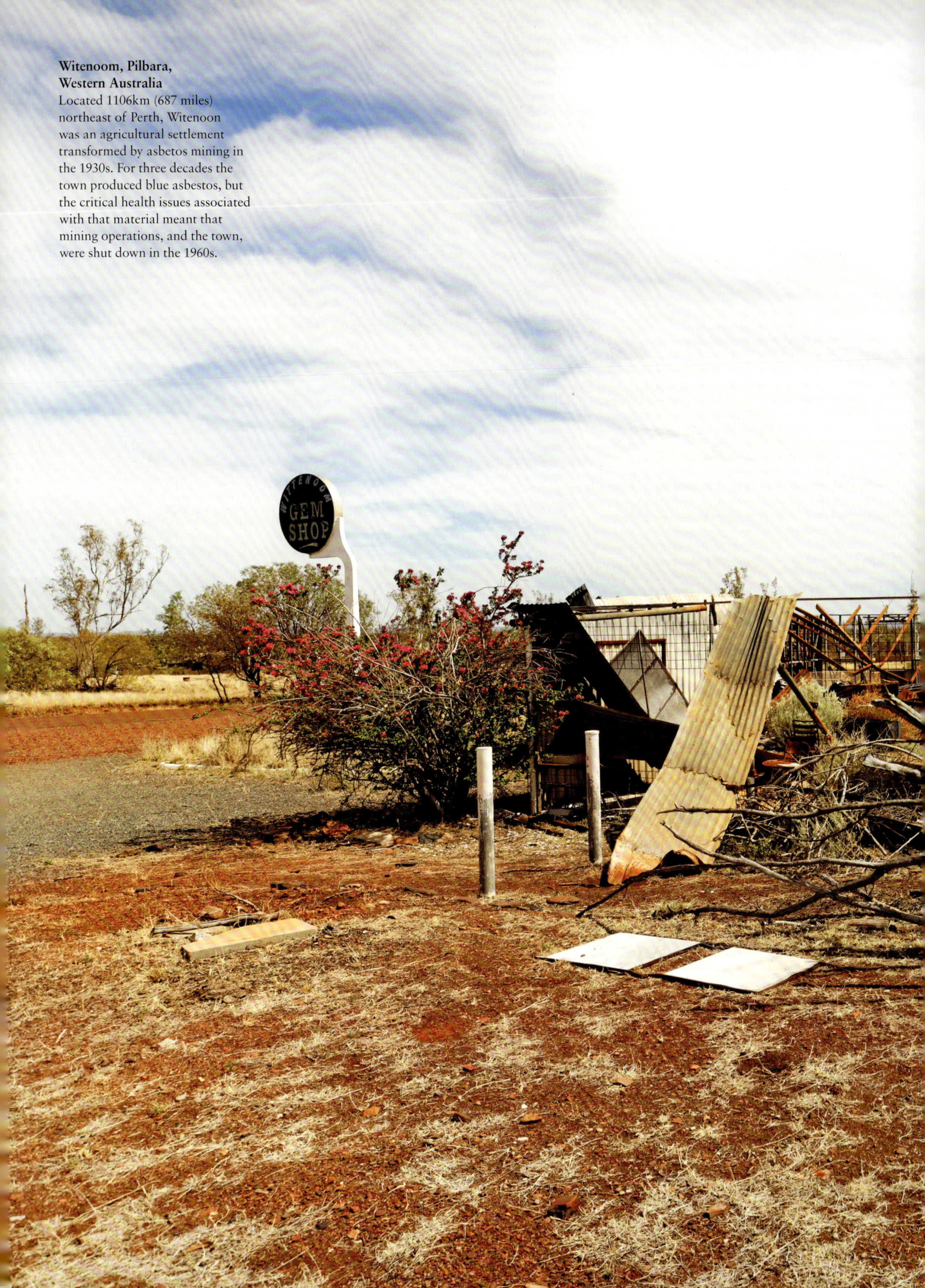

Witenoom, Pilbara, Western Australia
Located 1106km (687 miles) northeast of Perth, Witenoon was an agricultural settlement transformed by asbetos mining in the 1930s. For three decades the town produced blue asbestos, but the critical health issues associated with that material meant that mining operations, and the town, were shut down in the 1960s.

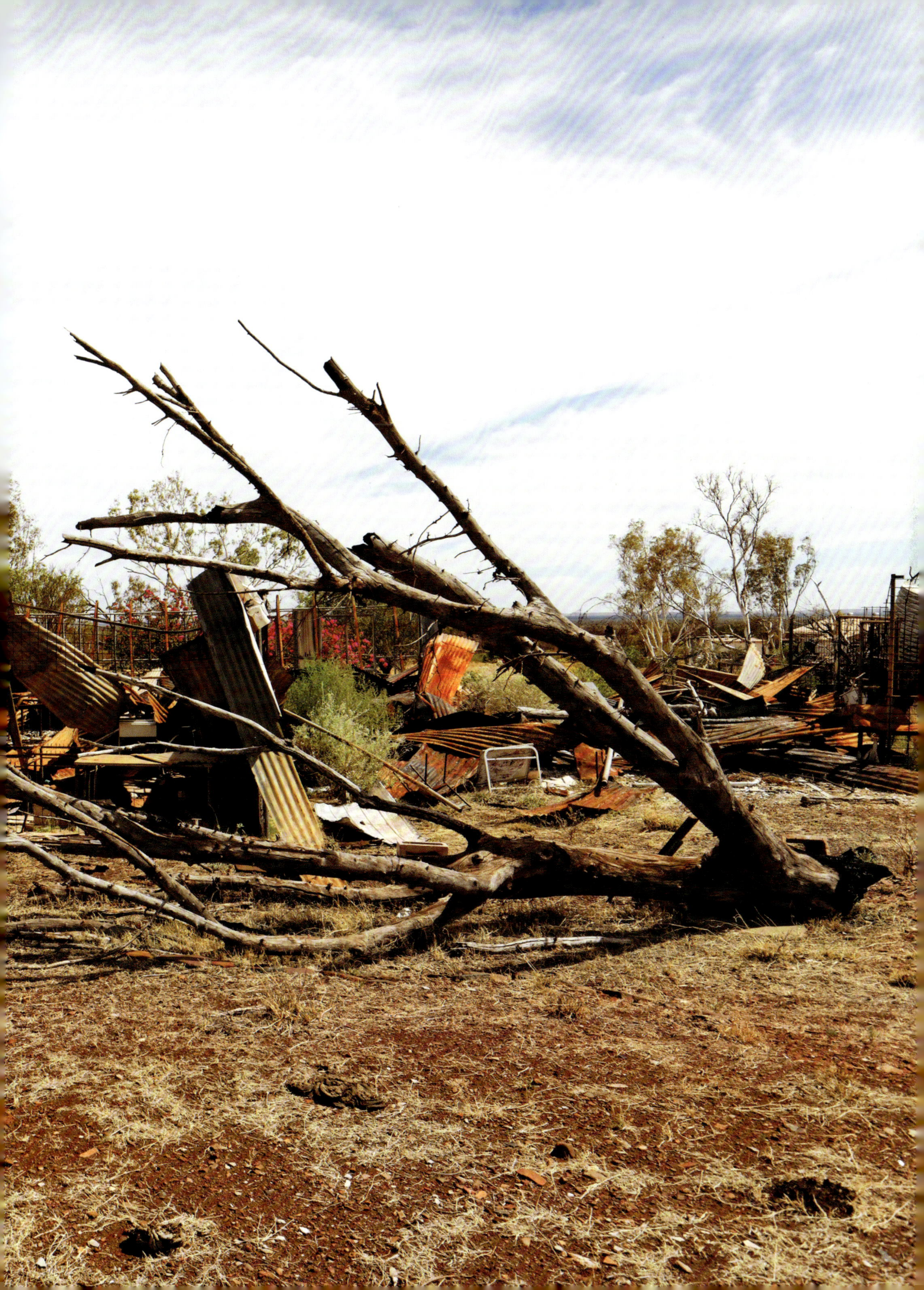

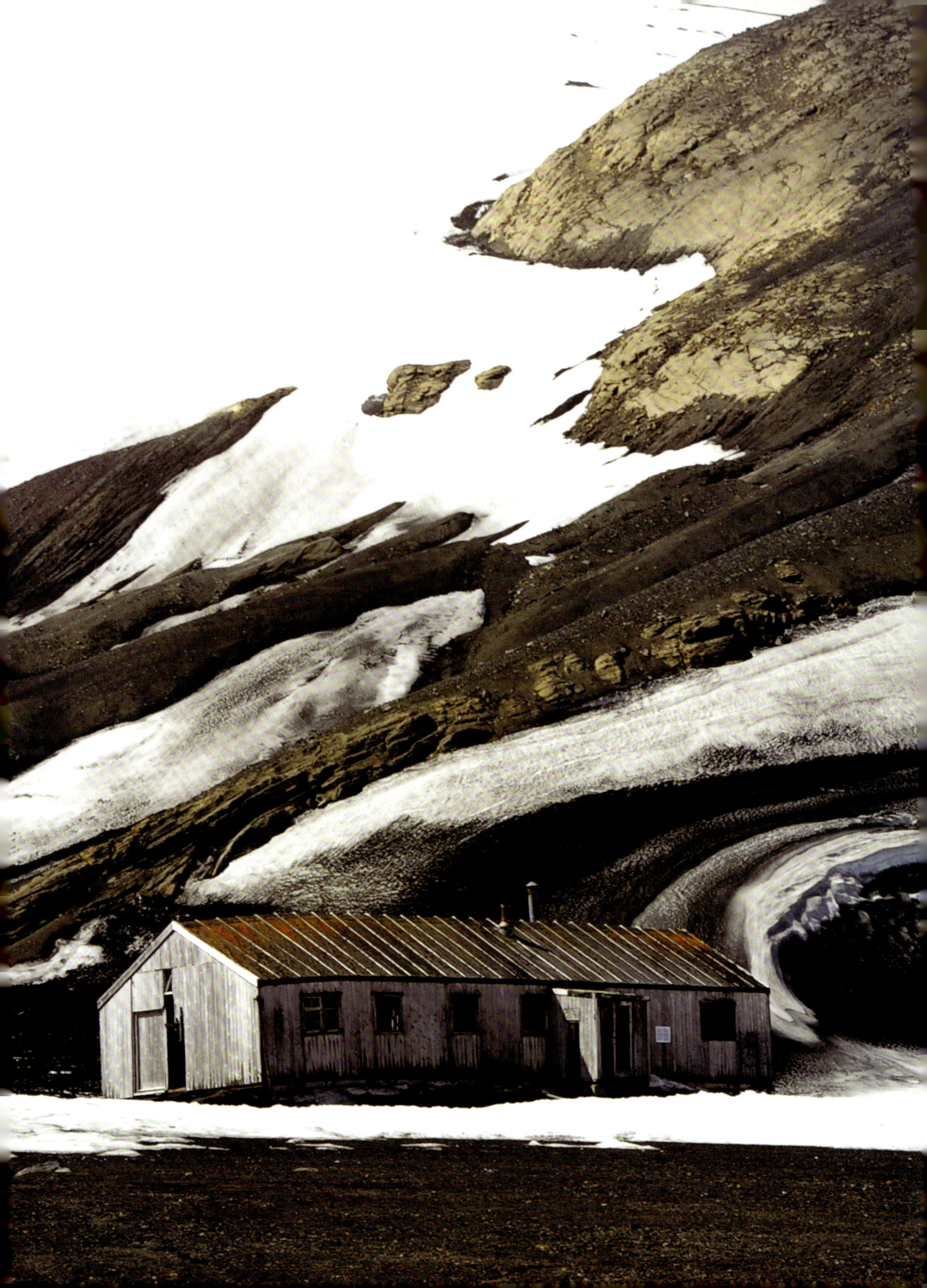

Antarctica

One activity dominates the following pages: whaling. The killing of whales for meat, oil, blubber and other products has an ancient history, but it was in the 19th and early 20th centuries in particular that it became the voracious industry that nearly wiped out many of the world's whale species. Roving whaling ships, armed with explosive harpoon cannon and fast enough to hunt down whales in open water, unleashed a slaughter on unprecedented scale. It is estimated that during the early 1900s more whales were killed than in the previous four centuries combined.

Until the advent of processing by the catcher vessel, most whale carcass handling was done at whaling stations like those featured in this chapter. The islands of Antarctica, being located close to some of the best whale hunting grounds, were popular sites for these stations. Given the current unpopularity of whale hunting, however, it is difficult to think sympathetically of those who toiled and occasionally died at these stations, often thousands of miles from home. Yet just a glance at the hard landscapes around whaling ghost towns immediately evokes just how grim and unrelenting this occupation must have been. When the whaling industry eventually collapsed in the 20th century, the victim of its own success and greater environmental awareness, the whaling stations were left to the erosion of the South Atlantic weather.

LEFT:

Deception Island, Antarctica

The evocatively named Deception Island was, between 1819 and 1920, a centre for the processing of seal fur and subsequently a whaling station. When whaling changed to offshore processing, the settlement collapsed, but was subsequently utilized as a base for scientific investigations, although its location in an active volcano has made it a precarious posting.

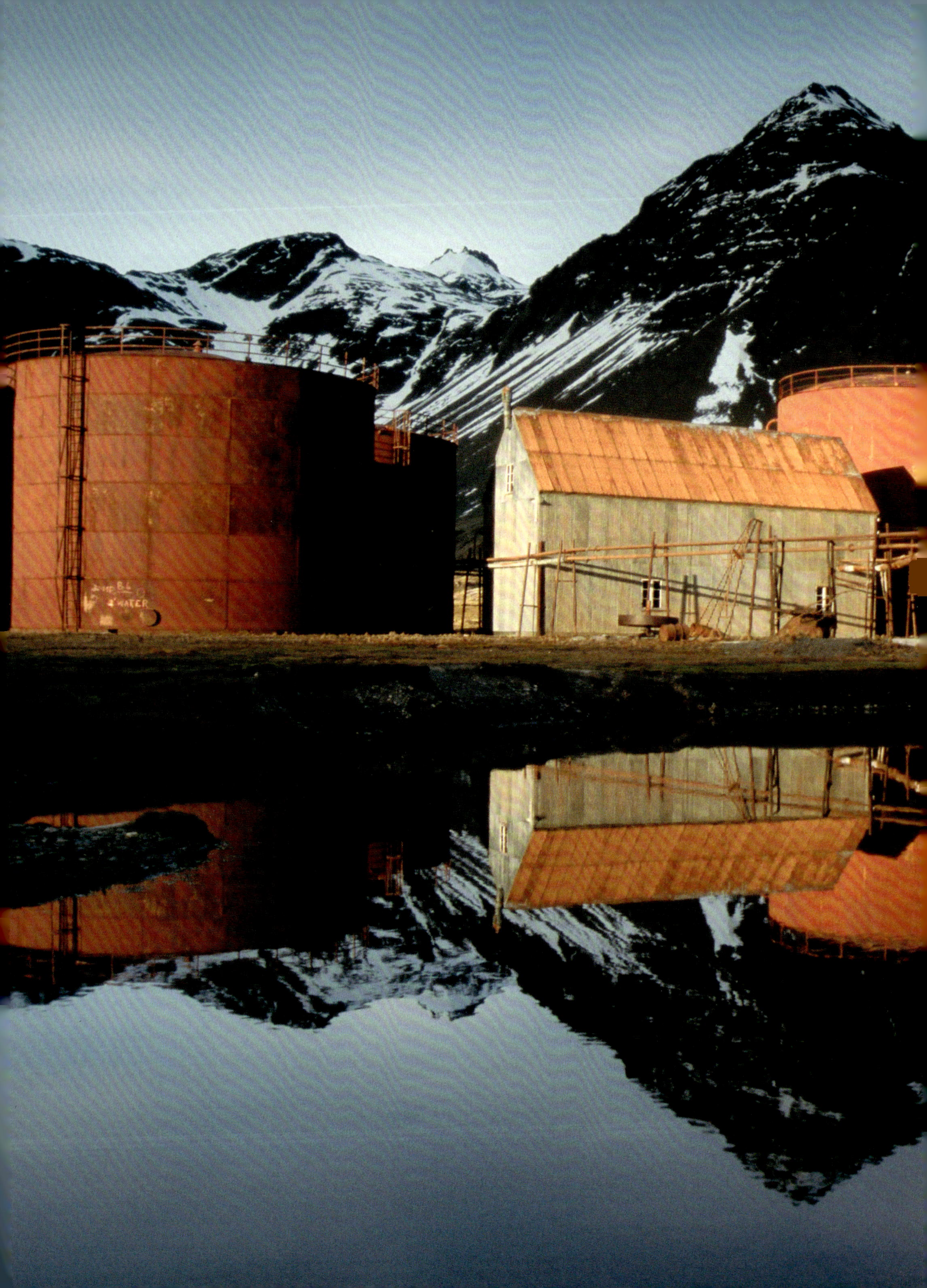
WATER

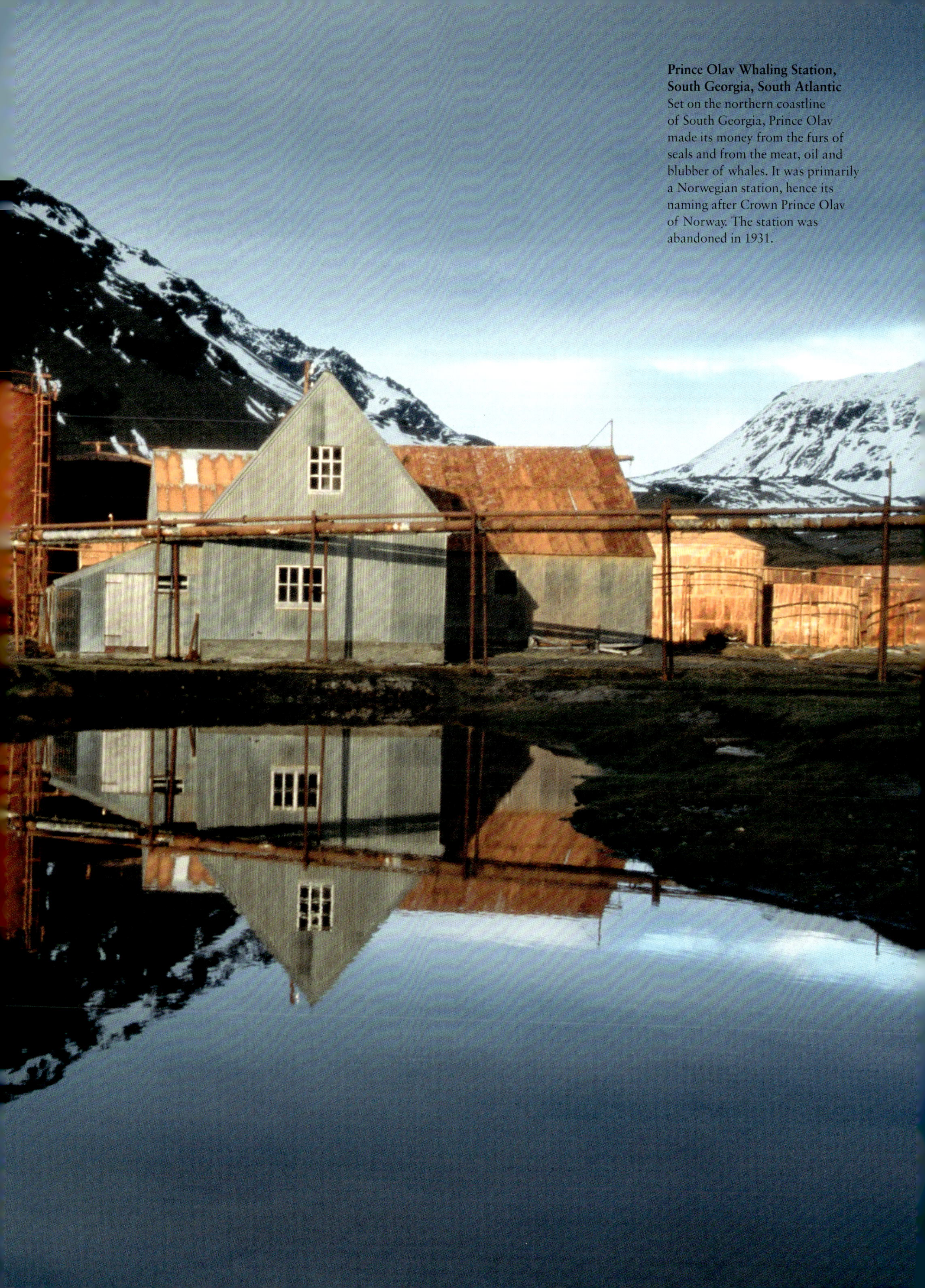

Prince Olav Whaling Station, South Georgia, South Atlantic
Set on the northern coastline of South Georgia, Prince Olav made its money from the furs of seals and from the meat, oil and blubber of whales. It was primarily a Norwegian station, hence its naming after Crown Prince Olav of Norway. The station was abandoned in 1931.

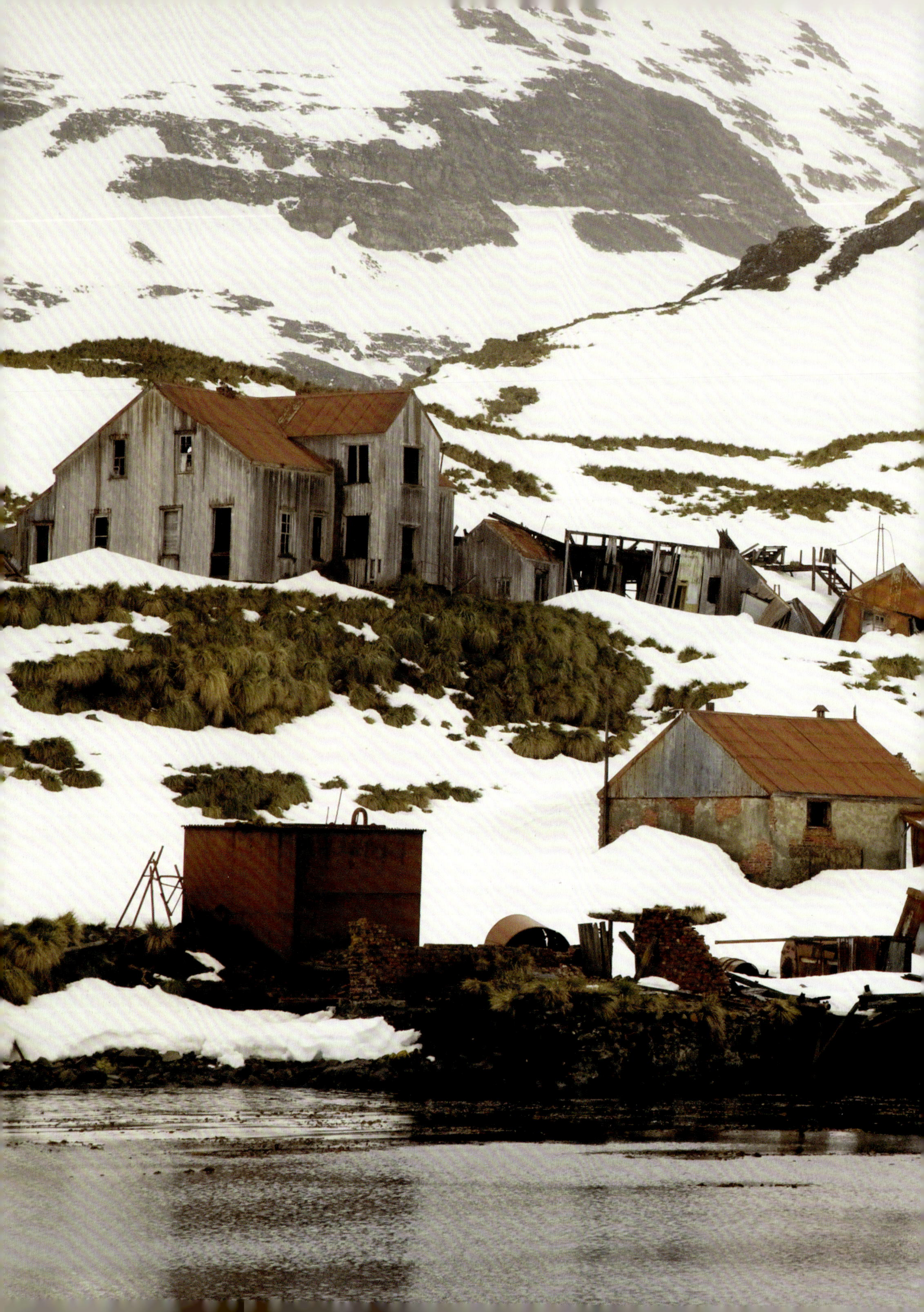

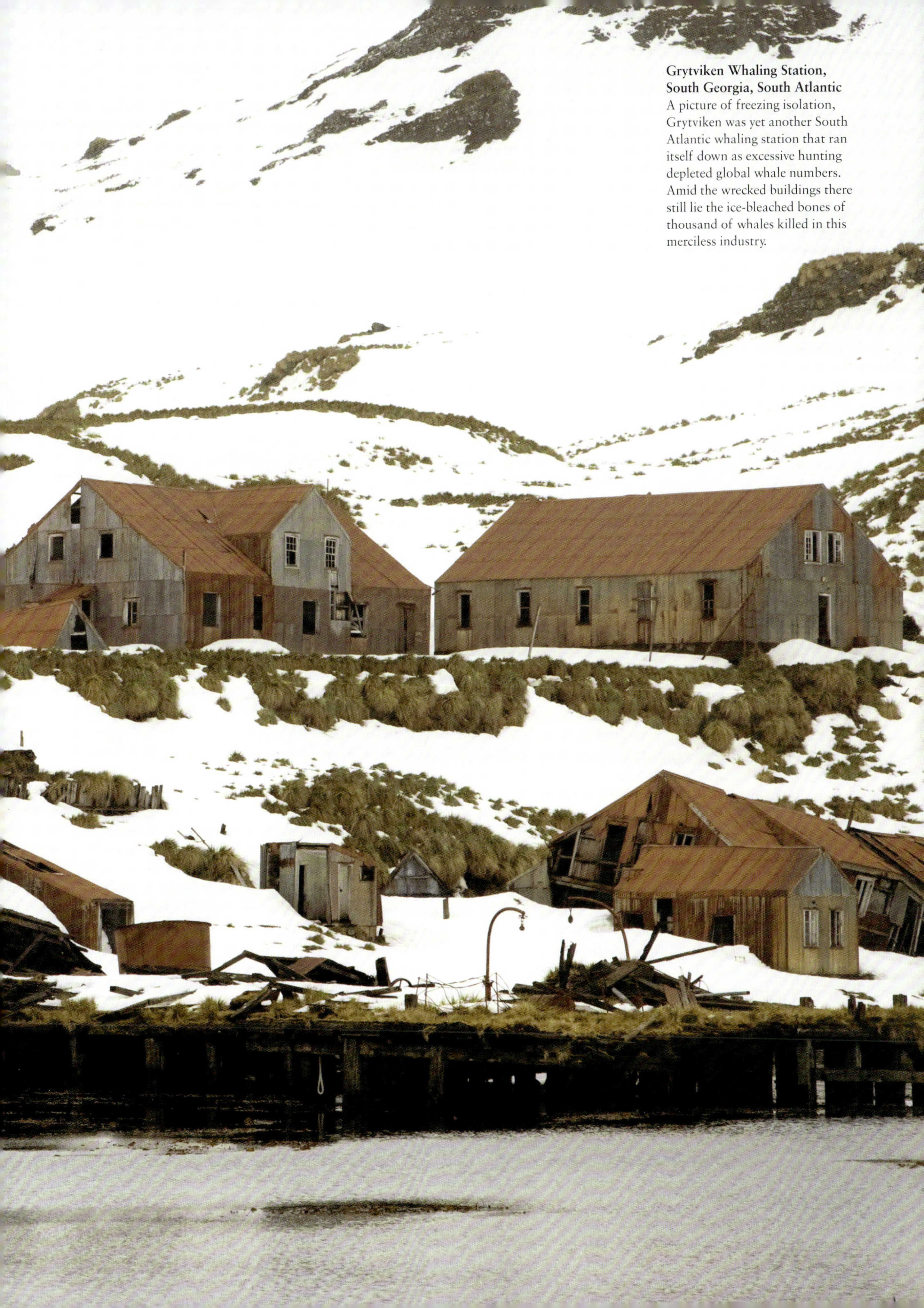

Grytviken Whaling Station, South Georgia, South Atlantic
A picture of freezing isolation, Grytviken was yet another South Atlantic whaling station that ran itself down as excessive hunting depleted global whale numbers. Amid the wrecked buildings there still lie the ice-bleached bones of thousand of whales killed in this merciless industry.

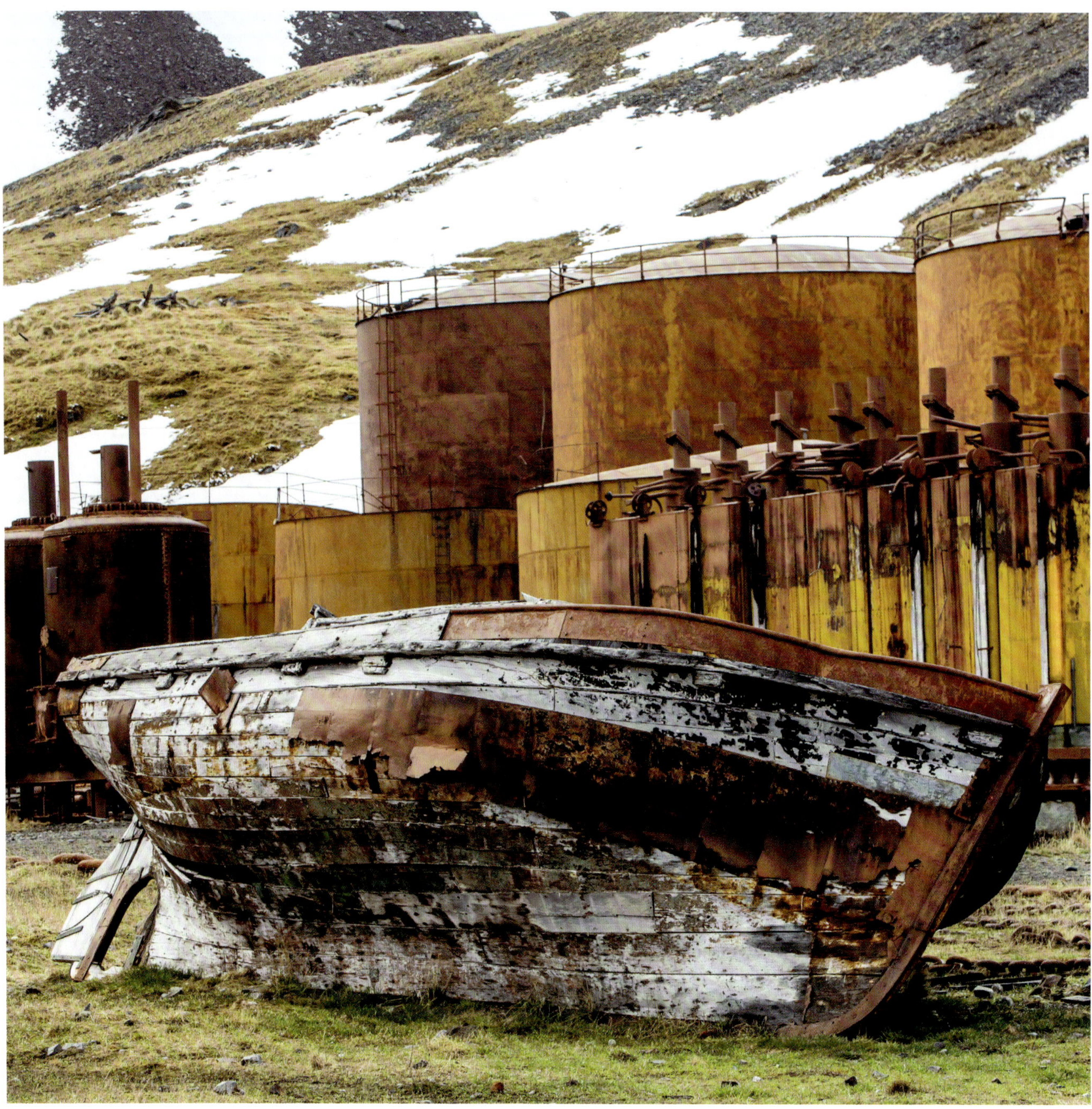

ALL PHOTOGRAPHS:

Grytviken Whaling Station, South Georgia, South Atlantic

A collection of images taken from around Grytviken Whaling Station perfectly capture the unforgiving nature of the environment in this remote part of the world. As storage tanks and buildings rot away, whaling ships sink along the quayside, their hulls holed by rust and frigid seawater. Despite its location, Grytviken has held the broader public imagination on several occasions throughout its history. The great British explorer Sir Ernest Shackleton used Grytviken as a base from which to launch a rescue attempt for men stranded during the ill-fated Imperial Trans-Antarctic Expedition in 1914–17. Shackleton's grave is actually located just south of Grytviken, surrounded by the graves of past whalers. Grytviken was also the site of one of the earliest battles of the Falklands War in 1982 when, on 3 April, Argentine marines were landed and engaged in a two-hour battle with a platoon of men from 22 Royal Marines. The heavily outnumbered Royal Marines were eventually forced to surrender, but their captivity was short-lived – the British forces returned just three weeks later and recaptured Grytviken on 25 April. Although the whaling station is derelict, Grytviken still has a population of about 20 people, to cater for the steady trickle of visitors. Indeed, the station has been declared an Area of Special Tourist Interest (ASTI), and the South Georgia Museum is today housed in the former whaling manager's property.

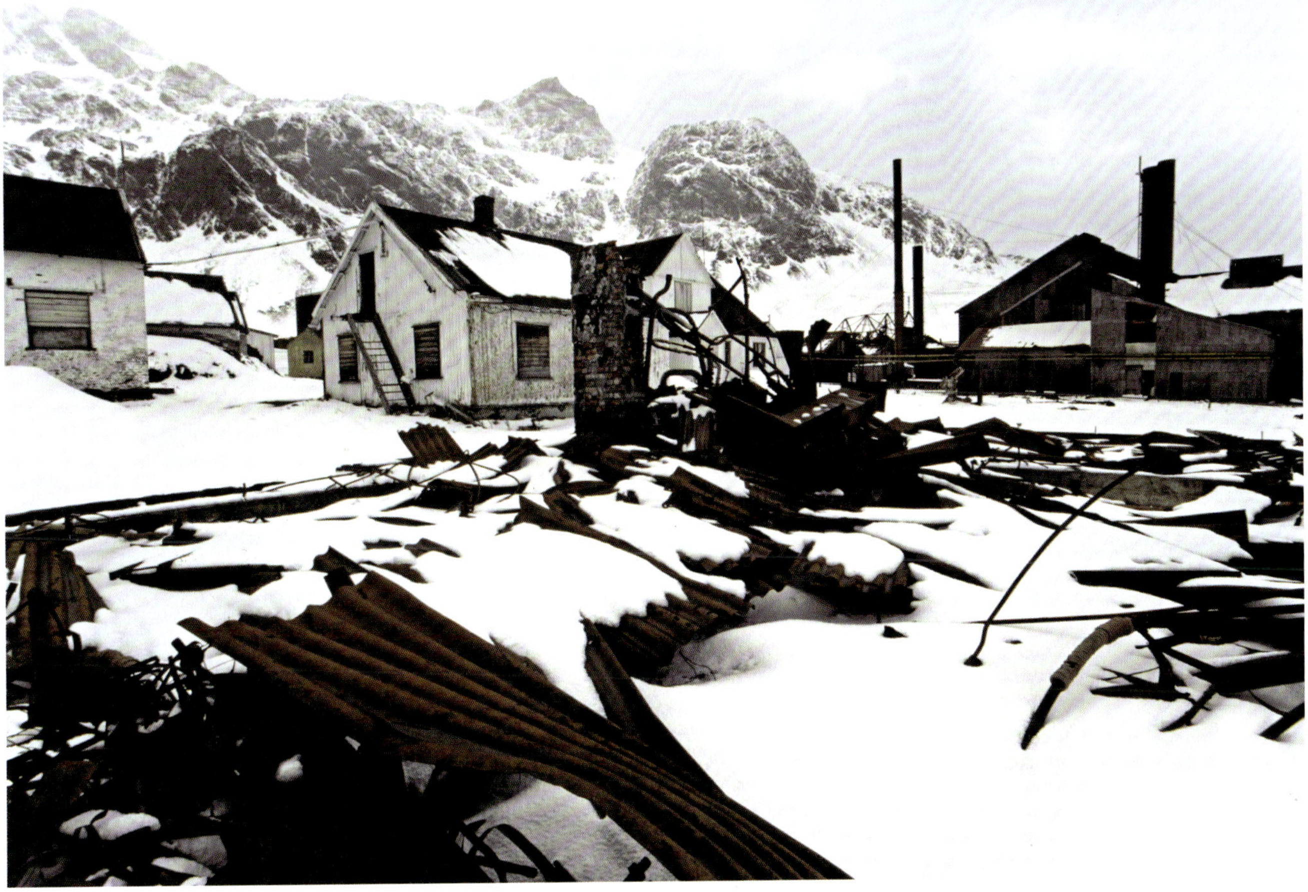

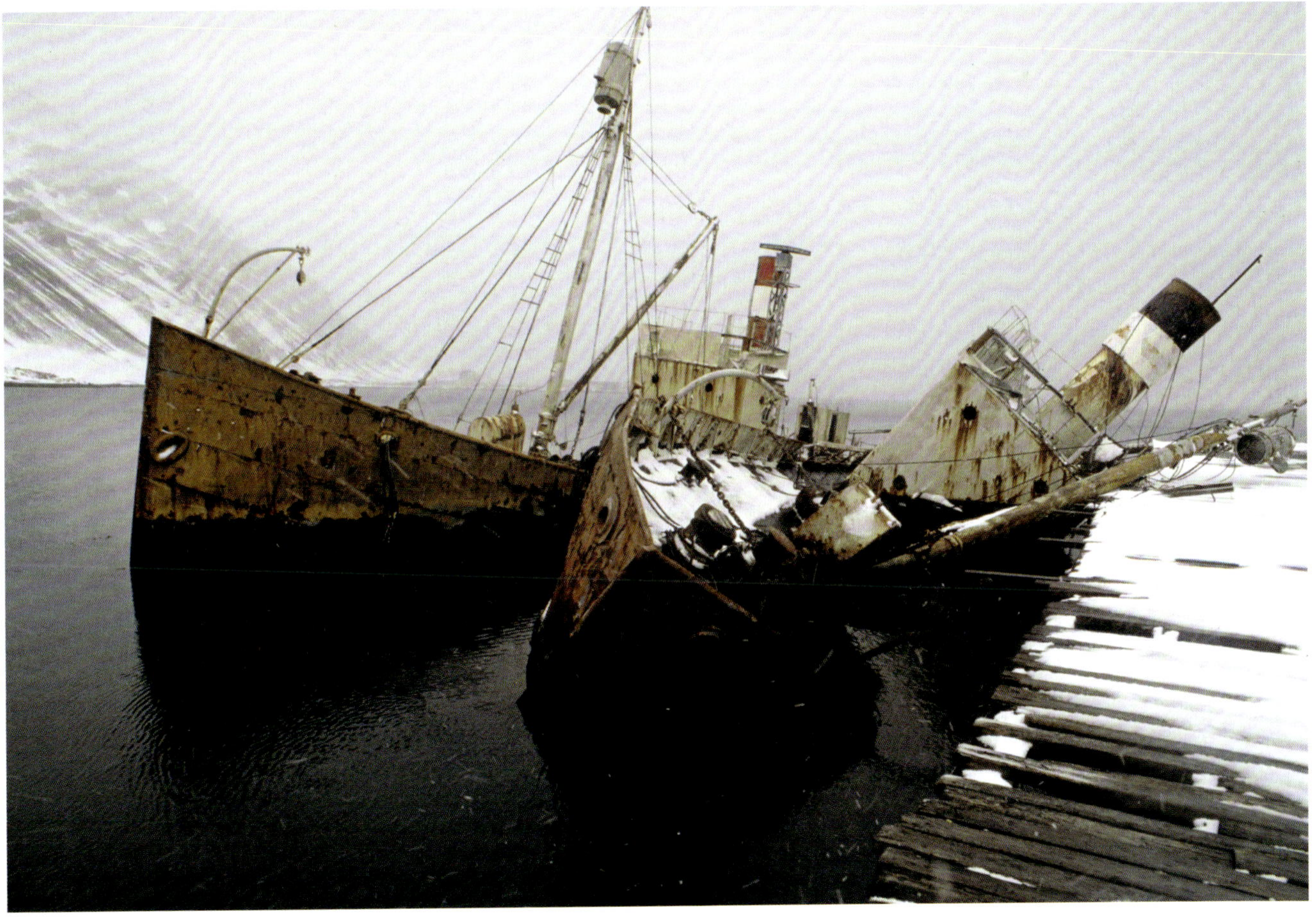

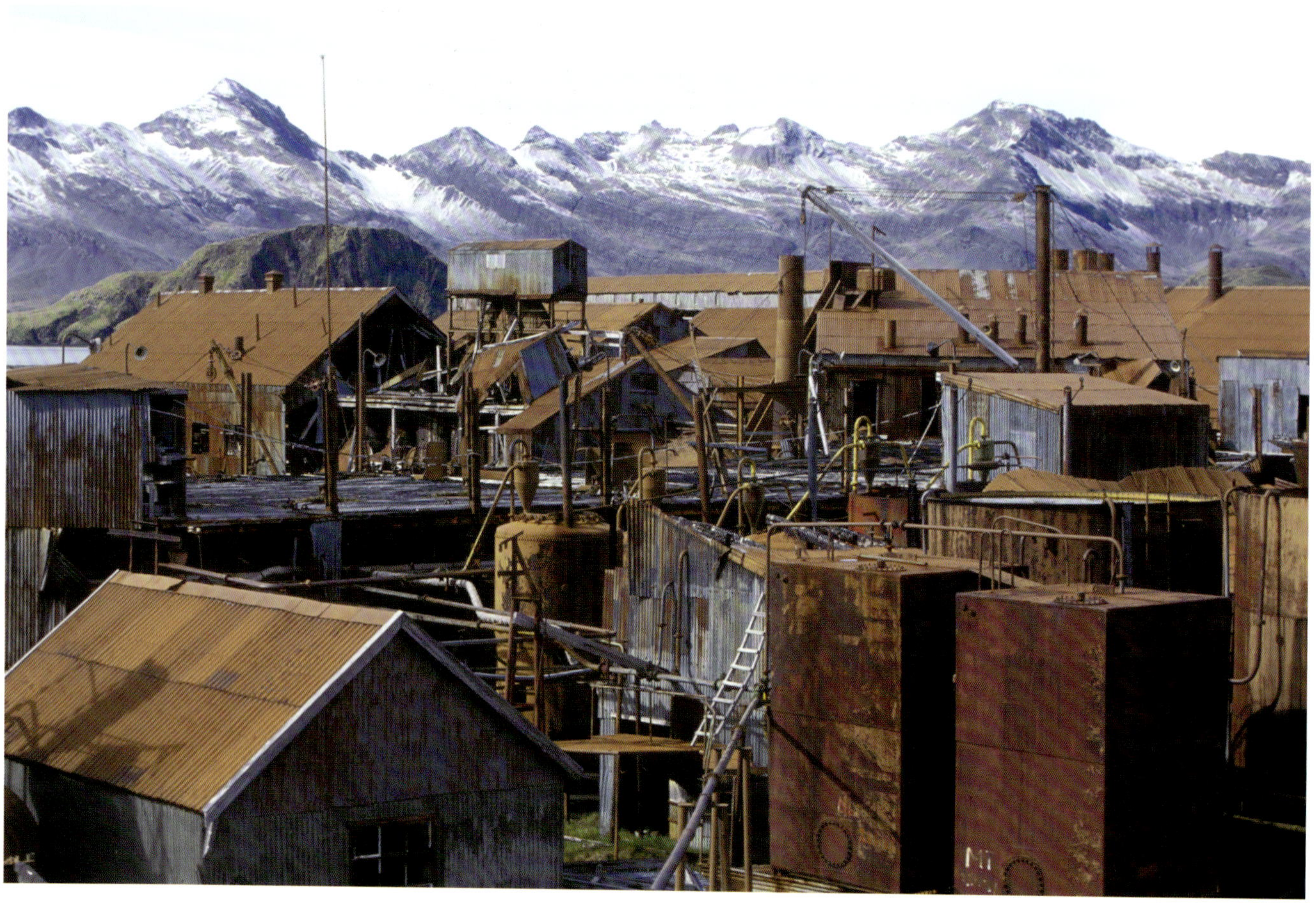

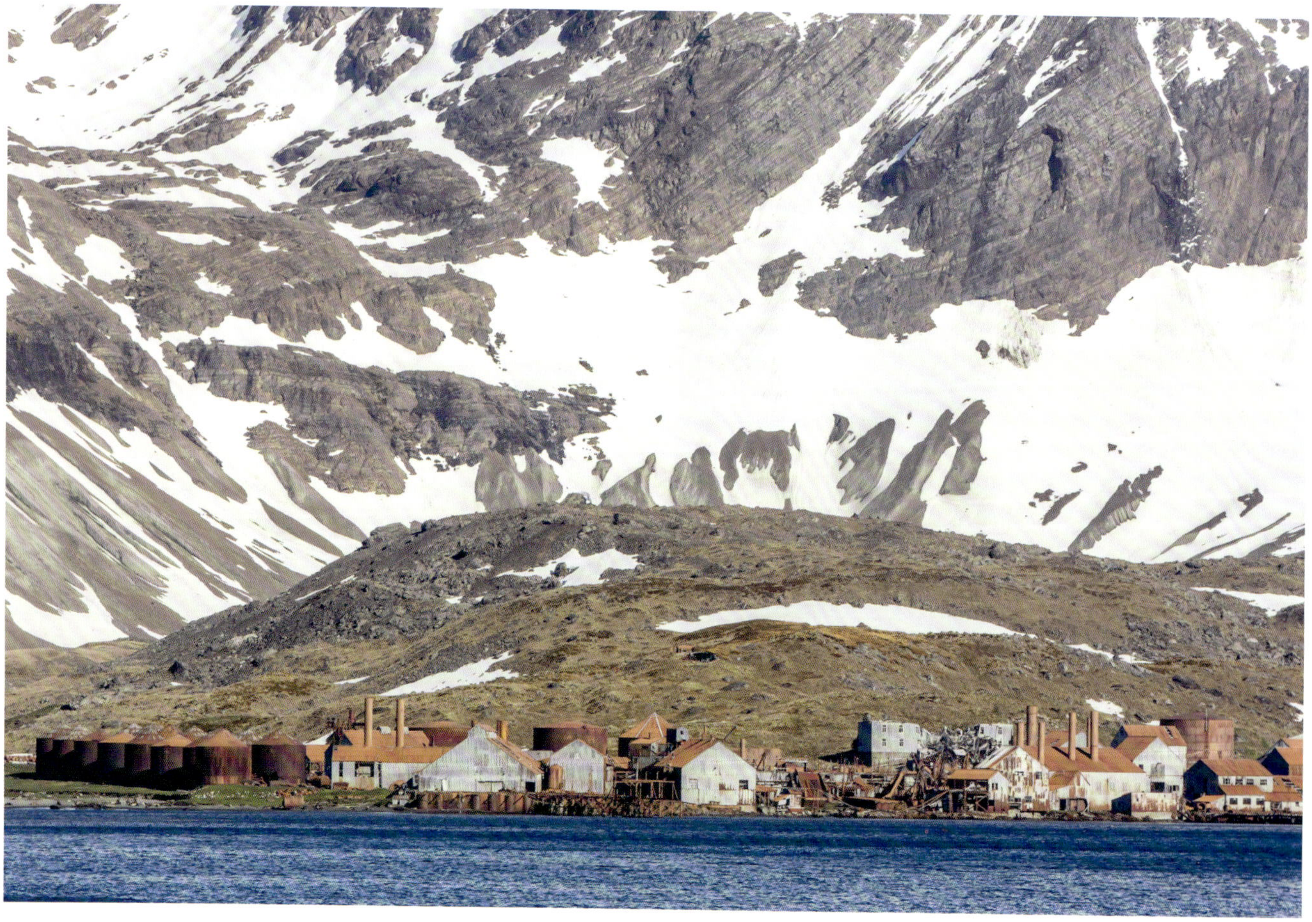

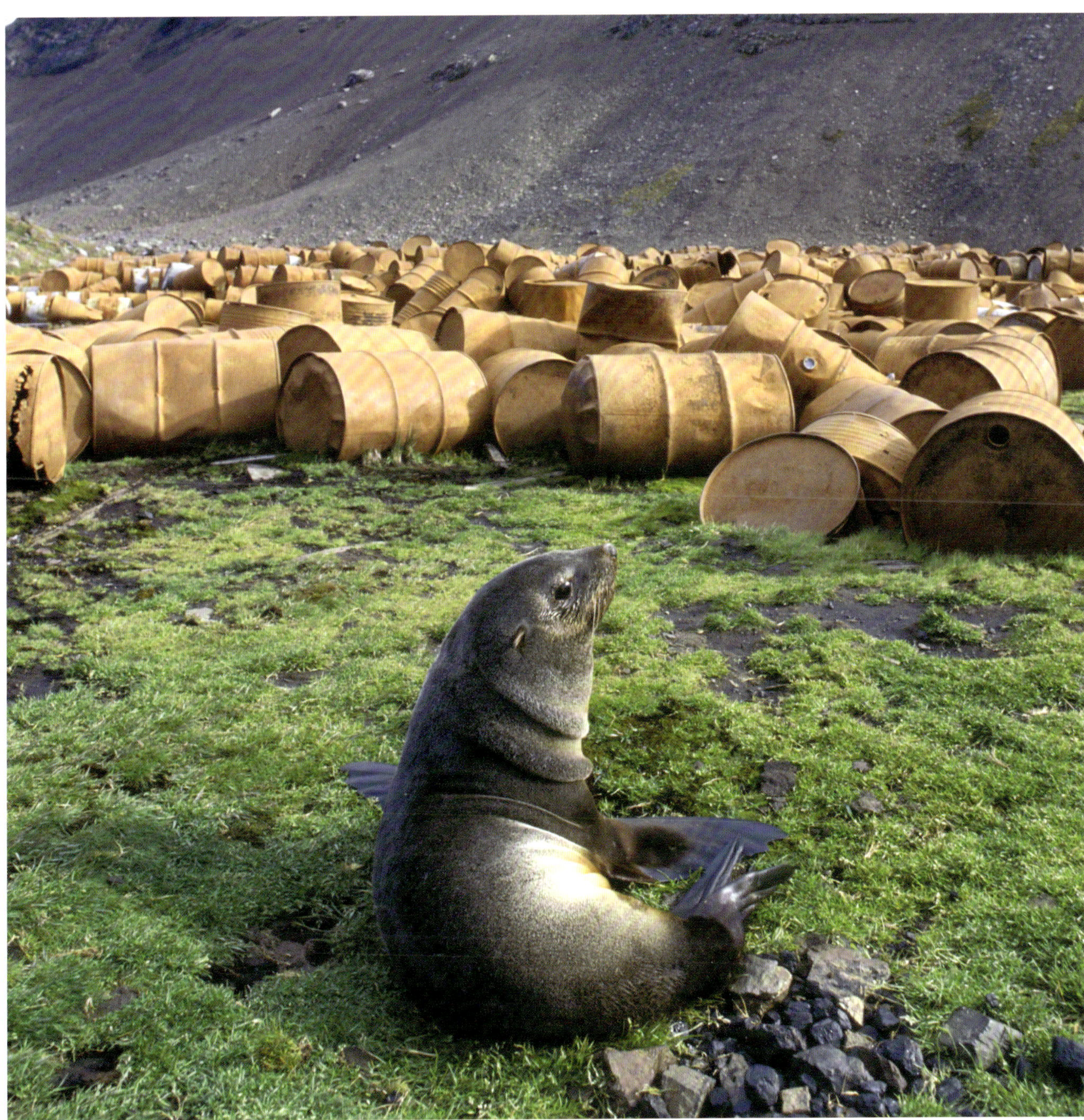

ALL PHOTOGRAPHS:

Leith Harbour, South Georgia, South Atlantic

Leith Harbour achieved the now-ambiguous honour of being the world's largest whaling station, and one of seven such stations dotted around the coast of South Georgia. During its operational years between 1909 and 1965, the station processed a dizzying total of 48,000 individual whales, the by-products of this industry including everything from margarine to fertilizer. (A notable statistic is that in 1933 a full 33 per cent of the fat in British margarines was provided by whale oil.) The station was run by Christian Salvesen Ltd of Edinburgh, and at its peak productivity it had a population of 500 extremely hardy men, who toiled for hours in conditions of extreme filth, cold and wet. Whaling activities continued until 1965, when the final seasons were held by two Japanese companies who leased the station, and thereafter the outpost was largely abandoned. Like the rest of the island, Leith Harbour was punctuated throughout its history by moments of military activity. During World War II (1939–45), the Royal Navy made patrols from the harbour in an armed merchantman ship, and during the Falklands War Leith was the first place occupied by the Argentines – 50 Argentines posing as scrap metal merchants took over the whaling station. Today, however, the major occupants of the harbour are seabirds, penguins and seals. The latter are actually quite dangerous during the mating season, when it is best to steer clear of the buildings.

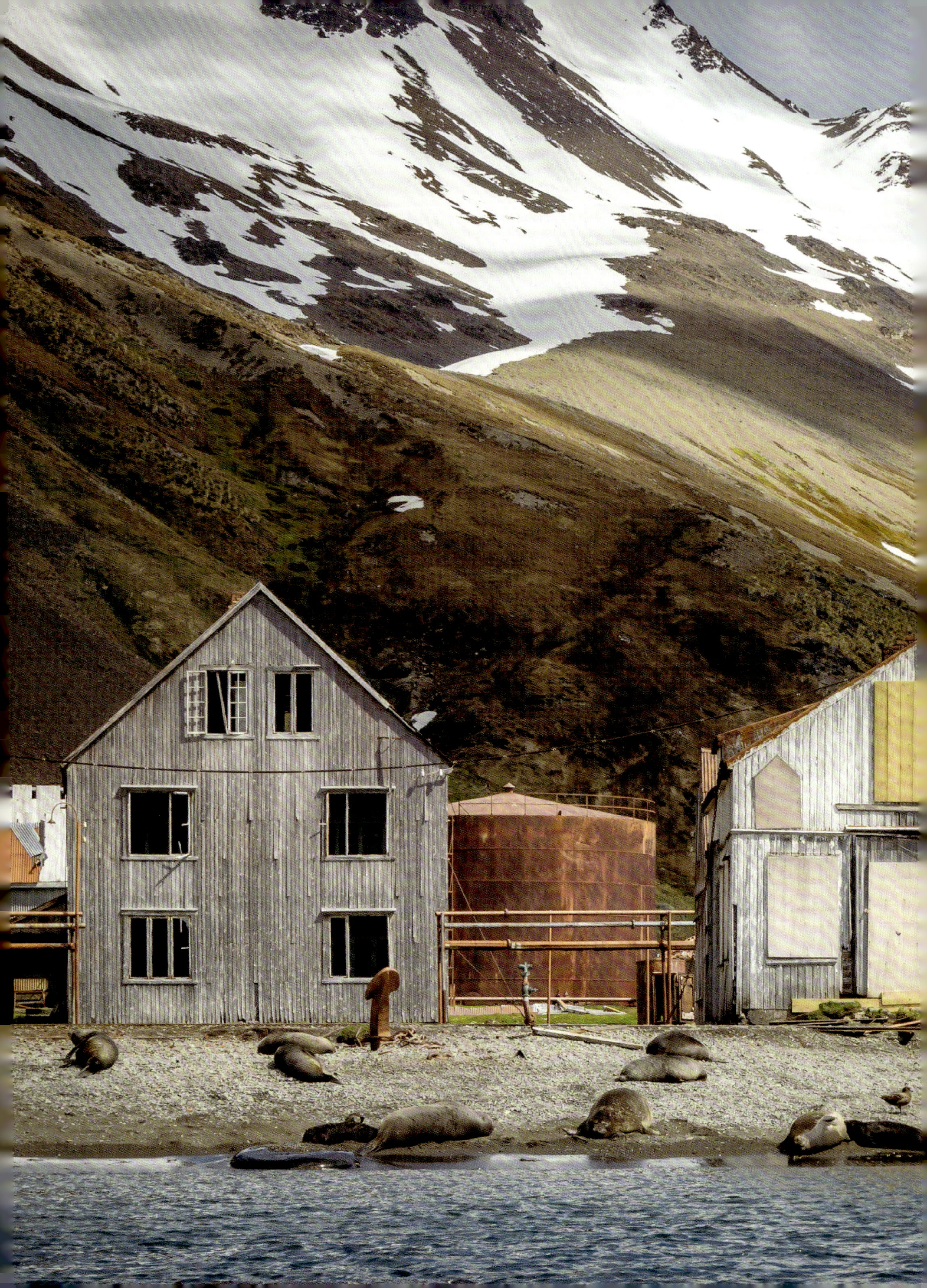

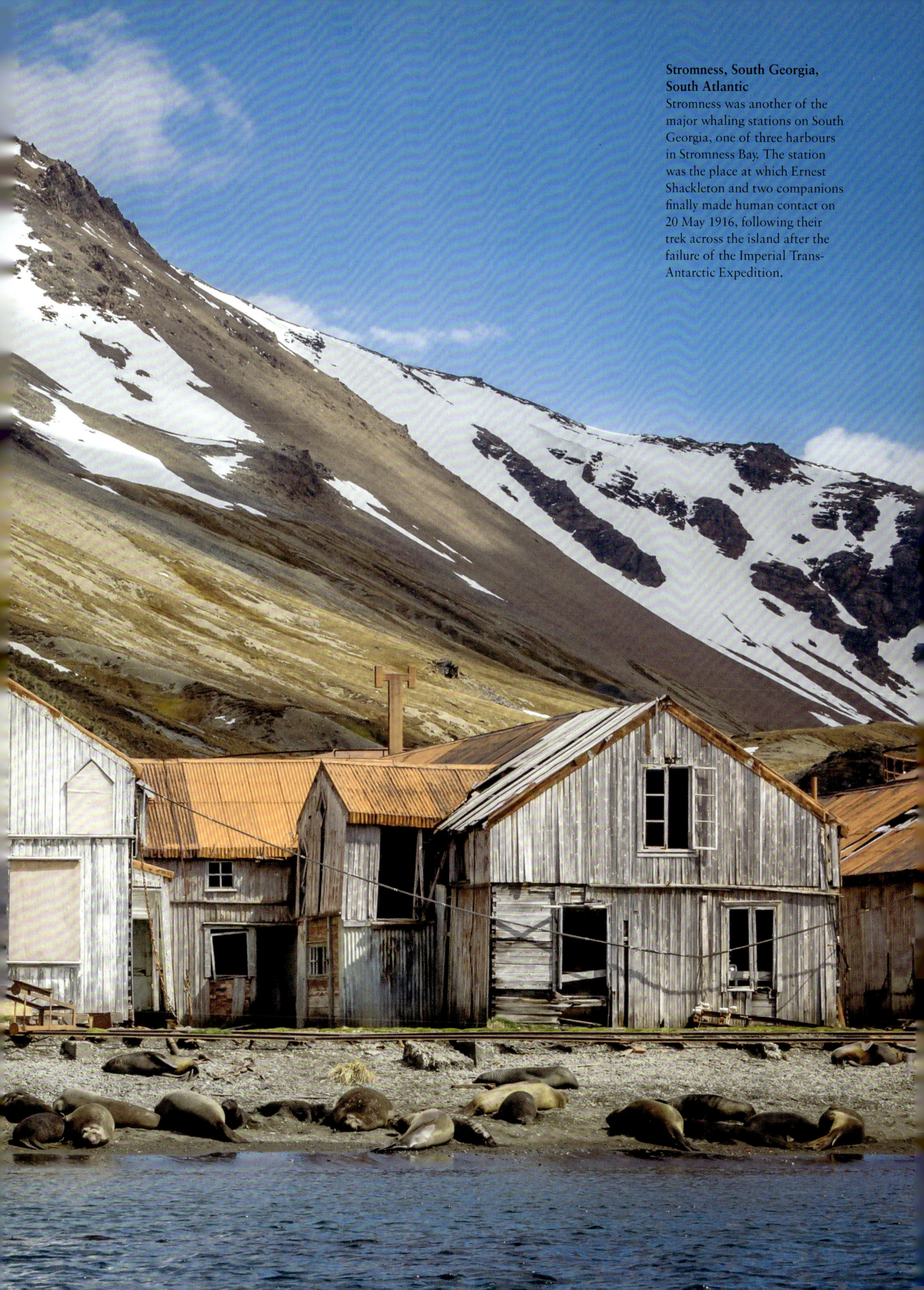

Stromness, South Georgia, South Atlantic
Stromness was another of the major whaling stations on South Georgia, one of three harbours in Stromness Bay. The station was the place at which Ernest Shackleton and two companions finally made human contact on 20 May 1916, following their trek across the island after the failure of the Imperial Trans-Antarctic Expedition.

Picture Credits

Alamy: 6 (Prisma by Dukas Pressagentur GmbH/Heeb Christian), 8 (Arcaid Images/Ryan Koopmans), 21 bottom (Eric Lafforge), 36/37 (Reuters), 44 & 58 both (Dinodia Photos), 59 (Travel India), 68/69 (GFC Collection), 70 (James MacKintosh), 71 both (Eric Nathan), 90/91 (Radius Images), 92 top (Reuters), 92 bottom & 93 (Michael Dwyer), 96/97 (Joana Kruse), 100/101 (Yavuz Sariyildiz), 132 bottom (Powered By Light/Alan Spencer), 133 top (Joana Kruse), 139 bottom (Slawomir Kowalewski), 140/141 (Urs Gautschi), 144 (Morten Larsen), 150/151 (RWP Photography/Rick Pisio), 152/153 (Jon Arnold Images), 158 top & 159 top (All Canada Photos/Mike Grandmaison), 159 bottom (John Zada), 162/163 (DPA Picture Alliance), 168/169 (Prisma by Dukas Pressagentur GmbH/Heeb Christian), 172 top (Leon Werdinger), 172 bottom (Wiltold Skrypczak), 196 (David Wall), 198/199 (Jeffery Drewitz), 202 & 203 top (David Wall), 210/211 (Paul Mayall Australia), 214/215 (Arco Images), 216/217 (Don Paulson), 218 (Robert Harding/Michael Nolan), 219 both (Mint Images), 220 top (Kevin Schafer), 220 bottom (Robert Harding/Michael Nolan), 221 (Worldfoto)

Manu Beaudon: 128/129

Depositphotos: 7 (Ivenks), 94/95 (Ivenks)

Dreamstime: 20/21 (Sean Pavone), 20 bottom (Leung Cho Pan), 28/29 (Prasit Rodphan), 30 (Igor Dymov), 32/33 (Dmitry Chulov), 34/35 (Ian215), 38-41 all (Vladimir Zapletin), 48/49 (Amreshm), 50 top (Dushyant Kumar Thakur), 50 bottom & 51 (Matyas Rehak), 52/53a (Stefano Ember), 54/55 (Aliaksandr Masurkevich), 56/57 (Snehitdesign), 60/61 (Michelle Liaw), 62/63 (Rajesh Misra), 64 (Ivan Stanic), 66 (Radiokafka), 72/73 (Amelie Koch), 74/75 (Brizardh), 76/77 (Anotella 865), 78 top & 179 (Irina Opachevsky), 80/81 (Asafta), 82 (Murat Tegmen), 83 top (Witr), 83 bottom (Asafta), 84/85 (Adonis1969), 86 (Moreno Novello), 88/89 (Catherine Unger), 102 &103 (Compuinfoto), 106/107 (Sinastraub), 108 (Faaabi), 110/111 (Freesurf69), 112 top (Alepuffo), 112 bottom (Tinieder), 114/115 (Actiacti), 116 top (Janka 3147), 116 bottom (Ppl5806), 117 (Electropower), 118/119 (Adeliepenguin), 120/121 (Anibl Trejo), 133 bottom (Ian Woolcock), 134/135 (Dmitry Chulov), 136/137 (Coddie), 138 & 139 top (Mirek1967), 142/143 (Enolabrain), 146/147 (Michele Cornelius), 148/149 (Celso Diniz), 156/157 (Light & Magic Photography), 158 bottom (Pictureguy66), 160 top (Paul Brady), 160/161 (Americanspirit), 161 top (Lisa McKown), 164/165 (Mtsue), 170/171 (Kelsey Martineau), 173 (Cynthia McCary), 174/175 (Lora Parks), 176 (Jesus Eloy Ramos Lara), 178/179 (Bluedeep), 180/181 (Juergen Schonnop), 182 and 183 top (Piccaya), 183 bottom (Dimitri Yrnd), 186/187 (Tupatu 76), 188/189 (Martin Schneiter), 192/193 (Marcelo Vildosola Garrigo), 194/195 (Jesus Eloy Ramos Lara), 203 bottom (Jubilist), 204/205 (Magspace), 206/207 (Ekays), 208/209 (Kaloramaphotos), 212 (Derek Rogers)

Fotolia: 65 (Taqitahmid), 78 bottom (mg1708), 190/191 (Nora Doa)

Getty Images: 10/11 & 12/13 (VCG), 14/15 (Corbis/Qilai Shen), 16 (VCG), 17 both (Guillaume Payen), 24/25 (Mohd Samsul Mohd Said), 42/43 (UIG), 46/47 (Motographer/Pixelia/Karthik Janakiraman), 98/99 (Reuters), 104-105 all (Andia), 113 (Ullstein Bild), 124/125 & 126/127 (Andia), 130/131 (Matt Cardy), 132 top (James Osmond), 154/155 (National Geographic/Pete Ryan), 166/167 (National Geographic/Pete Ryan), 184-185 all (Corbis/Colin McPherson), 200/201 (Lonely Planet Images/Manfred Gottschalk) , 222/223 (Mohd Samsul Mohd Said)

Carrie Kellenberger: 26/27 (CC by 2.0)

Shutterstock: 18/19 (Ben Richards), 22/23 (Abd. Halim Hadi), 122/123 (Vilu)